The Children's Crusade

Also by Gary Dickson

RELIGIOUS ENTHUSIASM IN THE MEDIEVAL WEST:
REVIVALS, CRUSADES, SAINTS

The Children's Crusade

Medieval History, Modern Mythistory

Gary Dickson

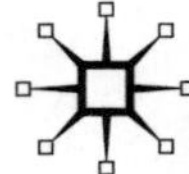

First published 2008 by
PALGRAVE MACMILLAN
Houndmills, Basingstoke, Hampshire RG21 6XS and
175 Fifth Avenue, New York, N.Y. 10010
Companies and representatives throughout the world

PALGRAVE MACMILLAN is the global academic imprint of the Palgrave Macmillan division of St. Martin's Press, LLC and of Palgrave Macmillan Ltd. Macmillan® is a registered trademark in the United States, United Kingdom and other countries. Palgrave is a registered trademark in the European Union and other countries.

ISBN-13: 978–1–4039–9989–4 hardback
ISBN-10: 1–4039–9989–9 hardback

This book is printed on paper suitable for recycling and made from fully managed and sustained forest sources. Logging, pulping and manufacturing processes are expected to conform to the environmental regulations of the country of origin.

A catalogue record for this book is available from the British Library.

A catalog record for this book is available from the Library of Congress

10 9 8 7 6 5 4 3 2 1
17 16 15 14 13 12 11 10 09 08

Printed and bound in Great Britain by
Antony Rowe Ltd, Chippenham and Eastbourne

To Rachel and Sarah
who left home
but did not run away

Contents

List of Illustrations x
Preface xi
Acknowledgements xiv

1. Introduction 1
   Agatha Christie's *Passenger to Frankfurt* (1970) 1
   Mythistory 3
   From Mythistory to Metaphor: Sixties Resurrection? 6
   In Search of Evidence 9
   History, Mythistory, Memory 15

2. History: The Pope and the *Pueri* 17
   The Papal Image 17
   Encounter in Perugia 19
   The Innocentian Epoch 21
   Religious Creativity and Impossibilism in the Age of Innocent III 23
   Innocent III, Papal Crusader 29
   Who were the *Pueri*? 33

3. History: Birthpangs of the Children's Crusade 36
   Pentecost 36
   Chartres 37
   A Burned-Over District 41
   Impetus—the Albigensian Crusade 46
   Stimulus—towards Las Navas de Tolosa 49
   Arousal—the Crisis Processions at Chartres 53

4. History: Charisma 59
   Weber's Charisma 59
   Charisma and Crusade 59
   From Kneeling Sheep to Pilgrim-Christ 63
   Stephen of Cloyes 66
   To Saint-Denis: the Pilgrimage of the Shepherd Boys 70
   Royal Dispersal 75
   Violence at Saint-Quentin 77

5. History: On the Road 83
Continuities 83
The Road to Cologne 84
Self-Imaginings 89
The Quest for the True Cross 94
Cologne—the Rhineland Journey Begins 98
A New Moses? Nicholas of Cologne 102

6. History: The Great Migration 107
A New Life—Nicholas of Cologne and the *Pueri* in Italy 107
Rome 111
Nicholas and Francis of Assisi in Egypt 115
Otto, the Last *Puer* 121
The Aftermath: Catastrophe or Pseudo-Catastrophe? 123
Epilogue: What was the Children's Crusade? 127

7. Mythistory: The Shape of a Story 131
"Based on a Real Event" 131
Mythistoricizing the *Pueri* 132
Child-Martyrs: the New Innocents 137
Searching for Villains 140
Eminent Mythistorians: Alberic of Trois-Fontaines 143
Eminent Mythistorians: Matthew Paris 147
Eminent Mythistorians: Vincent of Beauvais 151
Mythistory and the Spirit of Prophecy 155

8. Memory: The Echo of the Centuries—Fourteenth to Eighteenth 158
The Fourteenth-Century Chroniclers: Recitations and Surprises 159
Later Medieval Versions of the Children's Crusade 162
Renaissance and Early Modern Children's Crusades 164
Voltaire and the Enlightenment 169

9. Memory: The Echo of the Centuries—Nineteenth to Twentieth 173
Nineteenth-Century Romantic Medievalism 173
Academic Professionalism in Nineteenth-Century Germany 176
Nineteenth-Century Popular History and Historical Fiction 178
A Dreadful Warning? The *Pueri* in Children's Literature 182
Twentieth-Century Voices: Historians, Poets, Composers 186
Twentieth-Century Voices: Novelists 190
The Persistence of Social Memory 194

Chronology 197
Map: Europe of the Pueri 199
Abbreviations of Frequently Cited References 200
Notes 203
Bibliography: Specialist Scholarship 240
Index 241

List of Illustrations

Figure 1:	Gustave Doré, *Croisade des Enfants*, from Joseph-François Michaud, *Histoire des Croisades* (1879).	xii
Figure 2:	Bernardi Butinone (active 1484–1507), *Christ Child disputing with the Doctors*. National Gallery of Scotland.	5
Figure 3:	Pope Innocent III, upper register of fresco, church of Sacro Speco, Subiaco (c. 1216).	18
Figure 4:	Cathedral of Chartres, general view; photographer, Eric de Maré. RIBA Library Photographs Collection, Royal Institute of British Architects.	38
Figure 5:	Portrait of Stephen of Cloyes (reputed), chapel of Notre-Dame d'Yron, Cloyes (fourteenth century?). Courtesy of the photographer Bernard Legrand and Didier Caffot, librarian and archivist of the Société Dunoise, which authorized its reproduction.	68
Figure 6:	Cathedral of Chartres, Portail royal (twelfth century), *Shepherds led by an angel*. Éditions Houvet (reproduction prohibited).	69
Figure 7:	*Capture of the True Cross by Saladin*, drawing by Matthew Paris, *Chronica Majora*, MS 26, p.279. The Parker Library, Corpus Christi College, Cambridge.	95
Figure 8:	St. Antony Abbot holding the Tau Cross (early sixteenth-century woodcut from Lotharingia or the Rhineland). Paul Heitz (ed.), *Pestblätter des XV Jahrhunderts* (Heitz & Mündel: Strassburg, 1918), fig. 2.	104
Figure 9:	Simone Martini, *Christ Discovered in the Temple* (1342). Walker Art Gallery, National Museums, Liverpool.	136
Figure 10:	Andrea di Giovanni, *Holy Innocents adoring the Christ Child and the Mystic Lamb*, processional banner, church of San Ludovico, Orvieto (1410). ALINARI Archives, Florence.	139
Figure 11:	Jean-Antoine Houdon, Bust of Voltaire (1781).	170
Figure 12:	J. Kirchhoff, *Kreuzzug der Kinder*, steel engraving from Joh. Sporschil, *Geschichte der Kreuzzüge* (1843).	179
Figure 13:	*Stephen enlisting boys and girls for the Children's Crusade* from A.J. Church, *The Crusaders: A Story of the War for the Holy Sepulchre* (1905).	183

Preface

A sudden and inexplicable outpouring of crusading enthusiasm inflamed and unsettled troops of male and female youths, along with grown-ups, mothers with babes-in-arms, and the occasional family of peasants or townspeople, dislodging them from the towns and villages of early thirteenth-century France and Germany, severing their links with the strongest man-made force on earth, daily life, and sending them on a fervent quest to the Holy Land. This was the Children's Crusade, obscurely famous and famously obscure, one of the least understood but most memorable incidents of the crusading epoch.

In its successive guises and mutations it was the first popular crusade, the first medieval youth movement, the first Shepherds' Crusade, an ecstatic processional enthusiasm, a search for the True Cross, a charismatically-led Holy Land pilgrimage, an unarmed crusade of peasants and urban laborers, a collective migration of impoverished dreamers, folk art.

Born illegitimate at a time when crusading fervor gripped every level of European society, the Children's Crusade sprang to life in an era of extraordinary religious creativity. Amongst the period's most creative religious figures were the Poor Man of Assisi, St. Francis; St. Clare of Assisi, runaway and disciple of Francis; and of course the greatest of papal crusaders, Innocent III. No history of the Children's Crusade can ignore them.

But history is not the whole story. The Children's Crusade was also a child of the medieval imagination. The enthusiasts themselves were self-imagined, enclosed in a mythic world. Their earliest chroniclers incorporated mythic motifs into their fragmentary accounts. Already by mid-century a few talented writers were transmuting history into mythistory. Which means that by the time the Children's Crusade bid farewell to the Middle Ages and sailed into modernity, mythistory prevailed.

Nowadays what most people remember about it, besides its name, is an image of starry-eyed youngsters pitting themselves against the harsh realities of a pitiless world, exchanging their homeland, their freedom, and their lives for an impossible dream of Jerusalem regained. Gustave Doré, catching sight of these doomed runaways through the lens of late nineteenth-century French romantic medievalism, visualized fragile, fresh-faced, androgynous young people, dressed in flowing garments, gazing rapturously round and about, their mouths open in acclamation and song, one lad clasping his hands in prayer, another crossing his arms above his breast (Figure 1). Their apparent leaders, three youths heading an endless column, carry shepherds' crooks. As the youths stream into a faraway, Italianate city, young aristocratic ladies, glance downwards from a raised loggia at the vast processional troop of peasant

Figure 1 Gustave Doré, *Croisade des Enfants*, from Joseph-François Michaud, *Histoire des Croisades* (1879).

innocents. Whether their glances are impassive or compassionate is hard to say. Diagonally opposite these gentlewomen a sinister clerical figure positions himself near the front rank of the child-pilgrims, armed with a tall processional cross. Is this mesmeric, attentive figure their puppet master, their Svengali—the Pied Piper of these Lost Boys? What cannot be denied is that Gustave Doré was inspired by the mythistorical—not the historical—Children's Crusade.

This mythistorical "Children's Crusade" is one of the most evocative verbal artefacts to have come down to us from the Middle Ages. Centuries of usage have given it a name. That name—repeated in fiction and encyclopedias; on the web and the History Channel—is engraved in historical scholarship as well as in popular consciousness. Only a fool would tamper with it. But as we all know from commercial packaging, even standard brands sometimes mislead us about exactly what lies within. The "Children's Crusade" is just such a label. Neither "children" (Latin *pueri*), nor "crusade" (Latin *peregrinatio, iter, expeditio, crucesignatio,* etc.) is either entirely wrong, or wholly right. Both require clarification.

One of the most puzzling features of the historical Children's Crusade of 1212 remains largely unexplored. Out-of-control peasant crusaders in 1096, 1251, 1309, and 1320, swept through the Jewish communities in their paths, pillaging, massacring, and forcibly baptizing Jews. So why did the Children's Crusade alone leave no trail of Jewish corpses behind it? As Sherlock Holmes knew, dogs that do not bark are worth investigating.

Wonder and amazement accompanied these youthful, unconventional crusaders, attracting the attention of the chroniclers. Although generally hostile towards what was, after all, an unauthorized crusade, these same clerical chroniclers mythistoricized it so memorably that they preserved it from historical oblivion. But like mummification or formaldehyde, mythistoricization subtly—or not so subtly—distorts as well as preserves. Once provided with a mythistoricized afterlife, however, the Children's Crusade found a permanent niche in the uncatalogued and hopelessly cluttered museum that is the European and American imagination.

"Imagination always exerts a gravitional pull on historical events, bending them into confabulations, fictions, myths."[1] Imagination is the key to the transformative process which turns historical events into mythistory. But the secret is out. The postmodernists have let the cat out of the bag. In its hubristic imposition of order and coherence, historiography, too, re-imagines the past.

Gary Dickson
Portobello
Edinburgh
2007 C.E.

Acknowledgements

Expressing my gratitude to those who have assisted me in my research is not a duty but a pleasure. As long ago as 1977, the organizers of the Stirling Conference of the Scottish Medieval Group allowed me to air some of my half-formed—actually, half-baked—notions about the Children's Crusade under the chairmanship of Abelard's biographer, Michael Clanchy. Coincidentally, he was again my chairman when I spoke about the *pueri* to the Earlier Medieval Seminar of the Institute of Historical Research, London, in 1992. Within and well beyond these two dates, I hazarded various ideas on medieval revivalism and popular crusades at seminars and conferences too numerous to specify. To their organizers may I extend my blanket gratitude, especially as some of them had the additional burden of editing my prose. My attendance at these academic tribal gatherings was in several instances due to the partial or total benefaction of the Travel and Research Committee of the University of Edinburgh, which, in addition, enabled me to visit libraries and archives in Paris, Chartres, and Châteaudun in connection with this study. The Carnegie Trust for the Universities of Scotland subsidized my hunt for the elusive *pueri* in the Rhineland and Liège. The British Academy funded my appearance at the Tucson conference of the Medieval Academy of America.

In Châteaudun, my efforts were aided by the President of the Société Dunoise, Bernard LeGrand, and its Librarian and Archivist, Didier Caffot. In Chartres, I was assisted by the diocesan archivist Abbé Pierre Bizeau as well as staff members of the municipal library and the departmental archives. Equally helpful were the municipal librarians of Saint Quentin. As for Paris, it is best to maintain a diplomatic silence. In Rome, the Vatican librarians and archivists were unfailingly helpful and courteous, as were their counterparts in the British Library, London. Expert bibliographical scholars of Liège and the Rhineland benevolently guided me towards books and articles I would otherwise have overlooked. As always, the staff of the National Library of Scotland, and of the University of Edinburgh's Inter-Library Loans and its Special Collections gave service above and beyond the call of duty.

Particular individuals deserve to be singled out for their exceptional contribution to this book. Nicole Bériou then of the University of Paris-

Sorbonne (Paris IV) generously provided me with a transcription of a new manuscript text relating to the *pueri*; Jessalynn Bird, then of Queen's College, Oxford, discovered Otto, the last *puer*, while Andrea Tilatti of the University of Udine pursued him through the archives. As the endnotes testify, John P. Renwick of Edinburgh, Voltaire scholar *par excellence*, repeatedly responded to my queries. For emergency linguistic first aid, Edinburgh scholars—Philip Bennett, Jonathan Usher, and especially the patient and expert medieval Latinist Alan Hood—are owed a special vote of thanks. Finally, I am very grateful to Jonathan Riley-Smith of Cambridge for his perceptive comments on the completed typescript.

But to list the names of all those who shared their knowledge and wisdom with me—Edinburgh colleagues, first and foremost, but also old friends throughout the U.K., the U.S.A., France, Germany, and Italy—would overstretch these pages and try my publisher's patience. Please forgive your anonymity here. I look forward to thanking you in person.

Such acknowledgement doubles as formal exculpation. I take sole responsibility for any shortcomings found herein.

To my teachers, all now deceased, Gavin Langmuir of Stanford, Roberto Lopez of Yale, and Denys Hay of Edinburgh, is owed whatever merit this book may have. And to my wife—what can I offer? My apologies, or my thanks?

Acknowledgement for permission to publish copyright material

I am very much indebted to Professor John Shinners for his permission to make use of his translations of some of the major chronicle sources of the *pueri* in his valuable anthology, *Medieval Popular Religion, 1000–1500: A Reader* (Broadview Press: Peterborough, Ontario, Canada, 1997 © John Shinners).

Passenger to Frankfurt © 1970 Agatha Christie Limited, a Chorion company, all rights reserved.

All of the following © Oxford University Press: definitions of "mythistory" and "boy" from the *Oxford English Dictionary* (1989) ed. Simpson, J. and Weiner, E.; extracts from *The Sixties* (1998) by Marwick, Arthur; *Dictionary of American Biography* (1934) ed. Malone, Dumas; *Crusades* (1923) by Barker, Ernest; *History of the Jews in the Latin Kingdom of Jerusalem* (1988) by Prawer, Joshua; *Gesta Francorum/Deeds of the Franks* (1967) ed./trans. Hill, Rosalind.

Excerpt from Salimbene de Adam, *The Chronicle*, ed. Joseph L. Baird, Medieval and Renaissance Texts and Studies, Volume 40 (Binghamton, New York, 1986), pp. 4–5. © Arizona Board of Regents for Arizona State.

Patrick Harpur for an extract from © *The Philosophers' Secret Fire: a History of the Imagination* (Penguin Books: London, 2002).

Reprinted by permission of HarperCollins Publishers Ltd. ©: extract from Janet Morgan, *Agatha Christie: a Biography* (Collins: London, 1984).

Penguin Press: from *Chronicles of the Crusades by Joinville and Villehardouin* (1963) (trans./intro. M.R.B Shaw), © M.R.B Shaw, 1963.

Princeton University Press: extract from © *Meditations on the Life of Christ* (trans. Isa Ragusa) (1961).

Franciscan Press for © extract from Marion A. Habig (ed.) *St. Francis of Assisi: Writings and Early Biographies* (1973).

Ashgate Publishing Ltd. © extracts from Suzanne Lewis, *The Art of Matthew Paris in the "Chronica Majora"* (1987) and Peter W. Edbury (ed./trans.), *The Conquest of Jerusalem and the Third Crusade: Sources in Translation* (1996).

Kegan Paul for © extract from G.G. Coulton (ed.), *Social Life in Britain from the Conquest to the Reformation* (2004).

Yale University Press for © extracts from Rhodri Jeffreys-Jones, *Peace Now! American Society and the Ending of the Vietnam War* (1999) and Dorothee Metlitzki, *The Matter of Araby in Medieval England* (1977).

Librairie Arthème Fayard for © extract from Bernard Thomas, *La croisade des enfants* (1973).

Columbia University Press for © extract from Otto of Freising, *The Deeds of Frederick Barbarossa* (trans. Charles C. Mierow) (1966).

Todd Gitlin for permission to publish an extract from *The Sixties: Years of Hope, Days of Rage* (Penguin Books: Toronto, 1987; originally published by Bantam Books, a division of Random House).

Hodder Education for © extracts from Louise and Jonathan Riley-Smith (eds./trans.), *The Crusades: Idea and Reality, 1095–1274* (1981).

Extract from James A. Brundage (ed. and trans.) *The Crusades: A Documentary Survey* (Milwaukee, Marquette University Press, 1962). © Marquette University Press. Reprinted by permission of the publisher. All rights reserved.

University of St. Andrews for extract from © Walter Bower, *Scotichronicon* (D.E.R. Watt, gen. ed.), Vol. 5 (Simon Taylor, D.E.R. Watt, with Brian Scott, eds.) (1990).

Thames and Hudson for extract from © T.S.R. Boase, *Kingdoms and Strongholds of the Crusaders* (1971).

University of Chicago Press for brief © extracts from George Lakoff and Mark Johnson, *Metaphors We Live By* (1980); Edward Shils, "Charisma," in his *Center and Periphery: Essays in Macrosociology*, Vol. 2 (1975); Clifford

Geertz, "Center, Kings, and Charisma: Reflections on the Symbolics of Power" in Joseph Ben-David, *et al.* (eds.), *Culture and its Creators: Essay in Honor of Edward Shils* (1977).

James Clarke & Co. Ltd. for extract from © Eileen Heming's *Joan's Crusade* (1947).

Cornell University Press for brief © extracts from W.R. Cross, *The Burned-Over District* (1950) and Jeffrey B. Russell, *Lucifer: The Devil in the Middle Ages* (1984).

New York University Press for a brief © extract from Evelyn B. Vitz, *Medieval Narrative and Modern Narratology* (1989).

University of Pennsylvania Press for brief © extracts from *Roger Bacon, Opus Majus* (trans. R.B. Burke), Vol. 1 (1928); Norman P. Zacour, "The Children's Crusade," in Kenneth M. Setton (ed.), *A History of the Crusades* (1962), Vol. 2; and James M. Powell, *Anatomy of a Crusade, 1213–21* (1986).

Peter Smith Publisher, Inc. for a brief © extract from August C. Krey (ed./trans.), *The First Crusade* (1958).

Cambridge University Press for brief © extracts from John Moorman, *Church Life in England in the Thirteenth Century* (1945); Steven Runciman, *History of the Crusades* (1987); and Richard Vaughan, *Matthew Paris* (1979).

University of Glasgow for a short extract from V.H. Galbraith, Roger Wendover and Matthew Paris (Glasgow, 1944).

Extract from *The History and Narrative Reader* by Hayden White (New York and London, Routledge, 2001). Reprinted by permission of Taylor and Francis Books, UK.

Every effort has been made to trace all copyright holders, but if any have been inadvertently overlooked, the publisher will be pleased to make the necessary arrangements at the first opportunity.

1 Introduction

The turbulence of the Sixties protest movements, the drug-friendly love-ins of the flower children, and the drift of tiny but frightening direct-action groups like the Weathermen into "urban guerrilla warfare" generated a powerful counter-current of hostility against American youth culture in general and young radicals in particular.

Agatha Christie's *Passenger to Frankfurt* in 1970

Agatha Christie published *Passenger to Frankfurt* in 1970, when she was eighty. Nearly all the critics panned it, but *Passenger to Frankfurt* remained on the *New York Times* best-seller list for twenty-seven weeks. Miss Christie's biographer attributes its brisk sales to the fact that it "was timely:... everything seemed upside down... [Christie] hit raw nerves." Into her tirade against Sixties youth culture disguised as a novel, Agatha Christie poured her readings of European history, conversations with California prophets of hippiedom, and gloomy meditations on exploited innocence and perverted idealism.[1]

Trying to summarize *Passenger*'s convoluted plot risks bringing on a migraine; but the plot is immaterial. What matters is what lies at the heart of the book. An international youth movement is conspiring to undermine the civilized world. The youthful conspirators are a gaggle of neo-Nazis, pop-music fans, drug addicts, pushers, revolutionaries, nihilists, and dangerous dreamers—as unappealing an assortment of young undesirables as any octogenarian could wish for. A worldly-wise diplomat, Sir Stafford Nye (Miss Christie's mouthpiece as the voice of reason), dubs this unsavory gang of young people the "'children's crusade à la mode'," expatiating: "'this whole business is rather like the children's crusade. Starting with idealism, starting with ideas of the Christian world delivering the holy city from pagans, and ending with death. Nearly all the children died. Or were sold into slavery. This will end the same way unless...'"[2] But in "this business" death would not be the fate of self-sacrificial, young crusade heroes. Far from it. Instead, the murderous outcome of twisted idealism would be the death of countless others. Victims no longer, these youngsters are now the willing perpetrators of up-to-date horrors.

We are in the high Sixties. We hear the sound of embassy windows shattering. "'Again [deplores a female dinner-guest] it is those terrible students... they fight, resist the police—go marching, shouting idiotic things, lie down in the streets... We have them like a pest everywhere in Europe'."[3] Outbursts of youthful violence are coupled with threats of apocalyptical violence to come. Interspersed with bursts of action are musings about the medieval arch-villain, the Old Man of the Mountain, leader of the Assassins, together with ruminations upon that distant time "'when a yearning towards crusades swept... all over Europe'." Behind the crusades, we learn, were dreams and, more frightening still, visions.[4]

Agatha Christie thus imaginatively reworks the traditional picture of the misguided, pathetic, wide-eyed young people who ran off to join the Children's Crusade of 1212 into a photofit image of the young terrorists of the late Sixties. Rather than naively succumbing to devils, they were demonic themselves. Trick photography or historical mirage it may have been, but a good number of Miss Christie's readers saw contemporary events reflected in her pop-art picture. Implausibly but—all credit to her—ingeniously, *Passenger to Frankfurt* refashions a medieval tale to fit snugly inside a modern one.

That a popular writer like Agatha Christie (1890–1976) was able to allude to the thirteenth-century Children's Crusade, confident that it would not flummox her twentieth-century readers, is remarkable. It would have astounded the medieval chroniclers who foresaw not a glimmer of posthumous longevity issuing from it. Obituarists for juvenile folly, they carved their last words like epitaphs:

> After a short time all that came to nothing, because it was founded upon nothing.[5]... Their journey was brought to nought.[6]... But they succeeded not at all. For all, in different ways, were ruined, died, or returned.[7]

This is the way the chroniclers saw it. All that this overwhelming nullity left behind was disillusionment, discomfiture, and death. But the Last Judgment of the medieval chroniclers was overturned by subsequent generations. There was a trade-off. What the *pueri* (boys, children; youths, youngsters) lost historically, they gained mythistorically.

Mythistory

According to the respected Chicago world-historian and former President of the American Historical Association, William H. McNeill, man is such a producer of myths, and myths are so basic and necessary an element of group cohesion, that historians, sharing the assumptions of their audiences, and addressing their concerns, cannot help but write "mythistory."[8] The moderate triumphalism of McNeill's own *Rise of the West*, unashamedly subtitled *A History of the Human Community*, is a case in point.[9] Though this view of "mythistory" seems too despairing a relativism and perhaps too easy a cultural determinism, who can doubt that before historians became self-conscious demythologizers or postmodernists, myths, both as overarching explanations, and as self-contained narrative episodes, pervaded historical literature.

Mythistory, in fact, has a long history. Some would castigate its effects on historical writing as pernicious or subversive. Perceptively describing the mythistoricizing process, Roland Barthes argues that "myth... abolishes the complexity of human acts."[10] Myth, in other words, simplifies, clarifies, and reduces historical complexity to an essential meaning. Does that fatally undermine historiography or merely make it digestible?

Medieval historiography welcomed incidents which explored or confirmed the mysterious, sacral, or providential dimension to human affairs, the universe of wonder. Material of this sort found its true home in *exempla*, entertaining moral anecdotes inserted into sermons; in collections of *miracula*, miracle stories; and in *mirabilia*, antique legends and amazing tales. Wonders, marvels, and miracles, far from being intruders, were frequently honored guests in medieval annals and chronicles. Thirteenth-century historical anecdotalists such as Caesarius of Heisterbach and Thomas of Cantimpré presented "True Stories"—didactic, mythistoricized versions of private and public events—predigested for sermons. From this world of moralizing, theologizing, cautionary, prognosticating, *wundergeschichten* (miracle tales or "histories"), a select number of medieval mythistories outlived the Middle Ages and entered the modern world. One was called the Children's Crusade.

Sounding suspiciously like mystery, "mythistory" is not easy to vocalize in English unless it is either lisped or split in two, as in myth-[pause] history. Not by any means is the word a neologism. If anything, it is an archaism. As early as 1731, "mythistory" was defined as "history mingled with false fable and tales."[11] Unlike fable or folklore, however, or myths pure and simple, mythistories occur in real chronological time and real geographical space. Then again, unlike legends, their closest kin, mythistories are not so much additives (history plus) as new creations, hybrids. Nor do mythistories necessarily adhere to a biographical core, as so many legends do. Again, unlike legends, normally we do not encounter mythistories in an open-ended narrative cycle. An intriguing character like the Wandering Jew wanders in and out of mythistory as well as learned or folkloric legend,[12] and probably is wandering still. Conversely, a mythistorical figure like the Pied Piper (or Ratcatcher) of Hameln is typically confined to a self-contained, non-cyclical, anecdotalized episode rather like the Children's Crusade. Accused of musically bewitching and luring away the vanished children of Hameln, the Pied Piper has also been implicated in the disappearance of the—equally enchanted?—Lost Boys of 1212. Then, too, like the *pueri*, their near-contemporaries, the technicolored, mythistorical, twelfth-century English Green Children, are part and parcel of the grand, recurring mythic motifs centered upon uncanny or exceptional children.[13]

Myths have always surrounded the child prodigy or *wunderkind* and the *puer-senex*, the Wise Child with an old man's head on his shoulders. A perfect example is the runaway, twelve-year-old Jesus discovered by his distraught parents listening and putting questions to the venerable doctors of the synagogue (Figure 2). There are echoes of the missing boy-Jesus in some accounts of the Children's Crusade. One English chronicler, for example, maintains that none of the *pueri* was older than twelve.[14] Medieval ideas of childhood, combining notions of purity, divine election, and martyrdom, were strengthened by contemporary allegations of the Jewish ritual murder of Christian boys and by the cult of the Holy Innocents, themselves martyrs for the sake of the Christ child. These were mythic motifs lying in wait to impregnate historical events.

Fundamental to the idea of mythistory is generic location. Authenticating historiographical forms or genres have always provided a purpose-built, ideal habitat for mythistories. Despite the distancing techniques employed by medieval annalists, chroniclers, and historians (e.g. "it is said that"), the placement of mythistories in a generic context was more than camouflage. After all, historiography from its Herodotean inception was universally paraded as truth-telling. Constantly reiterated from classical antiquity to the Middle Ages, veracity was its sterling silver. "Histories," Isidore of Seville (d. 636) declares, "are true things that have taken place."[15] Once embedded in historical narrative, stories acquired

Figure 2 Bernardi Butinone (active 1484–1507), *Christ Child disputing with the Doctors*. National Gallery of Scotland.

historicity by contact. On the one hand, authors of medieval epics and romances brazenly sought to appropriate the truth-claims which gave medieval historical writing its cultural prestige and authority. On the other, sophisticated medieval chroniclers and self-conscious medieval historians, following in the footsteps of their Greco-Roman predecessors, tirelessly insisted that historiography was a true record of the past. Not only that, it was the sole truthful mode of representing that which had occurred before or during the historian's lifetime. This claim to unique and exclusive primacy was supported, not only by authoritative classical texts, but also—something which should never be forgotten, but often is—by biblical histories (the Book of Chronicles, Kings, Luke's Acts of the Apostles, among others). Scriptural histories were nothing less than the canonical vessels of God's truth. Wholly conscious of the dignity of their craft, medieval chroniclers and historians passed up few opportunities to trumpet it.

Once mythistoricized, the narrative of the Children's Crusade was not so much history deformed, as history outgrown, transfigured. Disengaged from linear events, liberated by mythic motifs, the medieval runaways, now equipped for time travel, hurtled through the centuries. Then, every so often the *pueri* would be released from suspended animation and taken on a tour of the ever-multiplying cultural media—encyclopedias; histories, both scholarly and popular; verse; illustrations; children's literature, novels for grown-ups; music; films; TV documentaries. Such a moment came not so long ago when the culturally mummified spirit of these forever youthful crusaders stirred and reawakened. Mythistory, history's stepchild, had come of age. It was now the proud parent of metaphor.

From mythistory to metaphor: Sixties resurrection

"Tireless, peripatetic, full time crusaders" was how the Director of the CIA, Richard Helms, reporting to President Lyndon Johnson, summed up America's leading anti-war activists in 1967.[16] Many of these activists, joined by thousands of university students—"college kids" to headline writers—streamed into Senator Eugene McCarthy's anti-war campaign for the Democratic presidential nomination in the months leading up to the New Hampshire primary of March, 1968. Post-grads, undergrads, veterans of many a demonstration for black civil rights or against U.S. policy in Vietnam, all marched together under McCarthy's banner on campuses across the country. The press christened their movement a "children's crusade." Journalistic shorthand triumphed. The label stuck.

Its meaning was clear. Just as the naive idealism of the medieval youngsters resulted in their abject failure, so, too, would Eugene McCarthy's youthful, well-intentioned but unworldly, campus crusaders suffer the same fate. The beauty of the metaphor was its taut way of allowing journalists to praise, pity, and mock McCarthy's college kids all at the same time. Meanwhile, "Clean for Gene" was the watchword. College students wanting to doorstep prospective voters first had to shave off their beards. Their enthusiasm transfigured their hero. No longer was the Senator from Minnesota an "unsatisfactorily stiff and proud academic" figure.[17] No, now he was the messianic leader of a new, American-style Children's Crusade. Consciously or not, he evoked the thirteenth-century leader of the German *pueri*, Nicholas of Cologne, whose dream it was to lead his followers across the Mediterranean Sea, just as Moses once had led the Children of Israel across a less daunting body of water. Like another Moses (or a latter-day Nicholas of Cologne), Senator McCarthy proclaimed: "My strategy is to walk through the Red Sea dry-shod. Any of you who want to follow me before the waters close in are welcome to do so."[18] Campaign apocalypticism indeed.

Eugene McCarthy's fervent supporters of 1968, along with the emergence of the young radicals and hippies of the late Sixties and early Seventies, gave the medieval *pueri* their 15 minutes of fame.

> There was enormous anxiety about whether the prevailing culture could hold the young... It became easy to imagine that the whole of youth was regressing, or evolving, into—what? Barbarism? A new society unto itself, a Woodstock Nation? A children's crusade?[19]

With its title on so many lips, *The Children's Crusade* by George Zabriskie Gray (1870) was reprinted, unrevised, in 1972. It was now deemed marketable. A less commercially-minded reason why a book of such amateurish scholarship should be back in print a full century later was offered by the journalist and political commentator Thomas Powers in his Foreword to Gray. His answer, more or less, was look around. The present crisis justifies, indeed demands, such a book. Powers goes on to highlight the uncanny parallels between the young American radicals of the Sixties and their youthful medieval forerunners. The same moral idealism fired and inspired them both. Both were utterly convinced of the rightness of their cause. Both were youthful idealists and moral crusaders. Analogous to the Children's Crusade, he argued, were the civil rights movement, the anti-war demonstrations, and the McCarthy campaign of 1968.[20] To Powers, the only diference between the thirteenth-century *pueri* and their young American counterparts of the Sixties was that the medieval youngsters paid the higher price for their idealism.[21]

Powers was not alone in finding the idea of a reborn Children's Crusade compelling. Indeed, during the American Sixties and early Seventies metaphorical crusades were plentiful. Although, for the most part, their body-count was lower than that on the distant battlefields of medieval crusades, this is not to deny that the "crusades" for civil rights and against the Vietnamese war also had their honorable casualties—martyrs some would say—like Medgar Evers (1963) or the students of Kent State (1970).

The fact remains that no matter how nobly men and women struggled in their respective causes, these were only metaphorical "crusades."

Yet this was not something new. America can boast of a long and proud tradition of metaphorical crusading, either *for* a great cause or *against* a perceived enemy of the people. These "crusades" began with Thomas Jefferson's call for a "crusade against ignorance" (1786)[22] and gained momentum with the nineteenth-century's "crusade for abolition." A pro-slavery advocate lashed out at the "clerical fanatics... [who] have... invited all men to join in the holy crusade [against slavery]" (1861).[23] The one common quality which the American anti-slavery "crusade" shared with the First Crusade of 1095–99 was that both were uniquely successful.

American metaphorical crusading thundered full-steam ahead with the Temperance movement's "crusade" against the demon rum in the later nineteenth century, culminating in Prohibition (1919–33), a success which failed. While the outcome of America's late-twentieth-century "crusades" against poverty and drugs is still in doubt, the fate of the early twenty-first century's "crusade against terror" remains anyone's guess. Not unexpectedly, the use of the highly-charged word "crusade" with its Christian and colonialist associations in the Middle East has prompted angry protests by Muslims.[24] However, American metaphorical crusading has generally elicited admiration, if not for the nature of any particular cause, then for the idealism of its adherents. Viewed as battles joined for the noblest of reasons, fought for the purest of motives, they have become the American secular or civic-religious equivalents of the medieval holy wars.[25] Thereby an imagined past could be enlisted in the service of the present.

"The primary function of metaphor is to provide a partial understanding of one kind of experience in terms of another."[26] That is fine, providing *partial* is emphasized, and the danger signals warning of *misunderstanding* are kept switched on. Historical metaphors invite anachronism, for historians the deadliest of the deadly sins. Thanks to the postmodernists, writers of history are now very well aware of how readily tropes—figures of speech, metaphors in particular—have infiltrated historiography.[27] We have been warned. Metaphors need to be taken metaphorically.

When Gray's grizzled *Children's Crusade* came back from the dead in 1972, Thomas Powers celebrated its rebirth with a ringing endorsement, which denied any need of revision. Nothing of importance has been learned about the Children's Crusade since the time Gray wrote his book.[28] Really? Between 1870 and 1972 eight substantial essays on the *pueri* were added to the scholarly canon, making Gray's inadequacies embarrassingly clear. Long before its second coming, his book was superseded.[29]

It was also during the mid-Sixties that the eminent crusade historian and bibliographer Hans Eberhard Mayer called attention to a remarkable lacuna in crusade scholarship—the absence of an acceptable modern study of the Children's Crusade.[30] Despite the fact that all the signs were pointing to a continuing popular interest in the subject,[31] no new book on the *peregrinatio puerorum*—the pilgrimage or crusade of the *pueri*—has appeared. Why?[32]

In search of evidence

Why indeed? First impressions are encouraging. Over fifty narrative texts written in Latin prose before 1301 refer to the extraordinary enthusiasm of the *pueri*.[33] So if the Children's Crusade left such a rich textual trail behind it, where are the packs of historians baying at the scent?

Across half of medieval Europe, from Scotland to Italy, from Brittany to Austria, wherever monks, hungry for news, feasted on incidents in the great world beyond the cloister, monastic scriptoria were at work. In regions too remote to catch a glimpse of the *pueri*, monastic chroniclers copied and embellished the texts that reached them, for medieval chroniclers shared the same work ethic as the early medieval masons who quarried Roman antiquities for building materials. Creative recycling encouraged the migration of texts from one manuscript codex to another. Then, too, pilgrims, merchants, travelling clerics, peasants returning from market, brought rumors and good stories, stirred and mixed with scraps of information. Yet some solid, newsworthy items got through. For example, certain Austrian chroniclers, though at some distance from the route of the *pueri*, were surprisingly well-informed.

Unsurprisingly, however, the contemporary chroniclers best placed to note the passing of the *pueri* were situated relatively near the pilgrims' line of march—i.e., north-central France, Lotharingia, the Rhineland, and northern Italy—in major cities such as Liège, Cologne, Piacenza, and Genoa, or in abbeys dotted along their path. Some of these chroniclers were very probably eye-witnesses. Coming face-to-face with the *pueri*, did they ask: "What in God's name do you think you're doing?" Then, having put them to the question, did they transcribe their answers faithfully, or—as ventriloquists in the guise of reporters have done for centuries—did they put their own words in their mouths?

What at first sight looks like a treasure trove of original sources is in reality less promising than the aggregate number of items in the dossier suggests. Out of a total of fifty-six chronicle entries in Latin prose dating from the thirteenth century, fifteen, including replicates, consist of a bare one or two printed lines. These annalistic notices merely label the event, state the year it occurred (oftentimes the wrong year), and nothing more.[34] True, knowing the annalist's monastic house helps in tracing the diffusion of information, while an interpretation can be encapsulated in a single phrase. Thus Herman of the Bavarian abbey of Niederaltaich, writing about sixty years after the pilgrimage of the *pueri*, mockingly dismisses it as a "ridiculous expedition of children" (*derisoria expedicio puerorum*), to which he appends two lines of verse: "In the year one thousand, two hundred, and twelve,/ Foolish children (*stultorum puerorum*) marched on pilgrimage (*iter*) to the sea."[35] *Iter* and especially *expeditio* were synonymous with crusade. Of course Herman knew it, but to him, this was not a true crusade; it was a Feast of Fools, and had these *stultorum puerorum* ever managed to take ship, Herman might have called it a Ship of Fools.

Next come eighteen, short-to-middling notices of the *pueri* (including replicates), comprising approximately three to six printed lines. A good illustration is the last entry in the chronicle of Sicard (d. 1215), Bishop of the northern Italian town of Cremona. At once terse, enigmatic, and intriguing, it announces the arrival of "an infinite multitude of paupers coming from Germany" led by a "child (*infans*) younger than ten" who declare that "without a ship they would cross the sea and recapture Jerusalem." Sicard never claims to have gazed upon this huge horde of German paupers or their infant leader with his own eyes; nor does he place them in his home city of Cremona, nor anywhere else in Italy.

Sicard was Innocent III's legate in Lombardy, and during 1212 he was occupied with papal business, mainly in northeastern Italy, including Treviso.[36] There his presence could coincide with a reported sighting of the *pueri* recorded in a late thirteenth-century chronicle from Salzburg. According to the Austrian chronicler, Pope Innocent sent cardinals to Treviso to repulse an expedition made up of a multitude of men and women of various ages, heading overseas.[37] Now if this chronicler *was* well-informed, and if Sicard *was* that papal agent (legate, rather than cardinal)—twin hypotheses impossible to confirm—then, just possibly, Sicard's chronicle entry was based on more than hearsay.

One formidable obstacle blocks Sicard's credibility: the implausibly tender years of his anonymous wee commander. Could this little chap really be Nicholas of Cologne, the acknowledged leader of the Rhenish *pueri*? Nicholas's age is not mentioned elsewhere, although it is true that one German chronicler calls him a *little* boy (*puerulus*).[38] The image of an infant leader is striking. Even more striking is the realization that without him the notion of a youth movement vanishes, for without a little child to lead them, Sicard's "infinite multitude" of German paupers turns into an undifferentiated mass of poor folk. No doubt that the demography of medieval Europe means that a very high percentage of these German immigrants were bound to have been young people. The question arises: did Sicard hear rumors about (or choose to exaggerate) the wondrous youth of their leader as a vivid device for thrusting the youthfulness of this army of German paupers into the spotlight? Or had this bedraggled invading host—whether or not it was the contingent led by Nicholas of Cologne—actually chosen a "child younger than ten" to lead them?

Whatever was the case, this swarm of poor migrants arriving in Italy unannounced in 1212 could only belong to the Children's Crusade. Their German origins and raggle-taggle status perfectly match contemporary accounts from Piacenza and Genoa. And if further confirmation were needed, we have their faith in a sea-crossing without ships and their ambition to reconquer Jerusalem. Following the French phase of the movement, both of these themes repeatedly resurface in the sources. Hence Sicard's mass of impoverished Germans must have been the *peregrinatio puerorum*—or a sizable contingent thereof—in its final stages.

The meatiest chronicles can be tasted last. Totalling twenty-three relatively extended passages, these run from around seven printed lines to a solid paragraph. Yet here, too, things are not quite what they seem. None of these relatively longer narratives present us with a trustworthy exposition of causes and consequences, let alone a reliable itinerary of the *peregrinatio puerorum* from its inception in northern Europe to its termination, not many months later, at the shores of the Mediterranean. Nonetheless, these chroniclers often bravely attempted to present an overview, indeed an interpretation, of the movement from its beginning to its end, despite the fact that their information was unequal to the task.[39] What the best of these scattered fragments of an unwritten narrative do manage to achieve, all the same, is to whet our appetite for more.

Take the *Annales Stadenses*, for example. It was composed between c. 1232 and 1256 by Albert, Abbot of Stade, a monastery located west of Hamburg in northern Germany, and so at a considerable distance from the route of the Rhenish *pueri*. Albert's tone is neutral, remarkably so:

> Around this time [1212] children (*pueri*) without a master, without a leader, ran together with eager steps from all the towns and cities of every region to parts beyond the sea. When people asked them where they were running, they answered, "To Jerusalem, to seek the Holy

> Land." The parents of many of them confined them at home, but in vain; for they smashed their locks or walls and escaped. The Pope [Innocent III] heard rumors about them, and, sighing, said: "These children reproach us, for while we sleep they race to recover the Holy Land." Even now it is unknown what happened to them. But many of them returned home, and when they were asked the reason for their journey, they said they did not know. Also around the same time naked women (*nudae mulieres*) ran through the towns and cities saying nothing.[40]

Emerging everywhere, all at once, for no discernible reason, are leaderless bands of *pueri*. Albert provides them with no birthplace and no birthdate except for the year 1212. Their movements are unmappable. They run together "from all the towns and cities of every region." That this was predominantly a peasant enthusiasm is left unsaid. Albert, however, does highlight what must have been the case. The crusade of the *pueri*, flowing from town to town, and from city to city, continued to pick up new recruits. Urban laborers and artisans, their families, and recent peasant immigrants to towns—all were swept along by a torrent of revivalist enthusiasm. Jerusalem was the magic name on their lips. The Holy Land was their land of dreams. Then Albert, magician-like, introduces another potent theme. Their parents, fearing the worst, imprison them, only for the *pueri* to stage a dramatic escape. Energized by the call for crusade, they break free. Like other contemporary escapees from parental control—Francis of Assisi (himself briefly a domestic prisoner) at twenty-four or so;[41] Clare of Assisi at around seventeen or eighteen; and her still younger sister, later, as a Franciscan nun, renamed Agnes—the *pueri* were runaways in an age of religious runaways.[42] For youngsters like these, running away was a conversionary experience, as it was for youthful converts to the crusade.

Now no less a figure than Innocent III steps forward. His self-reproachful, wholly fictive comment is Albert's way of rebuking the Pope for his failure to recover the Holy Land. Perhaps it is also Albert's way of interjecting a quiet note of sympathy. Writing twenty to forty years after the event, Albert discloses—"even now it is unknown what happened to them." Such candor was far from typical. A good number of his fellow monks, hearing titillatingly blood-curdling rumors of the terrible fate of the runaway *pueri*, translated rumor into fact; so have modern writers.

Finally, what do we make of the mysterious silence of the returnees? Were they dazed, bewildered, traumatized, humiliated? Or were they just reluctant to share their vision with non-believers? Their silence leads us directly on to that of the mute *nudae mulieres*, the naked women depicted by Albert as silently running through anonymous towns and cities, as if retracing the itinerary of the *pueri*. Here the inexplicable explains the inexplicable.

Albert of Stade's well-executed sketch of the *peregrinatio puerorum* is a work of art, rather than a mine of historical information. While little of Albert's art is mythistorical, a number of the other longer narratives are saturated with mythistorical emplotments and awash with mythistorical motifs. Indeed, three of these texts are crucial. The essential mythistory of the Children's Crusade rests upon them. Imaginative and gifted men of letters wrote them: the White Monk Alberic of Trois-Fontaines (d. after 1251); the Black Monk Matthew Paris (d. 1259); and the Black Friar Vincent of Beauvais (d. 1264). Elsewhere their works testify to their scholarly qualities and serious-mindedness, but not here.

Devoting a paragraph or so to the Children's Crusade, they confabulate what in our time would be the synopsis of a gripping, action-packed screenplay "based on a real event." As talented writers, they were doubly fortunate. They lived decades after the events in question; and had few facts at their disposal. Addicted to moralistic storytelling and lovers of the apt anecdote, they knew how to shape a story. Later medieval writers imbibed their rich concoctions without a second thought. These three, after all, were not anonymous nobodies, but reputable *auctores* (authors = authorities). It follows that these were the true accounts of what had befallen the *pueri*.

By the 1250s, when their work was completed, the pilgrimage-crusade of the *pueri* was well and truly mythistoricized. Thereafter, Alberic, Matthew, and Vincent were not only read, they were copied, paraphrased, embroidered. Their picturesque, thematically rich tales became the most widely diffused, most compelling, as well as the most authoritative representations of the Children's Crusade. No subsequent writer, medieval or modern, novelist, poet, or specialist crusade scholar, has entirely freed himself or herself from their magic spell. Privileged ever afterwards, these classic mythistorical texts have been ranked amongst the most valuable "contemporary sources" for "the history of the Children's Crusade." Not for the first or last time, art has proved to be more intellectually and emotionally satisfying, and more durable, than life.

Besides these Latin annalists and chroniclers, two official documents (one royal, one papal) also pertain to the crusade of 1212. In an age of increasing documentation on the part of church and state, this represents a pretty thin tally. An obvious example is the surviving registers of Innocent III, the Pope of the children's crusade—a Pope famously hungry for information. These yield not a single item relating to the *pueri*. However, a precious document, previously overlooked, has recently turned up among the curial letters of Innocent's successor, Honorius III. This papal letter of 1220 not only adds the name of a third *puer*, Otto, to the two others already on the short list (Stephen of Cloyes and Nicholas of Cologne); but also it carries the implication that the fate of Otto's erstwhile companions was much more varied and probably less darkly-colored than that painted by the mythistorians.[43]

Additional pre-1301 sources include a French vernacular verse chronicle, which puts a question mark over the notion that all the *pueri* were penniless; and two *exempla* or sermon anecdotes (one emphatically positive, the other brutally negative), which exemplify different modes of pulpit broadcasting. More perplexing are the verses of the *Chronicon rhythmicum Austriacum* or *Austrian Rhymed Chronicle* (to 1268). Its unknown author claims to reproduce the very words of the marching song sung by the German children *en route* to the Holy Land under the command of Nicholas of Cologne. If true, it would be the purest of pure gold, offering us unparalleled access to the heretofore hidden thought-world of the young Rhenish pilgrim-crusaders, male and female, revealing their innermost aspirations for eschatological peace, prophetic evangelism, and mystical sexuality.[44]

Lastly comes an indispensable, although indisputably problematic chronicler, John Le Long or John of Ypres. His *Chronica monasterii sancti Bertini* or *Chronicle of the Monastery of Saint-Bertin* holds out no promise of laying bare the secret soul of the *peregrinatio puerorum*, as the *Austrian Rhymed Chronicle* does. Rather, it promises something almost as glorious—anchoring it securely in the exterior world of events. Before that, a major problem needs to be surmounted. According to the conventional rules of historical evidence, John Le Long's statements must be kept farther than at arm's length, at least until subjected to severe critical scrutiny. The reason is plain. John Le Long died in 1383. If the mythistory of the Children's Crusade prevailed over its history from the 1250s onwards, how credible is a chronicler purveying stolen goods more than a century later? A strong case will be made in his defence nonetheless, because John Le Long's testimony is indispensable. On what he says the detection of the obscure origins of the Children's Crusade depends. Where he leads us, we must follow; and where he leads us is to the magnificent cathedral of Chartres.

History, mythistory, memory

So let us say amen to Hayden White: "One of the marks of a good professional historian is the consistency with which he reminds his readers of the purely provisional nature of his characterizations of events, agents, and agencies found in the always incomplete historical record."[45] The scattered, fragmentary, and enigmatic texts of the chroniclers of the *peregrinatio puerorum* intrigue us with what they say and frustrate us with their silence. All in all, the chroniclers have little to say about the aspirations and beliefs of the *pueri*; the circumstances governing the first stirrings of their movement; the traces of their footprints in northern France, then through Lotharingia and the Rhineland, until, over the Alps and destitute, they arrived in Italy, hoping for a miracle. Of their unmythistoricized fate, rigorous speculation is as good a guide as any. Overall, stray pieces of information and a few ambiguous phrases do not compensate for a lack of substantive material. Where are the defining landmarks of medieval reality—papacy, kingship, law, demography, rural economy, peasant society, urban development, scholastic theology, crusade preaching, and so on? There are occasional hints, but nothing more. Out of such exiguous material what kind of history can be fashioned? The positivists would have none of it.

The goal of late-nineteenth-century positivist historians was to construct a scientific history based upon a causal chain of factually ascertained events. For the positivists, the merest whiff of legend was obnoxious and repellent. Ruthlessly, historical wheat had to be separated from mythical chaff; the former to be used, the latter discarded. Any intermingling of the two was anathema, jeopardizing the scientific status of historiography itself. In 1902, the respectable French medievalist Achille Luchaire, having to decide on whether or not there really was a Children's Crusade, felt compelled to defend the historicity of "this strange episode" against historians—positivist zealots, no doubt—who "have questioned [its] truth... [and] have seen in it only the stuff of which a popular legend is made."[46]

The reign of positivism is well and truly over. Nowadays mythistory exists to be utilized, and certainly not discarded. To disjoin history from its Siamese-twin mythistory and send each of them off to separate households for adoption would be to misrepresent the past; indeed, to obstruct access to it, for the mythistoricizing of the chroniclers provides a port of entry into medieval mentalities. The social memory of the Children's Crusade, moreover, is largely grounded in its mythistory, not its history. So mythistory, too, has become part of its history. Over the centuries, what the Germans term *Leben und Nachleben*—the historical existence of the *pueri*, bound together with their posthumous historical continuance—have become almost surgically indivisible. However we configure the mythistory, history, and memory of the crusading enthusiasm of 1212, we encounter the imaginings and observations of the thirteenth-century chroniclers.

What these writers offer us above all are impressions, representations, images. In telling us about the *pueri*, they hold up a mirror to their religious culture as well as to themselves. Through them we glimpse the wonder on the faces of the spectators, as they stare, astonished, ill-at-ease, uncertain, torn between approval and disapproval, at this unparalleled *motio* (movement: people in motion) of ever increasing crowds of peasants and townspeople, a multitude of self-proclaimed crusaders processing past them, led, conspicuously so, by the young. The rhetoric of revivalism flavoring their accounts, the chroniclers cannot help but reveal the impact of the enthusiasm of the *pueri* upon those who stared hard at them, amazed:

> an outstanding thing and one much to be marveled at, for it is unheard of throughout the ages...[47] marvelous and unheard of in the whole world...[48] and this thing, unheard of in past ages, was a wonder to many...[49] they and many other shepherd boys in many localities were held by... the common people in great veneration because they believed that they too could work miracles...[50] A wonderful movement of youths... We believe that this was effected by magic arts...[51] For it is said this boy had received a message from an angel that he and his following should recapture the Lord's sepulcher from the... villainous Saracens.[52]

The *peregrinatio puerorum* was unheard of, miraculous, and more ominously, magical. Despite the barbs of the positivists, the rhetorical tropes and mythistorical motifs of the thirteenth-century chroniclers have retained their freshness and power. It is their images and representations of the *pueri* which have been preserved—airbrushed or enhanced—in the albums of social memory.

2
History: The Pope and the *Pueri*

Innocent III (1198–1216) fathered many a crusade, although, so far as the *pueri* of 1212 are concerned, his paternity has never been acknowledged. True, he never summoned the Children's Crusade; never had it preached; never granted it a plenary indulgence; never provided it with a papal legate; never encouraged, authenticated, or officially deigned to notice it. All of which means that the crusade of the *pueri* was born canonically illegitimate, without the merest whisper of a clerical benediction attending its nativity. Even so, it was Innocent's. The *pueri* were, so to speak, his illegitimate children.[1]

Innocent's crusades generated the popular enthusiasm which energized this extraordinary movement and set it in motion. Then, when all movement ceased, and the *peregrinatio puerorum* had run its course, he learned from it, and built on it. Innocent III was the central figure of an extraordinarily creative period. Set within the Innocentian era, the Children's Crusade begins to make sense.

The papal image

Years after his death, the Franciscan chronicler Salimbene, who also mythistoricized the Children's Crusade, recounts an apocryphal anecdote about him. Calling him an "audacious man, a man of great spirit," Salimbene relates that

> he once held up and measured to himself the holy relic of the seamless robe of the Lord, and it seemed to him that the Lord was a man of small stature. Yet when he put the robe on, he saw that it was far too big for him. And so he stood in great awe and reverenced it, as indeed was proper.[2]

Figure 3 Pope Innocent III, upper register of fresco, church of Sacro Speco, Subiaco (c. 1216).

Until he was thirty-seven, when he was given a new name—probably not one of his own choosing—he was Lothar of the Conti of Segni.[3] Office then eclipsed selfhood: "I am so much at the mercy of others... that I am almost deprived of my own self."[4] Max Weber, one of sociology's twin founding fathers, distinguishes personal charisma from charisma of office.[5] Innocent's charisma was of the second kind. To almost all of those who were ushered into his presence, it was his official persona which mattered. While his sometimes caustic wit and moments of sunlit relaxation were noted, it was the business of the church, his bride, which absorbed him.

So it was not entirely due to underdeveloped pictorial technique that his surviving thirteenth-century portraits depict the office rather than the man, for in a sense, the office was his true likeness. Gerhart Ladner, nonetheless, discerns what could be a naturalistic quality to his portraits in the "longish, rounded shape of the face" and his "relative youthfulness." Although he is always shown beardless, he does seem to be wearing a moustache in some of his early pictures.[6] The Subiaco fresco (c. 1216) unmistakably proclaims his hieratic power, clothing him in the costume of authority. Expressionless in his dignity, he faces the world outfitted in the full regalia of ecclesiastical monarchy—chasuble, dalmatic, tunicle, alb, fanon, pallium, and tiara (Figure 3).[7] These were the vestments of Pope Innocent III, spiritual leader of Latin Christendom.

Encounter in Perugia

Now in his late forties or early fifties, James of Vitry was one of the foremost modernizing clerics of the Innocentian era—a churchman after Innocent's own heart.[8] As a university-educated reformer; a writer (or soon-to-be writer) of travel letters, church histories, sermons, crowd-pleasing sermon stories (*exempla*)—as well as an experienced crusade preacher against Cathars and Muslims—James of Vitry's intellectual and moral credentials were impeccable. Recently he had been elected bishop of Acre in the distant kingdom of the crusaders. But before he could take up his episcopal post, he needed papal confirmation and consecration. So Vitry had business to transact with Innocent III, which was one reason why he was traveling across half of Christendom during the late spring and summer of 1216. Setting out from Flanders or the Rhineland, he headed southwards towards the papal state in central Italy.

Four years earlier the *pueri* had taken a similar journey. They faced danger, deprivation, and death on their pilgrimage. Unlike them, James of Vitry, a bishop-elect, rather than a poor peasant, would never have to beg for food, water, warmth, or shelter. Nor would the prospect of an Alpine crossing into Lombardy have terrified him. Indeed, the previous winter he had gone to Rome to attend the Fourth Lateran Council, where he may have heard Innocent himself deliver a sermon to the conciliar fathers.[9]

Besides obtaining episcopal confirmation, there was a second item on his agenda. James had vowed to plead at the papal court for the formal recognition of the Beguines, fervent religious women of the Low Countries and the Rhineland who had broken with the world's values, but continued to live in the worldliest of settings, the thriving and populous towns. The Beguines were Mary of Oignies's sisters in religion, and Mary, whose *vita* (saint's life) James had written, was his closest spiritual friend.

Perugia was then the temporary home of the papal curia, where Innocent III, his cardinals, and his army of clerical assistants were currently in residence. Here James of Vitry arrived on July 17, 1216. Dangling from his neck was the severed finger of Mary of Oignies, encased in a small silver reliquary. Three years before James set out for the papal court he watched Mary die. Her finger was then detached and given to him; she became his constant traveling companion. For a man to protect himself by wearing the relic of a saint—usually, but not always, a body part—was perfectly licit and not at all superstitious, argued the pre-eminent theologian of the Middle Ages, Thomas Aquinas.[10] While *en route* to the papal court, James attempted to ford a river in Lombardy. Mary's miraculous intervention saved him from drowning.[11] So when James of Vitry entered the cathedral of San Lorenzo in Perugia on that hot July day, Mary of Oignies, coffined in her pendant reliquary, came with him.

Coming into the papal presence, James encountered the great and illustrious Pope Innocent III, now a foul-smelling, virtually naked corpse decomposing in the summer heat.[12] On the eve of his burial, grave-robbers crept into the *duomo*, cooly inspected Innocent's corpse adorned in precious ecclesiastical vestments—much like those he is shown wearing in his Subiaco portrait—then stripped it bare. Such acts were not unusual. The cadavers of recently deceased prelates were almost routinely despoiled and their possessions looted, which is why it seems odd that the Pope's sumptuously robed body was left unwatched and unguarded. Vitry's comment was appropriate, if banal: "how brief and vain is the deceptive glory of this world."

What James of Vitry fails to mention is Innocent's funeral in Perugia. Perhaps still shaken by his gruesomely unexpected encounter with the Pope, or exhausted by his journey and the intense heat, he may not have felt strong enough to attend it. According to an undated, but probably contemporary Perugian source, Innocent's funeral was held later on that same Sunday. Quite naturally, the anonymous clerical author breathes not a word about the embarrassing nocturnal desecration of the Pope's remains, an omission which makes neither the Perugian text nor James of Vitry's report suspect.[13]

Crowding into the *duomo*—the scene of the pope's abject humiliation the previous night—"a copious multitude of clerics, and an innumerable multitude of [lay] men and women"[14] witnessed Innocent's entombment in a marble coffin placed in the chapel of Perugia's most celebrated local saint, Sant'Ercolano, whose altar Innocent himself had consecrated in June.[15] The very next day the assembled cardinals met and elected a new pope, Honorius III.

Innocent was eulogized, never sainted. It is Innocent the papal intellectual and orator whom the anonymous Perugian chronicler praises. Admirable was his learning in the seven liberal arts; his distinction in theology; his quickness of mind; the eloquence and fluency of his speech;

and the sonority, audibility, and intelligibility of his voice. Innocent's charisma of office is encapsulated in a phrase: those who beheld him respected and feared him. A final observation implies, perhaps, more than it says. Innocent's greatest achievement was the degree to which he exalted the Roman church.

Yet in spite of his charitable donations, undoubted Christocentric piety, and efforts to rescue abandoned infants, whose bodies bobbing in the Tiber horrified him, the alpine heights of holiness—let alone miracle-working—eluded him. Neither, try as he might, could he work miracles in the politics of Christendom.

The Innocentian epoch

The papal electors were at first hesitant about choosing him. His youth counted against him. No one of his age would normally have been considered *papabile*, eligible for the church's highest office. But circumstances favored him. The recent death of the German Emperor Henry VI left the affairs of Italy and the Empire in turmoil, offering the church rare opportunities for political self-assertion. Decisiveness was called for. What the church now needed was an active, vigorous, interventionist advocate; and Lothar's positive qualities outweighed any potential liability. For one thing, he had the right background—an aristocratic, wealthy, landed family with strong Roman connections. For another, he was well-educated, impressively so. As the author of his "deeds" (*gesta*) graphically puts it, he had "sweated out his studies" at the schools of Paris and Bologna.[16] These were the Harvard and Oxford of his day—the twin peaks of late-twelfth-century learning—and he had scaled them. He was well-traveled. While at Paris, he went on pilgrimage to St. Thomas Becket's shrine at Canterbury, probably with his fellow student Stephen Langton. Thirdly, the books he wrote as a cardinal-deacon testified to his biblical scholarship, liturgical piety, and moral self-confidence. His gloomy masterpiece *On the Misery of the Human Condition* became a classic text of in-the-world asceticism, appreciated by both Catholics and Protestants.[17] Finally—perhaps most important of all—he was an ecclesiastical insider. He had served his apprenticeship in the papal curia. He was elected on the second ballot.

Historians think the electors made a sound choice. Innocent's pontificate is regularly rated "the apogee"[18] or "the zenith"[19] of the medieval papacy. At a time when the church, institutionalized Christianity, enjoyed an unparalleled position in European politics, society, public values, and intellectual life, Innocent III was its pivotal figure. He was the architect of the Papal State; and it was during his occupancy of the papal throne that the church firmly and decisively insisted on its claim to the moral and religious leadership of Latin Christendom. It is true that during his reign as papal monarch, kings and emperors challenged and frustrated his political goals. Nonetheless, the prestige and spiritual influence of the Roman church were never greater.

Litigation was the focus of much of Innocent III's ecclesiastical business. The medieval church was at war with itself. The only victors were the canon lawyers. Endless cases required papal adjudication. Committed to dealing with a heavy workload of routine business, while simultaneously advancing his ambitious reform program—which included the herculean task of stamping out the culture of bribery in papal officialdom—Innocent struggled to renew the church's moral authority.

Innocent III's Fourth Lateran Council of 1215 was arguably the most important church council between Nicaea (325) and Trent (1545–63). It was the greatest parliament of the medieval church and the culmination of Innocent's pontificate. More than 1,200 churchmen, together with a sprinkling of laymen, came to Rome. A legislative package of cathedral-like proportions was the Fourth Lateran's monument—seventy decrees plus the crusade decree *Ad liberandam*. Like the Christian story pictured in the cathedral of Chartres, the decrees of the Fourth Lateran enclosed the entire Latin Christian universe from doctrine to devotion.

That was Innocent's world, but was it also the world of the young crusade enthusiasts of 1212, the *pueri*? To be sure, the assembled prelates did not come to Rome to discuss the religious aspirations of shepherds and peasants. Nevertheless, the religion of the Christian laity concerned them. Popular Christianity was vibrant, sometimes distressingly so. It was there to be regulated, curbed, channeled, encouraged—and, if necessary, strangled at birth. That is why the Fourth Lateran defined orthodoxy, condemned heresy, and promoted clerical reform. Reform was necessary to guard against clerical ignorance, immorality, and greed, all of which were driving the laity into the welcoming arms of the heretics. To safeguard the faith, the conciliar fathers decreed a new religious minimalism—obligatory annual confession and communion.

The last trumpet of the Fourth Lateran was loud and clear. It was the crusading decree, *Ad liberandam*. Two years earlier, about six months after the Children's Crusade, Innocent sent out a summons for a new crusade, the Fifth (April 19–29, 1213). In his bull, Innocent outlined an innovative, populist, all-inclusive recruitment strategy, which *Ad liberandam* confirmed. This was a major shift in papal policy. Instead of targeting the chivalric class—the great nobles and professionally trained military men, the knights—Innocent was opening up the crusades to anyone and everyone, regardless of age, sex, infirmity, or military suitability. The crusade vow could be taken without prior examination. Then, for those unfit for service, it could be redeemed for a cash payment. The inducement was the highly valued crusade indulgence, which brought spiritual rewards. That could be retained. Money raised by this transaction would pay for the services of battle-tested knights. The crusade vow was now a medium of exchange.

Innocent envisaged taking the cross as an orthodox outlet for lay zeal. Moreover, it allowed the laity active involvement in an increasingly clericalized church. As the central pillar of the religion of the laity, the crusade was a perfect alternative to heresy. The Children's Crusade persuaded Innocent that ordinary Christians still fervently embraced crusading ideals and would flock to take the cross, just as the *pueri* had done. How paradoxical that an impulsive popular movement could have inspired rational, clerical planning. How paradoxical that what Innocent took as a practical and achievable blueprint for crusading success was the end-product of creative religious impossibilism.

Religious creativity and impossibilism in the age of Innocent III

The Children's Crusade burst upon the scene unexpectedly to universal astonishment. While contemporaries struggled to comprehend what was happening, later observers have the advantage of being able to situate the crusade of the *pueri* in its native habitat—the flourishing religious creativity and impossibilism of the Innocentian age.

Characteristic of the Innocentian era was trust in divine providence, which was the bed-rock of religious impossibilism. Without it, the *pueri* would never have begun their journey. Providentialism saw God's hand ever-present in human history. That is why failed crusades demanded a theological explanation. God ruled history and gave the crusades his blessing. The success of the First Crusade confirmed that God willed it. So how could a crusade fail? The Second Crusade, preached by a charismatic living saint, Bernard of Clairvaux, failed miserably. St. Bernard's task was to explain why God, who favored the crusades, permitted the Second Crusade to fail. Scripture came to his aid. The Israelites—God's chosen people until the Christians replaced them—sometimes failed the test of battle because they were unworthy of their high calling. Bernard reaffirmed divine providence by applying biblical reasoning to the Second Crusaders, whose unworthiness stemmed from fractiousness and immorality, which, provoking God's anger, resulted in the failure of the Second Crusade.[20]

Echoing Bernard's harsh judgment on the Second Crusaders was the verdict of the chronicler Henry of Huntingdon (d. 1155):

> But God despised them, and their incontinence came up before Him... for they abandoned themselves to open fornications, and to adulteries... and to robbery and every sort of wickedness... Afterwards, they were destroyed by the enemy's swords.[21]

The scandal of sexual misbehavior in the crusader host was seen as crucial to the army's loss of divine favor. Even during the ultimately victorious First Crusade, the same issue had arisen.[22] This may shed light on a theme which appealed to commentators on the Children's Crusade, who implicitly contrasted the sexual purity and "innocence" of the *pueri* of 1212 with the debauchery of their grown-up crusade predecessors.

Crusade providentialism went hand-in-glove with a prophetic sensibility. It is no coincidence that the greatest of medieval prophets, Joachim of Fiore (d. 1202), was a child of the crusading epoch and in his alluringly cryptic world-historical conflation of past, present, and future, found a place for the war against the infidels. His personal intervention in the crusading movement came when he met Richard Lionheart, king of England, at Messina in 1190. *En route* to the Third Crusade, Richard requested a meeting with Abbot Joachim, "for this Joachim had the spirit of prophecy and used to foretell what was going to happen."[23] Whatever impression of a favorable outcome to the crusade which Richard may have taken away from his meeting with Joachim, it turned out, unfortunately, to be false.

Joachim taught that the new century which began in 1200 would see the tumultuous transition to a third epoch in human history, the age of the Spirit. The standard-bearers of the first age, that of the Father, were the elderly. Youths were the representatives of the second age, that of the Son. But symbolic of the third age, that of the Holy Spirit, which was imminent, were children, *pueri*. Joachim's disciples pored over his prophecies. Among the most enthralled were Franciscans like Salimbene, for the Franciscans saw themselves written into Joachite prophecy as an *ordo parvulorum*, an order of little ones, of *pueri*.[24] Although Joachite prophecy had no impact upon the *pueri* of 1212, revivalist enthusiasm itself encourages a spirit of prophetic elation. Later writers like Salimbene and the author of the *Austrian Rhymed Chronicle* added a prophetic element to the mythistory of the Children's Crusade.

So prevalent was the prophetic spirit that Innocent himself could not escape it. Summoning the Fifth Crusade in 1213, Innocent pronounced the days of Islam numbered. The sway of the beast in *Revelations* will last 666 years, he prophesied, "of which already nearly 600 have passed."[25] While the Fourth Lateran Council condemned Joachim of Fiore's theology of the Trinity, it ignored his prophetic system, even though Joachite prophecy came to influence the heretical beliefs of the Amalricians.

The Amalricians were a deviant sect of university-educated priests and lay converts who adhered to the teachings of the Paris theologian Amalric of Bène (d. c. 1206).[26] The Fourth Lateran pulled no punches. It hit out at "the utterly perverse opinion of the impious Amalric, whose mind the Father of Lies has blinded to such an extent that his teaching must be reckoned not so much heretical, as insane (can. 2)."[27]

Amalricianism was a potent concoction of gnosticism ("hell is nothing other than ignorance, paradise nothing other than knowledge of the truth"); antinomianism ("whoever knows that God is working within him cannot sin"); and pantheism ("whatever is, is God"). Operating subversively as priests within the parish structure, Amalric's adherents used their pulpits to fish for converts. This was what the church dreaded most—a clerical, intellectual heresy infecting the laity with its contagious toxins.

The death of their charismatic leader Amalric devastated the Amalricians. Probably it was during this unhappy time that they incorporated a sense of apocalyptical urgency derived from Joachim of Fiore into their previously static belief system. A new age, the Age of the Spirit, was about to be born. "The Son has worked up to now," they affirmed, "but the Holy Spirit begins to work from now on, even to the end of the world."

Prophecy demanded an eschatological deadline. No more than five years remained. Four plagues would herald the End. Famine would strike the people; the sword, the nobles; earthquake, the burgesses; fire, the prelates of the church. Those who were spared would be infused with the Spirit. They would become spiritual men, *spirituales*. Glorifying the French Capetian monarchy, the Amalricians assigned a providential role in the impending cosmic drama to King Philip Augustus's son, the future Louis VIII. Amalric had been his tutor.

Now if the clock on their eschatological time-bomb started ticking on the death of Amalric (c. 1206), the Amalricians pretty accurately predicted their own fate. Betrayed by their pseudo-convert Master Ralph of Namur, ten defrocked priests—virtually all the prominent leaders of the sect—were burned alive in Paris in 1210. A few others, along with some lay converts, were imprisoned rather than incinerated. Master Godin, the last known Amalrician intellectual, was thrown into the flames at Amiens about two years later. The sect, apparently, had ceased to exist. But if so, why did the Fourth Lateran call attention to Amalric's "insane" teachings in 1215? Was it because the Catholic polemics directed against them were circulating their doctrines? Oddly enough, in his two-paragraph-long *Life of Innocent III*, Martin of Troppau (d. 1279) devotes almost his entire second paragraph to the teachings of Amalric.[28] Perhaps the Amalricians had not been hunted to extinction after all.

Was it pure coincidence that the prophetic date of the Amalricians, 1212 (or near enough), was also the year of the Children's Crusade? Like the Amalricians, the French *pueri* seem to have had a messianic view of the Capetian monarchy, although their hero was Philip Augustus, the father, not the son. Then, too, there was a territorial link. The leader of the French *pueri*, Stephen of Cloyes, came from a village within the diocese of Chartres, while the cathedral city of Chartres was in all likelihood the birthplace of the Children's Crusade. Before Amalric of Bène became a Paris Master, he was raised and probably educated in the territory of Chartres, the Chartrain. Perhaps he attended the famous school of Chartres, whose scholars leaned towards Platonism and natural philosophy. That was where he may have acquired his taste for pantheism.

No Amalrician missionary preachers have been traced to the Chartrain. Yet the question remains—and it is an interesting one—were any of the dispersed Amalrician faithful active in that region around the year 1212? One art-historian argues that Chartres never forgot its heretical native son. She believes that an image of Amalric was sculpted on the tympanum above the right portal of the north transept of the cathedral, in the guise of one of Job's false comforters.[29] Alas, her case is unpersuasive. No matter how unsubstantiated, of course, prophetic possibilities of this kind are always tantalizing. Consequently, it should be stressed that no evidence whatsoever suggests that Amalrician prophecy ignited the white-hot enthusiasm of the *pueri*. Moreover, it is hard to see by what sleight of hand it could have done.

Although the Innocentian era was awash in heresy, no contemporary chronicler accused the *pueri* of holding heretical beliefs. But heretical Amalricians and Catholic *pueri* did have one thing in common. Both sets of believers were dedicated impossibilists, builders of dreams. As such, they were both authentic products of the Innocentian era's creative religious landscape—for what was heresy but a creative, if dangerous, variation on a theme? Heresy, a recurrent phenomenon in Christian history, is a typical manifestation of religious vigor and vitality.

But Innocent III would have found such a notion incomprehensible as well as reprehensible. To Innocent and the assembled prelates of the Fourth Lateran Council, heresy was an abominable perversion of the faith, a threat to the soul of Christendom, which is why thirteenth-century heretics faced unrelenting persecution. Of the major and obscure heretics of the Innocentian era—the Waldensians, Cathars, Amalricians, Speronists, Ortliebians, etc.—only the Waldensians survived long enough to become Calvinists.[30] Heresy thus exemplifies the perils of impossibilism, and in this respect, too, it can be likened to the crusade of the *pueri*.

Undertaken in defiance of worldly wisdom, impractical in the extreme, the Children's Crusade was impossibilism in motion. The spurning of workaday rationality in the teeth of parental and clerical opposition implies a quasi-monastic "contempt for the world" and the world's wisdom—a perennial, defining feature of Christian impossibilism. A conversionary disregard for what the world valued—markedly different from Innocent III's own moderate Christian stoicism—pervaded the playfully eccentric spirituality of early Franciscanism, just as it did the ascetic-ecstatic piety of the early Beguines. Among the Christian laity in both northern and southern Europe, monastic flight-from-the-world was beginning to yield to unworldliness-within-the-world, and despite the best efforts of the Innocentian church, impossibilism's ardent spiritual wings proved difficult to clip.

The spiritual trademark of the religious impossibilism of many of these groups was pious begging. Instead of enjoying an assured income from monastic estates, as the church preferred, impossibilists freely chose a precarious existence, happily reliant on divine providence, not knowing when next they would eat. Beguines, Franciscans, and several other new religious brotherhoods and sisterhoods favored such a lifestyle; and exactly the same holds for the multitude of *pueri* on the road in 1212. The *pueri*, like their fellow impossibilists, were pilgrims-in-the-world, exposed, vulnerable, subsisting on hand-outs.

First and foremost, the Children's Crusade was a revivalist mass movement, a community of believers on the march. The communitarian impulse, combining voluntary association with shared, sometimes quasi-utopian aspirations, was the seedbed of religious creativity. During the crusading centuries from the late eleventh to the late thirteenth centuries, more than fifty new religious orders were founded. And like the Cistercians and Franciscans, some of these religious communities had extensive networks of monasteries and friaries stretching across Europe from Scandinavia to Sicily, and from Portugal to Hungary.[31]

There is no better guide to the religious creativity and impossibilism of the Innocentian era than James of Vitry. Ever sensitive to new religious communities, Vitry, in the course of his travels, keenly observed the leading varieties of orthodox Christian impossibilism of his day, including the Beguines of Mary of Oignies, the Humiliati of Lombardy, the Friars Minor of Francis of Assisi, and the Poor Sisters, known also as the Clarissas, the female branch of the Franciscan Order, whose beginnings can be traced to a momentous night in 1212, the year of the Children's Crusade.

That year, on the night of Palm Sunday (18 March), a young woman of about seventeen or eighteen, the daughter of a prominent aristocratic family, slipped out of her home, and made her escape. The young runaway was Clare of Assisi. For about a year, chaperoned by a female friend, she had been having secret meetings with an eccentric fellow townsman, a devotee of poverty and penance. Francis, already a town character, revered by some, mocked by others, had converted to his strange new mode of life six years earlier, attracting disciples who included Clare's cousin, Rufino. Theatrically severing all links with his merchant father in the full glare of publicity by stripping off his clothes and handing them back, Francis was virtually a runaway himself. Thanks to the support of Guido, Bishop of Assisi, Francis's fraternity of pious beggars had been granted preliminary approval by Pope Innocent III in 1210. "And then Clare committed herself wholly to the counsel of Francis, considering him to be, after God, the guide to the life she wanted to lead."[32]

Clare's hair was cut; she took the veil. Then, not many days after her conversion, Clare's younger sister Catherine, aged fifteen, renamed in religion Agnes, became a second Franciscan runaway. Despite their family's aggressive efforts to reclaim them, both Clare and Agnes were now sisters in religion within the Franciscan family. Clare's hagiographer, probably Thomas of Celano, forgivably exaggerates the impact of her conversion on the young people of Assisi. He writes of crowds of young people, male and female, inspired by her example, abandoning the world and the flesh.[33] This brief outburst of conversionary enthusiasm was Assisi's version of the Children's Crusade.

Most, though not all, of Clare's impossibilist aspirations were ultimately frustrated. Relatively soon, she lost her first battle. She and her sisters-in-religion were not permitted to adopt the Franciscan lifestyle of wandering about begging. Instead, they were confined to convents on the Benedictine model. Later, she lost her second battle over her extreme fasting. Francis and Bishop Guido refused to allow her to abstain totally from food on some days, as she was doing, and instead insisted, by virtue of her obedience, that she consume no less than 1½ oz. of bread daily.[34]

Finally, in her third battle, fought over the question of Franciscan poverty, she did win a partial victory. Clare was absolutely determined never to abandon Francis's original vision of providential precariousness, meaning that a day without alms was a day without food. Grudgingly, the papacy allowed her a limited victory. The religious house she ruled, and the first convent of her order, San Damiano, would be an exception, but the majority of the other houses of Poor Sisters were forced to follow the pattern of female Benedictine or Cistercian convents whose lands yielded an assured level of income. That was the price of papal acceptance. Although compromise was undoubtedly painful to her, she nevertheless secured a limited degree of Franciscan impossibilism.

Other Christian impossibilists, Francis of Assisi and Mary of Oignies among them, learned to make similar adjustments. Intent upon combating heresy by allowing scope for orthodox innovation, Innocent III responded favorably to religious creativity. Viability, however, also concerned him. The solution was a papally approved rule which insured that pristine impossibilism with its unattainable, extraterrestrial ambitions could be, if not wholly subdued, then at least moderated.

But the *pueri* of 1212, those fervent, expectant, enthusiastic converts to Christian impossibilism, never pursued an institutional path, despite breathing the same air as the other creative Christian impossibilists of the Innocentian era. Like the early Franciscans, theirs was a literalist, unqualified, popular appropriation of normative religious ideas, which in their case was the idea of the crusade. For them, too, it induced utopian aspirations, boundless horizons, and conversionary ferment. Part of the air they breathed in the Innocentian era was the crusade. Impossible or not, the crusade was Innocent's dream. The *pueri* were his dream-sharers.

Innocent III, papal crusader

World War II was in its death throes when the Big Three met at the Yalta Conference in 1945. Winston Churchill, whether seriously or not, proposed bringing the Pope into the allied camp. Stalin's supposed, often-quoted quip has become proverbial: "How many divisions does the Pope have?" Such a gibe, aimed at Pius XII and his hardly intimidating troop of Swiss Guards, could never have been directed towards Pope Innocent III. The armies he could summon represented a formidable fighting force. For when Innocent III called a crusade, potentially at least, all the knights of Latin Christendom were at his disposal.

Granted that listening to law suits ate up his time; that he was dubbed "the Solomon of our age" for his razor-sharp legal judgments;[35] that the incisive clarity of his thought was lawyer-like—all this may be true enough, but to pigeon-hole Innocent III as a lawyer-Pope is to misconceive his papacy. He was a warrior-Pope. Admittedly, he never personally led his troops into combat, like his bellicose predecessors Leo IX (1049–54) and Innocent II (1130–43), both of whom paid the price for their combativeness through defeat, capture, and imprisonment on the battlefield. Nor was Innocent III insensitive to the crippling financial and human costs of war. Yet the inescapability of warfare for someone of his status and background was a cultural axiom, part of the nature of things.

Political circumstances made him a warrior-Pope. Medieval rulers used warfare as an instrument of policy. So, too, did Innocent III, but only, it could be argued, as a last resort. The Papal State was his creation. He ruled it in conjunction with local communal governments. Having territory to defend, he needed an army. Unlike today's miniscule Vatican City, the thirteenth-century Papal State was a broad bandanna wrapped round Italy's midriff.[36] To protect and enlarge his papal kingdom, and to fight his campaigns in Sicily, Innocent utilized Rome's army; troops sworn to serve him in the lands he ruled; and mercenaries from outside the Papal State. Assisted by his brother Richard and cousin James, Innocent recruited his cavalrymen to fight for the church's sake and God's. Ecclesiastical warfare shaded imperceptibly into holy war, which, in turn, mutated into the finest weapon in the papal armory, heaven-sent for the triumph of Christendom, the crusade.

It was the central thread in Innocent's pontificate and uppermost in mind. 1187, the year Lothar of the Conti of Segni began his clerical career as a sub-deacon, was the same year the True Cross was lost at Hattin, Jerusalem fell, and the Third Crusade was proclaimed. From that date onwards and throughout the whole of his papacy, Innocent never lost his "ardent aspiration to liberate the Holy Land from infidel hands" (Fourth Lateran: can. 71).[37] Less than six months into his pontificate, he summoned the Fourth Crusade; and ten weeks before he died in Perugia, in neighboring Orvieto, in the pouring rain, Innocent preached his last crusade.

On Sunday, May 1, 1216, those who came to hear his crusade sermon received a partial indulgence, a spiritual inducement which was Innocent's innovation. But no such incentive was necessary to draw a crowd that morning in Orvieto. Expectation of the papal presence was enough to fill a church and a nearby piazza. A much larger crowd was anticipated that afternoon, which required a change of venue. The chosen site was a spacious meadow just inside the city walls.

As the rain fell uninterruptedly, young lads climbed trees to see and hear Innocent preach his crusade evangelism from a specially built platform. A local chronicler reports that "the number of those who took the cross… was more than 2,000 men, while the women were few." The meadow rapidly became a swamp. Holding aloft an improvised *baldacchino*, a cortège of nobles escorted the Pope back to his lodging. The incessant rain, in addition to fatigue caused by preaching the crusade, might have weakened the Pope and precipitated his fatal illness in Perugia. One scholar thinks so.[38] And if he is right, then the first fatality of Innocent III's last crusade was Innocent himself. A papacy which commenced with one crusade, terminated with another.

Crusading energies drove Innocent's pontificate. His Christian soldiers were deployed not only on the frontiers of Christendom, but within Christendom itself. Innocent III was the first Pope to act upon the idea that the crusades could serve as an all-purpose instrument of papal policy, foreign and domestic. His papacy was a time of unparalleled crusading activity. The number, scope, and variety of Innocent's crusades were unprecedented and never replicated. Only Urban II (d. 1099), the initiator of the crusading movement, could rival him as a papal crusader. If we count the Children's Crusade as Innocent's—which it was—plus the Fifth Crusade (which he organized and preached, but did not live to see), then Innocent was responsible for a total of seven crusades. But two additional crusading ventures which never came to pass are visible just below the horizon. One was envisaged to compel Milan to stop harboring heretics (1212); and another was threatened against England's disobedient King John (1212/13). If both of them had been preached, then 1212 would have been a year of four crusades. Or five—counting the Children's Crusade. Yet it has to be said that relatively few of Innocent's crusades achieved what he intended them to achieve.

Geographically, Innocent III's crusading activities covered a huge swathe of territory—northwards to the Baltic; southwards to Sicily and Languedoc; eastwards to Byzantium and (after Innocent's death) Egypt; westwards to Spain. The borders of Innocent's Christendom were crusading frontiers. When heresy seemed to be subverting the unity of Latin Christendom, Innocent called for a crusade. By so doing, he Europeanized the crusading movement. Innocent's crusaders confronted a wide variety of foes, who included Christian political enemies (the Markward of Anweiler and his Sicilian supporters); Christian schismatics

(Orthodox Greeks); heretics (Cathars); pagans (Livonians); and Muslims (both North African Moors and Egyptian Arabs).

The crusades were the wars of Christendom. By allowing Christendom to fulfil its neo-Israelite, providential mission of carrying out God's plan on earth, the crusades were perceived as a continuation of sacral history. More of an idea than a land-mass, Christendom (*Christianitas*) was a clerically-constructed, papally-promoted ideology which pre-existed the crusades, but which grew to maturity during the crusading epoch. The idea of Christendom provided a myth of unity for a patchwork of fragmented loyalties. As such, it was the heir of ancient Rome's cultural imperium (*Romanitas*) and the precursor of modern Europe's self-imaginings (*Europa*).[39]

To clerical intellectuals like Innocent III, the unity of Christendom was at once religious, political, territorial, and cultural. Its fundamental premise was the unity of all Christian nations under the leadership of the papacy. For the clergy, the common language of Christendom was Latin. For the illiterate laity, it was the readable iconography of Christian art. The annual rhythm of Christendom—its major feasts, fasts, and holy days—was virtually the same throughout the Latin west. Christendom's sacred geography was dotted with pilgrimage shrines, although its territorial boundaries were elastic, expanding through crusading conquest and missionary success, contracting wherever crusading armies were defeated.

The cross was the universal symbol of Christendom's unity. It was omnipresent—conspicuous in the countryside; in the marketplace; on mountain tops; in cemeteries; at the boundaries of landed properties; at commemorative sites; places of sanctuary; on churches; and, of course, at crossroads.[40] So the cross was simultaneously a religious and a political symbol. Heretics, consequently, rejected it twice over. Full of rage, they burned it, the way a national flag is burned nowadays.

The defining symbol of Christendom, the cross was unquestionably the defining insignia of the crusades. Crusaders wore it on their right shoulder or their chests. They even tattooed it on their flesh, as the corpses of drowned crusaders revealed. So when a large troop of German *pueri* arrived in Piacenza and in Genoa in 1212 wearing the cross, they were proclaiming wordlessly, to all the world, their status as crusaders.[41]

The idea of Christendom gave Christians a collective identity. Overarching one's identity as a Frank or a Lombard, a Londoner or Perugian, was membership in the *populus christianus*, the chosen-peoplehood of Christians, whose common destiny was bound up with the destiny of the Holy Land, Christ's own country. Testifying to the peoplehood of Christians were popular crusades, such as the Children's Crusade.

Nor was the idea of Christendom the private property of clerical intellectuals, too abstract for poor peasants like the *pueri* to grasp. A crusade acclamation that the *pueri* shouted out in French was heard and recorded: "Lord God, exalt Christendom!"[42] That outcry was the *populus christianus* loudly endorsing Innocent III's idea of Christendom and his dream of a crusade. Spiritual affinity is what made the *pueri* Innocent's offspring.

Who were the *pueri*?

They were the leading actors of the Children's Crusade, and yet we know precious little about them. The snippets of information supplied by the medieval chroniclers are just enough to whet the reader's appetite without being able to satisfy it. So any attempt, like this one, to base the history of their *peregrinatio* (pilgrimage, crusade) on evidence rather than on flights of fancy must, paradoxically, employ hypotheses, suppositions, conjectures, and yes, informed speculations, labeled as such.

Medieval childhood provided the richest and mythistorically the most seductive of all the themes, motifs, and tropes embedded in its history. From the aftermath of the Children's Crusade onwards the youthfulness of the *pueri* captivated the mythistorical imagination, so that over the centuries the *pueri* not only retained their youth, but tended to grow younger and younger until nowadays they sometimes appear closer to infancy than to adolescence.

Perhaps it was this exaggerated popular image of the *pueri* which tempted Paul Alphandéry, a fine scholar, to put the medieval idea of childhood at the very heart of his interpretation of the Children's Crusade.[43] Excess leads to excess. So it was natural that the mythistorical youthfulness of the *pueri* would provoke a reaction. Not quite that; it provoked an overreaction.

Enter Peter Raedts, demythologizer extraordinaire. Aiming a deathblow at the popular mythistorical image of the Children's Crusade, Raedts strenuously denied that "the crusade of 1212 was exclusively an action of little children."[44] Yet almost without exception contemporary chroniclers maintained nothing of the sort. That notion comes later. It is mythistorical, not historical.

The chroniclers, in fact, endowed the *pueri* with multiple identities. At different stages of their crusade they were: workmates (fellow shepherds); a liturgical-processional grouping; a socio-economic stratum (poor peasants, male and female servants, urban laborers); and members of an age-group; or more than one of these simultaneously. The nametag "*pueri*" also came to be pinned on all those participating in the *peregrinatio puerorum*. For that way the later chroniclers were able to differentiate the enthusiasts of the Children's Crusade from those of the Shepherds' Crusades (1251, 1320), who largely belonged to the same agrarian underclass as the *pueri*.

Admittedly, as an age category the term *pueri* was used flexibly and loosely (much like American "kids"). It could also have an extended meaning of social subordination (as with "boy" for waiter or bell-hop). Raedts, however, seems to suggest this kind of elastic usage made *pueri* meaningless as an age category. Yet this was not the case. *Pueri* retained its designation as a term denoting age, even if the outer boundaries of *pueritia*, childhood, fluctuated. That was the case, for example, if "child" implied child-like qualities, say, inexperienced in the ways of the world, innocent, naive ("he is but a child").

Isidore of Seville's scheme set the upper limits of infancy at seven, restricting childhood in its narrowest sense to the years from seven to fourteen. Isidore's scheme proved to be extremely influential, but not absolutely dominant. Then there was canon law, which following Roman precedent, fixed the legal age of adulthood at fourteen for boys, and twelve for girls.[45] The chroniclers of 1212 make it abundantly clear that the *pueri* and *puellae* (girls) belonged to a distinct age-group, never more so when they declared that later on adults, mature women, babes at the breast, and older people joined their crusade. Consequently, the Children's Crusade was not, possibly never, composed *exclusively* of young people. Nevertheless, nearly all the chroniclers single out the youthful *pueri* as its core group, as well as its most visible and most remarkable element. At the sight of these young people marching off to the crusades, we can almost sense the amazement of spectators and chroniclers alike.

Raedts disputes this. According to him, the *pueri* were by no means an age-group. On the contrary, they were a social group. Citing the research of Georges Duby,[46] he argues that the *pueri* were socially marginalized, landless peasants of indeterminate years, who worked for meager wages as servants or day-laborers, farm-hands, or shepherds. Younger sons with nothing to inherit, they were too poor to marry. (In medieval village society, marriage brought social adulthood. The *pueri* would thus be "boys" regardless of their age.)

True, a good number of the *pueri* of 1212—and *puellae*: unmarriageable daughters, working as servant girls—probably would have fitted this description. But that does not rule out their actual youthfulness.

It is important to keep in mind that the chroniclers singled them out in relation to other age-groups. In fact, the two senses of *pueri* were far from being mutually exclusive. Raedts, therefore, sets up a false antithesis between two overlapping categories. Others have arrived at a broadly similar conclusion.[47]

Like many of today's underdeveloped societies, thirteenth-century Europe, was, despite high infant mortality, "positively teeming with children,"[48] with perhaps around half the population under twenty-one, and a third under fourteen.[49] These are rough estimates, but the impression of a youthful society remains. The youthfulness of the *pueri* partially accounts for the astonishment of the chroniclers. Seniors in medieval society were supposed to govern juniors. Leadership by the young was a disturbing reversal of the natural order of things, as was their departure in the teeth of parental opposition. Other qualities they manifested were more typical—rashness and youthful fervor (*fervore juvenili*).[50]

Medieval children were supposed to assume the responsibilities of work early. In so doing, they were expected to emulate and to imitate adults. *Imitatio* was stressed, as with piety.[51] Going on crusade was a good example of imitative Christian behavior, and, it could be argued, imitative social behavior as well, for by taking the cross these peasant *pueri* were imitating the chivalric elite. The young were attracted to the crusades, and it was widely believed that young men made ideal crusaders,[52] which is what the *pueri* of 1212 imagined themselves to be.

"In this extraordinary adventure," remarks Pierre Riché *apropos* of the Children's Crusade, "children and adolescents mingled together."[53] Unquestionably, the *peregrinatio puerorum* was a youth movement. In this regard, it is highly significant that the leading expert in the agrarian history of the medieval region of Chartres, André Chédeville, has never come upon the term "*puer*" in the archival documents of the region to mean other than child or young man.[54] Why is this significant? The Chartrain was the birthplace of the Children's Crusade.

3
History: Birthpangs of the Children's Crusade

Pentecost

Eastertide—the juvescence of the year—meant renewal in early-thirteenth-century Europe. The annual agrarian cycle recommenced; passable roads made military campaigns possible; and pilgrims and crusaders were now able to board the ships of the Italian maritime cities for their regular spring or Easter passage to the Levant (*Passagium vernale*; *Passagium paschae*). Chivalric lyrics and romances invested the season with amorous sociability—a season of love-games, tournaments, and the gathering of troubadours. It was a time of flowers. In scenes of the "labors of the months," April was the flower-bearer.[1] Pentecost at Chartres cathedral was signaled by the descent of multi-colored flowers falling from the lofty vaults of the choir, symbolizing the tongues of fire in the descent of the Holy Spirit. A dove was then released: another Pentecostal symbol of the Holy Spirit.[2]

It was then that the Children's Crusade was born: "Between Easter and Pentecost... many thousands of *pueri* from all of Germany and France" abandoned their rural labors and took the cross.[3] This is what a contemporary German chronicler, a monk of Cologne, reports. But where it began, he does not say.

Not unusually in monastic culture, calendrical time was marked by its liturgical season. Especially interesting is that several medieval religious revivals were also Pentecostalist movements. The four major popular religious enthusiasms of the thirteenth century—the Children's Crusade of 1212, the "Great Hallelujah" of 1233, the Shepherds' Crusade of 1251, and the Flagellants of 1260—all commenced during springtime.

James of Vitry divided the Christian year into four parts, corresponding to his quadripartite scheme of Christian history. To James, the span from Easter to Pentecost signified the world historical process from redemption to conversion (*tempus reconciliationis*), while the period from Pentecost to Advent (*tempus peregrinationis*) represented the Christian people's pilgrimage or march through the centuries.[4] Pentecostal conversion—stepping forward to take the cross, for example—thus preceded Pentecostal pilgrimage. That was precisely the pattern followed by those medieval Pentecostalists of 1212, the French *pueri*. Their *tempus peregrinationis*, the inception of their Long March across half of Europe, coincided with the last day of the octave of Pentecost. Time is the first co-ordinate: the season when it began.

Chartres

The second is place: the territory where it began. Chartres was an episcopal city, the diocesan center of a region known as the Chartrain;[5] and the Chartrain was part of the Île-de-France, whose leading city, Paris, was beginning to emerge as the capital of the Capetian kingdom. The glory days of Chartres' once-famous school were behind it, now that the University of Paris put every other educational institution in France in the shade. Chartres' location on the western edge of the fertile Beauce plain was the key to its prosperity. By profitably exporting cereal grains grown in the Beauce, the merchants of Chartres reaped the benefits of feeding Paris.[6] But Chartres lacked urban dynamism; its money economy was secondary; it belonged very much to the landed, seigneurial world of the Chartrain. The peasant population of the Chartrain continued to increase during the twelfth century, peaking in the 1250s. Thirteenth-century rural overpopulation, along with the unavailability of new land, led to a steady trickle of emigration, especially to towns and cities in the Île-de-France like Paris and Saint-Denis.[7]

The diocese of Chartres, one of the largest in the medieval Kingdom of France, was part of the archdiocese of Sens. At the time of the Children's Crusade, the Archbishop of Sens was Peter of Corbeil. He owed his position to the gratitude of a promising former theology student of his at Paris, who became Pope Innocent III. A snatch of undoubtedly apocryphal comic repartee has it—Innocent III: "I made you bishop." Peter of Corbeil: "I made you Pope."[8] Peter was the ecclesiastical superior of the Bishop of Chartres, Reginald of Bar (or Mouçon), through whose energetic promotion and fund-raising the building of the great new Gothic structure of Notre-Dame de Chartres was pushed forward (Figure

4). Bishop Reginald was himself a contributor to the building fund, but donations were also solicited and obtained from the cathedral canons, local guilds, visiting pilgrims, the lords of the Chartrain, the royal house of France, and even prelates from outside the diocese. Further contributions were generated by taking portable reliquaries on fund-raising tours. The cathedral's construction was not yet complete in 1212, although Chartres' solemn liturgies were long-established and meticulously performed by its canons and choirboys known as *pueri*.

Figure 4 Cathedral of Chartres, general view; photographer, Eric de Maré. RIBA Library Photographs Collection, Royal Institute of British Architects.

Chartres was an important shrine-city, drawing in pilgrims from all over the region, especially for major church festivals. Every year during the octave of Pentecost a processional rite was held which took the form of a diocesan pilgrimage. Priests and parishioners from churches scattered throughout the diocese set out on an obligatory pilgrimage to their mother church, assembling there with their parish crosses, banners, relics, and offerings. This gathering of the diocesan faithful coincided with both the usual time for synods (Pentecost), and the stipulated date for the payment of dues owed by parish churches to the cathedral church.[9] At such times, peasants and shepherds, along with local lords and their retinues, knights and pilgrims, would flow into Chartres, temporarily adding to its resident population of clerics, cloth and grain merchants, local traders, money-changers, artisans, students, laborers, and the urban poor. In addition to strengthening diocesan unity, seasonal rituals of this kind reinforced the centrality of the cathedral church.

The pride of Chartres' relic collection was the *sainte chemise*, said to be the shift or tunic which the Virgin Mary was wearing when she gave birth to the baby Jesus.[10] Knights believed that if their tunics touched the reliquary of the *sainte chemise*, they would be unscarred in battle. Thanks to its precious relic, Chartres became the Île-de-France's major sacral shrine. But to call Chartres "the Lourdes of the Middle Ages" (as one writer does) is putting it too exuberantly. Chartres never joined the ranks of Latin Christendom's four premier western pilgrimage sites—Rome, Santiago, Cologne, and Canterbury. Which is not to say that during the thirteenth century, the miracles which the Virgin performed at her cathedral in Chartres were not widely celebrated—and publicized— both in Latin and the vernacular.

Miracles are indicative of popular devotion; publicizing them demonstrates promotional acumen. Of the many forms of medieval devotion, the most conspicuous was pilgrimage to find a miracle cure; and Mary was known to heal her devotees. Devotion, it should be said, was no mere response to human frailty. Complicated feelings—personal piety, loyalty to a patron saint, momentary exaltation—were intermixed in it. Essentially, devotion was an individual matter. But multiplied many times over and intensely focused upon a single object of veneration at a single shrine, personal devotion would become a crowd phenomenon.

The indispensable incubator of medieval revivals like the Children's Crusade was the mixed religious crowd. Thrown together in exceptional circumstances were people of different social ranks, animated by a single impulse. This coming together of noble and peasant, rich and poor, male and female, young and old, was relatively uncommon in the hierarchical society of the Middle Ages, so much so that at times it seemed quasi-miraculous. Medieval revivals like that of the *pueri*, although often communitarian and populist in their initial phase, could differ profoundly in their original impulse. For example, urgency and crisis may have ignited the Children's Crusade, but not all revivals began that way.

At Chartres, more than fifty years earlier than the crusade of the *pueri*, there occurred a revival which turned crowds of pilgrims into unpaid hauliers. Scholars have dubbed it either the "cult of carts" or a "cathedral-building crusade" (*croisade monumentale*). Thinking of it that way is not too far off target, although the 1145 "cult of carts" had nothing to do with the Second Crusade, proclaimed later that same year. But like the popular crusades, the "cult of carts" was also an episode of medieval collective enthusiasm. Apparently, it was triggered by a sudden paroxysm of devotion to the Virgin and her church; but how it arose remains unexplained. No doubt the preachers of Chartres encouraged it, although no evidence suggests they instigated it.

Several chroniclers describe dramatic scenes of crowds of pilgrims converging on Chartres from near and far, determined to raise the towers of the new Romanesque cathedral. Pilgrims coming from Normandy exported the "cult of carts" to their homeland. Human horse-power was then put to work to raise Norman churches.[11] Like animals, pilgrims of every age-group, status, and gender harnessed themselves to haulage wagons. This was back-breaking work. Covered in sweat, they dragged cartloads of heavy building materials from outlying areas to the construction sites—stones, wooden beams, lime, as well as foodstuffs for the laborers employed on the job. Supervised by the clergy, these energetic volunteers made donations to the Virgin of Chartres, zealously performing acts of self-flagellation.

An eye-witness, Haimo, Abbot of Saint-Pierre-sur-Dive, says that in addition to adult enthusiasts, "children and very young children" toiled just as hard as their elders in struggling and straining to pull cumbersome, heavily laden wagons. Little children (*puerulos et infantes*) had themselves penitentially flogged by weeping priests, while invoking the pity of the Virgin on behalf of sick people praying for a miracle cure. One can almost picture Haimo shaking his head in wonder and admiration: "whose stony heart would not be softened as he watched the pious humility of the innocent children dragging their naked ribs on the bare ground?"[12]

"Innocent children" is a motif which resonates with the *peregrinatio puerorum*. Perhaps that explains why Paul Alphandéry—a fine historian who responded imaginatively to the silences of the Children's Crusade—was tempted to inflate the role of the young people in the "cathedral-building crusade" of 1145.[13] Yet contemporaries never spoke of the "cult of carts" as a youth movement. Youngsters were certainly involved in it, but they did not predominate, and they never assumed leadership roles. So, contrary to Alphandéry's interpretation, this was in no way a forerunner of the Children's Crusade. In fact, Haimo is unique among chroniclers of the "cult of carts" in singling out the *puerulos et infantes* for special attention.

But what this fervent church-building revival does show is that Chartres was an established focal point for pilgrims, miracles, and dramatic outpourings of collective zeal several decades before the coming of the Children's Crusade. This was demonstrated once more when the Romanesque cathedral of Chartres caught fire and burned down in 1194. Then, too, crowds assembled, and crowd scenes were re-enacted. Just as before, pious pilgrims painfully manhandled heavy wagons. But this time they hauled them towards the construction site of a splendid new Gothic edifice. And just as before, miracles testified to the fervor of the revivalist cathedral-builders.

A burned-over district

People of medieval Chartres and the Chartrain experienced the crusading movement from the First Crusade (1095) to the mid-thirteenth century, and beyond. It was not something remote; it impinged upon them directly. The crusades offered opportunities for individual salvation which hinged upon life or death decisions—whether to follow one's lord and enlist, or to remain at home. Crusades were times of collective excitement and individual decision-making. Understandably, the crusades left behind rich layers of personal and collective memory. Such an extended, multi-generational period as the crusading epoch creates its own dynamic and character, which French historiography terms a "long interval" (*longue durée*).

Nor can long-term exposure to the crusading movement be reduced to a series of one-off, ephemeral events. Exposure to the crusading movement was reflected in a continuing awareness of the Holy Land and its needs, as well as in crusade institutions like the military orders. Returning crusaders shared their experiences with others. The presence of the crusade inhabited the region. Crusade culture in the Chartrain became part of local tradition. Aristocratic families, for example, remembered their kinfolk who journeyed to the Holy Land, shed their blood there, and never returned. Their names were memorialized through annual recitation in the necrologies of the cathedral or of the local monasteries which these same families endowed as ancestral custom dictated.

Other cherished mementos, like the veneration of the relics of saints brought back from the crusader East, and the stained-glass windows of the cathedral, reminded the people of Chartres of their collective heritage. Of course, there were periods of relative quiescence, when the crusading temperature of the area seemed to have cooled. But the crusading fires of the Chartrain were never entirely extinguished. All it took was a papal summons to a new crusade to reignite them. Repeatedly inflamed by successive crusades, the Chartrain was, archetypically, a "burned-over district."

The notion of a "burned-over district" stems from American revivalism. Originally, it was applied to western New York State in the first half of the nineteenth century, where wave after wave of religious revivalism swept over the area, creating new churches like the Latter Day Saints or Mormons, as well as countless sects and cults. "Upon this broad belt of land congregated a people extraordinarily... devoted to crusades aimed at the perfection of mankind and the attainment of millennial happiness."[14]

For nineteenth-century millenarian "crusades" there exist plausible medieval analogues. Chief among them were recapturing the hallowed city of the Last Days, Jerusalem, along with the True Cross—the Holy Grail of the crusaders. These were non-literary medieval quests, millennial dreams in action. Where better, then, to situate the revivalism, religious creativity, and impossibilism of the Children's Crusade than in the Chartrain, a district well and truly "burned-over" after a "long interval" of crusade enthusiasm?

Crusade enthusiasm spread to the Chartrain almost as soon as the First Crusade was launched at Clermont on November 27, 1095.[15] It was probably early in 1096 that Stephen, Count of Chartres and Blois, took the cross. Most likely, he was urged to do so by his domineering but dearly-loved wife, Adèle, the formidable daughter of the formidable William the Conqueror. It was said that the rich and powerful Count Stephen possessed as many castles as there were days in the year. Once Stephen became a crusader, the Chartrain's ruling aristocracy followed him *en masse*.[16] And when the lords vowed to go on crusade, their men—knights, squires, sergeants, and foot-soldiers—likewise stepped forward to take the crusader's oath. As a result, Chartres emerged as a major recruitment center for the First Crusade.

One of the First Crusade's leading chroniclers, the chaplain Fulcher of Chartres, was besieged near Beirut along with his fellow crusaders from the Chartrain. Yearning for his distant homeland in the midst of foreign war, Fulcher sighs, "I wished very much that I were in Chartres or Orléans, and so did others." Although Fulcher did not personally witness the crusaders' capture of Jerusalem on July 15, 1099, he visited the holy city later that same year. Long residence in the crusader East altered his identity: "we who were Occidentals have now become Orientals."[17] He died in 1127, never having returned to Chartres.

Count Stephen was Fulcher's hero and villain. At once the most infamous and the most glorious of Fulcher's comrades-in-arms from the Chartrain, Stephen was both a deserter and a martyr. Admired by the crusading princes, he was chosen to preside over their assemblies and to maintain provisions for the troops. Fulcher concedes that Stephen's fateful decision in 1098 to flee Antioch and hasten home to France was "a disgrace to him... because he was a very noble man and mighty in arms."[18] The verdict of the anonymous author of the *Gesta Francorum* is less sympathetic: "that coward Stephen, count of Chartres... pretended to be very ill, and he went away shamefully..."[19]

Upon Stephen's return to France, he was excommunicated as were other crusaders found guilty of betraying their comrades and breaking their vows. Stigmatized as a contemptible renegade, pilloried by everyone—including his beloved Adèle—Stephen had but one course of action open to him. "To make up for what he had abandoned," he enlisted in the crusade of 1101.[20] That campaign was the first catastrophe in crusade history, an utter disaster. Stephen was captured by the Egyptians after the battle of Ramleh, then executed. Fulcher believed, as did most churchmen, that those who died on crusade were martyrs.[21] Stephen now joined their company. As for his beloved wife Adèle, she ended her days in a nunnery.

Throughout the twelfth century, crusading fires smouldered in the Chartrain. Not long after Stephen's execution, Bohemond, warrior-prince of Taranto and Antioch, came to Chartres in 1106 to marry the daughter of the King of France. While there, he preached a new crusade in the cathedral and was successful in gaining recruits.[22] Later, Hugh of Payen, the first Master of the Templars, was dispatched from the Holy Land to western Europe in 1128. His task was to return with military aid, which he did. Men from the Chartrain took part in Hugh's expedition of 1129.[23] When the Second Crusade was proclaimed, Robert d'Orrouer became one of the earliest fighting men of the Chartrain to take the cross.[24]

After the failure of the Second Crusade, there were renewed efforts. The next crusade needed a leader. Who he was to be would be determined at the Council of Chartres in May, 1150. Unusually, the Council chose a leader who was not a military man. Rather, he was a living saint. Their choice of Bernard of Clairvaux, a sick, aged Cistercian monk, shows that what the Council of Chartres wanted was not so much a crusade leader as a crusade messiah. With St. Bernard's death, any talk of such a venture ceased.

The catastrophic defeat of the Christian army at Hattin in 1187 resulted in the loss of the True Cross. The fall of Jerusalem followed quickly, imperiling the very existence of the Latin colony in the Levant. The response to this crisis was the Third Crusade. Along with other nobles from the Chartrain, Theobald V, Count of Chartres and Blois, combined forces with his nephew, Henry, Count of Champagne. Theobald, present at the siege of Acre in 1190, died there of dysentery in 1191. If some nobles and knights from the Chartrain managed to return to Chartres, more than a few died at Acre.[25] One survivor was the Bishop of Chartres, Reginald of Bar, a royal cousin of Philip Augustus.[26] Philip himself, abruptedly terminating his crusading service in the Holy Land, left what glory that remained to the brilliant general Richard Lionheart. Philip's hasty departure tarnished his reputation in France. That would be his last crusade; but not Bishop Reginald's.

The Third Crusade failed in its mission to re-conquer Jerusalem and liberate the Holy Land. Where its predecessor had failed, Innocent III's first eastern campaign, the Fourth Crusade, was intended to succeed. Instead, it slipped out of papal control. In contravention of Innocent's wishes, his crusaders captured the Christian city of Zara for the Venetians, then went on to conquer and pillage the Christian city of Constantinople in 1204. As late as the Fourth Lateran Council, Innocent naively believed that however deplorable the circumstances of reunion, the Latin and Greek churches were at last reunited under the Pope. That was Innocent's grand delusion. The brutality of the Latins drove the two churches farther apart than ever.

Responding to Innocent's summons to the Fourth Crusade were at least nineteen lords and prominent knights from the Chartrain.[27] This figure does not of course include all the anonymous knights, retainers, and common soldiers of the Chartrain who also took the cross. Immediately acknowledged as one of the leading figures in the crusading host was Count Louis of Blois and Chartres. The Fourth Crusade's major chronicler, Villehardouin, reports that Louis took the cross at the tournament of Écry in 1199.[28] Now twenty-eight, Louis had already gone to war with his father, the late Theobald V, on the Third Crusade. Too feverish to participate in the capture of Constantinople, Louis recklessly rushed into battle against the Cumans at Adrianople a year later, and ran straight into an ambush. Gravely wounded, he fell from his horse. Trying to save him, his loyal compatriot John of Friaize helped Count Louis mount his own horse. But Louis refused to withdraw, despite being urged to do so, exclaiming: "'God forbid I should ever be reproached with flying from the field and abandoning my emperor [the Latin crusader, Baldwin of Flanders]!'"[29] Louis and John both died on the battlefield. Their names were entered in the necrology of Notre-Dame de Chartres.

No greater contrast is imaginable than that between the hallowed names of fallen crusaders, and those whose names Villehardouin vilified in his chronicle. The latter were the dissidents in the crusader ranks, men who declined to fight their fellow Christians. Villehardouin despised them. To him, nothing was more important than the integrity of the army. Their disloyalty risked shattering it. Among the most prominent of those who chose to leave the army at Zara rather than violate the injunctions laid down by Innocent III, several were men of the Chartrain or near-Chartrain. At their forefront was the Cistercian abbot Guy of Vaux de Cernay, whose monastery was located just outside the diocese of Chartres. Abbot Guy vociferously opposed the plan to attack Zara, invoking the papal prohibition and using the threat of excommunication. He and other like-minded dissenters subsequently cut their ties with the army, and withdrew.

But the nay-sayer most respected by his fellow crusaders was the outstanding field-commander Simon of Montfort. His modest lordship of Montfort-l'Amaury and Epernon lay in the northeast quadrant of the diocese of Chartres. Like Guy of Vaux de Cernay, he strenuously objected to the storming of Zara, declaring, "I have not come here to annihilate Christians!"[30] While fully accepting that he was "one of the great barons in command of the forces," Villehardouin nonetheless condemns him unreservedly. "Having made a private agreement with our enemy the King of Hungary, [Montfort] went over to his side, and deserted us."[31] From Hungary, Simon traveled on to the Levant, then returned to his homeland.

The Fourth Crusade left its mark upon the crusading culture of the Chartrain, but the nature of its imprint is ambiguous. The war dead of the Fourth Crusade were naturally commemorated, just as its trophies of war were celebrated. Precious relics transported from the East, part of the enormous treasury of holy bones looted from Constantinople, found a new home in the Chartrain. A fragment of the head of St. Matthew and the cranium of St. Ann were solemnly and joyously deposited in the cathedral of Chartres, while the church of St. Mary Magdalene of Châteaudun received a knuckle-bone from the hand of John the Baptist.[32]

Yet in the Chartrain any triumphalist view of the Fourth Crusade was bound to be challenged. Returning after having abandoned the army rather than slaughter fellow Christians, these ex-crusaders felt they knew who the real sinners were. Nor were they the sort of men to keep their feelings to themselves and mouths tightly closed. Resounding through the region, the bitter, disenchanted voices of Abbot Guy, Simon of Montfort, and their aristocratic companions would have added more than a few discordant notes to the oral tradition of the Fourth Crusade. Gauging the impact of their embittered recollections upon the Chartrain's collective memory is hazardous. Possibly, one reaction was the re-emergence of a more papal, Innocentian vision of the crusades. Might reborn crusading ideals have cast a spell over the *pueri*? It is hard to say. Conversely, attitudes *towards* the *pueri* were most likely affected by the after-image of the Fourth crusaders. The contrast, even after eight years, was too great not to be noticed.

The role of the Fourth Crusade in the gestation of the *pueri* was doubly significant. First of all, it represents a symbolic closure. The return of the Fourth Crusade dissidents ended a century of recurrent crusading enthusiasm in what was by now a "burned-over district," the Chartrain. Second, it marks the transition to a new phase in the pre-history of the *peregrinatio puerorum*. For the aftermath of the Fourth Crusade in the Chartrain provides a direct link to a new crusading crisis which was much closer to home than either the Holy Land or Byzantium. More importantly, this crisis brings the birth of the *pueri* almost within sight. Now the span ceases to be *la longue durée*. It is the impetus of immediate events.

Impetus—the Albigensian Crusade

News reached Pope Innocent III in February, 1208, of the assassination of his legate Peter of Castelnau by an official of Count Raymond of Toulouse on January 14. This forced Innocent to act decisively against the heretical Cathars and their aristocratic protectors in the politically fragmented Languedoc of southern France. He did so. On March 10, he proclaimed the Albigensian Crusade.[33] Philip Augustus's unwillingness to participate in the crusade, let alone lead it, had no effect on the northern French church, which energetically endorsed it. The roll-call of northern French prelates who served in the Albigensian Crusade from 1209 to 1212 is impressive. It includes the Archbishop of Sens, the Bishops of Paris, Bayeux, Orléans, as well as the Bishop of Chartres, Reginald of Bar. In 1213, when Innocent III announced the date for the Fourth Lateran Council and the Fifth Crusade, he thought that the Albigensian Crusade had been won. He was premature. The war dragged on intermittently until Languedoc came under French control late in the thirteenth century. As for the Cathars, heretical dualists whose core beliefs were incompatible with Christianity, the Inquisition completed what the crusade began. The last Cathar burned at the stake perished in 1321.

Simon of Montfort had returned to the Chartrain from the Fourth Crusade by 1206. Less than three years later, he again took the cross. This time he vowed to fight, not the Muslims, but the Cathars and the lords of Languedoc who protected them. Montfort was known to be orthodox and pious; and his military brilliance and bravery, tested and proven in combat, guaranteed his high standing in the ranks of the crusaders. To demoralize his enemies, he employed terror tactics. One brutal instance will suffice. After a victorious siege in which many prisoners were taken, Montfort ordered that the noses of the captives should be cut off and their eyes put out, except for a single captive who was allowed to keep one of his eyes. Then, having assembled "a ridiculous procession of our enemies," Montfort commanded the one-eyed man to lead the blind ex-prisoners back to their base.[34]

Montfort's ambition to acquire land in Languedoc was far from unique. The dispossession of Languedocian nobles in favor of lords from the Île-de-France and their southern French collaborators was a predictable by-product of conquest. Created viscount of Carcassonne, Montfort finally achieved his ambition. He died, appropriately enough, on the battlefield, struck by a stone flung from a catapult.[35] To one chronicler, he was "truly a Maccabee of our time."[36]

Men from the Chartrain or near-Chartrain were among the thirty or so of Montfort's closest comrades-in-arms on the Albigensian Crusade. Their desire to join an unsullied holy war was probably strengthened by their defection from the army of the Fourth Crusade. The most notable of Montfort's fellow crusaders were Simon's brother Guy; Abbot Guy of Vaux de Cernay; Abbot Guy's nephew Peter of Vaux de Cernay—an important historian of the Albigensian Crusade, and a hero-worshipper of Simon— and Robert Mauvoisin, Lord of Rosni.[37]

During the years leading up to the Children's Crusade, there was ongoing recruitment for the Albigensian Crusade in the Chartrain. Montfort was already in Languedoc when "an enormous crowd of crusaders" from the Île-de-France, including the Bishop of Chartres, Reginald of Bar, together with a host of other prelates and notables, arrived in southern France in the early autumn of 1210.[38] Peasants were involved in the crusade from its inception, and they made up the bulk of the popular element accompanying the troops.[39] Serving in Bishop Reginald's retinue were also numerous attendants and foot-soldiers from the Chartrain. Reginald of Bar probably returned to his episcopal see during the winter of 1210–11. A crusade veteran, Reginald never would have allowed the people of his diocese forget for a moment that the holy war against the heretics in the south was still in progress.

Continuing recruitment in the Île-de-France reinforced popular awareness. Because crusaders were only obliged to serve for forty days to gain a plenary indulgence, there was a high turnover of fighting men, resulting in a constant demand for fresh troops. So Robert Mauvoisin, Lord of Rosni, was dispatched to northern France during the summer of 1211 in search of fighting men. About a hundred well-trained knights rode with him when he returned to Languedoc in early December.[40] Nevertheless, the shortage of manpower grew especially acute in the period from the winter of 1211 to the spring of 1212. Simon of Montfort's army was bogged down; little was being achieved. The crusade seemed to be going nowhere.

Desperate for fresh blood, the military turned to the pulpit. Christian oratory was a fine art. Crusading made it an eminently useful one. Sermons yielded *crucesignati* (the cross-signed, i.e. crusaders). As well as being superb propagandists, preachers were first-rate recruiting sergeants. Some exceptionally talented preachers were ready and willing to oblige. Two of them—William, Archdeacon of Paris, and the illustrious James of Vitry—embarked on an extensive preaching tour during the winter of 1211–12. Most likely their journeys criss-crossed northern France, as well as Flanders and the Rhineland, although Vitry's precise whereabouts in 1212 remains conjectural. But the power of their eloquence is demonstrated by the fact that from mid to late April 1212, "the venerable William, Archdeacon of Paris, and many other nobles and non-nobles from northern France" came streaming into the crusader camp almost on a daily basis.[41]

How many of these men came from the Chartrain is not known, but the best evidence for continuing support for the Albigensian Crusade in the Chartrain comes from a miracle. Reportedly, it occurred on a Sunday, sometime in 1212, while a crusade sermon was being preached outdoors to a large crowd of layfolk. Although the precise venue for the sermon is not given, the preacher was said to be the Cistercian Abbot of Bonneval, a monastic house located near Châteaudun, in the Dunois area of the Chartrain. Supposedly, this is what happened. As the abbot was urging the crusader's cross, miraculously there appeared in the sky a cross pointing straight towards Languedoc. The cross-in-the-sky motif may be typical of crusade-sermon miracles, but miracle stories often imply an atmosphere of popular excitation receptive to miracles. This may be indicative of the response of a Dunois congregation to the crusade message. The Dunois, incidentally, was the homeland of Stephen of Cloyes, future leader of the French *pueri*.[42]

Almost to the very brink of the Children's Crusade, therefore, incessant preaching to promote the Albigensian Crusade insured that the crusades were an ever-present reality in the Chartrain. A heady atmosphere of crusade ideology and propaganda implanted an awareness of the crusade as God's cause. Another point is that the Children's Crusade, as a revival of popular orthodoxy, implicitly repudiated everything the Cathars held dear.

The preaching campaign of the winter of 1211–12 would definitely have heightened popular crusading consciousness in the Chartrain. Yet it occurred too early to have served as a direct stimulus for the arousal of the *pueri*. Consequently, the Albigensian Crusade provided the impetus, rather than the stimulus, for the *peregrinatio puerorum*. That stimulus came not from Languedoc, but from across the Pyrenees.

Stimulus—towards Las Navas de Tolosa

In the Iberian peninsula a new crusading crisis posed an immediate and drastic threat to the territorial integrity of Latin Christendom.[43] Here the crusaders were not invaders, as they were in Languedoc; they were defenders. As the crisis deepened, Castile, not Languedoc, became the focus of papal anxiety. Arnaud-Amaury, the papal legate in southern France, and a hundred of his knights were diverted from the Albigensian Crusade to take up arms in the Spanish Crusade.

Latin Christendom's Levantine frontier with Islam began to crumble after Saladin's victory at Hattin in 1187. Now Christendom's western wall on the Spanish frontier looked increasingly shaky. Would it, too, collapse? What many were thinking, the troubadours dared to put into words. Aware of the ominous parallels between the eastern and western outposts of Christendom, they wondered if Spain's fate would mirror that of the Holy Sepulchre's.[44]

The gravity of the Iberian situation became apparent when in September, 1211, the castle of Salvatierra, held by knights of the Spanish military order of Calatrava, fell to the Berber invaders from North Africa. These were the Almohads, adherents of a fierce Muslim religious sect. Innocent III branded them *inimicos Christianitatis*, "enemies of Christendom," using that phrase for the first time.[45] The pope now feared for the existence of Christian Spain. Alfonso VIII of Castile, believing that a decisive battle would be fought during Pentecost, anxiously attempted to win the support of his fellow Christians beyond the Pyrenees. Mocking his frantic efforts, a Muslim chronicler imagines Alfonso's royal envoys scurrying through the entire Christian world from Portugal to Constantinople, crying "'Help, help; mercy, mercy!'"[46]

King Alfonso's three emissaries were Gerard, Bishop of Segovia, who was sent to Rome; maestro Arnaldo, the royal physician, who was dispatched to Poitou and Gascony; and Rodrigo Jiménez de Rada, Archbishop of Toledo, who was given a wider remit. Jiménez de Rada, one of the pre-eminent figures of the Spanish church, was entrusted to plead the Spanish cause to the *ultramontanos*, the faithful beyond the Pyrenees. For this he combined the twin roles of international diplomat and crusade preacher. His tour took several months to complete, and his itinerary is maddeningly uncertain, even though he was his own historian. By late March or early April of 1212, he had probably returned to Toledo, after most likely having visited Rome and other cities in Italy, Provence, possibly Germany. Perhaps he visited northern France as well, but no evidence exists of Archbishop de Rada conferring with either Pope Innocent III or King Philip II of France.

If the archbishop did travel to the Île-de-France, his mission yielded pitifully few crusaders at best. It is said that the last count of Blois and Chartres, the young, childless, Theobald VI, participated in the Spanish Crusade, where he contracted leprosy.[47] This, however, may be no more than a local tradition. To judge from its failure to recruit crusaders in the Île-de-France, the Spanish Crusade made a negligible impact upon the crusading consciousness of the Chartrain. This is a point well worth remembering, so far as the origins of the Children's Crusade are concerned, for it simultaneously give rise to a paradox, and resolves it. What serves as the stimulus for collective enthusiasm does not necessarily predetermine its direction.

The relatively few Frenchmen who, briefly, went to fight in Spain were mostly southerners or crusaders already participating in the conquest of Languedoc. The King of France failed to lend a helping hand. Neither the entreaties of de Rada were enough to sway him, nor, if she voiced them, those of Philip's daughter-in-law, Blanche of Castile. The one thing the French *ultramontanos* were prepared to offer their Spanish brethren in their supreme hour of need was—their prayers.

No man was better equipped to marshal the prayers of Latin Christendom on behalf of Christian Spain than Pope Innocent III. Very much aware that a decisive battle was anticipated on the octave of Pentecost, 1212,[48] Innocent first turned to his episcopal colleagues, then to his armory of ecclesiastical ritual. To invoke Divine Providence in order to ward off imminent calamity was nothing new. Since Carolingian times at least, western Christendom possessed a powerful liturgy of war.[49] But Innocent's new strategy for channeling spiritual energy towards the crusade was unprecedented. No previous Pope had utilized crusade processions to mobilize the support of the *populus christianus*, the Christian people. Mobilizing ordinary people in this way was Innocent's innovative expression of his Christian populism.

Processions of worshippers fervently imploring God's blessings at a time of crusading crisis were bound to have a galvanizing effect on the Roman populace. When the actual announcement came is unknown, but Innocent declared that a solemn "general supplication" would be held in Rome on the fourth day of the octave of Pentecost, May 16, 1212.[50] Innocent thus sought to focus the prayers of the people of Rome on the climactic battle that would decide the fate of Christian Spain.

There is no documentary proof, but still every reason to believe that on May 16, the Wednesday after Pentecost, large crowds of Romans, clergy and laity, assembled to march in public processions, except for those whose enemies had sworn to kill them on sight. These processions "for the peace of the universal church and for the Christian people" were intended to beg for God's favor in the fast-approaching struggle with the Saracens in Spain.[51] The Wednesday after Pentecost was a day traditionally set aside for penitential observances. Today the desire for penitence would be strengthened by an atmosphere of crisis. The church bells tolled, while three processions set off—one of men, one of women, and one of clergy—all marching separately along their respective routes towards the Lateran.

Crowds of barefoot, fasting, weeping and groaning Romans, marching in procession, now halted in front of the Lateran basilica. Each processional group was allocated a section of the square. There they impatiently awaited Innocent III's sermon. While they waited, a piece of the True Cross was put on display for them to venerate. Of course this was not the relic impiously plundered by Saladin at Hattin in 1187. Lamentably, that was still missing. This was another fragment of the True Cross, part of the treasury of holy objects which Latin Christians piously pilfered from Greek Christians at Constantinople in 1204. Whatever sermon Innocent preached to the massive Roman crowd that day is lost. But who can doubt that the assembled Romans, packed together in the Lateran piazza, heard a discourse inspired by what must then have been uppermost in the papal mind—the impending battle in Spain. Innocent would have been sure to solicit prayers for the survival of the Spanish church. Yet, as battle was about to be joined, desperate pleas for volunteers to go on crusade against the Moors in Spain were unlikely. The time for crusade recruitment sermons had passed.

Months earlier, in January, 1212, while the preaching campaign for the Albigensian Crusade continued in northern France, Innocent wrote a worried letter to the Archbishop of Sens and his suffragan bishops, including, naturally, the Bishop of Chartres, Reginald of Bar. In his letter Innocent sounded the crusade alarm, granting full indulgences for the holy war against the Moors in Spain and stressing that men and matériel were needed by the octave of next Pentecost, when Alfonso VIII of Castile expected the war to resume.[52]

Everything indicates that the octave of Pentecost was the crucial period. It was the key date in Innocent's letter to the bishops of the Île-de-France. It also was when Innocent chose to schedule his crisis processions in Rome. Finally, it both confirms and is confirmed by what the chronicler Alberic of Trois-Fontaines relates. Unequivocally, Alberic states that on May 20, the last day of the octave of Pentecost—and the octave was an integral part of the feast—"litanies and prayers were given in France for the Christians who were about to wage war in Spain."[53]

Alberic's Cistercian abbey was located in Champagne; thus the Île-de-France—and with it Chartres and the Chartrain—would have signified the heartland of France to him.[54] Now Alberic's isolated nugget of information about the liturgies of the Spanish crisis has the ring of truth, regardless of the fact that Alberic (or his interpolator) was an eminent mythistorian of the Children's Crusade. His information is credible for five reasons. First, his report on the Spanish conflict is entirely separate and quite distinct from his tale of the *pueri*. Second, there are no mythistorical overtones. As it stands, what we have is a simple, straightforward statement about the date of the French Pentecostal processions. Third, Alberic's precise date of the processions held in "France" has been accepted without murmur by at least one internationally respected historian of medieval Spain.[55] Fourth, Alberic's date (May 20) for the French processions corresponds well to Innocent's date for the Roman processions (May 16)—and both fall within the octave of Pentecost. Fifth, the monk of Cologne, the sole chronicler to hazard a liturgical season for the origins of the Children's Crusade, situates it "between Easter and Pentecost."[56] Thanks, therefore, to Alberic of Trois-Fontaines, the hypothesis that the Spanish crisis was directly linked to the coming of the Children's Crusade becomes increasingly plausible.

What is certain is that two consecutive crusading crises, one in Languedoc, the other in Spain, virtually intersected and overlapped with one another. Just as the Albigensian Crusade was the impetus for the Children's Crusade, so the Spanish Crusade became its stimulus. Exposure to these successive crises must have been psychologically cumulative, as more than a century of crusading tradition in the Chartrain was now re-energized by immediate events. Crisis, once translated into ecclesiastical ritual, infused it, animated it, and was not so much alleviated by it, as expressed and even dramatized.

As Edward Shils observes: "Rituals are parts of systems of belief directed toward averting danger... parts of a systematic response to crises, actual and anticipated."[57] Crisis processions, bringing members of a society together in a common ritual, allowed participants and spectators alike to take comfort from a demonstration of solidarity, physical compactness, and numerical strength. Innocent III's call for the traditional liturgical responses to crisis, preaching and processions, was heeded. What resulted, however, was unforeseen. The outcome of collective fervor, once aroused, confounds assumptions.

Arousal—the crisis processions at Chartres

A crisis confronting all of Latin Christendom now impinged upon Chartres. According to the Flemish chronicler John Le Long or John of Ypres (d. 1383), this was how it began:

> When at that time processions were being made throughout France to plead for God's grace against the infidels [i.e. the Moors in Spain], it came into the mind of a shepherd (*pastorello*) of the diocese of Chartres, that he would go to the procession; and he went.[58]

To the author of the *Chronica monasterii sancti Bertini*, this was Act One of the Children's Crusade. (John Le Long's account—obviously crucial to the argument of this book—has been dismissed out of hand on two grounds, neither of which can withstand criticism.)[59] Le Long's point of departure was the Spanish crisis. His "processions... being made throughout France" were clearly Alberic's processions of May 20. As for Le Long's "shepherd of the diocese of Chartres," where else would he have gone to join these processions, if not to the great new Gothic cathedral at the liturgical heart of his diocese—Notre-Dame de Chartres?

Like most northern European cities at this time, Chartres lacked an urban chronicler. A parallel instance will have to do—Innocentian Rome a mere four days earlier. Just as they would have done in Rome on the eve of battle, tightly-packed crowds of people congregated at Chartres.

The assembled mutitudes here, too, would have been urged to give vent to their emotions. Here too, as they marched in procession, weeping, groaning, chanting, shouting out liturgical acclamations, an atmosphere of urgency, exaltation, and imminent danger would have enveloped the crowd.

That the Chartres processions would have taken the same form as Innocent's is extremely doubtful. Chartres was not Rome; its liturgical traditions, like its topography, were peculiar to it. Instead of the separate but convergent male, female, and clerical processions that Innocent ordained for Rome, the Chartres processions would likely have been based on the northern European variant of the Roman major or sevenfold litany. Originally purpose-built for Roman supplications during plague-time in the early Middle Ages, it was equally serviceable for other crises in other cities.

The processional order of the sevenfold litany allocated the *pueri* a category of their own. They came fourth in the line of march, behind the secular clergy, the regulars (monks and canons), and the nuns, but ahead of "laymen over twenty-five years," widows, and married couples.[60] So the *pueri* were the first laypeople to be singled out in the processional ranks (unless minor clerics, perhaps choirboys, were marching among them). Sexually, the *pueri* also had a mediating role. Positioned as they were between the celibate clerics—presumed to be sexually inactive—and the sexually active (or potentially active) laity, the *pueri* were perceived to be sexual innocents.

Bishop Reginald of Bar's presence in the city around the time of the processions is attested by the charters he witnessed.[61] If the procedures laid down for Innocent III's Roman processions were observed, Bishop Reginald preached the sermon at Chartres that day. Whether the size of the crowd dictated that Reginald, like Innocent, preached outside the cathedral's portals or within its spacious enclosure cannot be determined. Assembled to hear him, in any case, would have been a sizable congregation, swollen by an influx of pilgrims from all over the diocese, including peasants and shepherds, such as John Le Long's *pastorellus*.

The Bishop, like the Pope, would have stressed the imminent dangers facing Christendom and called for penitence and prayer. But would the thrust of his sermon—Christendom's fate in the balance; the Saracen threat to the entire Christian people—have dissipated its specifically Spanish context? For if no plea was issued for crusaders to fight in Spain (and few, if any, from the Chartrain appear to have done so), then the strongest impression left on Reginald's congregation may have been that of a merciless Saracen foe poised to strike Christians at any moment.

Processions, like preachers, mobilized crowds, and in medieval revivalism the arousal of the religious crowd was oftentimes the initial step towards a full-fledged religious movement, which here, quite literally, means people in motion—processional ambulation. That was how the Children's Crusade began at Chartres. Once aroused, however, the religious crowd was left fired with revivalist zeal, but directionless. Heightened enthusiasm found no release. What seems to have happened next is that inflamed by endlessly repeated outcries for God to deliver Christendom from its enemies, the Pentecostalists of Chartres left the city to become itinerant processional evangelists, exporting the first stirrings of their revivalist enthusiasm beyond its birthplace.

Reports speak of a wave of revivalist fervor sweeping across northern France, which contemporary monastic chroniclers were unable to explain. None could say where it originated, let alone where it was headed. Chartres is never mentioned. Yet the nature of this diffuse and apparently leaderless enthusiasm in northern France betrays its origins. For this was a processional movement. So it seems highly likely that this wave of extraordinary popular revivalism, directionless and seemingly on the road to nowhere, was the lineal descendant and immediate consequence of the crisis processions at Chartres. Here there was continuity, but, as we would expect, also signs of evolution.

Captured by a chronicler's snapshot, these itinerant enthusiasts are caught for a brief moment in live performance. Just as in so many medieval revivals, their behavior is exuberant, expressive, pentecostal. Two Norman chronicles contain pretty much identical prints of the same image.[62] On balance, the chronicle of the Cistercian monastery of Mortemer is the most likely original source:

> [I]n the realm of France, boys and girls (*pueri et puellae*), with some more mature males (*adolescentulis*) and old men, carrying banners, wax candles, crosses, censers, made processions, and went through the cities, villages, and castles, singing aloud in French, "Lord God, raise up Christendom! Lord God, return to us the True Cross!" They sang these words, but also many others, because there were many processions, and each procession varied them, to its own liking. And this thing, unheard of in past ages, was a wonder to many, because, as they believed, it was a portent of future things, namely, of those which came to pass in the following year.[63]

The Mortemer chronicler's information is compressed and vividly conveyed. He describes vocally animated, excited layfolk eagerly joining together in many and varied processions *in regno Francorum*, i.e., the Kingdom of the French, which, to a Norman chronicler of the period, would have meant the Île-de-France,[64] a further positive pointer towards the Chartrain.

Marching at their head were the *pueri et puellae*. Prominently placed, just as in the postulated processional order at Chartres, the *pueri* were at the forefront of the laity. Here, too, processing beside them, and equally conspicuous, were their age-mates, young women, girls, *puellae*—the sole representatives of their gender. More mature men came next.[65] Finally, trudging along, bringing up the rear, were the old men.

These *pueri et puellae* were not yet synonymous with the revival as a whole. Their name was not yet attached to it. When the Mortemer chronicler clicked his camera, the *peregrinatio puerorum* was still in its formative, incubatory phase. Nonetheless, the other age-groups appear to be subordinate to the *pueri*.[66] Significantly, it was the spectrum of age-groups which caught Mortemer's camera eye, rather than social divisions among the marchers, if they existed. Indeed, the social status of those processing is ignored.

A more remarkable omission from Mortemer's snapshot of the processionists were the clergy. Invariably, they were the stage-managers as well as the starring actors in ecclesiastical performances such as these. Here they seem to have vanished. If they have vanished, however, it is not without a trace, because Mortemer meticulously enumerates all the liturgical props which the clergy habitually employed in church-led processions—banners, wax candles, crosses, and censers. These were items usually kept secure in clerical custody. The clear implication must be that, at one time anyway, they were utilized in an official liturgical procession that was once firmly under ecclesiastical supervision.

Where have all the clergy gone? Himself a monk and so unlikely to ignore his fellow clerics, the Mortemer chronicler overlooks them completely. The answer might be that these lay enthusiasts, having left Chartres—though perhaps not the Chartrain—and currently processing "through the cities, villages, and castles" of the Île-de-France, have emancipated themselves from ecclesiastical authority. They have broken free. Now they were on their own.

Outside clerical control they may have been, but theirs was an orthodox popular crusade revival, not an incipient heretical movement. Ideological proof comes from their acclamations. Declaimed not in the clerical Latin of the official liturgy, but in the layman's own vernacular, their chanted outcries articulated a terrible anxiety for the cause of Christendom and its people. "Lord God, raise up Christendom!" (*Domine Deus, exalta christianitatem*!), besides evoking Innocent III's idea of Christendom, was an acclamation drenched in the blood of Christian combat against the Saracens, so much so that it even predated its crusading associations. For an outcry on the eve of a nervously awaited battle, it was wholly appropriate. "Lord God, return to us the True Cross!" (*Domine Deus, redde nobis veram crucem*!), on the other hand, has nothing whatsoever to do with the Spanish crisis, and everything to do with the restoration of Christendom's most sacred politico-religious insignia. Lost at Hattin twenty-five years earlier, the True Cross had never been forgotten. Now it was the enthusiasts' Holy Grail, their symbol of a lost Jerusalem.[67]

Altogether there can be little doubt that the enthusiasts preserved a sense of crusading crisis, engendered by the preaching and processions which were originally intended to stir and arouse them to the dangers facing Christendom. The crusade alarms that rang in Chartres were now internalized. Much like the clergy, however, the Spanish context has disappeared, as if, in the midst of crisis, the crusades had returned to their natural homeland, the Christian East. And if there are hints in their voices of an implicit program—to recover the True Cross and with it Jerusalem—that lies in the future. For these were cloudy, boundless, powerful aspirations, the stuff of prophetic and millenarian dreams.

For the immediately post-Chartres, processional stage of the French *peregrinatio puerorum*, the Mortemer chronicler brings us as close to the actual enthusiasts as we are likely to get. Certainly, they were not all *pueri*, that is, actual youngsters. Many later observers of the Children's Crusade were careful to point this out. Despite the fact that other age-groups joined them from the very inception of the enthusiasm, the movement as a whole adopted their name—and continue to bear it—not without reason. The Mortemer chronicler already underlines the prominence of the *pueri*, perhaps indeed, their collective leadership role. Here and later on as well, the presence of actual *pueri* was such a singular and conspicuous feature of the crusading enthusiasm that it became its defining feature. Those participating in the *peregrinatio puerorum* were, therefore, the *pueri*, whether actual or nominal.

So to conclude: clearly displaying the birthmarks of their origins, the ardent post-Chartres enthusiasts of late May, 1212, marched and sang as they processed across the Île-de-France. As yet, they were not seeking out any specific destination. They were itinerant Pentecostalists. Theirs was neither a pilgrimage, nor a crusade. Nor were the *pueri* synonymous with the enthusiasm, however conspicuous they were. All that would come. This was indeed a popular religious revival, but one lacking a leader. That, too, would come. Collective arousal, such as occurred at Chartres, generates its own dynamic and trajectory, providing the ideal environment for the emergence of a charismatic leader. As momentum builds, movement follows.

4
History: Charisma

Weber's charisma

Not celebrity, not iconic status, not presence, not animal magnetism; pop-stardom, least of all—charisma is none of these. According to Max Weber, who picked up the idea and ran with it, personal charisma is a particular kind of authority, one which does not depend on office, whether inherited or elective. It is a gift. For some, a gift of God. Once recognized, it compels assent. "The holder of charisma... demands obedience and a following *by virtue of his mission*" (my italics).[1] That must be stressed: commentators neglect the degree to which a sense of mission is incorporated in charismatic attraction. Charisma overpowers, rather than persuades. Followers do not so much consent to charismatic authority, as succumb to it.

Followership is the true determinant of charismatic leadership; and what followers give, they can also take away. So Weber emphasizes the vulnerability of personal charisma, its inherent precariousness. Its lifespan is relatively short. One moment it is held; the next, it is lost. To Weber, the possessor of charisma is exceptional in some way. But charismatic exceptionalism first has to be recognized, perhaps by "miraculous" signs or "revelations." Once the authority of a charismatic leader is recognized, adherents will not be slow in coming. Not to be forgotten is another point that Weber makes. Charisma arrives when the time is out of joint. Charisma, Weber believes, is born of crisis, when a collective emergency fractures the customary routines of daily life.[2]

Charisma and crusade

What, then, could be a more propitious circumstance for charisma to reveal itself than at the launch of a crusade? Summoned in an atmosphere of prophetic urgency—the providential "now" (*nunc*) of St. Bernard's charismatic preaching of the Second Crusade[3]—the crusades superimposed themselves on the structures of daily life, shattering them. Immediately after the Council of Clermont in 1095, Pope Urban II went on a preaching tour in France, trawling for First Crusaders amongst the military aristocracy. Exploiting his charisma of office to the full, he brought along an impressive entourage and baggage-train. Such a magnificent retinue of prelates and attendants worked in his favor, as he knew it would. Onlookers were made very much aware that here in their midst was a former prior of Cluny, an aristocratic Frenchman much like themselves, save for one thing—he was the Roman pontiff.[4]

Around the same time in central France, recruiting crusaders of a different sort, was the outstanding popular preacher of the First Crusade, Peter of Amiens, known as Peter the Hermit. His charismatic authority, unlike Urban's, was personal. This is not to say that his status as a hermit, inseparable from his identity, did not endow him with a certain charismatic aura of holiness. Of course, it did. Granted, too, there were other wandering, eremitical preachers in late-eleventh-century France who attracted popular followers. Yet Peter was special. "He was surrounded by such great throngs, received such enormous gifts, and was lauded with such fame for holiness that I do not remember anyone to have been held in like honor," reluctantly concedes Guibert, Abbot of Nogent. What was peculiarly distasteful for Guibert, no lover of popular cults, was the fact that Peter was "regarded as little short of divine" to such an extent that "hairs were snatched from his mule as relics."[5]

No Sherlock Holmes is needed to pinpoint what legitimated Peter's charismatic authority. Observe first his eremitical appearance—muddy, dirty, barefoot; garbed in a plain woolen, ankle-length shirt and sleeveless cloak. Next, note his thin face and slight frame, instantly confirming the penitential harshness of his ascetic life. Finally, there was his voice, which preceded him. Vast, expectant crowds responded to a renowned medieval preacher before he uttered a word.

Above all else, one unimpeachable credential put Peter's charismatic authority beyond dispute. A fair number of chroniclers reported what people were saying about him. Peter carried a letter which had fallen from heaven. Reputedly, the celestial letter which Peter the Hermit possessed was an exhortation to take the cross, then to drive the Saracens from the Holy Land. Mysterious letters raining down from the sky were nothing new, although during the crusading centuries the volume of precipitation increased notably.[6]

Peter's preaching produced a raggle-taggle army of peasants, along with more than a sprinkling of battle-tested knights. Separate bands of his forces perpetrated the ghastly Rhineland massacres of the Jews. Peter's sway over his followers, however, was relatively short-lived. He began preaching the crusade in early December, 1095. By October of the next year, the Turks had wiped out his army. Peter was not present. His fate came later. In January, 1098, he fled Antioch and was brought back to the crusader camp in disgrace. It is hard to know if Peter's charisma ever fully recovered from this shameful incident, although it is true that the crusade commanders chose him as an envoy to their Turkish enemy Kerbogha; and also that after the conquest of Jerusalem, Peter organized public prayers before the battle of Ascalon.[7] More than likely, however, Peter's former peasant followers no longer looked upon him as the charismatic leader he once was.

Less well-known than the career of Peter the Hermit is the story of Durand of Le Puy, a poor carpenter with a wife and a son, who founded the White Hoods (the *Caputiati* or *Chaperons Blancs*). The details of that story are extremely sketchy, but Durand's career trajectory has all the ingredients of a classic charismatic drama—beginning with a crusade-like crisis, followed by the revelatory gift of charismatic authority; then cut short, probably brutally, by uncontrollable forces.

The crisis afflicting Durand's home country in southern France can be likened to the war zone the crusaders faced in Saracen territory. The Third Lateran Council (1179) was so concerned about the worsening situation in the region that it offered those bold enough to oppose the Cathar heretics and the *routiers*—murderous, freebooting, mercenary soldiers—the same spiritual and temporal rewards bestowed on the crusaders. To the anxious bishops of the Third Lateran, the courageous men who dared to challenge the *routiers* would be Christian heroes, like the crusaders. Durand of Le Puy's volunteer peace army of *Caputiati* took up the challenge four years later.

They were called the White Hoods, because of their distinctive woolen or linen costume. They were a militant peace confraternity—crusaders, in effect—sworn to fight the *routiers*. Their motto, affixed to a piece of parchment (or banner), along with an image of the Virgin and Child, perfectly summed up their millenarian-pacific-military ideals: "Lamb of God, who takes away the sins of the world, give us peace." Durand's spiritual calling was revealed to him in late November, 1182. His mission, it was said, came to him in a vision either of the Virgin Mary of Le Puy or of Christ. From that vision came the parchment with its image and motto. It was Durand's charismatic legitimation, the equivalent of a celestial letter.

Commanded by the Virgin to found the White Hoods, Durand gained the support of the Bishop of Le Puy, Pierre de Solignac. His confraternity was open to all, men and women, rich and poor. On Assumption Day, August 15, 1183, Durand's charismatic authority reached its peak. At Le Puy, in the midst of a great crowd which had assembled for the festival, he spoke to the people from a raised platform, holding aloft his parchment with the image of the Virgin and Child. As Durand fervently revealed the God-given purpose and rules of the *Caputiati* brotherhood, his voice broke with emotion.

Durand's confrères multiplied. Confraternities similar to the White Hoods sprang up throughout the region, and elsewhere. Military victories against the dreaded *routiers* made them a force to be reckoned with. But by 1184 the great secular lords and the prelates of the church began to suspect that these largely peasant militias were a threat to their own authority, an insurrection in the making. The *Caputiati* were suppressed. Survivors were fined and punished. Compelled to renounce their White Hoods and go bareheaded for a year in summer heat and winter cold, they suffered a humiliation which amounted to symbolic emasculation.[8]

Of Durand of Le Puy we hear no more. Whatever his fate, the violent suppression of the *Caputiati* dealt a death-blow to his charismatic authority. Durand's charisma rested precariously, as Weber knew, upon the successful outcome of his mission. His charismatic ascendancy probably lasted only for little over a year, yet that in itself is remarkable. For Durand was a layman of low social standing. He was, after all, a poor carpenter who possessed neither the quasi-religious status, nor the revivalist preaching skills of a Peter the Hermit. If any mesmerizing qualities irradiated Durand's personal charisma, none have been recorded.

A single, overwhelming encounter with Divinity prepared him for his mission. The story of his encounter, often retold, authenticated by a parchment, an image, and a motto, was enough for Durand to win charismatic recognition and adherents. The career of Durand the lowly carpenter remarkably parallels that of the leader of the French *pueri*, the shepherd-boy, Stephen of Cloyes. Like Stephen, Durand was a lay charismatic leader emerging in quasi-crusade circumstances, armed with the equivalent of a celestial letter. Although Stephen's charismatic drama unfolds almost thirty years later than Durand's, both might well have been scripted and directed by the same man, Max Weber.

From kneeling sheep to pilgrim-Christ

Act Two of the Children's Crusade begins with the chronicler John Le Long's surprising account of what happens next when his anonymous shepherd from the diocese of Chartres, after having taken part in the crusade processions held "to plead for God's grace against the infidels" in Spain, returned home.[9] Le Long fails to say if he returned immediately after the processions, or if some other incident intervened.

So the unanswerable question is this: did the unnamed shepherd, swallowed up in the fervent religious crowd at Chartres, leave the city as a wandering evangelist in a revivalist outpouring of itinerant processional enthusiasts? Had he, in fact, found a place in the processions among the Pentecostalist *pueri* so vividly described by the Mortemer chronicler? Along with them, did this obscure shepherd from the Chartrain sing aloud in French, "Lord God, raise up Christendom! Lord God, return to us the True Cross!"?[10]

The way John Le Long recounts it, the shepherd's homecoming coincided with an extraordinary moment of charismatic recognition, the moment when he gains a new flock:

> Returning [to his home in the Chartrain], he found his sheep almost consuming the grain, and when he wanted to drive them away, they kneeled to him, as if begging pardon. When news of this reached the common people, he was honored excessively. To him, in a short space of time, from every part of the kingdom [what follows is taken from William of Andres], there poured in an enormous multitude of children (*parvulorum*)....[11]

Charismatic recognition often presupposes a religious awakening, a consciousness of mission, on the part of the future charismatic leader. There is no trace of either in Le Long (or his lost source). Yet, if the anonymous shepherd returned to his home in the Chartrain filled with enthusiasm after marching in the exuberant post-Chartres processions, a new-found sense of personal mission was not an improbable prelude to the miraculous.

But those kneeling sheep of Le Long's were not necessarily extras borrowed from some medieval miracle play. In the month or so preceding the July harvest in the Chartrain,[12] the discovery of straying sheep in a field of ripening grain would not have been unusual. Nor would it have been out of the ordinary for an aggressive peasant farmer to come to blows with a negligent shepherd, especially if he were a mere lad. Angry fracas between peasants and shepherds over crops damaged by sheep were regular occurrences.[13]

The motif of kneeling sheep "as if begging pardon" can be found in saints' lives as well as in records of popular beliefs, for it was a motif rooted in agrarian society. Those same roots were also buried deep in unmiraculous reality. Foot-rot is a disease afflicting sheep; in the past it was widespread. When sheep suffer from it, they appear to "kneel" as they graze.[14] Whether such an incident actually happened or not, here it is its symbolic function which matters. Kneeling before their shepherd, offering him homage, as if to a lord, the sheep symbolize unquestioned assent to charismatic authority. There was no celestial letter addressed to Le Long's shepherd. None was required.

The kneeling sheep conclude John Le Long's passage on the anonymous shepherd, which leads directly to a short extract on the Children's Crusade whose source, unlike the unattributable text on the shepherd, is known. Le Long takes it from the chronicle of William of Andres. Although the outburst of mass enthusiasm recorded by William of Andres is leaderless, when Le Long welds the two texts together, the refashioning could not be more Weberian. Crowds of adherents respond to charismatic recognition: "in a short space of time from every part of the kingdom [of France]," "an enormous multitude of children"[15] pour in, ready to follow the charismatic shepherd from the diocese of Chartres wherever he might lead them. Along with the kneeling sheep, they are now his flock.

While John Le Long makes extensive use of William of Andres, he completely ignores the important early-thirteenth-century *Chronicon universale* of the Laon Anonymous, which is our sole source for the charismatic career of the shepherd-boy Stephen of Cloyes, leader of the French *pueri*. Le Long never names his shepherd, knows nothing about Stephen, and betrays not a hint of indebtedness to the Laon Anonymous anywhere in his chronicle. All the more remarkable, then, is the fundamental compatability of both chronicles, strengthening the case for their basic reliability.

John le Long, in fact, supplements the Laon Anonymous without contradicting him. So much so, that in a screenplay the narrative of Le Long's shepherd, up to, and perhaps even including, the kneeling sheep, would be filmed as the prequel to the Laon Anonymous's story of Stephen of Cloyes. The seamlessness of such a sequence is almost uncanny. So effortlessly does Le Long's nameless shepherd inhabit Stephen of Cloyes' pre-history that his name, one imagines, was Stephen.

The Anonymous chronicler of Laon, an English Premonstratensian canon living in France, took a keen interest in the political as well as the religious life of his time. His chronicle terminates in 1219, making him a contemporary of the *peregrinatio puerorum*. However laced it is with anecdotes and popular stories, his chronicle is generally thought of as trustworthy.[16]

Much like James of Vitry, the Laon Anonymous was intrigued by new kinds of lay religious creativity and impossibilism, whether orthodox or heretical, and was often surprisingly well-informed. Accordingly, he chronicles Valdes of Lyons and the Waldensians (devotees of poverty who wanted to preach, in spite of the clerical monopoly); the Humiliati of Lombardy (who wore plain clothing, would not swear oaths, and also wanted to preach); Durand of Le Puy (to the unsympathetic Laon chronicler, a simple-minded carpenter duped by a canon into believing that the Virgin Mary spoke to him); Alpais of Cudot (a medieval hunger-artist, who miraculously lived without eating); Amalric ("a most subtle man, but evil-minded") and the Amalricians, including Master Godin (all consigned to the flames); and Matilda ("a holy woman and lover of poverty") who died in the diocese of Laon in June, 1212—the same month as Stephen's pilgrimage.[17]

Whenever he can, the Laon Anonymous deals with new religious movements biographically. What engages him is the inspiration and aspiration of a single individual, which his account of the pilgrimage of the *pueri* exemplifies. At its center is the extraordinary story of the charismatic Stephen of Cloyes. The Laon Anonymous begins by setting the stage:

> In the month of June of the same year [1212] a certain boy (*puer*), by occupation a shepherd (*pastor*), of a village named Cloyes near the town of Vendôme, said that the Lord had appeared to him in the form of a poor pilgrim, had received bread from him, and had delivered letters to him to be taken to the king of the French. When he came, together with his fellow (*coevis*) shepherd-boys, nearly 30,000 people congregated around him from diverse parts of France. While he stayed at Saint-Denis, the Lord worked many miracles through him, as many have witnessed. There were also other boys (*pueri*) who were held in great veneration by the common multitude in many localities, because they were also believed to work miracles; to whom a multitude of boys came together, wishing to proceed to the holy boy Stephen under their guidance. All recognized him as master and prince over them. At last, the king, having consulted the masters of Paris about this assembly of boys, they returned to their homes at his command; and so this boyish revival (*puerilis illa devocio*) was terminated as easily as it had begun.

> But it seemed to many, that by means of such innocents (*innocentes*) gathered of their own accord, the Lord would do something great and new upon the earth, which turned out to be far from the case.[18]

Almost on a note of regret the Anonymous chronicler of Laon thus concludes his all-too-brief narrative of the mission of the shepherd boy, Stephen of Cloyes.

Stephen of Cloyes

The June date is highly significant. According to the Laon Anonymous, Stephen's encounter with the pilgrim-Christ and his pilgrimage to Saint-Denis both fell within that month. So if we preface his narrative with the (amended) account of John Le Long, beginning with the Chartres processions of May 20, while allowing time for the Mortemer phase of itinerant processional revivalism before the shepherd's return to the Chartrain, then the chronological jigsaw pieces fit snugly together.

Chronologically, the distances involved also make sense. Chartres is little more than thirty-five miles from Stephen's home village, Cloyes. The journey from one place to the other was hardly onerous. Moreover, another chronicler comes close to confirming Cloyes as Stephen's point of departure. Noting that the excitement of the *pueri* (*commocio puerorum*) spread through many cities, towns, and villages of France, the contemporary Norman chronicler of Jumièges asserts that it began in Vendôme.[19] Now Vendôme is a mere seventeen miles from Cloyes. Although the Jumièges chronicler refers neither to a leader nor to a destination, his commotion of the *pueri*, which commences in Vendôme, would surely have been the movement led by Stephen of Cloyes. For a Norman chronicler, Vendôme was a better geographical marker than an obscure village in the Dunois. To avoid perplexing his readers, the Anonymous of Laon came up with a similar solution: "Cloyes near the town of Vendôme."

Situated in a valley, and bridging both banks of the River Loir, Cloyes was about eight miles from Châteaudun, the largest town of the Dunois. The Loir powered water-mills, but could not serve as a roadway, so thirteenth-century travelers used the plateau above the Loir valley. Meadowlands provided abundant pasture for sheep, but marginal and scrub lands were equally suitable for grazing. Many of Stephen's fellow shepherd-boys would guard the family flock, walking from farm to field, rather than having to tend their sheep over long distances. The age of domestic, non-professional shepherd-boys typically varied from around eight to about fourteen.[20]

From the twelfth century Cloyes had four churches, Saint-Séverin, Saint-Lubin, Saint-Georges, and the church or priory chapel of Notre-Dame of Yron.[21] The last of these Romanesque churches houses a small, probably fourteenth-century fresco inside a circular border or medallion. It is a representation of an adolescent youth with short wavy hair. Depicted in profile, he is open-mouthed, as if speaking or shouting (Figure 5). Local tradition has it that this youth is none other than Stephen of Cloyes, shown preaching the Children's Crusade.[22] Nothing proves this was ever intended to be a portrait of Stephen, although discovering the origins of this local tradition would be interesting. One suspects it is post-medieval. Nonetheless, it is pleasant to reflect that some memory of Stephen survives on his home ground.

Stephen was both *puer* and *pastor*, a shepherd-boy. His fellow shepherd-boys were his workmates, as well as his age-mates (*coaevus*: one of like age). Given the Marxist theory of friendship as arising from shared work, they were also his best mates. When the heroine of the thirteenth-century tale *Aucassin and Nicolette* comes upon a group of young shepherds, they are eating together.[23] That sort of day-to-day comradeship must have been commonplace. So if Stephen went to the crisis processions at Chartres, it is unlikely that he went alone and unaccompanied. Much more probably, some *pueri* from the Dunois— including some who would later join his pilgrimage to Saint-Denis—walked alongside him. They would become his core group, the nucleus of his charismatic adherents. At Chartres and at the post-Chartres processions afterwards, they marched by his side. During the interval when his revivalist zeal and sense of mission developed simultaneously, they kept close to him.

In the Chartrain, the traditional period for sheep-shearing was between Easter and Pentecost. After that, and during most of May, the shepherds were temporarily at leisure. Even during the shearing itself, the full-time shepherd was no more than a spectator. In June, there came an interval of relative calm. Shepherds were then primarily concerned to keep the sheep away from harmful plants, and lead them to thistles in the fallow fields.[24]

At Chartres for the processions of May 20, Stephen and his fellow shepherd-boys might have glanced upwards and seen themselves in stone. For sculpted on the Portail Royal, the south portal of the west façade of Chartres cathedral at the right corner of the lower register, were figures of contemporary shepherds (c. 1140).[25] These are beardless youths, wearing short tunics, holding staves cut from tree branches; one is playing the pan-pipes. Armadillo-like grazing sheep put their occupation beyond any doubt (Figure 6).

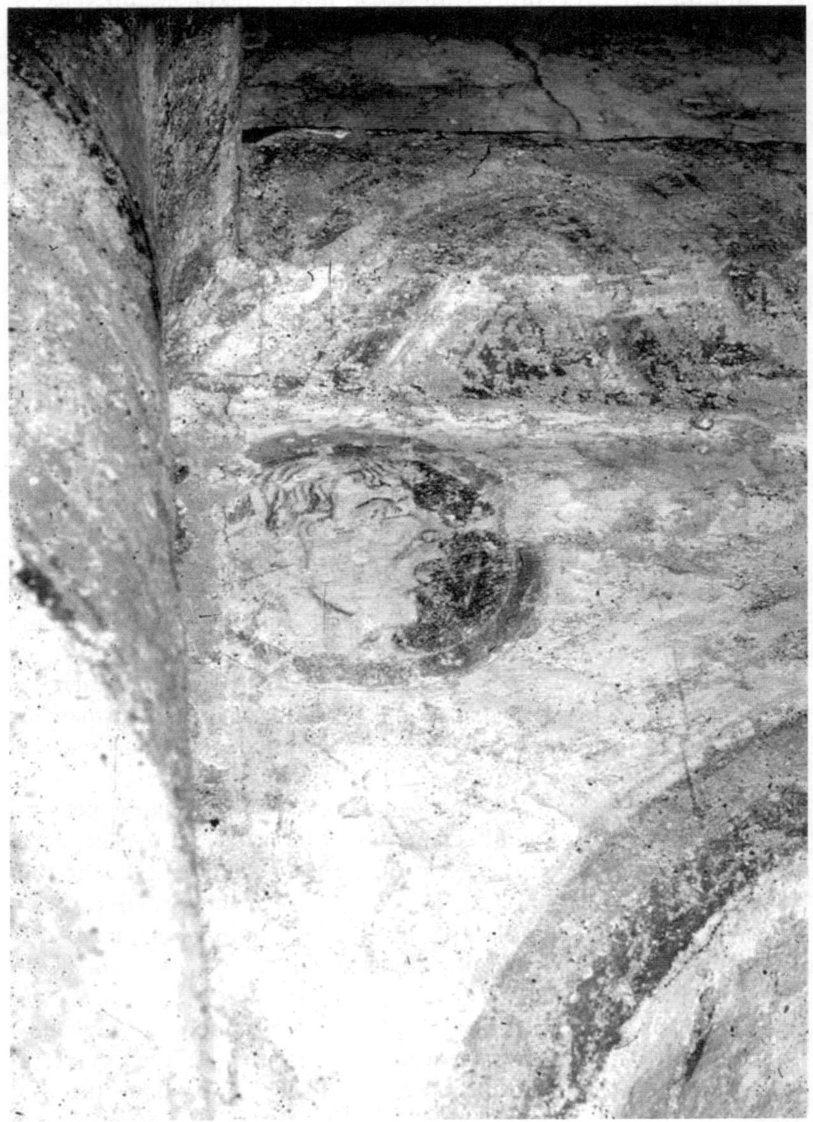

Figure 5 Portrait of Stephen of Cloyes (reputed), chapel of Notre-Dame d'Yron, Cloyes (fourteenth century?). Courtesy of the photographer Bernard Legrand and Didier Caffot, librarian and archivist of the Société Dunoise, which authorized its reproduction.

Figure 6 Cathedral of Chartres, Portail royal (twelfth century), *Shepherds led by an angel*. Éditions Houvet (reproduction prohibited).

Led by an angel, the three shepherds (the third represented by an arm and half a torso), approach the site of the Nativity scene at the center of the lintel. The sculptural program takes a degree of artistic liberty with the biblical text. In Luke (2:8–17) the angel who comes upon the shepherds out in the fields, keeping watch in the night over their sheep, tells them of the birth of Jesus, then rapidly ascends to heaven. The shepherds make their own way to the manger. So, strictly speaking, the scene at Chartres is neither a proper Annunciation to the Shepherds, nor a proper Adoration of the Shepherds (who are not yet at the crib), but combines elements of both.

In the clearest possible way the stone shepherds of Chartres sent out a message to their counterparts, the flesh-and-blood shepherds of the Chartrain. Be proud of your place in Christian history. You are privileged. You belong to a spiritual elite. Not only were you the first to see the baby Jesus (according to St. Luke), your biblical role stretches from David, the bold young shepherd, to that descendant of the royal Davidic line, the Good Shepherd himself. Bishops, as everyone knew, were the pastors of their spiritual flock—their crozier was a shepherd's crook, and part of the repertoire of Christian drama in the Middle Ages were shepherds' plays. There, watching medieval actors impersonate them, real shepherds in the audience saw themselves mirrored in sacred history.

This consciousness of their elect status found expression in the crusading movement. Shepherds' Crusades in 1251 and again in 1320 ended up as bloodbaths for Jews and clerics; and a good many of the shepherds perpetrating the atrocities were youths, *pueri*. Exceptionally, however, the very first Shepherds' Crusade—the Children's Crusade of 1212—was non-violent. As the Marxist historian Rodney Hilton notes, "herdsmen would very likely be the younger and more mobile of the rural population: the young peasants on the Children's Crusade… [were] mainly shepherds."[26] For the French *pueri* who followed Stephen of Cloyes on his pilgrimage to Saint-Denis, this was indeed the case.

To Saint-Denis: the pilgrimage of the shepherd boys

Far from concealing the ultimate source of what he knows about Stephen's pilgrimage, the Laon Anonymous reveals it almost immediately. Stephen "said (*dicebat*) that the Lord had appeared to him in the form of a poor pilgrim…." That sums it up: Stephen's story emanates from Stephen's own lips. Subsequently told and retold, it eventually reached the ear of the Laon chronicler. Whatever that story omits, the Laon Anonymous does not pretend to supply, however conspicuous the omission. Always making allowances for Chinese whispers, it is this profound silence at the heart of his narrative of Stephen's mission which inspires confidence in the Laon Anonymous, and his retelling of Stephen's story.[27] Stephen himself, of course, was the guarantor of its veracity. Like the stories of Peter the Hermit and Durand of Le Puy, the function of Stephen's story was to secure and maintain charismatic legitimacy, for, once his mysterious celestial letters were surrendered to the King's men, all he had left was his story.

In the beginning was the poor pilgrim-Christ who, appearing to Stephen, "received bread from him." Stephen behaved charitably towards the divine wayfarer, as Christians were taught to do. Soon the *pueri* would themselves be pilgrims, begging for their bread. Trying to unmask the "true" identity of the pilgrim-Christ may be an exercise in futility, but that has not deterred amateur detectives like George Z. Gray and Corrado Pallenberg. To Gray, he was "undoubtedly a disguised priest" intent upon manipulating Stephen, naturally.[28] To Pallenberg, quite the contrary, he was an actual pilgrim going to or returning from Santiago de Compostela in Spain, one of many such pilgrims who did in fact pass through Stephen's Cloyes.[29] Undoubtedly, this tenuous suggestion of a Spanish link to Stephen's venture is tempting, given the distinct possibility that Archbishop Jiménez de Rada tried and failed to enlist Philip Augustus in the Spanish cause. But Pallenberg's supposition, alas, is just that.

The pilgrim who was Christ then "delivered letters to… [Stephen] to be taken to the king of the French." Outside of Stephen's story, there is no evidence that this divine pilgrim, not to mention the letters he reputedly handed over, ever existed. Within that story, they did exist. Armed with celestial letters, and fortified by his story, the charismatic Stephen of Cloyes became God's postman.

Dispatched to Saint-Denis by the pilgrim-Christ,[30] the *pueri* embarked on their pilgrimage to the King of France. To get where they were going, they had to hike over ninety miles. "When he [Stephen] came, together with his fellow shepherd-boys, nearly 30,000 people congregated around him from diverse parts of France." 30,000 people? Perhaps the Anonymous's grand total should be taken in the same non-statistical spirit as the "vast multitude" or "infinite number" of other chroniclers of the Children's Crusade. Another guesstimate, this time from a contemporary English chronicler, halves this figure, which still makes it seem generous. He reckons an "estimated" 15,000 *pueri* came "streaming together through the cities of France" to "the great wonder of the spectators." Where this swollen stream of *pueri* started to bubble up, he does not say; nor does he say who led it, or what it was about. What he does disclose is its destination. The *pueri* were heading for Paris.

As a near-miss, Paris is perfect. The town of Saint-Denis was not much more than ten miles from Paris. Saint-Denis, nowadays, is one of Paris's less prosperous suburbs. Then it was not yet engulfed. The very next entry in that same English chronicle, dated July 10, 1212, further boosts confidence in the Laon Anonymous,[31] because it increases the likelihood that June was indeed the month that Stephen's congregation of *pueri* assembled at Saint-Denis. This once again confirms the essential trustworthiness of the Laon Anonymous chronicler, notwithstanding his inflated statistics and modicum of miracles.

Roughly three-quarters of the Anonymous's short narrative is devoted to the *pueri* at Saint-Denis. This suggests a local informant, probably a fellow cleric, who heard a recitation of Stephen's story and appreciated the newsworthiness of his mass pilgrimage, although he was not privy to its innermost secret, and so was unable to pass it on to the Laon Anonymous chronicler. Whatever was inscribed in the letters of Christ-the-wayfarer was evidently for King Philip's eyes only. It was not intended for public consumption, which is untypical of celestial letters. Normally left unsealed, they were scripted for pulpit broadcasting. A good example is the celestial letter that the Norman Abbot Eustace of Flay brought with him to England in 1201 to preach observance of the Lord's Day and excoriate Sunday trading.[32]

So why Saint-Denis? Why there? Why then? The short answer is that Stephen's mission impossible occurred in a historically plausible setting. The links between Saint-Denis and the Dunois, both secular and spiritual, were well-established. First, in the Chartrain, as in many parts of thirteenth-century Europe, rural overpopulation led to emigration from the countryside to the expanding cities. In search of a better life, peasants throughout the Chartrain, including the Dunois, targeted Paris and also Saint-Denis.[33] That meant Saint-Denis was known to the *pueri* as a place of good hope.

The season of their pilgrimage was also propitious. The arrival of the *pueri* in June coincided with the famous Lendit fair, held in the Plain of the Lendit between Paris and Saint-Denis. Thanks to privileges granted by the Crown, the great abbey of Saint-Denis gained important financial benefits from the Lendit fair, which became one of the most important markets in thirteenth-century Europe.[34] At the Lendit the merchants of Paris regularly turned out in droves, erected their stalls, and displayed their goods. In search of profits, merchants from the Dunois would also come. There, Stephen and his large and steadily growing army of followers camped out and awaited events. "While he stayed at Saint-Denis," says the Laon Anonymous, "the Lord worked many miracles through him, as many have witnessed." Crowded with buyers, vendors, and spectators, the Lendit fair was an ideal venue for the performance of miracles.

For centuries the royal abbey of Saint-Denis, the pilgrimage goal of Stephen and the *pueri*, had been at the juncture of French royal and religious life. Besides the relics of its titular saint, Saint-Denis claimed an impressive collection of relics, including hair from the Christ Child taken from the relic spoils of Constantinople in 1204. But the abbey Saint-Denis was not only a place of Christian religious pilgrimage. It was the Capetian monarchy's holiest shrine.

In Clifford Geertz's striking phrase about the geography of charisma, the royal abbey of Saint-Denis was "a locus of serious acts."[35] The first of the great Gothic churches, it was the necropolis of the Kings of France. Nurtured by the sacral-royal myth, St. Denis, patron saint of the abbey, was rapidly becoming the protector of all of France, a truly national saint. The abbots of Saint-Denis were the counsellors of kings; its royal annals chronicled Capetian achievements; and its propagandists championed the mystique of Capetian kingship. The Oriflamme, the battle standard of French kings, was stored in the abbey. When Kings of France like Philip Augustus departed on crusade, the Oriflamme went with them.[36]

Memories of the crusades were piously preserved at Saint-Denis, and visibly so. Here there were scenes depicting the battles and heroes of the First Crusade, including the conquest of Jerusalem. Stephen and his followers may well have seen them.[37] The present King of France had also been a crusader, and despite the damage done to his reputation by his hasty departure from the Third Crusade, perhaps for shepherd-boys like the *pueri* something of the prestige of an ex-crusader still clung to him. Although Philip Augustus habitually turned down offers to serve in further crusades, the continuing appeals which came to him, and not only from Innocent III, indicate that he was still perceived as a potential crusade leader. Just as the crusading movement remained a popular focus for dreams of Christian renewal, so, too, the King, whatever his personal shortcomings, remained a plausible leader for a new crusade. For those inclined towards divine revelations, he could serve as a messianic figure.

If Stephen did have letters to surrender to the King's men at Saint-Denis, and did so, he was now awaiting a response. Here the Laon Anonymous's narrative takes a surprising turn. Unexpectedly, attention is switched away from Stephen. "There were also other *pueri*... held in great veneration by the common multitude in many localities, because they were also believed to work miracles...." So where did these other groups of wonder-working *pueri* come from? They neither belonged to Stephen's original circle of shepherd-boys from the Dunois, nor, up to that point, recognized his charismatic leadership.

Working miracles is charisma in action. These miracle-working *pueri* held crowds of common people (*turbis vulgaribus*) spellbound. Was this pious fascination extended to the *pueri* as a distinct grouping or to particular charismatic individuals among them? Medieval collective charisma was uncommon. Typically, it was the product of awesome ritual. A good example would be the later medieval processions of semi-naked flagellants beating themselves until the blood flowed. Their penitential ritual was believed to be salvific. So people soaked cloths in their blood and retained them as relics. The church was not pleased.[38] Although charisma of this sort would rarely have outlasted the flagellant processions, highly emotive processional behavior such as this may offer a clue to the miracle-working *pueri* of 1212.

If this wider outpouring of the miraculous among the *pueri* was occurring while Stephen was at Saint-Denis, perhaps it began prior to Stephen's pilgrimage. Does this imply a common point of origin? Collective charisma, if such it was, would then have originated in the post-Chartres processions described by the Mortemer chronicler, in which the *pueri* marched to the fore, but did not march alone. Other groups would then have either fallen away or else disappeared from view, eclipsed by the spectacle of the massed ranks of *pueri*. The mid-century chronicler of the Norman abbey of La Vieille-Lyre (Évreux) concentrates entirely on the *pueri*. Under the wrong date, he sums up the revival in one laconic phrase: "the *pueri* held processions."[39] Could it be that it was their processional behavior, with its ecstatic, Pentecostal singing and thunderous acclamations, which charismatically empowered the *pueri* in the eyes of those who beheld them?

Thereupon, according to the Laon Anonymous, "a multitude of boys came together, wishing to proceed to the holy boy (*sanctum puerum*) Stephen... All recognized him as master and prince over them." Stephen's charismatic reputation had spread well beyond his original adherents from the Dunois, and his charismatic authority was now undisputed. *Pueri* from over a wide area were converging on Saint-Denis *en masse*. They shared Stephen's social identity: they, too, were youthful peasants and shepherds. As their encampment on the Plain of the Lendit continued to expand, Paris officialdom—perhaps including the King's counselors—began to take the threat of public disorder seriously.

Right at this juncture an adept teller of tales would have inserted a dramatic face-to-face encounter between Stephen of Cloyes and Philip Augustus. This was a scene no director of a Hollywood blockbuster would fail to shoot. Quite rightly, the Laon Anonymous chronicler ignores it. No such scene could have taken place. While Stephen's *pueri* were at Saint-Denis, Philip Augustus was elsewhere. But his itinerary does show that he was near enough to the abbey to have been readily contacted about any matters requiring a royal decision.[40]

Royal dispersal

In reaching his decision about the worryingly large assembly of peasant youths on his doorstep, King Philip consulted the Paris Masters. In 1212 the Paris Masters were already recognized as a prestigious body within the university, which itself was granted papal statutes in 1215. In 1200, after a town-gown (townspeople vs. students) riot in which several students were killed, Philip II, fearful that the Masters and their students would abandon Paris, as they threatened to do, took their side and granted them a charter spelling out their privileges.[41]

The Paris Masters were learned churchmen. For the King, their advice on what to do about the *pueri* would have been both valuable and authoritative. Whatever Stephen's business was, the gathering of his large flock at this "locus of serious acts" had religious, and perhaps religio-political, implications. If the Paris Masters were consulted, it is very probable that more than a concern over public disturbances was involved. A close reading of the situation suggests complicating factors. The mass pilgrimage led by Stephen to the royal shrine of Saint-Denis was an acknowledgement that to the *pueri* Philip Augustus was indeed the *rex christianissimus*, the most Christian King of France. The *pueri*, in other words, were true believers in the cult of sacral kingship, and more specifically, Capetian messianism. If so, what utopian proposals might Stephen have conveyed to the King's men? A new crusade to rescue Jerusalem and return the True Cross, perhaps?

The Paris Masters may already have noted the presence of the *pueri* during their annual ceremonial visit to the Lendit fair to purchase their supplies of parchment.[42] But their deliberations about the fate of the *pueri* took place in Paris. When the outcome of Stephen's mission to the King was under discussion, the shepherd-boy from Cloyes was presumably not present. Once more, the Laon Anonymous laudably forgoes a tale-teller's great opportunity for a classic confrontation, this time reconstructed on the model of the twelve-year-old runaway Jesus's precocious question-and-answer session with the doctors of the temple in Jerusalem (Luke 2:46–7) (Figure 2, p.5). Reticent as always, the Laon Anonymous maintains his silence about what was said.

Thus much remains obscure and conjectural. Because of this, scholars have been led to question whether Stephen's mission to the King had anything to do with the Holy Land or indeed the Children's Crusade.[43] On the contrary: if we accept that the ultimate origins of Stephen's pilgrimage to Saint-Denis lie in the Chartres processions provoked by the Spanish Crusade together with their aftermath in the processional enthusiasm that followed, then a connecting thread leads directly to Stephen's *pueri*—the True Cross, the plight of Christendom, and the crusades. One scrap of evidence that such a connecting thread did exist comes from the same English chronicler who gave Paris as the destination for the *pueri*. Responding to questions about what they hoped to achieve, their reply, he says, was to recover the True Cross.[44] Perhaps this indicates that the sentiments recorded in the Mortemer acclamations were alive and kicking at Saint-Denis. The same connecting thread to the True Cross will bind Stephen's French *pueri* to their counterparts, the Rhenish *pueri* of Nicholas of Cologne.

Finally, the royal dispersal: "At last, the king, having consulted the masters of Paris about this assembly of boys, they returned to their homes at his command." But not all of them, surely. Some of the *pueri* would have remained as immigrants, either in Saint-Denis or Paris. Nor was the timing of the royal dispersal left to chance. The right moment would have been carefully chosen. The Lendit fair lasted for about eleven to sixteen days, concluding no later than St. John the Baptist's Day (June 24).[45] The date of the closure of the Lendit fair was an opportune time for the dispersal of the *pueri*. Afterwards, little trace of Stephen's sprawling, ramshackle encampment on the Plain of the Lendit would have remained. The mission of the holy *puer* Stephen at Saint-Denis was at an end, and with it, in all probability, Stephen's always precarious charismatic authority as well. What became of the shepherd-boy of Cloyes thereafter is unchronicled.

In his farewell to the *pueri*, the last words of the Laon Anonymous are enigmatic as well as elegiac:

> And so this boyish revival (*puerilis illa devocio*) was terminated as easily as it had begun. But it seemed to many, that by means of such innocents gathered of their own accord, the Lord would do something great and new upon the earth, which turned out to be far from the case.

Was the Anonymous chronicler of Laon among the "many" whose hopes and dreams were excited by these "innocents"? His tone, certainly, is one of crushing disappointment, of high expectations dashed. So what was this tremendous, far-reaching, biblical-sounding, "something great and new upon the earth" that "many" believed the Lord would accomplish "by means of such innocents," the *pueri*? If only we knew.

Triumph followed tragedy in the Anonymous's next chronicle entry. On July 16, the long-anticipated, decisive battle of the Spanish Crusade produced a triumph—the overwhelming Christian victory at Las Navas de Tolosa. The contrast could not have been greater. For with the royal dispersal at Saint-Denis prophetic hopes had been reduced to ashes. Whatever it was the *pueri* attempted to carry out on the Lord's behalf "turned out to be far from the case." Whatever it was, it failed. But does this failure pertain only to Stephen's mission at Saint-Denis? Or does that failure also extend to what Stephen championed, and what he dreamed would follow from his mission? That is to say, does the Anonymous's cryptic phrase imply a later, post-Saint-Denis stage of the *peregrinatio puerorum*?

Violence at Saint-Quentin

After the forced evacuation of the *pueri* from Saint-Denis, their footprints grow faint to the point of near-invisibility, so that trying to track their itinerary from northern France to the Rhineland is more a matter of guesswork than roadwork. Reports of diverse, leaderless bands of French *pueri* on the march are one thing; attempting to determine whether or not they were refugees from Saint-Denis is another. In any case, the post-dispersal *pueri* were unlikely to have formed a single group, all marching off in the same direction.

Their reported direction was neither Paris, nor Saint-Denis. Yet Stephen's phase of the movement, it would seem, was now over. The same contemporary Norman annalist of Jumièges who traced the origins of the "commotion of the *pueri*" to Vendôme—thereby identifying it with Stephen's pilgrimage—totally ignores the encampment at Saint-Denis. Instead, he reaches beyond it. Using indirect discourse, he paraphrases what the *pueri* said: they are searching for God. (Their pilgrimage, consequently, was a journey to God; and where was He to be found? Where else, but in the Holy Land?) The *pueri* cannot be restrained. (By whom, one might ask? Parents and clergy is the obvious answer.) Gnawing hunger compels them to return home. (So, despite themselves, they are forced to obey the King's command.)[46] For these French *pueri*, this represents closure. For them, there would be no pilgrimage to God.

William, abbot of the monastery of Andres in the pas-de-Calais, was writing in the early 1230s, about twenty years after the annalist of Jumièges. Much later, John Le Long utilized him to round off his account of the anonymous shepherd. William fails to specify whether the "enormous multitude of children (*parvulorum*)," who came from "diverse cities, castles, towns, and villages," were French or German. Yet the location of his monastery points clearly to the former. While Stephen and Saint-Denis are not mentioned, William, like the Jumièges annalist, portrays this mass movement of children as leaderless and diffuse. Here too, as with Jumièges, there is more than a whiff of parental disapproval.

The children's fervor puzzles and dismays their "parents and others" (clergy?), who demand to know where they are going. In one voice—their own, not William's—the *parvuli* answer them: "Almost in one breath, each and all of them replied: 'To God!' (*Ad Deum*!)." Shouted out in unison, such a response sounds very much like a processional acclamation, even if it is presented as a reply to a question. This is an echo of Jumièges, and its implication is clear. The youngsters are setting out on a pilgrimage to God's dwelling place.

But in one crucial particular, William of Andres' account differs from Jumièges'. William records no famished return home, no closure. His *parvuli* are "hastening *towards* [my italics] (*versus*) the Mediterranean Sea." They have not yet reached it. Their adventure was not over. Unlike the German chroniclers, or later French mythistorians, no denouement awaits them at the water's edge. More significantly, William declares their intention of journeying to the Mediterranean before he records their cry, "To God!" If, as it seems, their royal road to God stretched across the Mediterranean, then their ultimate destination, in all probability, was the Holy Land.[47] Unlike Philip II, King of France, God would not fail them.

What confounds expectation is that, unlike Peter the Hermit's Crusade or the later Shepherds' Crusades, the march of the French *pueri* was not punctuated by sporadic outbreaks of anti-Jewish violence. A mass movement composed of youthful, God-intoxicated, roving bands of peasants and shepherds might have been expected to attack Jews in the towns where they were residing, and butcher them. On the contrary. When the *pueri* passed through Chartres, Saint-Denis, Paris, and Saint-Quentin in Picardy, they left the French Jewish communities they found there undisturbed and unmolested.[48] Had there been widespread assaults, pillaging, or massacres of Jews in the wake of the Children's Crusade, the

French monastic chroniclers, who hated social disorder, even if mob fury was directed against the Jews, would have condemned the perpetrators. Nothing of the sort was reported. So the passage of the unarmed crusade of the *pueri* through France was generally peaceful and left the Jews unharmed.

The only recorded incident of social disorder in France which refers to the *pueri* has nothing to do with the Jews. Preserved in the French royal archives is an official document dated June 18, 1213. As indisputable evidence of the Children's Crusade, it is remarkably early. This unique document contains a judicial verdict and sentences resulting from a civic disturbance in northern France.[49] It situates the *pueri* in a specific locality, the village of Rocourt (*Roocort*),[50] close to the town of Saint-Quentin, itself about 140 miles to the northeast of Saint-Denis.

At some unspecified time, presumably in 1212, a disagreement between the canons and the townspeople of Saint-Quentin turned into a full-fledged riot. Its cause is not stated. Although the *pueri* were somehow involved in it, they were not accused of participating in, let alone instigating it. Since none of them was punished, they were effectively exonerated. Yet even if they did not land blows or throw stones in the midst of this outbreak of mob violence, their presence was judged to be relevant, perhaps materially so, to the civic uproar. For the document is careful to note that the rioting occurred when the *pueri* were in town (*occasione puerorum*). Such a reference counts for more than a temporal marker. What it implies is clear enough—that the presence of the *pueri* in Rocourt somehow occasioned the violent confrontation between clergy and townsfolk.

Count Gaston de Janssens first drew attention to the significance of the Rocourt riot in his unduly disparaged, pioneering essay of 1891.[51] However unverifiable, De Janssens's hypothesis is certainly plausible. In his view, the tumult was triggered by the coming of the *pueri*. The cathedral canons of Saint-Quentin, if not openly opposing the crusade of the *pueri*, made their utter lack of sympathy towards it all too clear by refusing to disburse any of their charitable funds to assist it. De Janssens believed their stance enraged the townspeople, who, led by the mayor and jurors, attacked the canons as well as their goods, "wishing to take by force that which had not been offered with good grace."[52] The judicial penalty imposed upon Saint-Quentin's civic leaders, in addition to the permanent forfeiture of their offices, was public, ritual humiliation coupled with a penitential pilgrimage to Rome to seek absolution from Pope Innocent III. Punishment, including a substantial cash settlement, was also meted out to those townsmen found guilty of joining in the rioting and looting.

But the canons were also found to be at fault. Two members of the chapter were temporarily banished, and they, like the guilty townsmen, were obliged to undertake a pilgrimage to Rome. The canons of Saint-Quentin were plainly a contentious bunch. As recently as 1211 they had been implicated in local conflicts with the agents of Countess Eleanor of Saint-Quentin.[53]

Following De Janssens's lead, Paul Alphandéry postulates that it was the canons' hostility to the unofficial movement of the *pueri*, together with their clerical avarice, which provoked the reaction of laymen sympathetic to the cause of the *pueri*. The canons, for their part, were punished for their excessive zeal in defending themselves.[54] As both sets of punishments demonstrate, the authorities took a dim view of the eruption of mob violence at Rocourt.

Vitriolic disputes between the clergy and the laity which flared up during the German phase of the *peregrinatio puerorum*, probably in the Rhineland, strengthen De Janssens's and Alphandéry's case. The Marbach annalist, active in southern Alsace after 1230, alludes to several such hot-tempered exchanges without localizing them:

> when the clerics and certain others of sounder mind judged that pilgrimage or crusade (*iter*) [of the *pueri*] vain and useless... the laity vehemently objected, saying the clergy were unbelievers (*incredulos*), whose opposition was based on envy and avarice rather than truth and justice....[55]

Like so many medieval religious revivals, the Children's Crusade divided communities, as well as united them.

Given that divisive local clashes of this kind occurred here and there along the route of the Rhenish *pueri*, the likelihood increases that something similar had happened earlier with the French *pueri* at Rocourt. Simmering local antipathies came to the boil when the *pueri* begged for alms. Perhaps the vociferous clerical nay-sayers were trying to channel the donations of generous layfolk towards the church, or were defending the papal prerogative to call a crusade, or were simply being realistic about the immense practical difficulties that these naively hopeless crusaders faced in attempting a voyage to the Holy Land.

Whatever their motives, the clergy lost no time in speaking out against this ramshackle, pseudo-crusade of poor peasants and shepherds. Their harsh words exhorting the faithful to have nothing to do with it ignited the latent anticlericalism of the laity. Adding fuel to the flames was the belief, devoutly and ardently held by some townspeople, that this extraordinary child-led expedition to the East was indeed God's will, signifying "something great and new upon the earth."

Like other medieval revivalists on the march, the *pueri* saw their numbers continually fluctuate as some enthusiasts lost their enthusiasm, and dropped out, while others suddenly had their enthusiasm kindled, and so joined up. At Saint-Quentin as well as in the Rhineland, members of the urban underclass were themselves often recent peasant immigrants. Fascinated by these extraordinary pilgrims, they imbibed the dreams they dreamed, were converted to their cause, threw in their lot with them, and ran off. Townsfolk of greater means and a more sceptical disposition may have felt that by tossing a few coins or handing over a pouch of food and some water, these destitute crusaders would quickly move on to the next town and do their begging there.

Winning converts among the working urban poor would have contributed to their total assets, but these bands of *pueri*, like other impoverished pilgrims, always remained heavily dependent on donations given to them by charitable folk in the various towns and villages through which they passed. If alms dried up altogether, their journey risked being terminated abruptly. According to the Jumièges annalist, hunger forced the *pueri* to return home.[56] That might have been predicted. Yet there were numerous bands of *pueri*, and the Jumièges annalist does not tell us what proportion of them returned home. So while the Marbach annalist comments on their "empty purses," he also relates that people "aided them with provisions, furnishing them food and other necessities."[57] Not unreasonably, the comparatively late French verse chronicler Philippe Mousket (d. c. 1243) claims that groups of these youthful crusaders found lodgings with "good people" (ll.29216–17), and that a few of the children (*li enfant*) who took the cross had some money (l.29218).[58] This is a credible statement. Among the *pueri* were wage-earning urban artisans and laborers, and even poor peasants and shepherds were not necessarily penniless.

The Saint-Quentin document makes no mention of any leader of the *pueri*, nor does it provide any clue as to whether the enthusiasts were heading towards Saint-Denis, or away from it. Yet the Laon Anonymous's description of "a multitude of boys... [coming] together, wishing to proceed to the holy boy Stephen" appears to indicate that their journeys to Saint-Denis were trouble-free. Had there been incidents *en route* of anti-clerical aggression like that directed against the cathedral canons of Saint-Quentin, regardless of who was responsible for it, the canon-regular of Laon would have instantly withdrawn his sympathy towards Stephen and his followers. A further point is that news of the riot would have reached him quickly, for Laon is only about a third of the distance from Saint-Quentin as it is from Saint-Denis. But he says nothing about it.

All in all, the Saint-Quentin document is the closest we come to a signpost pointing towards a possible route from the French to the German phase of the *peregrinatio puerorum*. The Saint-Quentin document may not be a stepping stone; but as a tantalizingly ambiguous road sign, it will have to do. For the *pueri* were once again on the march. What cannot be proved can at least be hypothesized. Groups of French *pueri*, Stephen's followers most probably among them, were on the road to the Rhineland.

5
History: On the Road

Dana Carleton Munro (1866–1933), the founding father of American crusade historians, owed his intellectual formation to the German seminar, which kept him chained to the documents. At his death his grand project, "a detailed and scholarly history of the Crusades based upon an exhaustive and critical use of the contemporary sources," was left unfinished.[1] Amongst his many published articles was the first essay in English on the Children's Crusade. In his essay, diligent if uninspiring, Munro did achieve one thing. He left meat for his successors to chew on: "There were two movements in 1212, one of French, the other of German children; if they were in any way connected, as seems probable, such connection cannot be proved from the extant sources."[2]

Continuities

About the first point, Munro is spot on. The probability of a connection between the French and German *pueri* is so high it teeters on the edge of certainty. Here were two extraordinary peasant movements— both headed by *pueri*, both with crusade associations, both with similar aims and ambitions, and both on the march within months of each other. In the absence of a common ignition key, an identical starting mechanism, contact between them—rather than coincidence—seems a reasonable conclusion.

Munro's second point, on the contrary, creates a quandary where none exists. To the honest eye, the link between the French and German phases of the Children's Crusade—precedence and sequence—is transparent.

First, no fewer than five contemporary chroniclers mention the French and German *pueri* in the same breath. They do so, simply because they perceive both movements as part of a single, unitary phenomenon.[3] Aside from the Lotharingian, Renier of Liège, the four remaining chroniclers who refer to both the French and German *pueri* are German.[4] None of the French or English chroniclers (who are dependent on French sources), refer to the German *pueri*. A sign of precedence and sequence, perhaps?

Second, chronology confirms this. The French movement dates from May 20 (the processions at Chartres) to around June 24 (the end of the Lendit fair at Saint-Denis). The German phase of the Children's Crusade began, as we will see, in the latter half of July.

Third, without the propellant of the French *pueri*, the German enthusiasm was (and remains) inexplicable.

Fourth, motifs common to both the French and German phases of the Children's Crusade bind the revival together. To take one such motif amongst others—parental opposition. Bewildered French parents tried to restrain their runaway offspring, while German parents went further, imposing house arrest as preventive medicine for juvenile crusaders.[5]

Fifth, continuity in word and deed. The French *pueri* sang; so did the Germans.[6] The French *pueri* carried banners; so did the Germans.[7] The French *pueri* invoked God; so did the Germans.[8]

Sixth, ideological continuity. In the course of the movement ideas were elaborated; goals were made more specific. Flesh was added to bare bones. On the road from France to Germany, ideas and beliefs evolved, yet stayed rooted in what had gone before. This is precisely what one would have expected—enrichment rather than attenuation.

Altogether, at its core, the *peregrinatio* of the *pueri* was one and the same, whether it attracted adherents in France or in Germany. What does differentiate the two phases of the enthusiasm is the gradually broadening age range and social composition of its adherents in Germany. The revival in the Rhineland became more heterogeneous, with urban workers, older people, mothers, babies, perhaps entire families joining it. While retaining its name and character as a youth movement, it was now a full-fledged popular crusade. Quite unlike the so-called People's Crusade of Peter the Hermit, however, the Children's Crusade marched with no hermits, priests, armed knights, or feudal barons in command; nor, so far as we know, within its ranks.[9] Which means that the first true popular crusade was the *peregrinatio puerorum*.

The road to Cologne

These arguments are crucial. What follows depends on them for the obvious reason that direct evidence is lacking. The assumption must be that somewhere on the road to Cologne, perhaps in the Lotharingian borderlands, the missionizing French *pueri* began to attract proselytes. But the fact remains that the whereabouts of the *pueri* cannot be documented between their last known stopping place in France, Saint-Quentin, and Cologne, the point of departure for their transalpine adventure.

One hypothesis—and it is no more than that—may partially account for their route to Cologne. Their path from France to Germany came remarkably close to replicating the road taken by Peter the Hermit's motley army of First Crusaders. Peter's peasants and knights trudged and rode from Berry to the Île-de-France; then, through Lower Lotharingia to Trier and Cologne. Similarly, the *pueri* probably passed through Trier, although not while *en route* to Cologne, but after leaving it. Still, there is an undeniable resemblance. Conscious mimicry, perhaps? Did some vague folk-memory of Peter the Hermit's ill-assorted warriors trooping off to Cologne inspire the remnant of the French *peregrinatio puerorum* to trek northeast to the Rhineland?

On the other hand, if they were intending to go "to the sea," getting there via Cologne seems a strange choice. Peter's men took the land route to the Holy Land—the Rhineland, across Hungary and Byzantium, before crossing the Bosporus.[10] So this conjecture may be a blind alley. For whatever reason—or impulse—their road "to the sea" directed them to the Rhineland. Then it led them up the Rhine, over the Alps, into Italy, and finally, at long last, to the shores of the Mediterranean.

At Liège, there is the faint glimmer of an eyewitness. Renier, prior of the Benedictine monastery of St. James, composed the annals of his abbey from the late twelfth century until his death in 1230. Concentrating almost entirely on contemporary events, Renier filled his chronicle with the living history of his monastery, his city, and its surrounding region, while never losing sight of the great news stories of Christendom, like the crusades. Renier was by no means confined to quarters in Liège. On several occasions he traveled on monastic business to Rome. His raw materials were what he himself observed, and what reliable informants told him. Generally, he jotted down his notes as things occurred; later on, he added new information, then he wrote up the entry for his chronicle. Almost every year, Renier recorded precise and accurate data about climate, harvests, and prices. Miracles rarely graced his pages. Modern scholars show they respect him: they listen to what he has to say.[11]

In Renier's day, Liège was becoming increasingly prosperous. There was urban growth; the textile industry was developing; merchants were profiting from the cloth trade; new monasteries and convents were being built; the money-changers were active, always a sign of vibrant commerce.[12] On the whole, in the early thirteenth century the city of the River Meuse was doing well. Then came a crisis. On May 3, 1212, Liège was invaded and pillaged for four days by the forces of Henry, Duke of Brabant.[13]

The year 1212 was doubly memorable and doubly unfortunate for Renier of Liège. In addition to the attack on his city, on December 31 his mother, Judith, passed away. Clothed in the habit of a *conversa*, she died near his monastery of St. James. During that same year as well, there occurred a most remarkable incident:

> A wondrous movement of children (*motus puerorum mirabilis*) as well from the Roman [i.e. French] as from the Teutonic [i.e. German] kingdom, and chiefly of shepherds (*maxime pastorum*), both of the male and female sex. But those whose fathers and mothers would not permit to go away wept most profusely... But it was their intention to cross the sea, and what the powerful and kings had not done, recover the sepulchre of Christ, but because this work was not of God, it had no effect. The heat was extremely great in the first fifteen days of July.[14]

Renier of Liège had no information about where or how the *motus puerorum* started, although he knew it ended in failure. Three of Renier's themes—parental opposition; the intent of the *pueri*; and the fact that previous crusaders, powerful men, had failed to retake the Holy Land—are also remarked upon by the Cologne Continuator.[15] Yet there is no evidence of collusion between them. Monastic chroniclers, like modern journalists, shared a common culture and elaborated similar themes.

And on one crucial matter of reportage, Renier and the Cologne Continuator differ absolutely. On the one hand, the Continuator reports peasants and cowherds, "many thousands of children" taking the cross in a near frenzy of revivalist zeal.[16] Like all the rest of the German chroniclers, he fails to mention shepherds or shepherdesses. Renier, on the contrary, singles them out as the preponderant element, the most conspicuous group amongst the *pueri*. Does this mean that the shepherds had become invisible by the time the child-crusaders came to Cologne? How could the occupational composition of the enthusiasm have altered so radically between Liège and Cologne? The answer may be that the impressive numbers of new Rhenish converts which the Continuator observed at Cologne overwhelmed and submerged a relatively smaller contingent of young shepherds, for Renier does not indicate the scale of the phenomenon he is describing. Yet by highlighting the importance of young shepherds, Renier immediately evokes Stephen of Cloyes' earliest adherents—the shepherd-boys of the Chartrain. In other words, the French *pueri*.

Moreover, like the Cologne Continuator, Renier sounds as if he is describing what he has actually seen. So the next question is—if Renier did observe a "wondrous" procession of French *pueri* parading in front of him at Liège (or near it), when did he do so? Helpfully, Renier supplies a timeframe. Hard on the heels of the *motus puerorum* comes this laconic sentence: "The heat was extremely great in the first fifteen days of July." The implication could not be plainer. At some point within this fifteen-day interval, at Liège or near it, an astonished Benedictine monk named Renier watched as shepherds and shepherdesses strode across his field of vision, determined to complete their pilgrimage to the sea.

Speculative itineraries are risky; speculative rates of march, more so. All estimates of this sort are naturally subject to correction. In attempting to nail down the marching rate of the *pueri* of 1212, brave souls have come up with figures ranging from sixteen to twenty-five miles per day.[17] Taking the median, 20.5 miles per diem, offers at least a basis for a rough calculation. So: if the *pueri* left Saint-Denis on the date of the Lendit dispersal, June 24, they would have arrived in Saint-Quentin on June 30, which means they could have reached Liège on July 8—well within Renier's fifteen days.[18] Of course, the presumption of a constant rate of march is unrealistic. Variables such as the good spirits or fatigue of the travelers, rest-stops, the availability of provisions, or the odd disturbance (such as the Saint-Quentin riot) need to be factored in. Therefore, it seems reasonable to allow for, say, one or two days off the road. That still leaves Renier's timeframe intact.

Their next likely port of call on the road to Cologne was less than two full days' march from Liège. It was Aachen, city of the renowned medieval emperor Charlemagne (d. 814). When Emperor Frederick Barbarossa had Charlemagne's bones dug up at Aachen and instructed his tame antipope to canonize him in 1165, the Emperor Charlemagne emerged, resurrected. He was now St. Charlemagne, a growth in stature which boosted the stature of Aachen. The next year Barbarossa granted a privilege to Aachen, denoting it a *sacra civitas*, a holy city.[19]

Thereafter, just as the royal abbey of Saint-Denis was a shrine to French kingship, the cathedral of Aachen became a shrine to German imperial power. It was there in 1215 that the Hohenstaufen Emperor Frederick II was crowned; and, there, too, virtually at the same moment, Frederick took the cross for the Fifth Crusade.[20] Ready for Frederick's coronation was the splendidly ornate reliquary-shrine of St. Charlemagne on which work had begun in the late twelfth century.[21]

The *pueri* may have come under the spell of Charlemagne well before they encountered him at Aachen. Although the Charlemagne window at Chartres (1225?) had probably not yet been fashioned when Stephen's shepherds were there,[22] Saint-Denis did offer an opportunity for visual contact with the Emperor. Most likely commissioned by Suger in the 1140s (and destroyed during the French Revolution), the windows at Saint-Denis included representations of Charlemagne. Juxtaposed to them were a series of battle scenes of the First Crusade, among which was the conquest of Jerusalem. So, less than fifty years after Jerusalem became Christian again, on the eve of the Second Crusade, First Crusaders—unsainted Christian warriors—were already portrayed on the walls of a monastic church. Mere laymen were deemed worthy of emulation. Nor was the celebrated Emperor Charlemagne overlooked. Positioned in close proximity to these images of First Crusade victories was a series of windows devoted to Charlemagne's fabled adventures in the exotic Muslim and Christian East.[23] However odd it may seem historically, this conjunction of Charlemagne, the Levant, and the First Crusade was no accident.

There was an excellent reason for bringing these images together. The church of Saint-Denis appears in the French poem *The Pilgrimage of Charlemagne*. Rather like a mock epic, with heroic as well as humorous interludes, this is a pseudo-narrative of the Emperor's legendary voyage to Jerusalem and Constantinople. Critics have dated it to the early or mid-twelfth century. Its plausible source is an earlier Latin text which links the royal abbey of Saint-Denis to the legendary adventures of Charlemagne.[24] This legend recounts the story of Charlemagne's military pilgrimage to Jerusalem. At the urging of the Patriarch, Charlemagne liberates Jerusalem from the infidels. Then he and his army travel on to Constantinople, where the Byzantine Emperor rewards him with precious relics, which Charlemagne donates to Aachen and Saint-Denis on his return.[25]

By the time of the First Crusade it was widely believed that Charlemagne had already led a triumphant crusade of his own to the East. It was reported that Pope Urban II, preaching the First Crusade at Clermont, invoked the magic name of Charlemagne to inspire the French nobility to take up arms. Across Germany the rumor spread that Charlemagne had risen from the grave. Marching across Hungary, the troops in Peter the Hermit's army were convinced they "traveled by the road which Charlemagne, the heroic king of the Franks, had formerly caused to be built to Constantinople."[26] Could the young crusaders of 1212 have imagined they were following, not so much in the footsteps of Peter the Hermit, as in those of that illustrious "crusader," the sainted Emperor Charlemagne himself?

Aachen's relic collection—including, it was said, the swaddling clothes of the infant Jesus[27]—began to attract pilgrims from the eleventh century onwards. But it was during the twelfth century that the growing cult of St. Charlemagne lured increasing numbers of pilgrims to Aachen. Remarkably, there was a new development at the shrine of the sainted Emperor in 1212. For the first time, the donations of pious pilgrims were judged to be substantial enough for an agreement to be signed which split the proceeds of pilgrimage revenues between the Aachen cathedral chapter and the church provost, William.

What prompted this unprecedented agreement is unclear. One attractive possibility is that an unusually large crowd of pilgrims flocked to Aachen in the summer of 1212. Why then? The document setting out the agreement designates the three days of the liturgical year, when, implicitly, pilgrimage revenues were expected to peak. These three days were the cathedral's feast of dedication and the two days preceding it—July 15–17.[28]

Having left Liège, the *pueri* perhaps would have found themselves in Aachen, say, around July 11 or 12. The question now arises: if this new agreement to divide pilgrimage donations was indeed the result of an exceptional influx of pilgrims in July, 1212, could such an increase in pilgrimage traffic be at least in part attributable to the presence of the *pueri* in Aachen around that time? It goes without saying that, far from contributing to Aachen cathedral funds, the *pueri* would have been much more likely to have begged for alms than to have donated them.

All in all, the probable impression that the pilgrimage to Aachen would have made upon the *pueri* should not be underestimated. This was the shrine-city of Charlemagne the crusader. Here their desire to reach the crusader East would have quickened. Perhaps, after visiting Aachen, they imagined themselves as Charlemagne's heirs, the youthful beneficiaries of his crusading legacy.

Self-imaginings

Long before historians and mythistorians imagined them, the *pueri* imagined themselves. As they began their arduous trek to the sea, ideas of election, notions of providential chosenness, sustained them. Becoming pilgrims, taking up the crusader's cross, gave them a privileged status which enhanced their collective identity. Like the Israelites before them and innumerable neo-Israelites after them, the *pueri* of 1212 experienced moments of hope, doubt, despair, and certitude.

Common memories, often recounted, fostered collective identity. Revelations, as with Stephen and the pilgrim-Christ, empowered them. Never-to-be-forgotten collective experiences, like joining in the crisis-processions at Chartres and marching in the ecstatic, Pentacostalist processions thereafter, yielded a sense of solidarity. Their mass encampment at Saint-Denis was perhaps their formative collective experience. Their formidable presence there gave them confidence in having been chosen for a tremendous, divinely ordained enterprise. Experiences such as these made the *pueri* who they were. Credo and charisma were born of the crowd.

But collective experience recollected was not the sole source of their self-imaginings. Who they were depended equally upon self-perceptions based on actual social identities. Where so much uncertainty prevails, however, it is best to be undogmatic. Trying to imagine the *pueri* as they imagined themselves is a risky, some would say a foolhardy venture, rather like the Children's Crusade itself. Others would insist that any attempt to dream their dreams is an ambition best left to psycho-historians or novelists. *Per contra,* there is no reason why mental landscapes should be any more intimidating to reconnoitre than physical landscapes. Both make use of a safety rope—in this case, historical discipline.

Stephen himself, together with his earliest adherents, were shepherds. If, as Renier's chronicle strongly suggests, a good number of Stephen's core-group of young French shepherds transplanted the Children's Crusade to the Rhineland, they would not have forgotten their privileged role in the Nativity. From the shrine of the lactating Virgin of Chartres[29] to the cathedral of Cologne, where the Three Kings held sway, the role of shepherds in the cult of the *puer Christus* was an inseparable part of the Christian narrative. Even amongst the saints, there were former shepherd-boys. The Frisian Abbot St. Frederick (d. 1175), when he was a lad, was sent by his mother to tend the family's sheep, although he piously preferred to build model churches with tiny altars in them instead of playing worldly games with his workmates.[30] Accordingly, the French *pueri* of 1212 would have internalized the positive Christian image of the shepherd as a facet of their spiritual identity.

In stark contrast to the favorable medieval image of the shepherd was that of the lowly peasant. Two brothers—two archetypes. The former a just man unjustly killed, the first biblical martyr, and so a Christ-figure—that was Abel, the shepherd. The latter was his fratricidal brother, the evil, scheming Cain—a murderous peasant. Perhaps 85–90 percent or more of the people who lived in thirteenth-century Europe were peasants; regional estimates vary. On the Children's Crusade, the proportion of peasants may have been higher still. Medieval Europe had water power, wind power, and horse and oxen power, but its main source of energy remained peasant sweat. All of Latin Christendom's towering Gothic super-structure rested on the stooped backs of peasant laborers.

In Germany as in France, rural society was facing a crisis of overpopulation, resulting in land shortage and the growth of a marginal, landless class of wage laborers, a rural proletariat too poor to marry and establish a household.[31] German rural deprivation prompted migration *nach Osten*, to the East, or to the cities.[32] On the shores of the Mediterranean, the port-cities were booming, ready to absorb immigrant labor, while faraway in the crusader East there was another city, Jerusalem, awaiting those vowed to rescue it.

The mass migration of peasants known as the Children's Crusade was hastened by a potent combination of high ideals plus poor material prospects. Nor should a psychological stimulus be ruled out. Medieval peasants were subjected to negative stereotypes and literary caricatures. Townsmen sneered at them. They were likened to the beasts they tended. Vernacular and Latin literature defamed them as earth-bound creatures—small, dark, ugly, stupid, coarse, filthy, envious, lazy, crafty. To churchmen, they were little more than an irreligious pack of tithe-dodgers. Whatever literary praise they received—for their labor which fed the rest of Christian society, or for their simple piety—was doled out in modest portions. Mostly, the little there was of it appeared in the fourteenth and fifteenth centuries, when the Children's Crusade was but a memory.[33]

So the chance to exchange an imposed social identity saturated with belittlement and negativity, one inviting self-hate, for a new identity, freely-chosen, conferring prestige and quasi-chivalric status—that of a crusader—would have proved irresistible. Ever since the days of Peter the Hermit, peasants had made strenuous efforts to reinvent themselves as crusaders. Hence for these peasant *pueri*, going off on crusade implied something more than a voyage to God and Jerusalem. It was an opportunity to escape from vilification and exploitation, a means of running away from a selfhood brutally imagined by others.

Involuntarily poor peasants no longer, they would now be counted amongst the voluntary poor, Christ's poor, *pauperes Christi*. Luxuriating in spiritual poverty, they would enjoy the same exalted status as monks, pilgrims, and crusaders. For they, too, were pilgrims, imitators of Stephen's pilgrim-Christ. As such, they adorned themselves with emblems of their new identity. When the "great multitude of pilgrims" led by "the German *puer* named Nicholas" arrived in Genoa, they were "carrying crosses, [pilgrims'] staves, and also [pilgrims'] wallets."[34] Weapons of war are never mentioned; it was as if the crusade of the *pueri* was anachronistic, a throwback to the pilgrimage roots of crusading. In fact, the sacral geography of pilgrimage shaped their itinerary. Dotted along their route were shrine-cities—Chartres; Saint-Denis; Aachen (?); Cologne; Rome—way stations on the long, hard road to Jerusalem, which was Christendom's incomparable shrine-city.

The key to their self-imaginings was the crusade, and its quintessential attribute was the crusader's cross. That they wore it demonstrates that they saw themselves as real crusaders, "the cross-signed," *crucesignati*. In a sermon probably composed around the time of the Fifth Crusade (1213), an anonymous Paris crusade preacher praises the children (*parvuli*) who "the other year" became *crucesignati*.[35] Likewise, the verse chronicler Philippe Mousket (d. early 1240s) describes them as "children" who took the cross, and whose crosses were "firmly fixed" (to their garments?).[36] Large crowds of *pueri* signing themselves with the cross were also recorded by German chroniclers.[37]

John Codagnello, a citizen-chronicler of Piacenza, rather than a monk, was non-judgmental when it came to the *pueri*.[38] Describing the Children's Crusade entering his city, he chronicles the arrival of "some German *puer* called Nicholas, signed with the sign of the cross, with a great and countless multitude of German *pueri*, infants at the breast, women, and girls, signed with the sign of the cross of the Lord." All were "hastening to cross the sea" in order "to recapture the sepulchre of the Lord from the hands and power of the iniquitous and evil Saracens."[39] Whatever came of their grand design, he does not say.

Led by Nicholas, these self-imagined, unconventional *crucesignati* internalized the idea that God had chosen them, that they were an elect group. God had given them a mission; and they wanted the world to know it. "It was said" (i.e. they let it be known), an angel revealed their mission to Nicholas and foretold its success.[40] A German chronicler makes a similar affirmation: an angel commanded them to go.[41] (Angels will also figure in mythistorical accounts.) An unshakeable belief in chosenness runs through the French and German phases of the Children's Crusade, a belief made all the stronger by the extraordinary mass conversions in the Rhineland.

Like the Israelites, the chosen people of sacred scripture, they announced they would do "whatever God wanted them to do." That was how the Rhenish *pueri* responded to a crowd of gawping spectators in Cologne who declared they were foolish and imprudent for trying to achieve what in previous years so many mighty Kings, Dukes, and innumerable lesser folk had failed to achieve. That kind of self-confident and provocative reply from "youngsters with neither power nor strength to do anything"[42] would not have gone unchallenged. We can almost hear the mocking voices: "Well, tell us how you're going to do it!" The answer of the *pueri* was short and to the point: "We will cross the sea dry-shod, just as the people of Israel did in their flight out of Egypt."[43] This is what the *pueri* affirmed; this is what they believed. Were they, then, imagining themselves as the new Jews?

Nothing proves that their spiritual identification with the Children of Israel began in France, but there is every chance that the French *pueri* encountered non-biblical, living and breathing Jews in Chartres, or Saint-Denis, or Paris, or Saint-Quentin, all of which had established Jewish communities. Chartres' Jewish community, for example, may then have included the scholar Joseph of Chartres, who wrote a celebrated Hebrew elegy for the English Jews killed in the York massacre of 1190.[44] The point is—and it is altogether too remarkable to be purely coincidental— that at the time of the Children's Crusade the Jews of England and of northern and southern France were caught up in an astonishing pilgrimage revival of their own. More astonishing still, the pilgrimage goal of the European Jews and the *pueri* was the same—Jerusalem.

Known as the "pilgrimage of the 300 rabbis," this was an extraordinary Jewish mass movement, an outburst of medieval religious Zionism almost as difficult to explain as the contemporary pilgrimage of the *pueri*.[45] Ibn Verga's sixteenth-century account of it begins: "In the year 4971 [1211], God stirred the rabbis of France and the rabbis of England to go to Jerusalem; and they were more than three hundred."[46] Whatever their actual number, this mass pilgrimage to the Holy Land was probably triggered by a combination of factors—royal persecution in England and France; bitter internal divisions, especially in Provençal Jewry, between the rabbinic partisans of the great Jewish philosopher Maimonides and their rigidly tradition-bound opponents; and the sort of fervent messianic expectation always apt to bubble up during times of persecution. Messianic fervor was centered on the years 1209–10, and on the very year of the *pueri*, 1212. "It is just possible," comments Joshua Prawer, "that these messianic calculations are linked with the early waves of the migration."[47]

Prophetic enthusiasm, whatever its source, is readily communicable. The fact that western European Jews were suddenly departing for the Holy Land, created a vivid contemporary image of the Exodus from Egypt. This may well have strengthened the resolve of the *pueri* to cross, not the Red Sea, but the Mediterranean. So far as we know, the belief of the *pueri* in a biblical dry-shod crossing was first articulated in Germany, but it may have been part of the luggage the French *pueri* carried with them to the Rhineland. Parallel, simultaneous Jewish pilgrimages to Jerusalem may well have helped to engender a sense of spiritual affinity as neo-Israelites. Whether or not they imagined themselves as the new Jews, the *pueri* almost miraculously refrained from slaughtering the real Jews in their path. Earlier and later People's Crusades showed no such restraint.

These Rhenish *pueri* took up exactly the same cross and the same pilgrimage as their French confrères, whose self-imaginings they shared. Whatever the apparent differences which existed between them, these can be explained by an increasing sharpness of definition as the journey progressed. For example, while the destination of the French *pueri*—the crusader East—always remained implicit ("to the sea," "to God"), the German enthusiasts pronounced their goals unambiguously—to the Holy Sepulchre,[48] "the road to Jerusalem... to recapture the Holy Land."[49] Or, full-throatedly: "To Jerusalem, to seek the Holy Land!"[50] Their spiritual homeland was Jerusalem. They, too, were worthy of the tag the chroniclers pinned to the First Crusaders—Jerusalemites. Like the European Jews sailing to the Holy Land, the *pueri* were Jerusalemites.

The quest for the True Cross

"To Jerusalem, to seek the Holy Land!"—half-reveals, half-conceals something at the heart of the self-imaginings of these youthful crusaders. They were seekers—Holy Land-seekers, Jerusalem-seekers, God-seekers. Theirs, furthermore, was a quest for an object of awesome sacrality.

It was in France that their chant first rang out: "Lord God, return to us the True Cross!"[51] but similar outcries would probably have been heard in the Rhineland as well. In the Rhineland, however, their prayer for the reacquisition of the True Cross became a prayer for its liberation.[52] The change is significant. "Liberation" was the papacy's traditional term for the reconquest of Jerusalem; so perhaps in the minds of the *pueri* the search for the True Cross was synonymous with the liberation and repossession of Jerusalem. Saladin had seized them both. Now, apparently without arms, the *pueri* were seeking to liberate them both (Figure 7). Their quest for the True Cross thus coincided with their longing for Jerusalem. Proclaimed vociferously at the very beginning of their pilgrimage, their quest for the True Cross was no eccentricity on their part. What preoccupied the *pueri* was a central preoccupation of the age.

Only recently has the magnitude of the grief and spiritual distress suffered by Latin Christians at the loss of the True Cross begun to be

Figure 7 *Capture of the True Cross by Saladin*, drawing by Matthew Paris, *Chronica Majora*, MS 26, p.279. The Parker Library, Corpus Christi College, Cambridge.

appreciated.[53] Christendom was sorely wounded, and that wound was slow to heal. Just how long the painful memory of Christendom's loss remained raw is driven home by the passionate acclamation of illiterate country boys—"Lord God, return to us the True Cross!"—shouted out twenty-five years after the battle of Hattin.

Alleged bits and pieces of the True Cross were of course venerated in Latin churches long before the crusaders who sacked Constantinople in 1204 shipped supposed fragments of it westwards, although these stolen treasures immeasurably increased western holdings. The relic of the True Cross exhibited by Innocent III at his Roman crisis-processions, for instance, was possibly looted from Constantinople.[54] Yet for some reason all this pious booty failed to alleviate a terrible sense of loss. For the *pueri*—and one presumes for many Latin Christians—there was only one relic of the True Cross that mattered, and that was the True Cross of Jerusalem. Held hostage by the Saracens, a prisoner of war, it was the "real" True Cross.

The circumstances of its discovery guaranteed its authenticity. Probably on August 5, 1099, the newly elected Latin Patriarch of Jerusalem, Arnulf of Chocques, unearthed it in the compound of the Holy Sepulchre. Dramatically discovered at such an opportune moment, it boosted Arnulf's claim to legitimacy as Patriarch.[55] Significantly, too, finding the True Cross so soon after the Latin reconquest of Jerusalem (July 15) miraculously ratified the crusaders' victory, demonstrating that God had indeed willed it. From that point onwards, the history of Latin Jerusalem was symbolically intertwined with that of the True Cross. And not only their history: they would also share the same destiny.

Set in precious metals, then encased in a large wooden cross, the small fragment of wood from the True Cross was quickly elevated to the role of the Holy Land's most sacred emblem. Portable, ready to be taken into combat, it was a talisman, indispensable to morale on the battlefield. During the course of its military career in the kingdom of Jerusalem, the True Cross served in no fewer than thirty-one campaigns from 1099 until its final, fatal engagement at Hattin in 1187.[56]

After Hattin, an anonymous warrior-chronicler of the kingdom of Jerusalem lamented,

> Alas! should I describe with impure lips how the precious wood of the Lord... was seized by the damnable hands of the damned? Woe to me that in the days of my miserable life I should be forced to see such things...[57]

While from the enemy side, a Muslim chronicler shrewdly appraised the impact on the infidels of the capture of "their great cross, called the 'True Cross'": "This was one of the heaviest blows that could be inflicted on them, and made their death and destruction certain."[58]

News of the disaster reached the west quickly. A letter sent from the Holy Land at the end of July informed Emperor Frederick Barbarossa of the grim outcome of Hattin. Amidst all the gloom, one miracle offered inspiration. Saladin had the True Cross thrown into the flames to test its reputed sacrality. When it jumped free, the Muslim ruler, even though an unbeliever, was forced to recognize its miraculous powers.[59] Popular tradition in France also credited it with working wonders, even *in absentia*. The chronicler Rigord (d. 1209?) passed on this morsel of current folk wisdom. People believed that infants born after the time Saladin took possession of the True Cross had ten or twelve teeth fewer than infants born before it was seized.[60] The mouths of infants felt the loss of the True Cross.

An urgent letter from Patriarch Eraclius deploring the seizure of "the most holy and life-giving cross" as a consequence of Hattin[61] prompted Pope Gregory VIII to issue *Audita tremendi*, his summons to the Third Crusade (October–November, 1187). In it, Gregory broadcast the dismal news that "the Lord's cross… which used to afford a safeguard… against the invasion of the pagans" was now in the hands of the infidels.[62]

The story goes that when news of Hattin and the loss of the True Cross got to France in late October or early November, Richard Lionheart, on learning of it the previous night, took the cross the next morning.[63] Lending credence to the story is Richard's letter to Abbot Garnier of Clairvaux, written in October, 1191, after the Lionheart succeeded in taking Acre from Saladin. According to Richard, the reason men "eagerly" joined the new crusade was to "avenge the injuries done to the holy Cross." To Richard, it was as if these were injuries inflicted on Christ. In that same letter Richard mentions his failed effort to retrieve the True Cross from Saladin through diplomacy.[64] The Christian west hoped and waited.

Only one catastrophe was comparable to the loss of the True Cross. Henry of Marcy (d. 1189) was the cardinal-legate chosen by Gregory VIII to preach the Third Crusade north of the Alps. His treatise *De peregrinante Civitate Dei* contains the gist of his sermons of 1188.[65] Dwelling on the plight of the True Cross, Henry of Marcy calls it "the ark of the New Testament."[66] This powerful analogy between the Ark of the Covenant, lost by the Israelites to the Philistines, and the True Cross, lost by the Christians to the Saracens, could not be bettered. Clerical chroniclers also employed it: "the Cross of the Lord was carried away by the pagans... the glory has been removed from Israel; would that the Ark of the Lord is restored."[67]

Around the time of Hattin—just when this unbearable sense of loss was felt most keenly in Latin Christendom—Chrétien of Troyes was at work composing the first of the most famous quest romances of the Middle Ages, the quest for the Holy Grail. Chrétien's *Story of the Grail* (*Le Conte du Graal*) was left unfinished, probably in 1190. The Celtic-Arthurian and chivalric background to the quest for the Holy Grail has been investigated and re-investigated time and time again.[68] Yet the immediate crusading context in which Chrétien of Troyes was writing his romance must not be forgotten. Sometimes literature is not the only source of literature.

Chrétien's literary patron and the dedicatee of *Le Conte du Graal* was Philip of Alsace, count of Flanders, a man, according to the great Belgian historian Henri Pirenne, with a violent and brutal temperament as well as a keen appetite for literature.[69] For Philip of Alsace, the crushing Christian defeat at Hattin brought immediate personal consequences. He took the cross for the Third Crusade in 1189 and was killed at Acre in 1191, wearing the green cross of the Flemings. What was lost at Hattin cost the count of Flanders his life at Acre. Would the loss of the True Cross have escaped the notice of Chrétien of Troyes? Who can doubt that this universal experience of loss was a stimulus to the idea of a spiritual quest to recover an infinitely precious object.[70] For the *pueri*, the True Cross was their Holy Grail.

Cologne—the Rhineland journey begins

The home of the future leader of the German *pueri*, Nicholas of Cologne, was not the city of Cologne, but its rural hinterland (*a pago Coloniensi*).[71] Here in the Rhenish countryside, after a journey of a little over two days from Aachen, the youthful crusaders would have come into contact with local villagers, Nicholas quite possibly among them. Talking to folk much like themselves, they would have invited them to seek God, liberate Jerusalem, and recover the True Cross. Their fervent conviction and evangelical enthusiasm would have persuaded scores of young Rhenish peasants to become crusaders like them. New converts would have quickly carried the message to prospective converts.

The Cologne Continuator's breathless description of the headlong rush of the Rhenish *pueri* captures the astonishing dynamism of that initial conversionary moment preceding their arrival in Cologne— "many thousands of children from six years old up to the age of manhood [i.e.

14?],[72] abandoned the plows or wagons they drove, or the cattle they herded" and "suddenly ran, one after the other, and signed themselves with crosses."[73] An impetuous overflowing of conversionary zeal marked the beginning of the German Children's Crusade.

Like the Chartrain, the Rhineland was a burned-over district. More than a century of crusading activity prepared the ground for the popular enthusiasm of 1212. The First Crusade brought Peter the Hermit's army to the Rhine, sparking off the anti-Jewish Rhineland massacres led by the infamous count Emicho of Leiningen. At the start of the Second Crusade, Bernard of Clairvaux enlisted Emperor Conrad III to lead a large German contingent to the East. St. Bernard, attracting great crowds during his preaching tour of the Rhineland, also ordered the anti-Jewish, rabble-rousing, unauthorized crusade preacher Radulf to leave the Rhineland and return to his monastery. The Rhenish city of Mainz was first to hear the rallying cry of the great German army of the Third Crusade. There, on March 27, 1188, many thousands quickly followed the example of the emperor Frederick Barbarossa and took the cross. Then, after Barbarossa's death by drowning, his son the emperor Henry VI sent out a crusading force in 1197 which included a strong Rhenish element. In contrast, there was not a notable German presence on the Fourth Crusade.[74]

Again, like the men of the Chartrain, the Rhinelanders fought the Cathar heretics and their supporters in Languedoc. In mid-May, 1212, a substantial German contingent joined Simon de Montfort's army on the Albigensian Crusade. These German troops included Saxons, Frisians, Westphalians, and Rhinelanders, commanded by William, Count of Julich; Leopold VI, Duke of Austria; Adolf III, Count of Berg; and his brother Engelbert, the provost of the cathedral of Cologne. Probably they came as a result of the crusade preaching of James of Vitry and William, the Archdeacon of Paris, during the winter of 1211–12.[75]

The Spanish crisis, however, seems to have bypassed the Rhineland altogether. There is no documentary evidence that Innocent III lobbied the German prelates on the plight of Alfonso VIII or encouraged the Germans to join the crusade to defend the Spanish church. Only Leopold VI of Austria and his knights are reckoned to have crusaded in Spain, journeying there from Languedoc. But they arrived too late for the battle of Las Navas de Tolosa, which was fought and won without them.

Given the vital role of the Spanish crusade in the arousal of the French *pueri*, and especially of the crisis processions in the Chartrain, it is significant that there is no record of Innocent III calling for processions in the Rhineland, nor of any evidence that such processions were held there.[76] Consequently, there is only one identifiable precipitating event, analogous to that of the Spanish crisis-processions at Chartres, which could have inflamed the crusading passions of the Rhenish *pueri*, and that was the coming of the youthful crusaders from the west. Nonetheless, the immediate impact of their arrival must be set against the background of the Rhineland's strong tradition of involvement in the crusading movement.

Of the two contemporary Cologne chroniclers, the Continuator and the monk of St. Pantaleon, neither knew how or why the movement began. Neither states where it began, whether in France or Germany; neither claims German precedence; and neither refers to Nicholas of Cologne. Evidently, Nicholas was still a face in the crowd. He had not yet risen to prominence, let alone charismatic leadership.[77] On the other hand, what the monk of St. Pantaleon does indicate, if not in so many words, is that the enthusiasts were in Cologne sometime in July. He also sheds light on their pattern of recruitment.

First, he notices that "a multitude of youths (*iuvenum*) and women, marking themselves with the cross" came forward, and in doing so, they were following the "example" set by an initial group of "*pueri* of diverse ages and ranks (*conditionis*)."[78] While his remarks about the social diversity of the *pueri*, and especially about the participation of women in the movement, are important, even more revealing is his implicit acceptance of two distinct phases of recruitment. The initial phase was seemingly dominated by a core-group, while the second drew in more diverse adherents. In the Rhineland, the Children's Crusade was clearly attracting a broader age-range to its ranks. The *pueri*, defined solely as an age-group, were no longer alone, if they had ever been. So it seems that Cologne was the point of convergence, where a larger, more heterogeneous influx of popular enthusiasts flooded in to join the formative revival of the French *pueri*.

By 1212 Cologne had become the largest and wealthiest of the medieval German cities. Port and emporium both benefitted from the growth of trade, especially from the East. Muncipal administration was more and more in the hands of the urban elite rather than the Archbishop.[79] On the Christian map, Cologne was one of the four major pilgrimage destinations in medieval Europe, along with Santiago and its cult of St. James; Canterbury, the locus of the martyred St. Thomas Becket; and Rome, hallowed by St. Peter and St. Paul. Cologne owed its place in this privileged foursome by virtue of its claim to possess the relics of the Three Kings, the Magi, the bringers of gifts from the exotic East to the crib of the infant Jesus.

The Three Kings arrived triumphantly in Cologne on July 24, 1164, thanks to the imperial chancellor and archbishop-elect of Cologne, Rainald of Dassel, who snatched them from under the indifferent noses of the Milanese after Frederick Barbarossa destroyed their city in 1162. The locus of their cult was the cathedral of St. Peter, where construction of the shrine began in 1175. Soon, they were venerated as the patron saints of Cologne. They also protected the faithful against black magic—for as everyone knew, the Magi were masters of oriental occultism.

As pilgrims, the Three Kings had journeyed long and hard to venerate the Christ Child at Bethlehem. Pilgrims themselves, it was fitting that they should become the patron saints of pilgrims; and also fitting that from the later twelfth century onwards myriad pilgrims from across western Europe traveled to their shrine. A twelfth-century pilgrim's prayer invokes the Magi, who saw the star, and whom God had conducted from the East without danger. It pleads for their intercession, so that latter-day pilgrims would, as they did, arrive safely at the end of their pilgrimage.[80] Among the pilgrims at Cologne were the *pueri*. Ideas of holy pilgrimage, the Christian East, and the *Christus puer*—all would have held special meaning for them. Besides, reason enough for the *pueri* to visit the shrine of the Three Kings of Cologne was apprehension at the dangers that lay ahead.

While they were preparing for their arduous pilgrimage, the *pueri* were caught up in a dramatic incident in Cologne. The monk of St. Pantaleon recounts how "some evil men" infiltrated the movement under pious pretences, drawn to it by the scent of alms. "Furtively and wickedly" they stole items which the *pueri* brought with them, along with gifts the faithful were "daily" contributing to their cause. The thieves then ran off, clutching their stolen goods. One of the robbers was apprehended soon afterwards; and he was hanged.[81] To a monastic chronicler this was gratifying, a triumph of divine justice.

It was only to be expected that as new recruits for the *peregrinatio puerorum* were assembling in Cologne, thieves, ne'er-do-wells, and assorted religious con-men were taking a professional interest in the generous donations being given to the young crusaders. The atmosphere was one of feverish activity. Medieval revivalist movements thrived on momentum. Either they gathered pace quickly, or prolonged inactivity risked dissipating the zeal of their adherents. Delay would lead to a fatal loss of dynamism. If the *pueri* overstayed their welcome, they not only undermined their credibility, but also put at risk the supply of alms on which they depended. A limited period to rouse their fellow pilgrims from the countryside, to convert more city-dwellers, and to raise whatever support for their journey was forthcoming—and they were off.

Then, when the time came to depart, "in groups of twenty, fifty or a hundred, with their banners raised, they began heading for Jerusalem."[82] Banners held aloft, in an atmosphere of buoyant expectancy, the *pueri* left Cologne in groups most likely made up of peasants from the same villages, kinfolk, or urban workmates. These bands were self-selected, rather than organized. There is no way of knowing whether their mass exodus took place as a single unitary event or as a series of individual group departures. In either case, sometime around July 18 or so, the Rhenish *pueri* set out from Cologne and began their journey to the sea. Only the Cologne Continuator refers to the next stop on their itinerary—Mainz.[83]

After roughly four or five days on the road, they reached Mainz, where some of the *pueri*, perhaps already dog-tired or discouraged, turned back.[84] An ebbing and flowing of adherents was to be expected as the pilgrims passed through cities along their route. Fired-up new converts would readily embrace the crusade, while enthusiasts, now drained of enthusiasm, dropped away. Dropping out, however, did not necessarily mean turning back. There was a third option.

Mainz offered a powerful inducement to stay put. In the words of Otto of Freising (d. 1158), Mainz was a "great and strong" city, "closely built and densely populated... adorned with noble temples."[85] Dynamic economic growth and rapid urban development—from encircling walls to cathedral-building—were the cause and result of a surge in population. Here, too, peasants were leaving the land and pouring into the city.[86] To these peasants, and to some of the Rhenish *pueri* as well, Mainz was a city overflowing with possibilities. But for the majority of the *pueri*, Mainz was a temporary stopping place, and nothing more. As they resumed their journey to the sea, prophetic imaginings drove them forward. Yet for a minority of the *pueri* what Mainz promised its immigrants was nothing less than a new life.

A new Moses? Nicholas of Cologne

Pasted into the *Gesta Treverorum* is a close-up of Nicholas of Cologne. Included in it are details which make it hard to believe the writer did not see Nicholas with his own eyes; although whether or not the *pueri* actually set foot in Trier, he does not say. If they did make their weary way to Trier, it is unlikely they came via Mainz. Trier is approximately the same distance from Cologne as Mainz, and going from Mainz to Trier would have involved an improbable western deviation on the road southwards. Journeying to Mainz from Trier, on the other hand, defies subsequent chronology. The conclusion probably has to be that different bands of *pueri* were heading south by diverse routes. The earlier report of the Cologne Continuator of various-sized groups leaving Cologne seems to confirm this.

The nameless author of this section of the Trier chronicle (1190–1242) was likely to have been a monk at the Benedictine house of St. Eucharius (now St. Matthias) who was more interested in religious matters than in political events.[87] As was customary, each section of the *Gesta Treverorum* was alloted to the reign of a particular Archbishop of Trier. So the "marvelous and unheard of" movement of the *pueri* was inserted in the chronicle after the death of Archbishop John of Trier (July 15, 1212) and "a few months before" the election of Archbishop Theodoric II (at an unknown date, but before November 24, 1212).[88] Accordingly, if the *pueri* reached Trier, say, around July 22—in keeping with their estimated rate of march from Cologne—their arrival fell comfortably within the period when the archiepiscopal see was vacant.

Led by "Nicholas, a certain boy (*puer*) from Cologne," the *pueri* "assembled from all the towns and villages of Germany, almost as if divinely inspired," then "took the road towards Jerusalem, as if they intended to recapture the Holy Land." Although the Trier Anonymous does not say so explicitly, it is a fair assumption that they started out from Cologne. Nicholas, their "leader and head" (*dux et caput*), clearly fascinated the Trier chronicler, especially his distinctive emblem, which he found riveting. As if plucked from a fresco in a medieval church, it was Nicholas's iconographic attribute. It said everything about him—who he was, and what he was. It was the sign and warrant of his charismatic authority.

Predictably, the story of how Nicholas acquired it is not known. For him, however, it was the equivalent of a celestial letter, the charismatic credential which marked him out as a divinely appointed leader. As with Durand of Le Puy and Stephen of Cloyes, the classic charismatic paradigm necessitated a revelatory moment, an encounter with Divinity. Such a moment might have been the "message from an angel" which Nicholas was said to have received.[89] Authentication would then have been followed by charismatic recognition. Just as Durand obtained his piece of parchment with the Virgin's image, and Stephen his letters to King Philip, Nicholas somehow received his charismatic credential, his emblem. Later, probably at some stage after leaving Cologne, Nicholas ceased to be a face in the crowd. Instead, he became its charismatic leader.

Thirteenth-century churchmen were increasingly perplexed and troubled by the appearance of laymen with charismatic power. At its most disquieting this was manifested when a person of obscure origins assumed command of a religious crowd. What could be the source of his mysterious authority?[90] Right away, the Trier chronicler intuitively grasped the charismatic significance of Nicholas's emblem. Aware that it contained the secret of Nicholas's authority, he tried his best to peer at it. What he saw was Nicholas holding aloft a cross in the shape of the Greek letter *tau* ("T"). Most likely, it was positioned at the end of a rod, like a pilgrim's staff; or, as Miccoli suggests, like an episcopal crozier—itself a sign of pastoral leadership.[91] The writer of the *Gesta Treverorum* candidly admits that he could not discern exactly what kind of metal it was made of; an indication, if ever there was one, that he was staring at it. Yet he was not left in the slightest doubt about its charismatic function. To the Trier Anonymous, Nicholas's *tau* cross was a "sign of his sanctity and miracle-working powers"[92] (Figure 8).

Figure 8 St. Antony Abbot holding The Tau Cross (early sixteenth-century woodcut from Lotharingia or the Rhineland). Paul Heitz (ed.), *Pestblätter des XV Jahrhunderts* (Heitz & Mündel: Strassburg, 1918), fig. 2.

The *tau* was an immensely potent Christian symbol. Christian biblical exegetes equated it with the Prophet Ezekiel's "mark upon the foreheads" of those who sighed for the sins of Jerusalem. Only those marked with the sign of the *tau* would be spared from the slaughter of the wicked (Ezekiel 9:4, 6). So the "mark" of the *tau* was salvific. Those who bore it were members of an elect, destined to be saved. Pope Innocent III associated the *tau* cross with the cross of the crusader as early as June 1202. In a letter to the Catholicos of the Armenians, he singles out the army of the Fourth Crusade then embarking for the Holy Land from Venice as, figuratively speaking, marked with the *tau*.[93] Nicholas himself, along with his followers, were presumably wearing the crusader's cross. Even so, the crusading associations of the *tau* cross, if known to them, would have reinforced their identity as an elect band. Whatever the case, as a sign of protection and chosenness, as well as Nicholas's guardianship, it was their shield to hold up against dangers to come.

But there is a still more remarkable reason why the *tau* spoke directly to Nicholas of Cologne and to the *pueri*. Christian scriptural commentators interpreted the *tau* cross as the symbol of the Exodus of the Children of Israel from Egypt. It was the sign of the lamb's blood which the Israelites smeared on the door-posts of their houses in Egypt to ward off the angel of death (Exodus 12:7, 22). For the Rhenish *pueri*, that, too, would be their sign. As the climactic moment approached when they would re-enact the drama of the ancient Israelites by stepping into the water to cross the sea dry-shod, the *tau* would be there to keep them from harm.[94] Protected by the *tau*, these new Children of Israel were prepared for their own Exodus. Leading them was their new Moses, Nicholas of Cologne.[95]

Did he lead them southeast of Trier, to Speyer? A report from Speyer notes "a great pilgrimage" with as many males as girls, and old men as well as youths—"so many common people" (*tantum de plebe*). The date given by the Speyer annalist for the arrival of this plebeian mass of humanity is July 25.[96] Neither Nicholas nor the *pueri* are mentioned, which may be a significant omission. In addition, the Speyer annalist's date makes a journey from Trier unlikely. For if these pilgrims set out from Cologne and then passed through Trier, it would take them about sixteen days to reach Speyer, which would overshoot the annalist's date of arrival. If, on the contrary, the "great pilgrimage" came directly from Mainz, July 25 would be right on target. Hence it is reasonable to assume that those participating in "the great pilgrimage" at Speyer were not Nicholas of Cologne's band of pilgrims, but another, more heterogeneous army of popular crusaders, likewise heading towards the sea.

Nicholas of Cologne and his child-crusaders are next sighted south of Trier in Alsace, where a cluster of chroniclers devote at least a line to the *peregrinatio puerorum*. For example, from the diocese of Strasbourg there is this acerbic dismissal—"the same year (1212) there was a pilgrimage of foolish boys."[97] An altogether more substantial notice comes from the chronicle of the monastery of Ebersheim, near Sélestat, midway between Strasbourg and Colmar.

The Ebersheim chronicler was sure that the memory of such an unheard of event was worth preserving. It happened this way: "A certain little boy (*puerulus*) Nicholas, by name" from the countryside of Cologne, influenced by some unknown source, convinced "many *pueri*" he could cross the sea dry-shod and provide for them on their journey. When his message "resounded through the cities and towns," boys and girls "throughout all of Germany and France" then hastened to join him leaving their parents, taking the cross, and making ready to cross the sea. "An infinite number of young servant lads, servant girls, and maidens" followed Nicholas towards the sea.

Whether these young laborers, all apparently recruited in "cities and towns," were originally from a peasant or urban background is left unsaid. Where they went is equally problematic. The Ebersheim chronicler states they "came to Vienne (*Vienaiam*), which is a city near the sea."[98] This is puzzling, because Vienne is nowhere near the sea. One scholar thinks that some of these child-crusaders may have been heading towards the port of Marseilles by way of Vienne.[99] Marseilles, however, was not where Nicholas and his *pueri* were heading. In spite of hunger, thirst, and all the obstacles and rigors of the road, they were making their way up the Rhine, across the Alps, and into Italy, where their great migration would conclude—although not, perhaps, for Nicholas.

6
History: The Great Migration

Following the Rhine, Nicholas of Cologne and his travel-weary crusaders probably passed not far from the Augustinian abbey of Marbach, located near Colmar in Alsace. There the hostile Marbach annalist recorded his disdain for this "stupid multitude" in no uncertain terms:

> At the same time [1212], there occurred a futile expedition, as children and foolish men took the sign of the cross without any discretion... People of both sexes, boys and girls, not only minors, but also adults, married women with virgins... not only through all Germany, but also through parts of France and Burgundy.... [E]verywhere in the villages and fields... [they] left their tools and whatever they had in hand at the time and joined the bands as they passed by. And just as we are often a crowd, credulous in the face of such novelties, many thought this happened not through light-headedness, but by divine inspiration and a kind of piety....[1]

The Marbach annalist's unsympathetic account of the Children's Crusade may or may not be based upon direct observation of the passing *pueri*. Nicholas of Cologne is not mentioned. The *pueri* and *puellae* take pride of place, but older folk trudged alongside them. All these peasant crusaders endured the trials of the Long March. Once over the Alps, Italy awaited them.

A new life—Nicholas of Cologne and the *pueri* in Italy

There is no certainty about which Alpine pass or passes took them into Italy—the Great St. Bernard, the St. Gotthard, the Splügen, the Chur, and the Brenner have all been proposed. On balance, the Brenner might be the safest option.[2]

Sicard of Cremona's contemporary report of a horde of German paupers whose leader was a "child (*infans*) younger than ten" has been submitted in evidence that the *pueri* passed through Cremona, but, as previously argued, Sicard says no such thing. His extremely young child leader makes an implausible Nicholas of Cologne.[3] The fact that Sicard was then serving as a papal legate in northeastern Italy, including Treviso, points to another band of enthusiasts—one heading in an easterly direction, rather than westwards.

And westwards it was. Unlike Cremona, there are excellent grounds for confirming Piacenza as the first Italian city to catch sight of Nicholas of Cologne and his troop of Rhenish followers. On August 20, the town chronicler John Codagnello witnessed their arrival, when Nicholas, together with "a great and countless multitude of German *pueri*, infants at the breast, women, and girls" first appeared in Piacenza; then, "hastening to cross the sea," they "passed through" it.[4] But was their time in Piacenza quite as short as Codagnello makes it out to be? If Nicholas and his exhausted *pueri* spent a night in Piacenza, they could have taken advantage of Piacenza's long-established hospices for pilgrims *en route* to Rome—or Jerusalem.[5]

Next they came to Genoa, the thriving port city on the Ligurian coast of the Mediterranean. With a booming market economy, and strong trading links with Egypt and the Levant, Genoa was one of the success stories of medieval capitalism. By around 1300, it was among the most densely populated of Italian cities, boasting a population of 100,000. Maritime commerce was its life blood. Banking, overseas outposts and colonies, gold coins (first minted in 1252), participation in the crusades, merchant settlements in the crusader states, maritime insurance—these were Genoa's gifts from the sea.[6]

Like a Genoese businessman pressed for time, its civic chronicler, Ogerio Pane, quickly jots down the essential points about the sudden influx of a vast horde of *pueri* in his city. In terse, no-nonsense prose, Pane writes as if he is recording answers to a checklist of questions: When did they arrive? "Saturday, August 25." Who was leading them? "Some German boy named Nicholas." What was their purpose? "A pilgrimage [destination unspecified]." How do you know? "They were carrying [crusaders'] crosses, [and pilgrims'] staves, and wallets." How many of them were there? "There were men and women, boys and girls, more than 7,000 of them...." What became of them? "Sunday, the following day, they left the city [August 26]." All of them? "[No,] many men, women, boys and girls of that number remained in Genoa."[7]

At an estimated marching rate of 20.5 miles per diem, the *pueri* would have covered the distance from Piacenza to Genoa in roughly five days, corresponding reasonably well to a departure date of August 20 and an arrival date of August 25. If, however, Nicholas and his followers left Piacenza the next morning after a good night's sleep in a pilgrim hospice, the time-distance ratio would be that much closer. Whatever the case, there is no doubting the trustworthiness of Codagnello and Pane. More debatable, perhaps, is Ogerio Pane's assessment of the number of pilgrims who swarmed into Genoa.

"More than 7,000"—this is the first figure we have for the multitude of crusade enthusiasts since the guesstimates of the Anonymous of Laon (30,000 French *pueri* at the Lendit encampment) and the Peterborough chronicler (15,000 enthusiasts).[8] On the face of it, Ogerio Pane's relatively moderate figure is less implausible than theirs. But there are more convincing reasons for not dismissing it out of hand. First, Ogerio Pane was an eye-witness. Second, Italian mercantile culture lived or died by numbers. Basic literacy as well as numeracy were occupational tools in a society driven by commercial exchange. Sophisticated business operations in which large sums of money were at stake could not be bungled through inaccurate estimates. Mistakes such as the French noble Villehardouin's miscalculation of the number of troops supposedly coming to Venice and so needing purpose-built ships to the East—a gross overestimate which doomed the Fourth Crusaders to indebtedness to the Venetians—is unlikely to have occurred in a Genoese transaction of comparable significance. So Pane's figure ought not to be rejected out of hand.

Pane's 7,000-plus represents a depleted though still impressive army of Rhenish *pueri*, which included youngsters, individual men and women, and most likely families. Once across the Alps, linguistic and cultural barriers would have been formidable obstacles to replenishing the missing brethren through crusade evangelism. The heavy toll of hardship and deprivation occasioned by their Long March, combined with Lombardy's inviting prospects, would have reduced their ranks even further. Yet there is good reason for believing that Nicholas's contingent was not the only brigade of *pueri* to cross the Alps, possibly bringing the total number up to, say, 7,500 or even 8,000. The true figure is anyone's guess.

Italy transformed them. When the *pueri* crossed the Alps, they were still pilgrims and crusaders. Then, step by step, their collective identity as religious vagrants began to melt away. Their metamorphosis, almost imperceptible at first, resulted in a change of status. Crusaders no longer, they were gradually becoming immigrants. In Ogerio Pane's words: "many men, women, boys and girls of that number [the 7,000-plus] remained in Genoa."[9] A mixture of frustrated expectations and new opportunities accounted for what happened. But the seaside drama beloved of popular imaginers can safely be discounted.

We are asked to be present at a cinematic dénouement. There, at the edge of the sea—either in Genoa, or Marseilles—the *pueri* assemble in hushed silence while Nicholas of Cologne, holding high his *tau* cross, reverentially, delicately, expectantly, dips his toes into the waters of the Mediterranean. Then—*miserere*! Lord have mercy! The waters stubbornly refuse to part. At this juncture—sadly shaking their heads, muttering to themselves, or worse, angrily raising their fists—the dejected followers of the former Moses desert him *en masse*.

True, nothing attacks and destroys charisma like demonstrable public failure. But an alternative scenario is much more plausible, if less dramatic. Nicholas or a trusted lieutenant contact a Genoese captain and beseech him to transport the entire troop of *pueri* to the crusader East. They have heard that a ship from Genoa is due to depart on the "summer passage" (*passagium aestival*) towards the end of September.[10] Alas, without a substantial cash payment, theirs would have been a forlorn hope. It is nevertheless credible that some such unrealistic attempt was made to find ships in Genoa. Indeed, this is exactly what one chronicler— admittedly, a later chronicler—claims: that in Genoa they tried and failed to find sea transport.[11]

Undoubtedly, for a good number of the *pueri*, having reached the sea at long last, a major setback like this was enough to put an end to their crusading dreams. The picture was not altogether bleak, however. For the "many" ex-crusaders who chose to stay on in Genoa there was a good chance of ready employment. Whether in households, small workshops, or in the shipyards, there were jobs crying out for casual, unskilled or semi-skilled laborers, as most of them would have been.[12] These jobs, naturally, paid the lowest of low wages. The immigrant's lot was hardly paradisiacal, whether medieval or modern. People who emigrate to escape poverty usually rediscover it elsewhere.

On a more positive note, a small percentage of the artisans amongst them might have maneuvered their way through tight guild restrictions. The new immigrants might also have developed a predisposition towards mutual support, as a result of their long and painful journey together. Among them there must have been fellow villagers, kinfolk, and former workmates. Together, they had survived the Long March. Perhaps, for some, it was a bonding, community-building experience.

What is remarkable is that no chronicler (or mythistorian) accuses the Genoese merchant-seamen of enslaving the *pueri* or selling them on to the Muslims. Other Christian merchants faced just such accusations.

Rome

After Genoa, the *pueri* who chose not to stay, dispersed. One group probably headed for that other great Mediterranean seaport, Marseilles. The best evidence they did so comes from the well-informed and reliable Cologne Continuator, who states that, having left Cologne, the *pueri* stopped in four major cities—Mainz (already discussed), Piacenza (confirmed by Codagnello), Rome (to be discussed), and Marseilles. French pilgrims amongst the Rhenish *pueri* might have found Marseilles especially attractive as a port of embarkation.

According to the Cologne Continuator, some of the *pueri* returned to their homeland from Mainz, some from Piacenza, and some from Rome. Marseilles was the sole exception. From it, no one returned. "Others reached Marseilles, but whether they crossed the sea, or what became of them, is uncertain."[13] Unlike the mythistoricizing Alberic of Trois-Fontaines (or his interpolator), who famously elaborates the pathetic tale of the Lost Boys at Marseilles, the Continuator has nothing to say about betrayal, shipwreck, drowning, or mass enslavement.

The Continuator's confession of uncertainty inspires confidence. Mythistorians are invariably certain. It must be conceded, nevertheless, that, particularly in the later Middle Ages, Marseilles, like Genoa and other Mediterranean seaports, profited from a brisk trade in human flesh, especially foreign slaves.[14] As for trading with the enemy, churchmen castigated merchants both from Marseilles and the Italian seaports for supplying the Muslims with a range of prohibited goods necessary for crusading warfare.[15]

Leaving Genoa behind them, a sizable number of young and not-so-young crusaders would have taken the Roman road southwards. Perhaps they were still determined to wheedle or beg their way across the Mediterranean to the Holy Land. Perhaps Nicholas of Cologne still marched at the head of their procession, displaying his charismatic *tau* cross. That possibility exists because for some true believers, charisma, like prophecy, cannot be allowed to fail. Too much psychological capital has been invested in it.[16]

The mid-thirteenth-century chronicler Richer of Sénones relates that on entering Lombardy, groups of *pueri* headed for the maritime cities. Here they believed they would find the ships to take them overseas.

The two seaports which Richer names are Genoa and Pisa. The former is unchallengeable—confirmed by Ogerio Pane's testimony. As for the latter, doubts arise. Richer is the only chronicler to refer to Pisa, and he is a late source.

Yet Pisa would have been the logical next step for the *pueri*. If hunting for ships continued to be their primary objective, Pisa was perfectly positioned to meet their needs. Lying about ninety-nine miles down the coast from Genoa, Pisa was the leading seaport in Tuscany, and an aggressive commercial rival to Genoa and Venice. Until 1284, when it lost the battle of Meloria to the Genoese, it was a major Italian maritime power. In 1212, Pisa's urban population was expanding, and its prosperity was growing. Following the Fourth Crusade its outpost in Constantinople suffered losses. Despite this, trade with the Levant, Sardinia, southern Italy, and Africa continued to drive its economy forward.[17]

The *pueri* would have arrived in Pisa sometime around the 30th of August. Richer of Sénones remarks that in

> Genoa and Pisa and the other cities situated on the coast, they thought that they would find ships to make the crossing. And they did not find any. However, two ships loaded with them put out to sea; but it is as yet not known if they made it to port or to what parts they were taken.[18]

Richer's uncertainty about this last point enhances his credibility. His statement, however, leaves many questions unanswered. Which group of *pueri* managed somehow, somewhere, to take ship? But one thing does seem irrefutable. "And they did not find any" must mean that the *pueri* who came to Pisa experienced what had already been experienced in Genoa—failure.[19]

Which means that the *pueri* who reached Pisa by land, departed in similar fashion. All their efforts at finding ships to take them to the crusader East having failed, another decision was called for. To judge from their behavior in Genoa, a proportion of the *pueri*—perhaps a significant proportion—decided to make their home in Pisa. Here, too, was the same opportunity for ready employment, no matter how poorly rewarded. So the *peregrinatio puerorum*, hemorrhaging pilgrims and crusaders at each of its halting places, was simultaneously generating recruits for northern Italy's insatiable labor market. Despite its ever-thinning ranks, remnants of the unarmed army of *pueri* pressed on. Where would they go now?

Southwards along the coast of the Tyrrhenian Sea lay Rome. An approximately ten-day hike from Pisa would have got them there. The traditional route favored by the *romeì*, pilgrims making their way to Rome, was via Genoa and Pisa.[20] And how Rome loved pilgrims, sheep for the shearing. Rapacious keepers of inns and lodging houses, ingratiatingly pious sellers of devotional souvenirs, mendacious guides, high-priced canon lawyers at the papal court, bribable papal officials, multifarious vendors jostling to satisfy every conceivable daily need—all thrived on the bustling pilgrimage traffic which contributed so mightily to the Roman economy.

Rome's total population in the early thirteenth century was a relatively moderate 35,000, or so.[21] Yet its transient population—not only pilgrims in the strict sense, but also visiting prelates and their clerical attendants, litigants at the papal court, foreign princes and their retinues—added a constant throb of to-ing and fro-ing. Ecclesiastical special events filled the available accommodation in Rome to bursting point and brought processional crowds onto the streets. The Roman thirteenth century was sandwiched between two such remarkable events. Opening this greatest of papal centuries was Innocent III's Fourth Lateran Council (1215), and closing it was Boniface VIII's Jubilee (1300), the first *anno santo* or Holy Year.[22]

Rome, according to the Cologne Continuator, was the last stopping place of the *pueri* in Italy. Obviously, the choice of destination for the dwindling band of *pueri* depended on their motive, and one chronicler and one mythistorian suggest what that motive was—obtaining dispensation from their crusade vows. These were still binding, regardless of the fact their crusade was unauthorized. Without making any reference to Pope Innocent, the Marbach annalist relates that when some of the *pueri* came to Rome, those who were "below the age of discretion" (younger than fourteen) and those "burdened by old age" were released (*absoluti*) from their crusade vows; the others, not so.[23] Their crusading obligation would remain.

This idea naturally presupposes that all the crusade imaginings of the *pueri*, of recovering Jerusalem and the True Cross—imaginings which had sustained them during their long, hard transalpine trek—were over, done with, gone. Some would say that their failure to find ships, first in Genoa, then in Pisa, brought the curtain down on the Children's Crusade, which may be true. But there remains another possibility. Perhaps some of the *pueri*, Nicholas of Cologne among them, still retained a glimmer of hope for their expedition—the hope that ultimately they would be crusaders in more than name. In any event, before determining what to do next, they would have wanted to consult Pope Innocent III or, failing that, high-ranking, knowledgeable clerics attached to the Roman papacy. That in itself would have prompted a journey to Rome.

Innocent III passed the summer of 1212 in the hilltop town of Segni not far from Rome. This was Innocent's homeland, the land of the Conti dei Segni. From June 23 to September 18, he was in residence at Segni, but by September 28—quite possibly earlier—Innocent returned to the Lateran palace in Rome.[24] Since the *pueri* would have been in Rome by around mid-September, there was a good chance that the Pope and the *pueri* were in Rome about the same time, although there is no evidence they ever met. Nor is it likely that Nicholas of Cologne and his scruffy band of peasant followers would have been ceremoniously ushered into the papal presence.

Corroboration from the papal registers may be lacking, yet it is reasonable to suppose that curial officials kept Pope Innocent well-informed about this unauthorized crusade. A contemporary Austrian annalist records that Innocent learned "many people of both sexes and various ages, incited by false leaders" were intending to cross the seas. So he sent cardinals to intercept them at Treviso in order to turn them back.[25] Quite possibly, this very troop of *pueri* was making its way through northeastern Italy, *en route* to Venice and the sea, around the time Nicholas's pilgrims were in Rome. Besides the Austrian annalist, other thirteenth-century chroniclers take it for granted that Innocent knew about the crusade of the *pueri*.[26] For Innocent III had a voracious appetite for information, and whatever pertained to the affairs of Christendom, especially to the crusades, would not have escaped his attention.

Indeed, it was only six months after the *peregrinatio puerorum* that Innocent III announced a new crusade to the Holy Land. Now, for the first time, all the faithful were encouraged to step forward and take the cross. This fundamental shift in papal recruitment policy bore the imprint of the *pueri*. No longer would crusading be the exclusive business of the chivalric classes and their men-at-arms. A new papal appreciation for the crusading aspirations of the Christian people had come into being. Virtually all the *populus christianus* were now offered the opportunity to take part in the great enterprise of Christendom, to take the vow and receive the crusade indulgence, even if they redeemed their vow immediately afterwards for a cash payment. Thanks to the *pueri*, Pope Innocent was aware of continuing, deep-rooted, populist crusading sentiment, and he was determined to mobilize it.

On November 11, 1215, in his justly celebrated opening sermon to the Fourth Lateran Council in Rome, Innocent III invoked the mystic power of the *tau* cross. The supreme pontiff declared that he would "place the sign of the *tau* on the foreheads of the men who weep and lament... over the abominations which are performed in the midst of the church," and those not so designated, those who, in effect, scorned to take up the crusader's cross, would not be spared.[27] To Innocent, the *tau* would be the distinctive badge of a new crusader-elect. Innocent had used the *tau* as a crusader symbol previously, but at the Fourth Lateran it was also emblematic of church reform. The symbol, one feels, has been refreshed and re-energized. It may even be that Innocent's choice of the *tau* as his central sign of reformist and crusader chosenness reflects the memory and influence of Nicholas of Cologne's charismatic attribute.

Nicholas and Francis of Assisi in Egypt

The same question can be posed with respect to another, no less illustrious figure who valued the *tau* as much as Innocent did. Assisi's pre-eminent beggar and most celebrated son, St. Francis, chose the *tau* as his personal seal, his preferred signature at the end of his letters, and as the painted image on the walls of his cell.[28] When he came to cherish it cannot be ascertained, but Francis's adoption of the *tau* was once taken as proof that he was present at the Fourth Lateran Council and listened to Innocent III's sermon.[29] That may be so, although resolving the question really hinges upon something which still remains obscure—dating Brother Pacifico's vision of Francis with "the great sign *tau* on [his] forehead".[30] Interestingly enough, one scholar dates that vision to 1212.[31]

This same Brother Pacifico of the March of Ancona may have been one of Francis's unnamed companions when he traveled to Ancona sometime in October 1212, intending to take ship to the Holy Land, convert the Saracens, or die a martyr's death in the process.[32] Trying to explain *why* Francis sought passage to the Holy Land is not at all difficult. The missionary impulse, the longing for martyrdom—these were deeply held desires of the first Franciscan.[33] What has not been scrutinized so thoroughly is why Francis decided to travel to the Holy Land *when* he did.

The Franciscan historian Father Cuthbert believes that "the victory of Las Navas set men thinking of the crusade, and turned the thoughts of Francis towards the conversion of the infidels."[34] That is likely. Yet Las Navas occurred on July 16, while Francis probably sailed from Ancona, bound for Syria, in the autumn of 1212.[35] Las Navas may well have been the first step, but why should a summer victory in the West necessarily precipitate an autumn journey to the East? An Italian historian has come up with a better explanation for the timing of Francis's mission to the

Muslims. He wonders whether "the great event" of June–September—the *crociata dei fanciulli*, the Children's Crusade—so "strongly impressed St. Francis" that the idea of an eastward journey became irresistible.[36] It is in this context that the report that Francis visited Rome sometime in 1212 is certainly intriguing.[37]

So can the conjunction of the coming of the Children's Crusade to Rome (around mid-September) and Francis's sudden, seemingly inexplicable decision to venture East (undertaken no more than a few weeks afterwards) be altogether coincidental? Taken in tandem with the question of what prompted Francis to adopt the *tau* cross as his personal emblem, the idea of contact with or, perhaps more likely, hearsay about the charismatic leader of the *pueri* who carried the same potent symbol is attractive, though, of course, unverifiable.

What is demonstrable is that an enthusiast like Francis was readily responsive to enthusiasm. Embracing the shame of poverty rather than the aristocratic code of honor, Francis championed a radical Christian spirituality which turned the world's values upside down. In all likelihood, the sudden appearance of a host of eccentric and paradoxical crusaders—unarmed *pueri* bound for Jerusalem—would have fired his imagination and roused him to pursue his missionary dreams. As Thomas of Celano recounts it, the story of Francis's abortive mission to the Saracens in Syria is swiftly told. His ship was blown off course. After landing on the Dalmatian coast, Francis and his companion found a ship sailing back to Ancona, but, lacking funds to pay for their passage, they stowed away. A miracle or two later, and back they were in Ancona.[38] Endowed with "the best natural harbor in central Italy," Ancona had long-established trading links with the crusader kingdom and was the chosen port of embarkation for crusaders from central Italy.[39] Later, when St. Francis embarked for the Fifth Crusade in 1219, he set sail from Ancona, as he had done in 1212.[40]

Near the heel of Italy, approximately 360 miles down the Adriatic coast from Ancona, lies Brindisi. Here there is a reported sighting of Nicholas of Cologne and the *pueri*. Given its place in crusade history, situating Nicholas in Brindisi is not surprising. Latin Christian warriors on the First and Second Crusades took ship from Brindisi,[41] and at the Fourth Lateran Council, Innocent III, declaring that the goal of the Fifth Crusade was to "liberate the Holy Land from the hands of the impious,"[42] enjoined combatants to rendezvous at Messina and Brindisi on June 1, 1217.[43]

The Trier Anonymous affirms that when Nicholas of Cologne and the *pueri* arrived in Brindisi, "the local bishop sensing a deception, did not permit them to cross the sea."[44] Such a scenario does seem plausible. In

1212 the *pueri* were clearly not participating in any papally approved enterprise. A sensible bishop would have questioned their motives, and tried to discover anyone who could speak up on their behalf. Was their proposed crusade a fraud of some kind? Puzzled, perhaps, about what course of action to take, Bishop Dominicus (1203–16) of Brindisi[45] might well have decided to consult Rome concerning the legitimacy of the so-called crusade on his doorstep. If so, the papal instructions would probably have been along the same lines as those addressed to the cardinals at Treviso—verdict: negative; intercept them, turn them back. And if Nicholas and his crusaders were audacious—or foolish—enough to beg for episcopal funds to subsidize their dubious adventure to the East, then, surely, the good bishop's patience would have run out. Once again, the crusading aspirations of Nicholas and the *pueri* were frustrated, for the time being at least.

The Trier chronicler's account of the incident at Brindisi seems to be based on solid information. But the rest of what he says is confused and transparently mythistorical. Nicholas's father is revealed as the villain of the piece. Under the influence of demons, at some point he is alleged to have betrayed the *pueri* by selling them to unbelievers (the Saracens?), as a result of which he meets a "bad death" (suicide?) in Cologne. Rather suspiciously, the "bad death" of Nicholas's father calls to mind the fate of the Cologne robber who was hanged for stealing the goods of the *pueri*.[46] And if the *pueri* never left Brindisi, how could they have been sold to the heathens? Evidently keen to wrap things up quickly, the Trier chronicler falls back on rumors. Nicholas is abruptly killed off. There are no details.

Not so. Quite the contrary, according to the Austrian chronicler of Admont abbey. His version of events has it that instead of dying in an undisclosed location in total obscurity, "Nicholas, a certain *puer* of Cologne," having served as *dux* (leader) of the *expeditio puerorum* of 1212, enrolled in a later crusade. Nicholas himself probably did not think of it as a new crusade. To him, it would have been the continuation, the prolongation—indeed, the final chapter—of his *expeditio puerorum*. According to the Admont chronicler, Nicholas set out on his "pilgrimage of the Holy Cross" (*peregrinatione sancte crucis*) "not long after" the Children's Crusade.[47] But this time things were different. Nicholas's crusade was papally sanctioned.

The question is—how long was "not long after" 1212? Was it 1213, when Innocent III proclaimed the Fifth Crusade? Or 1215, when Innocent III at the Fourth Lateran Council laid down the departure dates at the ports of Brindisi and Messina? Or was it 1217, the year preordained for the ships to sail, when Innocent promised to bless the departing crusader host? (Death's intervention abrogated Innocent's promise.) All in all, 1217 seems the most likely date for the commencement of Nicholas's career as a papal crusader. How, then, could he, and possibly a few of his companions, have managed to live in the interim? Charitable handouts might have helped at first, speedily followed by some sort of poorly paid employment in the local labor market. Nicholas—the *puer* who had traveled on foot, begging his way from Cologne to Brindisi—would have known whatever there was to know about survival in a world of strangers.

The Admont chronicler does not specify where Nicholas began his voyage overseas. Yet Brindisi, where Nicholas was last sighted, would be a prime candidate. One of the two ports designated for departing crusaders, Brindisi also had a new bishop in 1216. Bishop Peregrinus perhaps would have been more sympathetic towards Nicholas—and possibly a few of his *pueri* companions, steadfast to the last—than Bishop Dominicus had been.[48] For the situation had changed completely. There was now an official, papally-proclaimed crusade in progress, and Nicholas was a sworn crusader with a vow to keep. To fulfill his vow, Nicholas was intent upon serving in the papal army. A five-year wait was sufficient proof of his determination, and that was something which Bishop Peregrinus would have appreciated. It may even have persuaded him to assist Nicholas on his journey to the crusader battlefields in the East.

Sailing from Brindisi with an Italian force of crusaders, most likely late in the summer of 1217, was the strong-willed Spanish papal legate Cardinal Pelagius. It was his duty to see that the instructions of Pope Honorius III, Innocent's successor, were carried out. Pelagius arrived in Acre about mid-September, where he remained until late August, 1218. Then, learning of the fall of the chain tower which stood between the crusaders and their initial target, the city of Damietta, Pelagius, together with other Latin crusaders, left Acre for Egypt.[49] The Egyptian strategy dated from the Third Crusade. Richard Lionheart realized that Jerusalem could be retaken easily enough, but unless the Egyptian fortresses threatening the Holy City were secured, retaining it was a different matter. Victory in Egypt was thus perceived as a necessary prelude to reconquering Jerusalem. By the autumn of 1218, Pelagius was present at the siege of Damietta.[50]

Nicholas of Cologne may have left Brindisi in the company of Cardinal Pelagius's crusaders. Such a possibility arises because Nicholas's movements shadow those of Pelagius. According to the Admont chronicler, Nicholas, like Pelagius, was "at Acre and [then at] the siege of Damietta." The same chronicler maintains that Nicholas spent "almost two years vigorously fighting" there. Without Admont explicitly saying so, this suggests that Nicholas remained in Damietta at least until its capture by the Latin crusaders (November 5, 1219). But whether or not he stayed until Damietta was eventually surrendered to the Egyptian Sultan al-Kāmil (August 30, 1221) is uncertain. The terms of the treaty of surrender included al-Kāmil's pledge to return the True Cross, lost at Hattin, and the object of Nicholas's quest and that of the *pueri*. Nonetheless, the True Cross was never recovered.[51]

During the siege of Damietta in the late summer of 1219, a modest, unassuming figure arrived at the crusader camp. There he was observed by the bishop of Acre, James of Vitry: "We saw the founder and head of this order whom all the others obey as their prior, a simple and ignorant man, but loved of God and of men, by name Brother Francis."[52]

Francis of Assisi, accompanied by Brother Illuminato, joined the crusaders when battle was imminent. Francis told Illuminato what God revealed to him: it was the wrong day for such a battle; and so it was bound to fail. Was this because Francis could sense dissension in the crusader ranks?[53] Or was it because August 29th was a holy day, the feast of the beheading of John the Baptist?

Unafraid of opposition, he addressed the troops, "forbidding the war, [and] denouncing the reason for it." Whether Francis was preaching against fighting this particular battle, or against the general idea of the crusade is far from clear.[54] The troops mocked him; fought; and lost.[55]

While negotiations about a truce continued with al-Kāmil, there was a lull in the fighting. "To such a degree of intoxication and fervor of spirit was he seized,"[56] that Francis approached the papal legate Pelagius seeking permission to cross the Christian lines, enter the Saracen camp, and convert the Sultan to the true faith. Convinced that al-Kāmil would have Francis and his companion killed, Pelagius was understandably reluctant to grant what must have seemed a suicidal request. Somehow Francis persuaded him to do so.

Much later (c. 1260), Brother Illuminato, Francis's companion on that daring mission to the Sultan, was interviewed by Bonaventure, the illustrious minister-general of the Franciscan order and prominent Paris theologian, who was writing a new (and approved) saint's life of Francis. Despite its undisguised hagiographic purpose, Illuminato's belated account of events is the best source of what happened when the saint met the Sultan.[57]

When al-Kāmil's troops discovered them in their midst, the two friars were insulted, savagely beaten, chained, then dragged into the presence of the Sultan, who "asked them by whom and why and in what capacity they had been sent." Commentators speculate that al-Kāmil thought they were either messengers concerning the truce negotiations, or deserters from the crusade army wanting to convert to Islam. Francis replied that he was indeed a messenger—but one sent by God to proclaim the truth of the Gospel. He urged the Sultan and his people to convert.

To prove the truth of the Christian message, he offered to jump into a big fire, together with the Saracen "priests." The well-known scene, including the fire, of St. Francis before the Sultan is attributed to Giotto, and can be seen in the upper church of San Francesco, Assisi. Such an offer seems anachronistic, given that in 1215 the Fourth Lateran Council expressly forbade the ordeal by fire. In any case, al-Kāmil politely declined the ordeal—no fire was ever lit—or conversion, but instead offered Francis "valuable presents" to take with him. Illuminato makes it clear the Sultan respected Francis as a holy man. Now it was the turn of Francis, lover of poverty, to decline. Abandoning hope of converting the Muslims or of martyrdom, Francis found his way back to the Christian camp.[58]

Francis believed in the wisdom of folly. "And the Lord told me that He wished me to be a new fool (*novellus pazzus*) in the world and that He did not want to lead us by any other way than by that wisdom..."[59] Francis's strategy of peace with the Muslims through their conversion was the purest folly, as idealistic, or unrealistic, as the Children's Crusade. A shared devotion to religious impossibilism made Francis and the *pueri* kindred spirits. Did Francis's path cross Nicholas's at Damietta? One wonders. Both of these unconventional crusaders returned safe and sound from Egypt, Francis to Assisi, Nicholas to Cologne.[60]

All of Pope Innocent III's careful crusade planning had come to naught. Conducting a crusade was ultimately the business of the laity, the Christian warriors, not the clergy, the intelligentsia of Christendom. Poor, divided lay leadership; the non-appearance of the Emperor Frederick II; Pelagius's head-strong exercise of command; the march from Damietta towards Cairo, which ended in a shambles—the result was a strategic and tactical disaster. So like all the Holy Land crusades except the First, the Fifth Crusade failed in its objectives.

The history of the Children's Crusade was intertwined with that of the Fifth Crusade. From 1213, as already discussed, Innocent III's new recruitment policy for the Fifth Crusade was prompted by his awareness of continuing popular enthusiasm for the crusades. This, the movement of the *pueri* made plain for all to see. So it was altogether appropriate that the same venue should witness the final moment of both crusades. For the true terminus of the *peregrinatio puerorum*, if the Admont chronicler can be trusted, was not papal Rome. Rather, it was the crusaders' camp at Damietta, where Nicholas of Cologne, accompanied perhaps by a few fellow veterans of the Long March, at last managed to fulfill the vow he made several years earlier in the Rhineland when he took the cross.

Otto, the last *puer*

The history of the Children's Crusade is a history constructed out of textual fragments and buttressed by hypotheses. Reconstructing individual case-histories is out of the question. Indeed, what evidence there is for one new *puer*—a papal letter, plus documents which may (or may not) pertain to him—permits little more than conjectures. We start, at least, with a name, which is something. For out of the many thousands of youthful and not-so-youthful enthusiasts who ran off to join the crusade of the *pueri*, up to now only two names have surfaced in the literature—Stephen of Cloyes and Nicholas of Cologne. A third name can now be added. It is not that of a leader, but of a follower.

The papal register of Honorius III (1216–27) contains a letter dated August 19, 1220, addressed to the Patriarch of Aquileia and to Henry, Canon of Cividale del Friuli. The letter is an official response to the petition of a certain Otto, who pleads for a papal dispensation from his crusade vow.[61] If Otto had taken it when he was fourteen or older, or, if younger at the time, had ratified it when he reached the age of fourteen, that vow would still be binding.[62] This means that even if Otto was in his early teens when he took the cross in 1212, and was now in his early twenties, his vow continued to haunt him. It was as if he had an unpaid debt, and a threatening creditor was at the door.

Otto's situation was serious. Dispensation for the non-fulfillment of a crusader vow was a matter reserved exclusively for the pope.[63] The papal letter alludes to his anxiety; it is clear that the vow must have been weighing heavily on him. There was also a good reason why at that time he should have felt under particular stress. Recruitment for the Fifth Crusade was continuing in northern Italy. This would have intensified the pressure on him to honor his commitment and at long last go off on crusade, which he had vowed to do.

In the papal letter Otto is described as a *pauper scolaris*, a poor student or scholar. Some students were, of course, real paupers (*vere pauperes*), but the term "poor student" was conventional,[64] as conventional as the Lord presenting Himself to Stephen of Cloyes in the guise of a "poor pilgrim"[65]—poor pilgrim, poor student. But if Otto was really a poor student, that term applied perfectly to his present circumstances. It signified that Otto could not afford to go on crusade, or redeem his vow. The third option, commutation, substituting another pious project in place of the crusade, would probably have been impractical as well. All of which meant that if worst came to worst, and his plea for dispensation failed, Otto risked being condemned as a Christian outlaw—in other words, excommunicated. And if Otto the *scolaris* hoped for a glittering career in the Church, as an excommunicate his career would have been over before it began.

Someone had to pay the notary who drafted Otto's petition to the Apostolic Penitentiary (unless Otto, who was literate, managed to draft it himself). Then, too, someone had to pay the proctor who would have served as Otto's intermediary if he were to be spared the necessary trip to Rome.[66] But poor Otto apparently lacked the funds to pay. So at this point would an obliging patron—say, a senior churchman like one (or both) of the letter's addressees—have stepped in to cover the costs?

The papal letter brought tremendous relief. His petition was granted. Sworn in a moment of intense religious excitement eight years previously, Otto's crusade vow was now null and void, with the sole proviso that he had not bound himself by a subsequent obligation. According to the papal letter, when Otto took the cross along "with a multitude of other *pueri*," he was acting "imprudently." Such a mild rebuke is very different in tone from the comments of hostile chroniclers towards the Children's Crusade. On the other hand, the papal letter confirms the reports of the German chroniclers, by declaring that the *pueri* were "hoping to cross the sea [to the Holy Land] dry-shod." This statement implies that, when they took the cross, Otto and the other *pueri* believed God willed it. It may be that Otto himself acknowledged this in his original petition. But eight years had passed. Otto's youthful crusading ardor had cooled. His life had taken a different turn.

Otto's past or present whereabouts is never mentioned in the papal letter, but it is reasonable to assume that he was then living near one or the other of the two addressees of the letter—Aquileia, the home of the Patriarch Berthold de Méran,[67] or Cividale del Friuli, where Henry held his canonry. In this period, there was a series of patriarchs of Aquileia who, like Berthold, were of German extraction.[68] Otto's name, not particularly common in Aquileia at that time,[69] was German. So altogether, his name; his crusade vow as a *puer*; and his present location make it plausible that Otto belonged to the band of Rhenish *pueri* which Pope Innocent tried to intercept at Treviso. If that is so, Otto would have crossed the Alps, possibly via the Pontebba pass,[70] *en route* to Venice and the sea; then, finding himself in the Friuli, he decided to stay. It was a good place to study.

The schools of Friuli can be documented from the twelfth century onwards. Otto could have attended the cathedral school of Cividale del

Friuli, or either of two schools in Aquileia: one attached to the cathedral, or the other belonging to the provost's church, St. Felix.[71] Otto's student status raises some interesting questions. Had he begun his studies before he took the cross in 1212? Was he already in minor orders before he set out? At least one scholar believes that "priests and those in lesser orders" were present on the Children's Crusade, "although the number participating would be small."[72] Although mythistorical testimony alone supports such a conjecture,[73] yet if Otto had been in minor orders at the time he ran away with the other *pueri*, his peasant origins might be put in doubt. Just possibly, he sprang from that curious class of unfree German nobles, the *ministeriales*.

A document dated 1228, eight years after Otto's papal dispensation, may provide an answer to the question of where Otto pursued his studies, as well as how his later clerical career progressed. It concerns an *Otto Ruffus magister scolarum S. Felicis*.[74] Now was this Otto Rufus (Otto the Redhead?), "our" Otto? Could redheadedness be more indicative of German than of Italian stock? If it is "our" Otto, he has risen to be the master of the scholars of St. Felix of Aquileia, which could also have been the school where he himself studied. A later document (1232) refers to an Otto who was a canon of St. Felix and a senior official of the Patriarch of Aquileia. Now studying at the University of Bologna, this Otto (Otto Rufus?) has taken out a loan from some Sienese merchants.[75] The last notice of Otto Rufus, canon of St. Felix, comes from the necrology of the cathedral of Aquileia under the year 1240 and records that he held property in the area.[76]

Admittedly, this is speculative. Yet if these documents do refer to "our" Otto, the twenty years which followed his papal dispensation can be graphed as an ascending curve, the trajectory of a successful clerical career, the story of an immigrant who made good. In its roughest outlines, this, possibly, was the afterlife of one Children's Crusade survivor. So, contrary to the gloom and doom of the chroniclers, Otto's story might suggest that for those who survived the transalpine journey from the Rhineland to Italy, their fate was not necessarily a fate worse than death.

The aftermath: catastrophe or pseudo-catastrophe?

Contemporary chroniclers of the Children's Crusade could not say how it began. They left that tale to the mythistorians. How it ended was a different matter; that was something which the monastic chroniclers, the majority of them at least, claimed to know. There was little ambiguity in their accounts. Repeatedly, we hear of a series of calamities culminating in the unhappiest of unhappy endings. The mid-thirteenth-century mythistorians appropriated these views, embellished them, spray-painted them in bold acrylic colors, then inserted them in their volumes, which were deemed authoritative. Through the Middle Ages and into the modern era, these "contemporary sources" provided the standard narrative, which, in turn, became historical orthodoxy. It was their miserabilist interpretation which colored the received version of the Children's Crusade, creating an unforgettable after-image of unrelieved pain and distress. Once burned into the European consciousness, no other conclusion was imaginable.

What, allegedly, befell the *pueri*? *En route* to the sea, "many… perished in woods and desert places of heat, hunger, and thirst; others, having crossed the Alps, as soon as they entered Italy were despoiled and driven back by the Lombards…."[77] Still others, impoverished, starved in Italy or while attempting to return to their homelands.[78] Or, an alternative Italian welcome: "after this stupid multitude reached the regions of Italy, they were diffused and dispersed throughout the cities and towns, of whom many were kept [involuntarily?] (*detenti*) by the local inhabitants as servants and servant girls."[79]

Monastic culture privileged virginity, so sexual casualties could not go unnoticed: "many virgins were raped and lost the flower of their chastity." Others who left as virgins returned pregnant.[80] As for those unfortunates who reached the sea and managed to board ships, some drowned in shipwrecks, or were imprisoned by evil sailors, or were seized by pirates, enslaved, then transported to distant lands. They were human cargo—sold to the Saracens, and suffering God only knows what.[81]

It is true there was a minority report. Not all the northern European chroniclers professed to know the aftermath of the Children's Crusade. Some were more circumspect. "Even now it is unknown what happened to them."[82] "Whether they crossed the sea, or what became of them, is uncertain."[83] Some chroniclers who heard all the frightful rumors, evidently did not credit them. And of course there were good grounds for skepticism—the lack of specific details, for one thing.

Of all the chroniclers, the Italians were ideally situated to hear of human disasters in their part of the Mediterranean and especially in North Africa. But they say nothing about urban or rural enslavement in Italy, and nothing about the supposedly miserable fate of the *pueri* overseas. So is it sensible to argue that any seafaring calamities they suffered probably happened outside Italian waters, if they happened at all? Marseilles then becomes the obvious target, but this means that for the enduringly dramatic tale of the fate of the *pueri* who reached

Marseilles, we are forced to rely on the mythistorian Alberic of Trois-Fontaines (or his interpolator) later in the century.

Far removed from the scene of these alleged crimes, the German monastic chroniclers showed no restraint in trumpeting rumor as fact. At times they almost seem to compete with one another in cataloguing the sufferings which—or so they claim—deservedly rained down upon the heads of the runaways of 1212, those young people who had spurned the sound advice of parents and clergy.

With the returnees, the chroniclers' tales of woe continued. These *pueri* amounted to "many,"[84] or "some,"[85] or "barely a few"[86] of the former enthusiasts who, dejected and disillusioned, managed to slink back to their homelands. They returned confused, in disgrace, mocked and ridiculed. While they set out singing with jubilation, they returned abject, in silence. Kind-hearted, well-meaning strangers gave them alms on their outward journey, but as they straggled home barefoot, they received no alms and met no admirers. Instead, starvation stared them in the face. The same moral tune is played again and again. This was the price they paid for their ill-conceived venture; this was their self-inflicted wound. For who had blessed their pilgrimage? Neither God, nor his vicar, the Pope. Their utter failure was the surest sign of God's judgment.

Responsible for reporting more than his fair share of these negative outcomes was the unsympathetic Marbach annalist whose assertion that when they "reached the regions of Italy, they were diffused and dispersed throughout the cities and towns" is as close as he gets to saying that the great migration occurred. But then he goes on to add that "many were kept (*detenti*) by the inhabitants of the land as servants and servant girls." Possibly, but unverifiably, some were held against their will, virtually enslaved, in towns or rural estates, even though pilgrims (and crusaders) were supposedly a protected species.[87] Yet at one point even the Marbach annalist distances himself from the rumors which were flying about: "Others *are said* [my italics] to have reached the sea who were imprisoned by sailors and mariners, and transported to remote parts of the world."[88] This information, he acknowledges, may be unreliable.

So: catastrophe or pseudo-catastrophe? Undeniably, the Long March yielded its victims. Undeniably as well, the German chroniclers speak with some credibility of inglorious homecomings, even if the picture they paint of the bedraggled and humiliated returnees is too uniformly black to be entirely true to life. As for allegations of mistreatment in Italy or rumors of horrors abroad, they must remain unproven. All in all, the ideological bias and sermonic inclinations of the chroniclers guaranteed that their Last Judgments would be heavily weighted against the *pueri*.

Oddly enough, however modern the rhetoric, the chroniclers' voices can still be heard.[89]

While the German chroniclers insisted on finality, the reverberations of the Children's Crusade continued in France. The Mortemer chronicler relates that many saw the processions of the French *pueri* as

> a portent of future things, namely, of those which came to pass in the following year. For the Roman legate came within the borders of France, and signed an abundant multitude with the cross in the name of the Crucified One....[90]

Innocent III's choice as legate and crusade preacher in France was an Englishman, Cardinal Robert of Courçon (or Courson, or Curzon). By about June 1213, he was in Paris.[91]

Rather quickly, the preaching of the Fifth Crusade in France assumed a populist character. Much to the disgust of the usual beneficiaries of crusader status, the chivalric aristocracy, Innocent III's radical new recruitment guidelines opened the crusader's vocation to all and sundry.[92] This exposed crusade preachers to ferocious criticism. The chronicler William the Breton gives voice to the injured pride of the crusader nobility, when he accuses

> Robert de Courçon, legate of the Apostolic See, and many with him... [of] preaching throughout the whole Gallic kingdom... and ... sign[ing]... many indiscriminately with the cross, little children (*parvulos*), old men, women, the lame, the blind, the deaf, lepers....[93]

William begins his list of totally unsuitable crusaders with the absurd category of children, little ones, *parvulos*. How significant was that? Was it intended to evoke an episode of popular enthusiasm connected to the crusades which attracted a great deal of attention barely a year earlier?

A remarkable piece of recently discovered new evidence strengthens the case that the *pueri* were not forgotten during the preaching of the Fifth Crusade.[94] Originating in Paris or thereabouts is an anonymous early-thirteenth-century crusade sermon which can be dated to 1213, or shortly thereafter, because it alludes to the Children's Crusade as having taken place recently.[95] What is striking is that when the Paris crusade preacher refers to the "innocent children who became crusaders the other year" (*innocentes parvuli qui alio anno fuerunt crucesignati*), he felt no need to elaborate. Why not? Was it because the laymen and clerics who came to hear him knew exactly what he meant? Beyond a shadow of a doubt, this demonstrates that in the Île-de-France—the territory around Paris which included the Chartrain, birthplace of the Children's Crusade—people had not forgotten the *pueri* of 1212. But not only that. Contrary to what some modern scholars believe, it demonstrates that people regarded them as fully fledged *crucesignati*, as true crusaders.[96]

Said the Paris preacher: fresh, vigorous crusaders will spring forth from the growing tree of the Christian people (*arbor christianus populus*). Such a symbolic image was faithful to Innocent III's vision of a crusading Christendom infused with Christian populism. The thrust of his sermon was that these *innocentes parvuli* should be an inspiration to embryonic crusaders. What these *parvuli* had initiated, implies the preacher, the present campaign of crusade recruitment was now continuing and completing.

The most astonishing revelation of the Paris sermon is that a learned cleric has chosen an entirely unofficial, unauthorized crusade as an *exemplum* of true crusading fervor. Who could have imagined it—the Children's Crusade reborn as crusade propaganda! What a triumphant note on which to end.

Epilogue: What was the Children's Crusade?

Given the creative impossibilism of the entire enterprise, pontificating about the "failure" of the Children's Crusade is pure theatre of the absurd, as if "success" in whatever terms were ever a realistic possibility. The utopian impulse has always scorned realism. Another point: deprivation does not explain the crusade of the *pueri*. Their poverty was a condition, not a cause of the movement.[97] Their crusading zeal was neither the product of poverty, nor the consequence of a belief that poor people would play a providential role in the crusades.[98] Before and after the *pueri*, countless other impoverished medieval peasants fled the land and emigrated to the city. Particularly in its transalpine phase, the Children's Crusade was an urban migration, one of the geographically most impressive, large-scale urban migrations in medieval history.

Why, then, should the *pueri* of 1212 have chosen Jerusalem as their city, and set out in search of it, and the True Cross? The stimulus was a crusading crisis. Omnipresent in western Christian culture for a century before the *peregrinatio puerorum*, the idea of the crusade percolated through all levels of society, and persisted for centuries. Innocent III's crisis processions called to rally human and divine support for Christian Spain initially roused them, but the Spanish dimension quickly disappeared from view. It was as if, in the midst of their overwhelming processional fervor and pentecostal energy, the crusades returned to their natural habitat, the Christian East. Reacquiring Jerusalem and the True Cross now became the overriding ambition of the youthful crusaders. Popular crusading idealism found its outlet in collective enthusiasm.

Crusade revivals were one of medieval revivalism's interconnected families. Like the Children's Crusade, medieval revivals typically began with a religious crowd from which charismatic leaders emerged (or did not emerge), then progessed to the *motio* or movement phase (processions, pilgrimage). Here the active life of most medieval revivals ended. For a few, however, there was a life after death. Ordinarily, this took the form of new religious institutions, such as confraternities, which preserved or commemorated their fundamental spiritual ideals (for example, peace or penance). In exceptional instances, social memory conferred immortality.[99] As an archetypically tripartite medieval revival, the Children's Crusade passed through all of these stages. Although no new institutions sprang from it, what saved it from oblivion was social memory.

Good historicists insist upon the uniqueness of historical events, and rightly so. Nothing can wrench the Children's Crusade from its time, place, or circumstances. Yet patterns of behavior do recur, and the *peregrinatio puerorum* was the first born of two new species of crusade revivalism. The best known of these were the popular crusades, and heading the list is usually Peter the Hermit's People's Crusade of 1096. Yet Peter's crusade was an immediate popular response to Urban II's summons, and so was actually the first wave of the First Crusade. After the People's Crusade disintegrated, what was left of it merged with the official crusading armies. Peter's armies, what is more, had clerics and nobles in leadership roles. In contrast, the Children's Crusade could stake no claim to quasi-official status, and neither priests nor armed knights ever marched in its ranks. Consequently, it, rather than the crusade of Peter the Hermit, was the first popular crusade.[100] The first, but not the last.

The Shepherds' Crusades were a sub-species of popular crusades, and in its French phase, the Children's Crusade was a Shepherds' Crusade. Indeed, here, too, it was first of a line. Youthful shepherds, *pueri*, flocked to later Shepherds' Crusades in 1251, and again in 1320, but this is where comparison ends. For these later medieval Shepherds' Crusades turned to violence. Their target was not the Muslims abroad, but primarily the Christian clergy and the Jews at home.[101] In addition to the Shepherds', there were two further popular crusades, the Crusade of the Poor (1309) and the Hungarian Peasants' Crusade of 1514.[102]

But crusade revivals were not the only progeny of the Children's Crusade. Of all the descendants of the *pueri*, the later medieval youth movements are the least known, though the most remarkable. As in 1212, these were extraordinary collective enthusiasms, shrine-directed revivals, mass pilgrimages. As in 1212, successive waves of young people ran off towards a sacred shrine, seemingly without being prompted to do so. Unlike the *pueri*, however, these youths were neither crusaders nor Jerusalem-seekers, but in other respects the resemblance is uncanny.

These outbursts of youthful enthusiasm triggered the same response as there had been to the Children's Crusade—overwhelming astonishment reflected in the prose of the chroniclers. But this time, instead of a lost and inaccessible Jerusalem, the magnet which drew in these latter-day *pueri* was the venerable abbey of Mont Saint-Michel in Normandy, a sanctuary guarded by the sea. In 1333, without permission from their parents, shepherd youths from Normandy, Brittany, and Maine suddenly set off on a pilgrimage to Mont Saint-Michel. They sang, praised God, and danced *en route* to the abbey and on their return home.[103] Then, once again, in 1393, "children of the age of eleven, twelve, thirteen, fourteen, and fifteen years" gathered from Montpellier, parts of France, and other countries, to go to Mont Saint-Michel.[104]

Still again in the south of France, young people from some of the best families in Milhau began their long trek to Normandy during the summer of 1441, carrying a banner of St. Michael. Pilgrimages continued the next year. The local bishop named it a *motus puerorum* or *motus innocentum*, words highly evocative of the Children's Crusade. To Bishop Pierre Soybert, even if husbands and wives were included, it was definitely a youth movement.[105]

But what occurred in 1457–59 overshadowed all that had gone before. For it was then that the pilgrimage revival of young people to Mont Saint-Michel reached a new intensity, a veritable flood. Band after band, troop after troop of youths aged seven to eighteen, accompanied by others, the elderly included, made their way from the Low Countries, the Rhineland, Alsace, many other parts of Germany, and also western Switzerland, to the Norman abbey. Parental permission was disregarded. Begging for provisions along the way, these youths sang songs as they journeyed to St. Michael's sacred shrine, carrying banners depicting the Archangel.[106]

While contemporaries, predictably, struggled to find a reason for this bizarre mass movement, learned men were not slow to offer explanations, which, also predictably, hinged on moral judgments. Some blamed Satan and irrational superstition; others exalted childhood innocence and the veneration of St. Michael, the cult of St. Michael being particularly associated with childhood. It was also said that the *pueri* trusted the great Archangel to protect Christendom in its hour of need from the Turkish menace: Constantinople had fallen to the Ottomans in 1453. In the midst of this attempt to grasp what was happening, the Children's Crusade was recalled—more than two centuries after it was said to have vanished without a trace.[107]

What the Children's Crusade was is defined by its historical legacy: future crusades and crusade revivals, continuing labor migrations to the city, and later European youth movements of which it can claim to be the founding father. But where history ends, mythistory begins.

7
Mythistory: The Shape of a Story

Mythistory has insinuated its way into the historical record from antiquity to the present. Once fused together, myth + history becomes mythistory, a hybrid, which feeds on history and is unthinkable without it. Some might call it parasitic. As a response to the extraordinary in the workaday world—a myth-reading rather than a misreading of history—mythistory simplifies, but also elaborates. Medieval chroniclers exploited the devices of mythistory to the full, whether in the form of mythistorical motifs, which brought an extra dimension to historical texts, or as self-contained, enlivening anecdotes, sprinkled throughout an otherwise dutiful narrative. Readers of history were thereby invited to partake of the pleasures of the imagination.

"Based on a real event"

Aesthetically superior to history, mythistory clears away the fussy details that only create confusion and ambiguity. Once the historical context falls away, the story, isolated and anecdotalized, can reveal its essential, evocative, universal themes. Suddenly, everything is vivid, sharp, distinct. There are no quibbles in the name of scholarship. Mythistory laughs aloud at historical reality and obeys no rules other than those enjoined by the story itself, whereas historical writing, in theory at least, is confined to the prison house of actuality. Mythistory lays bare the gripping plotlines, and serves up in the most appetizing fashion the delectable motifs which the imagination craves. In the process, mythistory busily sets about reshaping, re-imagining, and reinventing, adding, subtracting, multiplying, and dividing, turning lead into gold. And what if historicity does become a sacrificial lamb, a burnt offering to the god of storytelling? Is that such a bad thing? Isn't a better story worth it?

"Purposeful blurring of the distinction between fiction and history" is taken for granted nowadays.[1] Well-paid blenders of stingy portions of historical fact and generous, tasty dollops of mythistorical fiction regularly offer us factoid films, docudramas, and "live" re-enactments of medieval battles. It is enough to make poorly paid historians, mere purveyors of truth, burst a blood vessel. Yet postmodernists relish informing us that historical narrative has storytelling in its bones.[2] Oddly enough, medievalists, while happy to acknowledge that the "cross between chronicle and story is... particularly common in the Middle Ages,"[3] sometimes give the impression that it was all one-way traffic, from chronicle to *roman*. It was not. Traffic flowed both ways. To be sure, medieval chroniclers may have expressed reservations, even tut-tutting disdain, but a good story was a good story, especially if the chronicler was telling it.

Mythistoricizing the *pueri*

Mythistorical motifs arise effortlessly from the nature of the story. Not unexpectedly, medieval ideas of childhood provided a rich storehouse of mythistorical motifs for the *pueri* of 1212. Images of uncanny, exceptional, or pure and holy children were part of medieval culture. No great leap of the imagination was required to superimpose stereotypical features on the blank faces of the *pueri*.

Ghosts are found in attics and basements, just as the border regions of age—the old and the young—are the promised land of strange stories. In the Middle Ages there was a dreadful non-place, the *limbus infantium*, the limbo for unbaptized babies, whose souls could be heard sobbing in the wind. Then, there were the changelings. Sound, healthy children were spirited away by the fairies, and sad, wretched, broken creatures were deposited in their place. Who could blame mothers for abandoning these malformed unfortunates? After all, they were never theirs.

Green children seemed so contrary to reason that the English chronicler William of Newburgh (d. c. 1200) was at first reluctant to record what he heard about them. Yet credible witnesses vouched for it, and that was enough for him to insert it in his chronicle. It was said that during the reign of King Stephen (1135–54), two children, a boy and a girl, "green at every point of their bodies, and clad in garments of strange hue and unknown texture" suddenly appeared in a field in East Anglia. The villagers fed and cared for them. Their new diet gradually de-greened them, and they learned to speak the language of their neighbors, after which they revealed how they were whisked away from their home in far off St. Martin's land, a Christian country of eternal twilight. "One day," said the child-shepherds, "we were feeding our father's flock in the field, when we heard a great noise... [and] suddenly we were rapt in the spirit and found ourselves in your harvest field." Both children were baptized. Not long afterwards, the boy died. The girl married and lived on. William of Newburgh concludes somewhat defensively: "Let all men say what they will... I for my part am not ashamed to have related this prodigious and marvellous event."[4]

A "prodigious and marvellous event" was how the late anonymous chronicler of St. Médard saw the Children's Crusade, which he noted under the wrong year, 1209:

> An innumerable multitude of infants and children (*infantium et puerorum*) from diverse parts, cities, castles, towns, camps, farms of France, going forth without the permission and assent of their parents, said that in quest of the Holy Cross they had undertaken to cross the sea. But they succeeded not at all. For all, in different ways, were ruined, died, or returned.

So much for the event. Already a mythistoricizing cast of mind is indicated by the "multitude of infants" among them. Next, without transition, the St. Médard chronicler delivers three reports of strange phenomena in the world of nature. Strangeness, perhaps, is what linked them to the *pueri*.

> They say indeed and affirm for a certainty, that every ten years before that wonder (*mirabile*) happened [i.e. the movement of the *pueri*], fishes, frogs, butterflies, birds, proceeded in like manner... At that time so great a multitude of fishes was caught that all marvelled greatly.

Here that *mirabile*, the Children's Crusade, is likened to a kind of biorhythm in the animal kingdom, or to a marvelous haul of a "multitude" of fishes.

A final "multitude" completes the story, but neither is it a "multitude" of *pueri*, nor of fish:

> And certain old and decayed men affirm as a certain thing, that from different parts of France an innumerable multitude of dogs gathered together at the town of Champagne which is called *Monshymer*. But those dogs having divided into two parties, and fighting bravely and bitterly against one another, nearly all slew one another in the mutual slaughter, and very few returned.

The intriguing story of the fierce canine warriors of Monshymer is credited to an oral folkloric source. Yet others writing in the 1240s told it as well, including the mythistorian of the Children's Crusade, Alberic of Trois-Fontaines.[5] Here St. Médard's phrase "and very few returned" echoes the fate of the *pueri*. In fact, all four of these episodes are bound together by a common unlikelihood. They were equally bizarre.

These things happen, the chronicler seems to be saying. The inexplicable explains the inexplicable.

The chronicler Salimbene de Adam was born nine years after the Children's Crusade. In 1233, when he was twelve, a popular revival in Parma called the Great Hallelujah laid the groundwork for his later conversion to the Franciscan order. When he was sixteen, he ran away from his prosperous, well-connected family to become a Franciscan. Salimbene's father, desperate and enraged, made repeated efforts to free his son from the clutches of the order—which had a reputation for snatching youngsters—but in vain. As a runaway, Salimbene was following in the footsteps of the founder of his order, St. Francis, and of his disciple, St. Clare. Whether he recognized it or not, he was also following in the footsteps of those other young religious runaways, the *pueri*.

In the 1280s, working on his chronicle, Salimbene lifted nearly all of his passage on the *pueri* directly from the *Codex Estensis*.[6] The relevant passage was probably written by Sicard of Cremona's secretary, a priest of Cremona, Peter de Crotta.[7] Salimbene slightly altered the original, but, once incorporated in his chronicle, the passage becomes Salimbene's:

> In that same year of 1212, three boys of about twelve years of age, who said that they had seen a vision, took the cross as crusaders in the region of Cologne. Persuaded by them, an innumerable multitude of paupers of both sexes and children took the cross and journeyed from Germany into Italy. With one voice and one heart, they said that they would cross the sea dryshod and restore the Holy Land of Jerusalem to God's kingdom. But almost the entire multitude simply disappeared. In that same year there was a famine so severe, especially in Apulia and Sicily, that mothers even ate their own children.[8]

"Three boys of about twelve years of age" is interesting because the contemporary Peterborough chronicler likewise states that of the estimated 15,000 *pueri* "none was older than twelve."[9] Why twelve?

That age may signify more than it seems. Joachim of Fiore, whose prophecies held Salimbene spellbound, made much of the symbolic number twelve. He especially associated it with the twelve-year-old Jesus's pilgrimage to Jerusalem with his parents, as recounted by Luke (2:41–9).

This was the sole incident of Jesus's childhood recorded in the Gospels, serving as the bridge between his infancy and his mature preaching mission. Jesus goes missing for three days, leaving Mary and Joseph frantic with worry until they finally discover him in the Temple, seated in the midst of the teachers, listening to them and asking them intelligent questions (Figure 2, p.5).[10] Jesus the runaway was mature beyond his years. In medieval terms, he was a *puer senex*.[11] He was represented as a wise and independently-minded child. Yet his escapade presented medieval biblical exegetes with a bit of a conundrum.

It was this. How could the child Jesus have gone about his Father's business, as, rebuking Mary, he said he was doing, while at the same time observing the Commandment to honor his distraught father and mother? For the Cistercian Aelred of Rievaulx, a monk sworn to obedience, there was no problem. His twelve-year-old Jesus is the perfect model of monastic virtue. He is deferential towards his elders, and humble and obedient towards his parents, whom he rejoins as soon as his Father's business has concluded. So there is and can be no conflict. Jesus willingly submits to both parental and divine authority.[12]

Conversely, for the fourteenth-century Franciscan John de Caulibus, the same incident was a family drama; and in a drama, conflict is what one would expect. Mary's anguish at losing Jesus is terribly real. She accuses herself: "Forgive me this time, for never again will it happen that I be negligent in your care. Or did I offend you in any way, my son, or why have you left me?" Mary's plaintive cry in Simone Martini's celebrated fourteenth-century painting echo those words: "Son, why have you dealt with us like this?" (Figure 9).

De Caulibus notes that after their reunion in the Temple, Jesus bowed to his mother's wishes and returned submissively to Nazareth with them. Yet the conclusion Friar John draws from this episode is unsentimental: "He who would approach God must not stay among relatives, but must leave them."[13] This recognition of conflicting spiritual obligations is quintessentially Franciscan. Like the twelve-year-old Jesus, Francis, Clare, and Salimbene were religious runaways; so, too, were the *pueri*.

Salimbene concludes his account of the Children's Crusade with the disappearance of the *pueri*—"almost the entire multitude simply diasppeared." Immediately thereafter he notes that the famine in Apulia and Sicily was so severe "that mothers even ate their own children." This memorably gruesome expression, derived most likely from Josephus, became part of the rhetoric of medieval famines.[14] Figuratively, it implies the fate of the Lost Boys. Betrayed, perhaps by those whom they most trusted, they vanished. In a manner of speaking, they were eaten, consumed, devoured.

Figure 9 Simone Martini, *Christ Discovered in the Temple* (1342). Walker Art Gallery, National Museums, Liverpool.

Child-martyrs: the New Innocents

Already young, they grew younger still. In his chronicle of Genoa written between 1295 and 1297, Archbishop James of Varagine, the Dominican author of the *Legenda aurea* (*Golden Legend*), borrowed most of his information on the coming of the *pueri* to Genoa from Ogerio Pane, but he embellished it with mythistorical details of his own. "Many of them were the sons of nobles," claims Varagine, "whom their fathers had provided with wet-nurses [what could this mean? For themselves? For the infants among them?]."[15] But it seems hard to credit such a touching sign of paternal concern, which flies in the face of known parental opposition. Their alleged aristocratic status also appears to be a mythistorical flourish. Although one might argue that Varagine was gesturing towards the unfree class of German nobles, the *ministeriales*, his comment about their noble birth must be rated as highly improbable. No other chronicler corroborates it. Nonetheless, Varagine's affirmation was taken seriously by post-medieval Genoese historians who were happy to gratify their fellow citizens eager to claim descent from the "noble" German pilgrims of 1212.

Other later medieval chroniclers did refer to the *pueri* as "infants" or "little ones,"[16] a hint of a note of tenderness, perhaps. One of the characteristic and appealing qualities of the very young was their purity. The illustrious medieval etymologist, Isidore of Seville, said that a child is called *puer* because he is *pura*, pure.[17] "And therefore for purenes of kinde innocence, such chydren ben called *pueri*, as saith Isydore."[18] The church affirmed that sexual sinfulness began at fourteen.[19] Had not Jesus said: "Suffer little children and forbid them not, to come unto me" (Matthew 19:14). And the twelfth-century exegete Anselm of Laon explained why Jesus said it. It was because little children were truly humble and truly chaste that they were permitted to approach him.[20]

Bernard of Clairvaux was another prominent figure who linked spiritual purity with pre-pubescent innocence. This emerges clearly from one of James of Vitry's moral anecdotes in a sermon composed especially for children and adolescents. One morning, so the story goes, St. Bernard was out riding when he saw children in the fields looking after the sheep, prompting him to say to his fellow monks: "'Let us greet these children, so that they may respond and bless us; and thus, strengthened by the prayers of these innocents, we may ride on today in safety.'"[21]

This sermon anecdote (*exemplum*) advances the idea that the prayers of these sexually pure, spiritually innocent, shepherd-boys would find favor in the sight of God. What, then, of the prayers of Stephen of Cloyes and his flock of shepherd-boys? After all, they were the ones the Laon

Anonymous referred to as "innocents," and the anonymous Paris preacher (c. 1213) praised as "the little innocent ones" who had taken the cross.[22] Both clerics would have shared the beliefs of St. Bernard, which meant that the prayers of Stephen and his workmates were equally privileged.

Of course, this was always a minority view, although some went further still, even daring to compare the *pueri* to the most famous of the child-saints. Widely thought of as martyrs, they were technically confessors, for they were not witnesses for Christ; rather, they died in place of Christ.[23] Slaughtered on the orders of King Herod, aged a mere two years old or younger, they were commemorated liturgically and lauded in drama throughout medieval Christendom. Often depicted, although not always depicted as infants, they were the Holy Innocents (Figure 10).[24]

Running like a golden thread through the medieval sources of the Children's Crusade is the motif of the "innocence" of the *pueri*. Their innocence, together with their ever-increasing youthfulness and the cruelty they suffered, intertwined their fate with that of the Holy Innocents, mythistorically and metaphorically. In Alberic of Trois-Fontaines's mid-thirteenth-century mythistory of the Children's Crusade, one of his unsubstantiated assertions is that Pope Gregory IX had a church built to house the uncorrupted bodies of the *pueri* who drowned at sea—a church dedicated to the New Innocents (*ecclesiam novorum Innocentum*).[25] Metaphorically at least, the *pueri* were the New Innocents. (But that even the mythistoricizing chroniclers actually imagined them as an army of two-year-olds seems hard to believe.)

The Lotharingian Richer of Senones (c. 1264) picks up on the same theme. Dwelling on the story of the famished *pueri*, he quotes the Book of Lamentations on the pathetic "little children" (*parvuli*) asking for bread. He then goes on to compare the Little People (*parva gens*) of 1212 with the Great Innocents (*magnis innocentibus*) who were killed for Christ.[26] For a later-thirteenth-century chronicler, to mention the *pueri* in the same breath as the Holy Innocents is startling. Certainly, as a manifestation of sympathy, it is out of the ordinary. Richer, however, was not alone in ushering these youthful crusaders into such exalted company. The unknown author of the *Austrian Rhymed Chronicle* (c. 1270) claims to have heard the very voices of these "Innocents" as they marched and sang with Nicholas of Cologne. Their fate would be similarly brutal.

The massacre of the Holy Innocents had one clear villain, and his name was Herod. The villain (or villains) responsible for the mythistorical fate of those New Innocents, the *pueri*, was not so easily identified. Several candidates were auditioned for that role. All of them were adult males. Not all of them were human.

Figure 10 Andrea di Giovanni, *Holy Innocents adoring the Christ Child and the Mystic Lamb*, processional banner, church of San Ludovico, Orvieto (1410). ALINARI Archives, Florence.

Searching for villains

The Judeo-Christian ethic postulates a cosmic economy of justice. For the innocent to suffer is troubling and distressing. However deluded the *pueri* were in their pursuit of the True Cross and Jerusalem, however wrong they were in disobeying their priests and parents, they were not inherently evil. They were only poor, credulous dupes, gulled by sinister figures. Mythistory, like history, sought causal agents. In that search there was a certain logic, a certain fearful symmetry. A foreboding presence at the start of the story made an eventual scene of carnage all the more inevitable. The search was on to find the guilty party.

What is surprising is that the Jews were never accused of this crime. Increasingly, whenever the corpse of a Christian boy was stumbled upon—only boys: young Christ-figures—the Jews were the prime suspects. Spurious allegations of ritual murder against the Jews began after the death of William of Norwich in 1144, and gained credence in the second half of the twelfth century.[27] Even so, to have blamed individual Jews or a Jewish community for what befell the multitude of young crusaders in 1212 would have required an elaborate stage set, special effects, and considerable literary talent. For one thing, the scale of such an alleged atrocity would have been unprecedented. For another, Jewish collective conspiracy theories, foreshadowed at Norwich, were still a long way off from the *Protocols of the Elders of Zion* (1917). As a mythistory, it probably would have been just too implausible.

So who did conspire to set the movement of the *pueri* in motion? Several chroniclers claimed to know. Singled out for plotting the doomed crusade was the shadowy brotherhood of magicians. "We believe this was done through the magic art," says an early chronicler.[28] The practitioners of magic were known to be capable of deluding the simple-minded. This is precisely what Richer of Sénones asserts when he blames magicians for the Shepherds' Crusade of 1251. At this point he puts forward the notion that the same culprits—evil enchanters (*incantatores*)—lay behind the crusade of the *pueri*.[29] In the later Middle Ages, clerical moralists and theologians spoke out fiercely against them.[30]

Victims of treachery, the juvenile crusaders of 1212 were no more than foolish, easily-led innocents. Their foredoomed adventure must have been the Devil's work, instigated by Satan's henchmen. Nicholas of Cologne's father was one diabolical arch-villain. Encouraged by demons, he sold the *pueri* to the heathens. A fitting, Judas-like bad end was his probable suicide in Cologne.[31] Demons, on the other hand, "are permitted by

God to kill children in order to punish their parents," argued William of Auvergne.[32]

Demonic influence was omnipresent. "An expedition of *pueri* of both sexes, and later of men and women of advanced age, came to pass through the incitement of the Devil."[33] The diabolical "spirit of deception"[34] tainted the venture. So "one can clearly see that this journey issued from the deception of the Evil Enemy because it caused so much loss."[35] The Devil, naturally, had partners in crime. In league with Satan were the sworn enemies of Christendom, his natural allies, who operated both within and beyond its frontiers. They even worked in tandem, as when heretics betrayed the *pueri* to the Saracens.[36] One of their favorite tactics was to have men disposed to do evil marching alongside the young people.[37]

These were men with unearthly, diabolical powers who enticed them away. Writing in 1267, the insufficiently appreciated English genius Roger Bacon (d. c. 1292) remembered that "less than sixty-four years ago, *pueri* of the Kingdom of France once followed in countless numbers after a certain evil man, so that they could not be restrained by fathers, mothers, friends, and were placed on board ships and sold to Saracens."[38] What triggered Bacon's recollection of the *pueri* was his face-to-face sighting of the charismatic leader of the Shepherds' Crusade, the Master of Hungary, and his observation of the Master's extraordinary technique for overpowering crowds, which Bacon—a crowd psychologist before there was such a thing—termed "fascination."[39] Someone, Bacon must have thought, had employed a similar technique with the *pueri*. Once "fascinated," they could easily be lured away.

Or would it have been the haunting notes of a silver flute that "fascinated" them? Charmed away, the children of Hameln left, never to return. How they came to be enthralled melodically, as if by a snake-charmer, is the subject of the earliest narrative of the Pied Piper:

> A wholly exceptional marvel (*miraculum*) took place in the little town of Hameln in the diocese of Minden in the year of the Lord 1284 on Saints John and Paul's day [*sic*] [June 26]. A certain young man of thirty, handsome and very smartly dressed, so that all who saw him admired the way he was clothed, came in over the bridge and by the Weser gate. He had a silver flute of a most unusual kind and began to play on it through the whole town. And all the children who heard the piper play, around 130 of them altogether, followed him out of Eastgate right to the place [known as] Calvary, or the Place of the Beheadings. Here they disappeared, and no one could find where even

> one of them remained. Mothers of the children ran from city to city, and discovered nothing.

The author, writing about 1430–50, says that he came upon this extraordinary incident in an old book;[40] but, like the missing children, the book has never been found. Before this short narrative, there are only late-fourteenth-century fragments, none of which shed any light on the historical circumstances of the so-called Hameln Exodus, and none refer to a lone piper. Much later, in the second half of the sixteenth century, the theme of the vengeful Ratcatcher of Hameln was pasted on to the story of the Pied Piper.

Now this tale of the splendidly attired, mysteriously attractive stranger, whose piping proved so charming—in the original sense of the word—that 130 children of Hameln were lost forever has been linked with memories of the Children's Crusade, and with good reason. The seductive piper could easily be made to fit the persona already sketched in by the chroniclers of 1212—the diabolical trickster, the malicious magician, the wandering hypnotist (à la Roger Bacon). Another congruent motif is the pathos of the vanished children, gone forever, their anguished mothers hunting for them in vain. Nonetheless, although the Hameln date is firm and precise, it is wrong for the *pueri*, while the crusade theme—an essential pointer to the *peregrinatio puerorum*—is entirely missing.

Perhaps the first to suggest a link between the *pueri* of 1212 and the *kinder* of Hameln was the illustrious German polymath Leibniz (d. 1716), but he rejected the idea.[41] Louis Backman calls the idea of such a link "no more than a shot in the dark," preferring his own pet obsession, the dancing mania of 1374.[42] Opinion now seems to be turning towards the theory that if the legend of the Pied Piper does have a historical basis it is connected to an exodus of the young men of Hameln, recruited by enterprising agents, *locatores*, who were actively promoting later-thirteenth-century German colonial settlement in the East.[43] It seems a credible hypothesis. With a persuasive recruiting-sergeant acting as their Pied Piper, a generation of Hameln's youth left as settlers, never to return.

Immigration—what an intriguing idea. The young men of Hameln, migrants to a distant land, disappear from history. Time passes. Then legend rediscovers them, brings them back from oblivion, and rewards them with immortality. But in 1212, seventy-two years earlier than the youth of Hameln were reputed to have done, a great multitude of German *pueri* likewise disappeared from history. Similarly as well, immigration was largely the reason for their disappearance. And even without a spellbinding piper, the chroniclers never ceased writing about them, mythistoricizing them, immortalizing them.

Thus the story of the *pueri* was evoked in sermons, mulled over by peasants in the fields, retold historically and mythistorically by the annalists and chroniclers of western Europe. Nevertheless, it was the literary skill of three eminent mythistorians—Alberic of Trois-Fontaines, Matthew Paris, and Vincent of Beauvais—which guaranteed that in the Children's Crusade, myth married history, so that the two became one flesh. Versions of their authoritative horror stories were reiterated down the centuries to the point of incontrovertibility.

Eminent mythistorians: Alberic of Trois-Fontaines

Alberic was a Cistercian monk of the abbey of Trois-Fontaines in the Champagne. The date he died is uncertain, but he wrote his great work, a universal chronicle, between 1227 and 1241. A decade later, the chronicle was revised and readied for publication, perhaps by Alberic, perhaps not. For his early entries, centuries before his own time, Alberic drew from around fifty or more chroniclers. He included original documents, such as charters; the lives of saints, their visions and miracles; official letters and canon law; epics, romances, and Arthurian legends.[44] His chronicle accommodated both history and mythistory. Although he often made use of German chroniclers, Alberic took nothing from them about the Rhenish crusade of the *pueri*. Just as Alberic's source or sources were exclusively French, so, too, was his Children's Crusade:

> This year [1212] there occurred a rather miraculous expedition of young children (*infantium*) coming together from everywhere. First they came from the area around the city of Vendôme to Paris. When there were around 30,000 of them, they arrived at Marseilles, as if they wished to cross the sea [and fight] against the Saracens. But ribald and bad men joined them and so corrupted the entire army that, some perishing in the sea, some being put up for sale, few of such a great multitude returned. However, the pope commanded those who escaped from there [where they were enslaved?] that when they came of age, they should cross the sea as crusaders.

Alberic's narrative is short, self-contained, and seemingly complete. From its first stirrings in the territory near Vendôme, this "rather miraculous expedition" proceeds to Paris, after which 30,000 "young children" eventually join it. The Norman chronicler of Jumièges agrees that it began in Vendôme;[45] and the Peterborough chronicler brings it to Paris.[46] The highest number of correspondences, however, belongs to the Anonymous chronicler of Laon—two indirect ("Cloyes near the town of Vendôme," and the encampment at Saint-Denis, close to Paris), and one direct ("nearly 30,000 people congregated around him from diverse parts of France").[47] Does this prove that the Anonymous was his source? It remains doubtful. Alberic ignores Stephen of Cloyes, Laon's hero, while the Laon Anonymous omits Alberic's destination, Marseilles.

Right from the start, mythistory enters Alberic's narrative. First, the extreme youth (*infantium*) of the entire 30,000-strong army is stressed. Next, the villains, "ribald and bad men" are quickly introduced. They corrupt the army of youngsters by the very act of joining it. Consequently, unlike most other chroniclers, Alberic in no way blames the children for what befalls them. He seems to be saying that only after coming into contact with these vile men is their purity compromised, and their innocence lost. As a result, disaster strikes. Finally, when only a "few of such a great multitude" return (presumably to northern France) does the tale appear to end. In conclusion, perfectly consistent with the image Alberic presents of very young children, he cites the papal command that "when they came of age [at fourteen], they should cross the sea as crusaders."

Then, just as it appears that Alberic has concluded his narrative, the story takes a sudden turn. The transition is handled clumsily, which suggests poor editing, almost as if something new has been tacked on at the last moment. Of attempts to explain this curious structure, that of Raedts is the most plausible, yet not altogether convincing.[48] Instead of another monastic chronicler supplementing Alberic's text, as he argues—and which remains a possibility—it may be that Alberic himself drafted an addendum to an already composed text. Perhaps, later on, he jotted down the exaggerated or fanciful testimony of an oral source. Whatever the case, Alberic (or his interpolator) resumes the story with a flashback to the "ribald and bad men" who betrayed the children, but this time the two chief villains are named:

> Now the betrayers (*traditores*) of these young children are said to have been Hugo Ferreus [Iron] and William Porcus [Pig], merchants of Marseilles, who, being captains of ships, ought to have conducted them across the sea without cost for God's sake [because they were pilgrims and crusaders?], just as they promised them.

For the moment, the two traitors, Hugo Iron and William Pig, are identified simply as merchants of Marseilles and ship captains. Later in the narrative we learn that they collude with the Saracens of Sicily in order to betray the Emperor Frederick II. Their plot fails, and afterwards the Emperor has both of them hanged on the same gallows as their Sicilian co-conspirator.

Zacour, however, picks gaping holes in Alberic's assertions about Hugo and William.[49] Both men were indeed historical figures, but neither Hugo nor William were merchants. Hugo Ferreus was the principal agent of the viscount in Marseilles.[50] William Porcus, on the other hand, was a Genoese captain, and one of Frederick II's admirals, who fled to Sicily in 1221, after losing favor with Frederick. Neither Hugo nor William were hanged, and there is no evidence that they ever met.

What became of the *pueri*?

> And they [Hugo and William] filled seven large ships with them [the youngsters]. When after two days at sea they came to the island of St. Peter at the Rock, which is called Recluse, a tempest arose, two ships were sunk, and all the young children on board those ships were drowned. It is said that after some years Pope Gregory IX [1227–41] built the church of the New Innocents on that island and appointed twelve prebendaries. And there are in that church the uncorrupt bodies of the young children which the sea cast up, and to this day they are shown to pilgrims.

The island of San Pietro is located four miles southwest of Sardinia. Of the two claims to have discovered the church of the New Innocents on that island, one is extremely implausible, while the other is at best problematic.[51] The lack of ecclesiastical documents, in Pope Gregory IX's registers, for example, confirming that such a church ever existed, is sufficient to make these claims unsafe.

In the magic realm of mythistory, however, the cult of the New Innocents gave the *pueri* a glorious, redemptive afterlife, their death at sea being a kind of martyrdom, cleansing them of any last trace of the contagion of sin carried by the "ribald and bad men." Proof of their sanctity lay in their "uncorrupt bodies." The New Innocents attracted the veneration of the faithful, and their tomb became (an unrecorded) place of pilgrimage.

What, then, became of those young children unfortunate enough to survive the cruel sea?

> But the betrayers managed to take the five other ships to Bougie and Alexandria, and there they sold all the young children to the princes of the Saracens and the merchants, of whom the Caliph purchased for himself four hundred, all clerics, because he wished to keep them separate from the others. Among them were eighty priests whom he treated more honorably than was his custom.

Lifelong enslavement to the Saracens—that was their destiny. The youngsters were shipped to North Africa from Marseilles, which for centuries had been a thriving and profitable slave market, although its great days were still to come.[52] The Cologne Continuator believes some of the *pueri* "reached Marseilles, but whether they crossed the sea, or what became of them, is uncertain,"[53] while the Ebersheim chronicler holds that they boarded ships, which were seized by pirates, and then sold on to the Saracens.[54] Neither statement provides a ringing endorsement of Alberic (or his informant).

Alberic's sizable round numbers—four hundred clerical slaves, of whom eighty were priests—likewise arouse suspicion. Moreover, Alberic is unique among chroniclers of the *pueri* in singling out priests in their ranks. But Alberic's tale of misery is not over. Seven hundred and eighteeen Christian slaves remain to be accounted for:

> That same year when the young children were sold, the princes of the Saracens assembled at Baghdad. In their presence, eighteen of the young children were martyred in different ways because they would by no means abandon the Christian faith. The rest were diligently reared in slavery. One who saw this—he was one of the clerics purchased by the Caliph—faithfully reported that he heard that not one of all these young children had apostatized from Christianity.[55] Eighteen years after this expedition [1230], he who reported this added that Mascemuch of Alexandria kept in good custody seven hundred [of these slaves], now no longer young children, but fully grown men.[56]

To the New Innocents who drowned at sea, Alberic now adds "young children [who] were martyred in different ways." Mercifully left unsaid is how "in different ways" they were martyred. (For graphic details, there were always the images of the early Christian martyrs exhibited in churches.) A total of eighteen brave child-martyrs refused to deny their faith and convert to Islam. Curiously, the number eighteen recurs. Eighteen years elapsed before Alberic's informant ("he who reported this")—presumably a runaway slave once owned by the Caliph—escaped to tell the tale. Was this recurring number a sign of literary invention or a pure coincidence?

Spurious exactitude, precise imprecision is part of the seasoned storyteller's repertoire. Here there is an oral tale—a story recounted, a story which has been told more than once, and grown in the telling. As one writer comments: "Critically evaluating Alberic's testimony, Norman Zacour cautions us against throwing out the baby with the bathwater. The real problem we have with Alberic, however, is finding that elusive baby."[57] What elements of Alberic's powerful and unhappy tale are trustworthy? In a Scottish court, the verdict returned at the trial of Hugo Iron and William Pig, or of any of the merchants of Marseilles, on charges of kidnapping and enslavement would have to be "not proven."

But historical unreliability and a propensity to exaggerate do not make Alberic a mythistorian. What does is his love of mythistory for its own sake. With Alberic mythistorical motifs are totally in command. He does not so much interpret the *peregrinatio puerorum*, which historians are obliged to do, as anecdotalize and mythistoricize it as an *exemplum* of Christian fortitude and heroic virtue in the face of Saracen and Christian evil. Alberic's infants are heroes of the faith, redeemed by suffering. Unquestionably one of the leading mythistorians of the Children's Crusade, Alberic is also its supreme hagiographer.

So far as villains go, Alberic's Hugo Ferreus and William Porcus perform rather well. But for sheer diabolical charisma they face stiff competition from our next candidate.

Eminent mythistorians: Matthew Paris

Matthew Paris (c. 1200–1259) was a hagiographer, cartographer, and artist who illustrated his manuscripts, illuminating them with pictures of people and events in history. He was also a student of heraldry, probably a gold and silversmith, and perhaps the most vital, imaginative, and idiosyncratic of all medieval English chroniclers. What he was to his fingertips was a Benedictine monk at St. Albans, devoted to his order, his monastic house, and its traditions. That is the key to his prejudices and to his most deeply held values as the chronicler of St. Albans. Anyone posing the slightest threat to the wealth or privileges of his fellow monks—the King, the Pope, the Franciscans—risked Matthew's censorious displeasure, evident to any reader of his *Chronica Majora*.[58]

As a chronicler, Matthew's contradictions are hard to reconcile. On the one hand, he valued documents, collected documents, and transcribed them in his chronicles. On the other, "his sporadic tampering with documentary sources and misuse of historical material, as well as his many errors, make him basically unreliable as a historical source." That is the harsh judgment of the acknowledged authority on Matthew Paris, Richard Vaughan.[59] Ambivalence characterizes the verdict of another fine scholar. V.H. Galbraith considers Paris's *Chronica Majora* "the high-water mark of medieval historical writing in England." Yet his plaudits are tempered. The chronicler excels "in scope and in method, if not in critical ability."[60]

How, then, to assess Matthew Paris as a historian? Galbraith comes up with a solution. Paris, he says, was a writer who could "turn a dull fact… into a good story."[61] Suzanne Lewis, an art-historian brilliantly equipped to appreciate Paris the visual and literary artist, makes the same point more elegantly: "[Matthew's] chronicles still possess the power to move us by transforming human history into the suspenseful drama of medieval fiction."[62] That, in a nutshell, is Matthew Paris, mythistorian.

My argument is that Matthew Paris was compelled to write about the Children's Crusade because what he had already written pre-supposed it. According to this hypothesis, his next step would have been to check the earlier portion of his *Chronica Majora,* the work of his predecessor at St. Alban's, Roger of Wendover (d. 1236). He would then have discovered that Roger had left it entirely unreported. Matthew now would have realized his cross-reference to the *pueri* was meaningless. This hypothesis, if valid, is significant for two reasons. First of all, the circumstances in which Paris came to write about the *peregrinatio puerorum* colored his negative perception of it. Second, if we can deduce roughly when he discovered Roger of Wendover's omission, we can more or less date when Matthew Paris's mythistory of the Children's Crusade was inserted in the *Chronica Majora*.

Paris wrote a stirring account of the violent, anti-clerical French Shepherds' Crusade of 1251 probably fairly soon after its death throes. He made no secret of his wholehearted revulsion for the *pastores* and their excesses. Heavily embroidered with mythistorical motifs as his report was, it was at the same time exceptionally well-informed. Paris's plot was well-crafted. An evil genius inspired it. He was a sixty-year-old, Hungarian-born, charismatic leader, who had "in his early years… imbibed the falsehoods and cunning emanating from the sulphureous pit of Toledo." Magic, in other words: Toledo in Spain was its traditional home. Later, the future Master of Hungary apostatized from Christianity, becoming "a servant and disciple of Mohammed." Subsequently, his abominable life unfolded in France. There, "about forty years ago" [1251 – 40 = 1211] "while he was still a beardless youth," he "infatuated the

French people, convoking an infinite multitude of *pueri* who followed him singing...."[63]

That is a truly astounding revelation. The fearsome aged leader of the Shepherds' Crusade had actually been the youthful prime mover of the Children's Crusade. They were one and the same. As mythistory, it is brilliant—a master-stroke. The leader of the Shepherds, known as Jacob, the Master of Hungary, now acquired a back-story, a prequel. Anti-heroes, like superheroes, like Jesus himself in the apocryphal gospel known as the "Pseudo-Matthew,"[64] must be endowed with a childhood thrilling enough to be worthy of their later years. So, leading the Children's Crusade was the young Master of Hungary's apprenticeship, paving the way for, indeed prefiguring, his unspeakably evil deeds to come. This creative mythistorical fiction—that one career bridged the two great popular crusade revivals of the thirteenth century—inevitably colored Paris's views of the Children's Crusade. Therefore, it follows that Paris composed a paragraph on the *pueri* sometime around 1251, which he then appended to Roger of Wendover's portion of his *Chronica Majora* under the year 1213.[65]

Like Alberic's, Matthew Paris's Children's Crusade was an exclusively French affair. His narrative was based on one, possibly two, French chronicles, plus his own fertile imagination:

> In the course of the same year (1213) [*sic*], in the following summer, there arose in France a certain heresy (*error*) never before heard of. For a certain boy (*puer*), instigated by the Devil, a boy indeed in years, but most vile in his way of life, went through the cities and towns in the realm of the French, as though sent by God, singing in French: "Lord Jesus Christ, restore to us the Holy Cross," with many other things added. And when he was seen and heard by other boys of the same age (*coetaneis*), an infinite number followed him, who, wholly infatuated by the craft of the Devil, left their fathers and mothers, their nurses and all their friends, singing in like manner as their teacher (*paedagogus*) sang.

It was a heresy, according to Matthew, and he was the only chronicler to stigmatize it as such. Heretics were damned; hence the enterprise itself was damnable; hence the Devil's role in instigating it. "A certain boy (*puer*)" accompanied by "other boys of the same age (*coetaneis*)" points to the Laon Anonymous as a source, but no mention is made of Stephen of Cloyes; nor is Stephen, or any of his age-mates, described as a shepherd-boy. Moreover, to the Laon Anonymous, Stephen was certainly not "most vile in his way of life."[66] The boys following their teacher, singing, seem to have come straight from a "song school" (ages seven to twelve).[67]

"Singing in French: 'Lord Jesus Christ, restore to us the Holy Cross,' with many other things added" is taken directly from either the Mortemer chronicle or the Rouen annals.[68] Yet here Matthew does something no French chronicler does. He joins the boy leader of the *pueri* (Laon?) to the processional movement (Mortemer or Rouen). In this instance, Matthew's imagination is historical, rather than mythistorical.

"Wholly *infatuated* [my italics] by the craft of the Devil," the *pueri*, marching and singing, follow their leader. For Matthew Paris "infatuation" was the equivalent of Roger Bacon's "fascination"—a technique for seizing control of a crowd, overawing it, stupefying it. According to Paris, the youthful leader of the *pueri* used it much the same way the Dominican inquisitor Robert le Bougre did in 1239 when he *infatuated* accused heretics before burning them in a huge, mass funeral pyre. Like Bacon, Paris was a crowd psychologist *avant la lettre*.[69]

Now comes the denouement. The fate of the *pueri* is death, naturally enough, although this time they escaped enslavement either to Christians or to Saracens:

> Nor, wonderful to say, could either bolts restrain them, or the persuasion of their parents recall them from following their aforesaid master to the Mediterranean Sea, which crossing, they marched on in orderly procession, singing. For now no city could hold them because of their numbers. But their master was placed in a wagon adorned with coverings, and was surrounded by shouting armed guards. But such was their number that they crushed one another through overcrowding. For he who could carry away some threads or hairs from his garments considered himself blessed. But at last through the machinations of that old imposter Satan, they all perished either on land or by sea.[70]

The motif of parental opposition regularly appears in trustworthy chroniclers, French and German, and so cannot be called mythistorical. As for "bolts [to] restrain them," Paris is virtually repeating what he says in his narrative of the Shepherds. But their crossing of the Mediterranean is not something Paris would have picked up from contemporary French chroniclers; and their "orderly" processing through (Levantine?) cities seems misplaced.

The cinematic close-up of the canopy-covered wagon with its armed guards protecting Stephen is an original visual touch. (Pictorially, the scene would have a future in children's literature.) The crush of crowds—

the fact that crowds could kill—was something that Paris, the crowd psychologist, was aware of. Paris knew very well that when "some threads or hairs from... [his] garments" were plucked off and carried away, it was a sign of the boy-leader's charisma (akin to Peter the Hermit's). Closure came swiftly: "all perished either on land or by sea." No further details are supplied.

Casting a dark shadow over the Children's Crusade from its beginning to its end is the lurking presence of the Devil. Their futile death-march? He instigated it. Their going to their deaths infatuated, blindfolded? His machinations engineered it. "All perished"—save for the young Master of Hungary who was purposefully spared to preside over an even greater spasm of satanic destruction. "That old imposter Satan" understood something to chill the hearts of parents: the vulnerability of young children. He was, after all, the "enemy of the human race" who originated the "new kind of false doctrine" (i.e. heresy) that became the Shepherds' Crusade.[71] This was a Devil who walked on earth, intervening in the affairs of men. He was not the abstract, disembodied *diabolus* of the medieval scholastics. For medieval "artists and mystics were able to grasp the diabolical reality more intensely and convincingly" than their academic contemporaries.[72] Such a literary artist was Matthew Paris.

Matthew's Children's Crusade was an *exemplum*, which contravened his Benedictine values and vindicated them by its dreadful end. Instead of God, Satan reigned. Instead of monastic stability, there was unmonastic pilgrimage, mere vagrancy. Instead of the duly constituted authority of an abbot, there was the illegitimate rule of a pseudo-master. The moral of the story was plain to see. When juniors cast off the rule of seniors, when ungovernable enthusiasm banishes well-regulated routine, then the outcome is a foregone conclusion.

Satan and his servants make formidable villains. But now a third mythistorian steps forward to challenge them and Alberic's slave-merchants as well. This new villain controls a band of murderers so terrifying as to rival even the mafia as a synonym for bloodlust and depravity.

Eminent mythistorians: Vincent of Beauvais

Vincent of Beauvais (c. 1190–1264) was the greatest encyclopedist of the Middle Ages. Centuries before Diderot's and D'Alembert's jewel of the eighteenth-century Enlightenment, the *Encyclopèdie*, Vincent's monumental *Speculum Maius* was the largest and most comprehensive encyclopedia in the western world. Its thirteenth-century compiler probably entered the Dominican Order in Paris around 1220, which makes him part of the first generation of Dominicans. Dominican giants of the second generation, like Thomas Aquinas, continued to enhance Paris's reputation as a dazzling intellectual center.

By 1246, Vincent was sub-prior of the Dominican convent of Beauvais. Then, through the intervention of King Louis IX of France, he became a lecturer (*lector*) in a royal foundation, the Cistercian abbey of Royaumont, not far from Paris, where he resided from c. 1246 to 1259/60. There he taught, preached, and prepared a number of works, the most famous of which, the *Speculum Maius*, was dedicated to Louis IX, who partially funded the burdensome costs of copying the manuscript. A team of friars assisted Vincent of Beauvais in collecting and organizing his material. He maintained he was not an author, merely an excerptor of the work of others.[73]

Included in Vincent's encyclopedia was a volume devoted to history, the *Speculum Historiale*. Often circulated independently of the rest of the work, it survives in about 200 manuscripts and was translated into French, Catalan, and Dutch—a clear sign of its European popularity. Five early Latin versions of the *Speculum Historiale* are known. The earliest dates from 1244/45. The last was the Douai version, completed after July 1254. Only this final version of the *Speculum Historiale* contains Vincent of Beauvais's entry on the Children's Crusade.[74]

Vincent divides his material on the crusade of the *pueri* into two distinct parts. Part One looks like a terse statement of fact, distilled by the compiler from his source or sources:

> Also in the above-mentioned year [1212] little children (*parvi pueri*), about 20,000 of them, as it is estimated, became crusaders, and coming in troops to various seaports, namely Marseilles and Brindisi, returned famished and without anything.

Their extreme youth is underscored—these were "little children, about 20,000 of them" (not the 30,000 of Laon or Alberic, nor the 15,000 of the Peterborough chronicle). They took the cross, became *crucesignati*, and headed for the sea. By the time Vincent was writing, the conventional opinion about where the French *pueri* were heading probably had settled on Marseilles. That was what Alberic thought. Brindisi, mentioned in no other French chronicle, was a novelty. Vincent's precise source has not been identified.

Part One closes with an extraordinary statement—the *parvi pueri* "returned famished and without anything." Is Vincent implying that *all* of them returned? That none died, and none were enslaved? Of course, they suffered destitution and disappointment, but this was a small price to pay for the failure of their expedition. Equally remarkable is that Vincent, a moralist and a friar-preacher, fails to rebuke them for their disobedience to parents and clergy. Nor is the illegitimacy of their crusade thrown in their face. To Vincent, the one charge that could be raised against them was their folly, and that remains implicit.

Part Two sees a dramatic change. All at once the sky darkens:

> But it was said that the Old Man of the Mountain (*Vetulus de monte*) who habitually used to rear the Assassins[75] from boyhood had detained two European clerics in prison, and would never let them go until he received a firm promise from them that they would bring him some boys (*pueri*) of the kingdom of France. By them, therefore, the said boys were thought to have been enticed by some false reports of visions and also promises to them when they took the cross.[76]

The discontinuity between the two parts of Vincent's encyclopedia entry could not be sharper. The apparently factual synopsis in the previous passage has vanished altogether, and something very different has taken its place.

History has suddenly been reshaped and re-imagined as mythistory, disconcertingly so. Everything has been turned round. What appeared to be an inexplicable, motiveless, and futile crusading episode, is now presented in an entirely different light. Events now have a cause, and it is sinister. We glimpse prior arrangements. Undisclosed up to this point is the plot hatched by the Old Man of the Mountain and his sworn agents, two western Christian clerics, blackmailed into becoming traitors.

Infamous in the West from the twelfth century onwards, the Old Man of the Mountain was the fearsome commander of the fanatical Assassins. A string of illustrious corpses established the Assassins' reputation as a ruthlessly efficient killing machine. Brandishing their knives, they struck down—more accurately, assassinated—such luminaries in the crusader East as Count Raymond II of Tripoli (1152), Conrad of Monferrat (1192), Raymond, son of the Prince of Antioch (1213), and Philip of Montfort (1270). Prince Edward of England was wounded, but escaped death (1272). The quasi-suicidal loyalty of the Assassins towards their *shaykh* (sheik = Elder, Old Man) became the stuff of legend. In the poetry of the Provençal troubadours, the absolute obedience of the Assassins to the dictates of the Old Man of the Mountain metaphorically mirrored the willing feudal submission of a lover to his beloved: "You have me more in your power than the Old Man his Assassins, who go to kill his mortal enemies…."[77]

This western image of the Old Man of the Mountain and his implacable Assassins underpins Vincent of Beauvais's mythistory of the Children's Crusade. Central to it is a recurring theme in the legend of the Old Man of the Mountain, which the chronicle of Arnold of Lübeck (to 1209) first brought to the attention of western readers.

Arnold cites a report from Emperor Frederick Barbarossa's envoy who traveled to Egypt and Syria in 1175, which describes how the Lord of the Mountain educates his juvenile Assassins. Many of the sons of peasants are taken to his palaces. There they are brought up from early childhood and are instructed in many languages. "From their earliest youth to their full manhood" they are taught by their teachers to obey every word and precept of their all-powerful Lord. If they do so, they will be granted all the joys of paradise. "Note that from the time they are taken into the palace as children, they see no man but their teachers and masters and receive no other instruction until they are summoned to the presence of the Prince to kill someone." Once in his presence, they throw themselves at his feet, fervently pledge their obedience, then receive a golden dagger from the Prince's own hand. Attached to it is a note with the name of their intended victim.[78]

Although he was referring to the Persian, rather than the Syrian Old Man of the Mountain, Marco Polo touched on the same topic. "All the promising youths of those parts from the ages of twelve to twenty" were indoctrinated and thus became his devotees.[79] Constant reiteration of this theme meant that "the Old Man of the Mountain was known to literature as a debaucher of youth."[80]

Which answers the question at the very heart of Vincent of Beauvais's mythistory of the *pueri*—for what reason did the Old Man of the Mountain devise an elaborate plot to ensnare the "little children"? His secret agents, the turncoat Christian clerics, were not supplied with drugs like hashish, or mind-altering beverages, or magical means. No: "false reports of visions and... promises" would be sufficient to "entice" them. In other words, theirs would be the standard bag of tricks (minus the false relics) that religious con-men were exploiting all over medieval Europe, something which good Dominicans like Vincent of Beauvais were only too aware of.

This, Vincent seems to be saying, was the ingenious plan of the Old Man of the Mountain. Duped into running away on a fool's errand, the French *pueri* would be reared and educated side by side with the native-born Assassins. Pledged to unquestioning obedience, and able to mingle unobtrusively with his Christian enemies, they would become ideal operatives in France. They would faithfully carry out whichever assassination he had in mind. As Vincent's text indicates, the same vocational training program in place during the "boyhood" of the Assassins would be followed with "the boys of the kingdom of France." The same curriculum meant that the latter would be just as professional in their line of work as the former. For some unexplained reason, however, the plot of the *shaykh* of the Mountain was foiled. So the *pueri* "returned famished and without anything."

From the fabled crusader East came mythic polarities—nightmares of drug-induced atrocities with the Old Man of the Mountain, and always-raised, always-dashed messianic hopes with Prester John. Revivalism kindled such hopes and roused the spirit of prophecy. For a medieval revival like the Children's Crusade, the spirit of prophecy was a predictable traveling companion.

Mythistory and the spirit of prophecy

Revivalist enthusiasm itself generates a prophetic sensibility. On the march, a conviction of divine election is validated by collective experience. Such a conviction infuses ultimate goals, and a prophetic self-consciousness emerges. In the case of the *pueri*, it is not difficult to see in their outcries and acclamations, prophetic exaltation as a consequence of revivalist zeal. Mythistorians of the *pueri* were also receptive to the prophetic spirit.

Of all the texts claiming to unlock the secrets of the *peregrinatio puerorum*, without a doubt the most breathtakingly audacious, perplexing, and potentially revelatory comes from the *Austrian Rhymed Chronicle* (*ARC*). It was composed around 1270 by an anonymous, Paris-educated cleric at a monastery of Augustinian canons in Klosterneuburg, near Vienna.[81] In composing the *ARC*, the versifying chronicler made use of earlier annals, some of which have been identified. None, however, would have provided him with the material for his extraordinary revelations about the *pueri*.[82] The late composition of these verses is sufficient to make them suspect; their unique status makes them doubly so.

Still, for the most insightful historian of the interior world of the crusaders, such concerns do not arise. To explore the mentality of the *pueri*, Paul Alphandéry focuses precisely on this passage from the ARC which its anonymous author presents as coming from the very lips of the *pueri*. [83] If this were so, as Alphandéry believes it to be, it would give us unrivalled access to the innermost thoughts of the *pueri*.

Jubilant with anticipation and captivated by millenarian dreams, they await the impending apocalyptical conversion of all the enemies of Christendom, swiftly followed by eternal peace and their own celestial glory. What initially seems very odd, however, is that these exuberant, celebratory verses are enclosed within the frame of a traditionally negative interpretation, painted in the blackest of colors. First as preamble and last as epitaph, it is the chronicler's gloomy, disapproving voice which we hear. All of this was a trick, a swindle. The *pueri* were deceived by "some magic art" through which evil was made to appear good. The boys were sold; the virgins ravished, and, as in scripture, Rachel weeps. She also weeps in the medieval *Ordo Rachelis*, the dramatized death of the Holy Innocents.[84] Deceit and disaster preside over their end. So far, so familiar.

Yet right in the middle of this funereal diatribe a joyous song bursts forth, a song which, says the rubricator, the *pueri* sang everywhere:

> Nicolas, servant of Christ, will cross the sea
> And with the Innocents will enter Jerusalem.
> Dry-footed, they will safely walk on the sea.
> Youths and virgins will chastely couple.
> To the honor of God they will achieve so much
> That cries of "Peace! Jubilation! Praise God!" will ring out.
> Pagans and the perfidious will all be baptized.
> Everyone in Jerusalem will sing this song:
> "Peace is now, O Worshipper of Christ; Christ will come
> And will glorify those redeemed by his blood.
> He will crown all of Nicholas's *pueri*."[85]

The song glows with prophetic wonder. It is the credo of the *pueri*. There will be miracles—the dry-shod crossing of the sea and the chaste, mystical coupling of young men and young women. At the end of days, Christians, Muslims ("pagans"), and Jews ("the perfidious") will all be one. As the *pueri* enter Jerusalem, they will usher in an age of universal peace. Christ will come again and crown Nicholas and his *pueri*. They will be blessed and triumphant at the close of history.

What are we to make of this? Did the *pueri* see themselves as actors in a prophetic drama? But was it prophecy lived, or prophecy invented artfully, *post factum*? The *ARC* writer, after all, reports the supposedly actual, joyous words of the *pueri*. Yet these are bracketed by the deep disillusionment of his comments. Such a stark contrast must have been intended. While Alphandéry uncritically rejoices in this rarest of opportunities to probe the thoughts and feelings of the young enthusiasts, his acceptance of their song for what it pretends to be seems naive. For one thing, its literary qualities are obvious. It is well-crafted; perhaps too well-crafted to be true. Second, for so late a text, it is suspiciously knowledgeable. So the problem then becomes one of searching for historicity within a prophetic mythistory.

Three of the motifs are traditional: the dry-shod crossing, the New Innocents, Jerusalem. On the other hand, the spiritual copulation of male and female enthusiasts; the arrival of millennial peace followed by the conversion of all unbelievers; and, the grand finale, Christ's coronation of the *pueri*—all these themes are entirely novel. The anonymous verse chronicler is able to name the Rhenish leader—"Nicolas, servant of Christ"—but he omits his charismatic attribute, the *tau* cross. True, the aspirational destination of the *pueri*, Jerusalem is historical, rather than mythistorical. Conversely, nothing is said about where their pilgrimage began, or where it actually ended. The opinion of one scholar is damning. The ARC's anonymous author yields "meagre historical information... colored by personal judgment."[86] Artistry is beside the point.

And yet... we *do* know that there were processional acclamations in the early days of the Children's Crusade, and it is not inherently implausible that the Long March of the *pueri* yielded pilgrimage songs.[87] Moreover, *Pax*! *Iubilacio*! *Deo laus*! are just the sort of short, sharp outcries which were characteristic of medieval revivals. A later manuscript rubricator calls the movement an "unheard of *devocio*,"[88] using the medieval equivalent term for "revival". So were these acclamations with their unmistakable prophetic overtones overheard somewhere by someone, if, almost certainly, not the *ARC*'s author? Were they the authentic substratum upon which a mythistorical, prophetic text was constructed? Whether or not the verses of the *pueri* proclaiming the good news of millennial peace and universal conversion—let alone the delicate prospect of mystic copulation—have any basis in fact, it may be best to keep a skeptically open mind. The mythistorical imagination expands to take in whatever it can.

As with Alberic, Matthew, Vincent, and the *ARC* writer, mythistory, the storyteller's art, can impose a shape, a pleasing curvature of meaning, that real history often struggles to attain. History has its satisfactions, but these are other than what one gets from a well-told tale. Thanks to mythistory, the *pueri*, those never-to-be-seen-again child-(better, infant) crusaders, became the Lost Boys of the Middle Ages. Not for the first nor for the last time, a once-historical incident was denatured—then fortified—with mythic motifs, the signatures of literary art. What mythistoricization insured was memorability.

8
Memory: The Echo of the Centuries—Fourteenth to Eighteenth

Astonishingly, the *pueri* were remembered—and not just for a short stretch of time, but over *la longue durée* from the thirteenth century to the twenty-first. The usual route for preserving the memory of medieval revivals was through commemorative rituals—saints' days, shrine dedications, processions, and gatherings of a religious and social nature. Typically, these were presided over by confraternities whose foundations stemmed from a particular revival. Sharing its original religious impulses, these institutions were effectively dedicated to its memory. But the Children's Crusade left no confraternal institutions behind it. For it, there would be no institutional vehicles of collective remembrance. So memories of the Children's Crusade had to travel by other means.

Thirteenth-century chroniclers and mythistorians lovingly embroidered it in their annals, deplored it, fantasized about it, and tearfully or coldly recorded that it ended miserably as a nullity which "after a short time all that… came to nothing, because it was founded upon nothing."[1] Yet what they negated, they publicized. Curiously, the memory of this supposedly foolhardy venture outlasted the crusades and outlived the Middle Ages, so that ultimately the Children's Crusade became an emblem of crusading idealism, whether deluded or inspired.

The forgettable became the unforgettable. Irresistible to storytellers and moralists, clerical or secular, the *peregrinatio puerorum* captured first the European then the American imagination. Changing while remaining the same, it was re-imagined, retold, and reshaped for century after century by chroniclers, historical scholars and popularizers, encyclopedists, novelists, poets, dramatists, and composers. They were the transmitters of social memory.

This chapter and the next explore how the Children's Crusade was re-imagined in response to the changing pattern of European cultural mentalities over the last seven hundred years. As comprehensiveness is too much to hope for, selectivity across the genres will have to do. Historiography, with its privileged truth claims, demands pride of place. Whatever its flaws, written history is the formal guardian and guarantor of social memory. Not unexpectedly, crusade historians have been prominent in refashioning perceptions of the Children's Crusade,[2] though only in the late nineteenth century did the *pueri* begin to acquire a specialist historical literature of its own.

Historical writing is both a creature and creator of western culture, yet not all of memory's landscape architects have been historians. Writers of European and American fiction—magicians of the imagination—nourished social memory. Crucial in this regard is the representation of the Children's Crusade in children's literature, where, since the nineteenth century, the subject has taken hold so strongly that it is impossible to do more than glance at a small sample of titles. To study the adult messages barely disguised in this medieval tale transmuted into a modern children's story would be a rewarding project for someone with the psychological sensitivity of a Bruno Bettelheim.[3]

A panoramic view of how the *pueri* of 1212 were re-imagined from the early fourteenth to the late twentieth centuries necessarily draws upon both history and mythistory. Whatever the tricks played upon the Children's Crusade either by bad history or good literature, the *pueri* proved to be as enthralling and intriguing a story for the modern age as it had been for the Middle Ages.

The fourteenth-century chroniclers: recitations and surprises

Medieval chroniclers unhesitatingly plundered their predecessors for material about events before their own times, thus preserving, recycling, and altering the historical record. Many fourteenth-century chroniclers described the Children's Crusade in virtually the same words as those used by their thirteenth-century sources, while adding errors of their own.[4]

The fourteenth century sees the movement of the *pueri* increasingly making its way into the vernacular, especially with translations into various languages of Vincent of Beauvais's *Speculum Historiale*. Amongst these, the French prose version of Jean de Vignay (d. c. 1348/50), the five-volume *Miroir Historial*, is probably the most notable.[5] During the fifteenth century, vernacular texts of Vincent's *Speculum* appeared in print. Translation from Latin implies laicization. Once the story of the Children's Crusade gained a non-clerical readership, it retained it.

When Fritsche (or Friedrich) Closener (d. c. 1384), a priest of St. Catherine's chapel of Strasbourg cathedral, included the *pueri* in his vernacular chronicle in 1362, they made their debut in German: "In 1212 foolish children had mounted a crusade [literally: a sea journey] with the intention of journeying overland with dry feet [dry-shod] to Jerusalem."[6] "Foolish" says it all. Their folly foretold the outcome of their journey.

Umberto Eco's highly successful medievalizing novel *The Name of the Rose* (1980), and the film based on it (1986), featured as one of its characters a real-life figure, the intimidating Inquisitor Bernard Gui. Of all the fourteenth-century chroniclers of the Children's Crusade, Bernard Gui must be the best known. Like his fellow Dominican Vincent of Beauvais, Gui had an all-consuming interest in history, particularly church history. Neither the administrative burdens he undertook on behalf of his Dominican brethren, nor his ecclesiastical office as Inquisitor, hindered his scholarly productivity. He was a hagiographer, liturgist, and librarian, as well as a prolific historian. His prolonged service to the papacy was rewarded, late in life, by his appointment as Bishop of Lodève. Well-qualified through his experience of conducting heresy trials and punishing heretics, he wrote a manual of good inquisitorial practice.[7] He also produced nine editions of his chronicles—*Flores chronicorum* or *Catalogus pontificum romanorum*—the last edition of which was extended to and issued in 1331, the year he died.[8]

Gui places the Children's Crusade in the frame of a brief survey of the life and pontificate of Innocent III. This was a shrewd choice and a historiographical novelty, even if the *pueri* are entered under the wrong date, 1210.[9] Gui's chief, and most likely only, source was Vincent of Beauvais. Yet he uses Vincent's text selectively. For one thing, he completely ignores Vincent's villain, the Old Man of the Mountain.

Could it be that for Bernard Gui the Inquisitor, moral responsibility had to be shifted from an outside agent, however diabolical, onto the protagonists themselves, now judged to be culpable for their own wicked deeds? Right away we hear the judgmental tone of the Inquisitor. Vincent of Beauvais's "little children" (*parvi pueri*), with its hint of innocence and pathos, is disallowed. Gui emends it to read "vicious (or bad) children" (*pravi pueri*), perhaps unconsciously alluding to his depraved heretics.[10] To explain his antipathy towards the *pueri*, one only has to point to his horror at the violent, anti-clerical outrages perpetrated by the Shepherds'

Crusades of 1251 and 1320, the latter of which he lived through. All three movements had a very similar, if not virtually identical, social composition, so perhaps he assumed that the *pueri* were cast from the same rebellious mould.[11] Gui emphasizes their unofficial status. While Gui knew that the Pope alone could call for a crusade, the crusading call of the *pueri* came to them fancifully, through dreams.

According to Gui, the army of child-crusaders was enormous. Instead of Vincent of Beauvais's 20,000 *pueri*, Gui's total is a majestic 90,000. Unless there was a defect, his Ms. copy of Vincent (or in our printed versions of either of the two texts), such an inflated figure, surely counts as an instance of statistical mythistory. Is it indicative of Bernard Gui's inquisitorial mentality? Was this huge horde of 90,000 *pueri* the product of Gui's unconcealed fear of large-scale religious and social disorder?

In what is often misconceived to be an impersonal genre, other chroniclers likewise reveal their individual approaches to events. The anonymous Austrian author of the *Leobiensis Chronicon*, for example, includes mythistorical details never replicated elsewhere. Towards the mid-fourteenth century, this unknown Dominican compiled his annals, either in Vienna or Krems, beginning with the birth of Christ and terminating in 1343. Aside from two lines of verse about the *pueri*, which he probably took from an earlier Austrian chronicle, his source is unknown.[12] Either it came from someone else's imagination, or from his own.

Pueri of both sexes from Burgundy, Lotharingia, the Northern Ardennes, and East Franconia, aged about twelve and under, left their parents, taking nothing with them and giving no reason for their journey. Ever-increasing numbers of them journeyed from place to place (*de loco ad locum*), visiting the sacred shrines, although Jerusalem is not mentioned. Nothing connects these pilgrims with the crusades, and that seems strange, because the crusades were by no means moribund in the first half of the fourteenth century.

As a mysterious child-pilgrimage to nameless Christian shrines scattered throughout the world, the journey of the *pueri* remains enigmatic. Its conclusion is unique: there is no tragic end to this mythistory—no capture by pirates, no enslavement, and no mass slaughter. There is only a last known sighting of the wanderers at the island of Patmos in the Aegean Sea (*ad mare Oceanum in Pathmum*). Never before has Patmos been named as the final destination of the Children's Crusade. Although its significance is by no means clear, a reference to Patmos sends a strong signal of apocalyptic prophecy, for Patmos was supposed to be the location where the script of the last act of Christian world-history was written, St. John the Divine's Book of Revelations.[13] After Patmos, the *pueri* were never seen again. Was it believed they would have a role to play in apocalyptical events to come?

Later medieval versions of the Children's Crusade

Walter Bower (c. 1385–1449) was the scholarly Scottish abbot of the monastery of Inchcolm, a tiny island in Edinburgh's Firth of Forth.[14] Here during the 1440s he wrote his massive *Scotichronicon*, greatly amplifying the earlier chronicle of John of Fordun, which makes no reference to the Children's Crusade, and extending it from the 1380s to 1437.[15] Beginning with the Egyptian birth of the Scots, mythistorical elements happily co-habit with history in Bower's chronicle which is both universal and Scottish in its scope. Lest there should be any mistake, Bower's concluding comment shows where his loyalty lies: "Who this book does not please, O Christ, he is nae Scot."[16]

Trained in canon law and theology, perhaps at Paris, more likely at St. Andrews, Walter Bower drew upon the recognized authorities in the approved medieval fashion.[17] This well-educated Scottish abbot was a nostalgic partisan of the crusades, and his *Scotichronicon* has been called "the closest thing to crusading propaganda in mid-fifteenth-century Scotland." To Bower, the conquest of Jerusalem occurred in a distant, golden age of Christian unity ("O how far removed are present-day princes from those there were at that time!"). Reflecting traditional Scottish politics (the "auld alliance"), he sees the French as generally vigorous proponents of the crusade ideal, while the English either impeded or even subverted it.[18] For the Children's Crusade Bower took what he wanted from Vincent of Beauvais's *Speculum Historiale*, which, more than two and a half centuries after it was compiled, continued to retain its status as an authoritative work.

But Bower did not simply recycle Vincent of Beauvais. He glosses and emends him to stress the crusading zeal of the *pueri*. First, their motive: they "were zealous to recover the Holy Land." Second, why they failed: "because no one cared to transport them." Thus it was the unresponsiveness of others, not the dastardly machinations of the Old Man of the Mountain, which doomed the *pueri*. As a canonist, Bower might have pronounced upon the illegitimate nature of a crusade which the papacy had not authorized, but he does not do so. Moreover, by omitting Vincent's Old Man of the Mountain, Bower leaves the memory of the *pueri* better than he found it.[19]

Bower the chronicler now departs, and Bower the angry moralist and preacher steps into his shoes:

> So while these tender youths who had not even reached adolescence, these mere boys (*pueri*), were so fired with enthusiasm to come to the aid of the Holy Land, what will you say, you bearded soldiers, you who daily attack churchmen and tillers of the soil, and who along with your accomplices live off their estates, and off plunder to fight against justice, what will you say when at the Last Judgment the Lord says: "Suffer little children, to come unto me; of such is the Kingdom of Heaven" [Matthew 19:14]? And turning to sentence you, he will say: "Cast ye the unprofitable servants into outer darkness" [Matthew 25:30].[20]

Wonder of wonders, Vincent of Beauvais's negative verdict has been reversed. Bower's ringing historical *exemplum* is positive—almost uniquely so—in the homiletic uses of the Children's Crusade.

Walter Bower grasped "the implications of past experience for the problems of his own day,"[21] and the disorderly conditions of contemporary Scotland appalled him. These "tender youths," whose venture belonged to the great crusading past, gave him an ideal opportunity to berate, and possibly convert, the marauding, unchristian soldiery of Scotland. Like Catherine of Siena, and her vain efforts to persuade the *condottiere* to satisfy their aggression and love of booty by crusading in the East,[22] Walter Bower was a crusade idealist; so his Children's Crusade, as opposed to Vincent of Beauvais's, was not a monument to diabolical folly, but a symbol of hope.[23]

In absolute contrast to Bower, Werner Rolewinck endorses the prevailing, negative view of the Children's Crusade. Rolewinck (1425–1502), a Carthusian monk of the abbey of St. Barbara in Cologne, wrote practical and edifying theology as well as historical works, one of which was his *Fasciculus Temporum*, a compilation which begins with Adam and concludes in the later fifteenth century. First published in 1474, Rolewinck's *Fasciculus* was a traditional, grand-scale, medieval universal chronicle, which survived into the age of printed books. Thrived, in fact, rather than survived: Rolewinck's compendium went through more than thirty Latin editions during the lifetime of its author and translations into German and other languages followed.[24]

Annalistically, under the year 1204, Rolewinck juxtaposes a short summary of the Children's Crusade, coupled with a brief word about the Shepherds' Crusade.[25] Both movements were linked. Rolewinck speaks of the crusade of the *pueri* as the father of the crusade of the shepherds. But just how they are linked is not explained until the last line of Rolewinck's discussion: "And thus it is clear that the Devil also preached his own crusades."

Rolewinck believes that the biblical verse *ex ore infantium* was used to justify the claim of the *pueri* to divine election: "Out of the mouth of babes and sucklings hast Thou ordained strength..." (Psalms 8:2) or perhaps: "Out of the mouth of babes and sucklings Thou hast perfected praise" (Matthew 21:16). Yet their miserable fate—some drowned, others sold to the Saracens—proves that their crusade was of diabolical origin. Consequently, any claim to divine election implicit in *ex ore infantium* must be false.

Renaissance and early modern Children's Crusades

Several decades before Werner Rolewinck's *Fasciculus Temporum* was first published in Cologne there emerged amongst the humanists of Renaissance Florence a new kind of elegantly crafted, self-consciously classicizing historical writing. Around the same time some of these Florentine scholars had begun to develop a new interest in the post-classical past, an interest which today we would call medievalist. The parallel streams of Renaissance medievalism and humanist historiographical technique came together in a new history of the crusades, Benedict Accolti's *De bello a christianis contra barbaros gesto pro Christi sepulchro et Iudea recuperandis*. For the most part, Accolti recasts in polished, humanist Latin, an imperfect French translation of Archbishop William of Tyre's narrative of the crusades and the crusader states which terminates in 1184. Accolti's history of the crusades appeared in 1464, the same year that Pope Pius II himself embarked on a fresh crusade against the Ottoman Turks, the still menacing conquerors of Constantinople (1453). Accolti intended to show Florence's commitment to the new crusade, while also attempting to stimulate Florentine enlistment in it. Neither then, nor for centuries afterwards, did the post-medieval west reckon that the age of the crusades had passed.[26]

Like William of Tyre, Accolti ended his chronicle before reaching the Children's Crusade, but a sixteenth-century German writer, much less gifted than Accolti, did manage to reach it. Illegitimate, impoverished, and so unable to complete an academic education either in his native Germany or in Switzerland, Johannes Basilius Herold (1514–1567) was employed as a translator, proof-reader, and editor for several Basle publishers. The author of a wide variety of works in Latin and in German, he produced "historical compilations of doubtful value."[27]

One of these was his *De bello sacro continuata historia*, written in 1549. It was intended as a supplement to William of Tyre, bringing the crusades down to 1521.[28] That both William of Tyre's and J.B. Herold's books were at some point bound together is an apt symbol of sixteenth-century perceptions of the crusades—past and present bound as one. For post-Reformation Europe, the crusades were no medieval anachronism. The anti-Turkish crusade, and with it the crusading movement, remained a living issue.

However much it lacked the eloquence of humanist historiography, Herold's *De bello sacro* was history in a rhetorical mode. For instance, by stressing the depravity of the Latin colonists in Syria—a familiar medieval theme—Herold highlights the value of moral innocence without which the Holy Land could not be secured or held. Innocence provided a smooth transition to the *pueri*.

Herold's rather incoherent narrative of the Children's Crusade fundamentally consists of embellishing his main source, Vincent of Beauvais, with additional material.[29] Thus the appearance of the "senior of the Assassins" (the Old Man of the Mountain) prompts a digression on the magic arts. The *pueri* arrive at Genoa, Marseilles, Brindisi; many settle in Narbonne, Calabria, and Liguria; others return to their homeland. "According to the example of the Hebrews," they anticipate a dry-shod crossing between parted walls of water and expect ships to come to their aid. They were "insane" and "deluded."

Herold makes two astonishing assertions. First of all, among the 7,000 *pueri* who followed Nicholas to Genoa were "many girls wearing male clothing." This mythistorical assertion of transvestism in the ranks of the *puellae*—the young females marching along in the Children's Crusade—is unique. Where it originated is open to speculation. Could it have arisen from the fact that in describing their pilgrimage and crusader insignia the Italian chroniclers did not differentiate between the genders? Second, Herold implies that *all* of Nicholas's *pueri* belonged to the German nobility. While this notion must ultimately derive from James of Varagine's Genoese chronicle, Varagine's name does not appear among Herold's authorities,[30] and Varagine says "many" (*multi*) of the *pueri* were "sons of nobles," not all.[31] Re-imagined as it was recollected, the *peregrinatio puerorum* was still capable of yielding more arresting details than contemporaries—however mythistorically inclined they were—ever dreamed of.

Another sixteenth-century historian who wrote about the German children's crusade was the Umbrian exile Pietro Bizzarri (1525–after 1586). Constrained to leave Italy because of his anti-Catholic opinions, Bizzarri wrote historical works while resident in Antwerp. Here he composed a massive, annalistic history of Genoa, the *Senatus Populique Genuensis*, which he published in 1579. His hopes that the city of Genoa would appreciate (and generously reward) his efforts were dashed when Genoa's official historiographer bitterly attacked his book, drawing attention to its pedantic style, poor historical judgment, and numerous heresies. It was this whiff of heresy which caused Bizzarri's Genoese history to be put on the Index in 1590.[32]

Viewing the Children's Crusade exclusively from a Genoese perspective, Bizzarri took his information from an unacknowledged reading of James of Varagine's Genoese chronicle, while adding some mythistorical embroidery of his own. Expatiating on the dry-shod crossing motif, he says the *pueri* believed that the drought would be intense enough that year to cause the sea to dry up from Genoa to the Holy Land, thus allowing them to walk along the dry seabed all the way to the Holy Sepulchre.

But Bizzarri's most remarkable contribution to the mythistory of the Children's Crusade is saved for last. What Varagine states, Bizzarri inflates. Varagine's "many" of the German *pueri* were nobles becomes Bizzarri's "the majority" of them. Without divulging where he got his information, he then claims to know the fate of the noblest of the new immigrants, those who chose not to return to their German homeland, but to stay on as permanent residents of Genoa. According to Bizzarri, the Genoese Senate granted them citizenship. Later, these most noble ex-*pueri* were admitted into the order of patricians.[33]

The result, or so Bizzarri maintains, was that several of the wealthiest and most powerful clans of sixteenth-century Genoa, including the illustrious house of Vivaldi, could trace their descent from the noblest of these noble German youths. Whether this was a legend circulating amongst Bizzarri's Genoese friends in Antwerp, or whether a supposed descent from veterans of the Children's Crusade, who, luckily enough, happened to be German nobles, did become part of the clan foundation myths of later-sixteenth-century Genoa, would be an interesting question to pursue.

The seventeenth-century English writer Thomas Fuller (1608–1661) was an Anglican clergyman who published more than thirty books of history, biography, treatises, and essays during an extremely productive literary career.[34] Popular in his own time, he fell out of literary favor in the eighteenth century, only to regain it in the nineteenth, when his amusing quaintness, wit, worldly wisdom and Christian morality were much admired. Coleridge put him in the same company as Shakespeare, Milton, and Defoe. Charles Lamb published witty "specimens" from Fuller's writings—e.g., *Intellect in a very tall person*: "Oft times such who are built four stories high are observed to have little in their cock-loft."[35]

Thomas Fuller's literary career began with the success of his *The Historie of the Holy Warre* (1639). Such was the demand that a fifth edition was needed in 1651. Apart from an edited translation of William of Tyre printed by William Caxton in 1481,[36] Fuller's was the earliest history of the crusades in English. Making no pretence of original research, Fuller followed the medieval authorities available to him, usually citing them in the margins. His Anglican bias can be seen in his hostile tone towards the papacy, although a similar attitude was already present in Fuller's English sources.

Fundamentally, the *Holy Warre* was a compilation dependent on medieval narratives, which robustly but fairly set out the several arguments used at the time and afterwards to justify the crusading movement ("God set his hand to this warre..."), or to condemn it ("this warre was a quicksand to swallow treasure, and of a hot digestion to devoure valiant men").[37]

Matthew Paris was the sole source for Fuller's Children's Crusade:

> ...this accident (whether monstrous or miraculous) fell out: in France, a boy (for his yeares) went about singing in his own tongue,
>
> *Jesus Lord, repair our losse,*
> *Restore to us thy holy crosse.*
>
> Numberlesse children ranne after him, and followed the same tune their captain and chanter did set them. No bolts, no barres, no fear of fathers or love of mothers could hold them back, but they would to the Holy Land to work wonders there; till their merry musick had a sad close, all either perishing on land or drowned by sea. It was done (saith my authour) by the instinct of the devil, who, as it were, desired a cordiall of childrens' bloud to comfort his weak stomach long cloyed with murdering of men.[38]

A French *puer* sings a line of English verse. But it is mistaken to think that Thomas Fuller's delightful and picturesque seventeenth-century English is simply a translation of Matthew Paris's thirteenth-century Latin.

Fuller is his own man. While Paris blames the Devil, Fuller keeps his distance ("saith my authour"). There is a suggestion of doubt ("whether monstrous or miraculous"), and even a hint of pathos (the *Table* reads: "children marching to Jerusalem wofully perish"). Finally, bloodthirsty as he is, there is something slightly comic about Fuller's English vampire. Such a piquant anecdote was bound to be remembered.

The first significant early-modern French historian to discuss the Children's Crusade at any length was the controversial Jesuit Louis Maimbourg. Although notable, his *Histoire des croisades* (1675–76) was by no means the most distinguished scholarly work produced during a century of flourishing medieval and crusade studies.[39] Medievalism, however, was not the only cause of a renewed contemporary interest in crusade history. There was a political dimension to it as well. Efforts were being made to promote a crusade against the Ottoman Turks. The young Leibniz, the papacy, and scholars like the pre-eminent Du Cange were among those seeking to push the crusade forward. In his dedicatory epistle to Louis XIV, Du Cange praised the French king by comparing him to his medieval namesake, St. Louis, while in his epistle, Maimbourg likened King Louis to the heroic crusaders of the medieval past.[40]

Louis Maimbourg (1610–1686) was a prolific author of church histories. Because of his Gallican sympathies, he was expelled from the Society of Jesus in 1681 and several of his works—but not his history of the crusades—were placed on the Index. Louis XIV, however, granted him a pension,[41] and his ecclesiastical histories gained an influential secular readership. Fueter says of Maimbourg: "he knew how to satisfy the taste of the *grand monde*."[42] Indeed, a certain eighteenth-century gentleman from Virginia, one Thomas Jefferson by name, owned a set of Maimbourg's *Histoire des croisades*.[43] Maimbourg's *pueri* crossed the Atlantic more easily than they traversed the Mediterranean.

The most gripping part of Maimbourg's narrative of the *peregrinatio puerorum* was its tragic finale. This was appropriated from Alberic of Trois-Fontaines, but from an Alberic stripped of many of his mythistorical details. Evidently, these were no longer plausible. Partially concealed under Maimbourg's traditional theological certainties, a rationalizing historiography was at work. Items now perceived as incredible were excised to make way for a new narrative rationality. By the third quarter of the seventeenth century, the story of the Children's Crusade needed re-editing.

Maimbourg's crusade "of young children" was a "strange illusion, or rather, kind of frenzy, which spread like a plague." The Devil has vanished. Where he stood, inexplicable secular phenomena now defined the nature of the movement; but these secular agencies functioned no less mysteriously than the Devil once did. Maimbourg differs from previous historians of the *pueri* in another respect. He isolates an event which he thinks precipitated the enthusiasm. According to Maimbourg, what provoked the "disorder" were letters sent by Pope Innocent III to "all Christians." It is unclear, but he may have been referring to the papal summons for the Fifth Crusade in 1213. In that case, his chronology is to blame. His Children's Crusade occurs in 1213.[44] Nevertheless, the suggestion of a precipitating event is a milestone in the modern historiography of the *pueri*.

"Disorder" was abhorrent to Maimbourg. So the unhappy outcome of the Children's Crusade ("one of the greatest disorders that had been seen in all the previous Crusades") both validates the providential order and allows him to conclude on a theologically optimistic note:

> It is true [says Maimbourg] that God... derived this benefit from so great a disorder... that a number of these poor innocents, whom these Infidels wished to make renounce the faith persisted [in it] ...so that they were chopped to pieces rather than abandon...[Christ] and thus became Martyrs by a fortunate consequence of their fantastic and entirely irregular undertaking.[45]

Condemning "so great a disorder," Maimbourg simultaneously celebrates its victims. As to their brutal deaths, it could be that Maimbourg was recalling his former confrères, the Jesuit missionary martyrs of Japan, as well as the Japanese lads crucified among them.

Voltaire and the Enlightenment

Voltaire (1694–1778) was too much of an Enlightenment ideologue ever to be a medievalist, although his far from uninformed, shrewdly pointed rationalist observations, combined with a fierce antipathy to the medieval outlook, paradoxically contributed to the romantic reaction in favor of medieval studies (Figure 11). In spite of a strong current of Enlightenment anti-medievalism, literary and scholarly medievalism by no means ceased during the eighteenth century.[46] And even Voltaire, who greatly admired the erudite philological research of Du Cange, considered the Middle Ages worthy of serious historical study.[47] In seach of appropriate material on the crusades and other medieval topics for his path-breaking history of civilization, the *Essai sur les moeurs et l'esprit des nations* (1756), Voltaire carefully quarried the ecclesiastical history of Claude Fleury, while at the same time deriding Fleury's failings as a historian.[48]

Figure 11 Jean-Antoine Houdon, Bust of Voltaire (1781).

Amongst Voltaire's historical works is a scarcely known history of the crusades, for which one of his major sources was Fleury. Voltaire's criticisms of the crusade, however, were far more stinging and ironic than Fleury's.[49] Initially published in 1750–51,[50] Voltaire's *Histoire des croisades* was appended to his *Micromégas* the following year, and subsequently incorporated in his *Essai sur les moeurs*. Before the *Essai* appeared in print, many of his caustic observations on the crusades had already found their way into the article "Croisades" in Volume 4 (1754) of Diderot's and D'Alembert's great vehicle of the Enlightenment, the *Encyclopèdie*. From the relevant passage in the *Histoire*, which was reproduced in the *Essai*, it is plain that the few lines he wrote on the Children's Crusade were derived neither from Maimbourg nor Fleury. Rather, when he writes about the *pueri*, Voltaire seems to be bringing together garbled notes from the chroniclers (or from an unknown intermediate source) plus the workings of his own imagination:

> The widow of a King of Hungary took the cross with a few women, believing that heaven could be gained only through this journey. She died at Ptolemaïs [Acre]. This *maladie épidémique* [epidemic disease—meaning crusade enthusiasm] spread even to children. Thousands of them, led by their schoolmasters and monks, left their parents's homes on the faith of these words: "Lord, you have drawn your glory from children." Their leaders sold some of them to the Mussulmen; the rest died of poverty.[51]

Maladie épidémique recurs more than once in Voltaire's crusade history. It sums up his Enlightenment view of collective religious enthusiasm or fanaticism.[52]

Matthew Paris, who calls the leader of the *pueri* their "teacher" and "master," was possibly the source of Voltaire's "schoolmasters." But where did that unbiblical verse "Lord, you have drawn your glory from children" come from? Voltaire himself? Unlike Maimbourg, Voltaire blames the clergy for betraying the *pueri* to the Saracens.

The *Encyclopèdie* goes badly, ludicrously, wrong when it seeks to reproduce Voltaire on the Children's Crusade:

> A Queen of Hungary took the cross with some of her women. She died at Ptolemaïs of an epidemic disease, which carried off thousands of children conducted into these territories by monks and schoolmasters. There has never been an instance of madness (*frénésie*) so unvarying and so general.[53]

Surprisingly, the redactor of the *Encyclopèdie* article, who misunderstood Voltaire's *maladie épidémique*—turning it into a real disease which killed thousands of children—was none other than Diderot himself.[54] Nevertheless, the fact that the Children's Crusade is singled out as an unprecedented example of collective madness maintains the spirit of Voltairean rationalism.

Claude Millot's *Élémens de l'historie de France* (1768) was one of the earliest French national histories to allude to "the ridiculous Children's Crusade." More than 50,000 strong, they were led by "a great number of priests."[55] The prevailing view of the medieval chroniclers is thus turned upside down. Instead of the *pueri* defying clerical authority, they fall victim to it. What we now have is collective irrationality manipulated by clerics, the formula which perhaps best encapsulates Voltaire's and the Enlightenment's attitude towards the Children's Crusade.

9
Memory: The Echo of the Centuries—Nineteenth to Twentieth

Bonaparte's Egyptian expedition of 1798–99 may not have led to the recapture of Jerusalem, nor even to the reconquest of Acre, but its galvanizing impact upon French orientalism and with it the historiography of the crusades is indisputable. Oriental learning, once placed at the service of imperial power, not only became less exotic, but even assumed contemporary relevance in a new age of European expansion.[1] Napoleon's campaign in Egypt, rekindling, as it did, memories of St. Louis's Egyptian crusade, also helped to revivify crusade studies. The Enlightenment interpretation of the crusades was perceived to be inadequate, and the European significance of the crusading movement once more became an intellectual and historiographical problem. In 1806 the Institut de France announced a prize essay competition concerning "the influence of the crusades on the civil liberty of the peoples of Europe, upon their civilization, and upon the progress of their culture, commerce, and industry."[2] The very wording of the essay proposal implies a complete redirection of emphasis away from the primarily negative views of the French Enlightenment. But the salient factor in challenging the dominance of the Enlightenment assault upon the Middle Ages was the coming of romanticism, and without a doubt the growth of an idealized, conservative medievalism owed a very great deal to the romantic Christian inspiration of Vicomte François René de Chateaubriand (1768–1848).

Nineteenth-century romantic medievalism

Chateaubriand's highly-colored, aesthetic apologia for Christianity, the *Génie du Christianisme*, was published in 1802. In G.P. Gooch's judgment, "few books possess less of the historical spirit, but few have had a more far-reaching influence on historical studies."[3] Chateaubriand was one of the seminal figures who, like Sir Walter Scott, ushered in the new romantic appreciation for the Middle Ages. In the *Génie* his allusions to the crusades are not especially numerous, but they occur, significantly, in the midst of discussions of heroic poetry and of chivalric, Christian valor. According to Chateaubriand, Tasso's sixteenth-century masterpiece *Jerusalem Delivered* showed that the crusades could inspire the highest literary art. "In modern times," writes Chateaubriand, "there are only two noble subjects for epic poetry, the crusades and the discovery of the new world."[4] The crusades belonged to Chateaubriand's idealized Christian past.

Inspired by Chateaubriand's, anti-revolutionary, romantic vision of the Christian Middle Ages, the conservative Parisian journalist and editor Joseph-François Michaud (1767–1839), a Catholic royalist who survived a death sentence in the French Revolution, began work on his multi-volumed *Histoire des Croisades*, which appeared between 1811 and 1822 and went through five editions in his lifetime, with a sixth edition issued posthumously in 1840. Michaud was made a Member of the Académie Française in 1813, and his *Croisades* earned the warm praise of both Chateaubriand and Pope Gregory XVI.[5]

The book attracted a readership which was learning to share the same romantic vision as its author. Michaud gave his readers a view of the medieval crusading era as a marvelous, absorbing spectacle, strange and distant from the present. At the same time, he retained the Enlightenment's legacy of judging the past, however anachronistically, according to notions of human progress. Nostalgia for a vanished age and sympathy for its beliefs were thus held in unresolved tension with a reasoned critique of the past—the heritage of the *philosophes*—but moderate in tone rather than polemically shrill. Michaud himself, aware of this tension, articulated it as a conflict between "reason," which severely censured the barbarism of feudal mores, and "imagination," which took its poetic and patriotic inspiration from the "spectacle of generous passions" and ancestral deeds of prowess of medieval times.[6]

Michaud takes up the story of the Children's Crusade, the like of which, he says, "had never occurred even in times so abounding in prodigies and extraordinary events." This "juvenile militia" sprang into being because "some ecclesiastics blinded by false zeal had preached this crusade." Even if Michaud does reproach these (unidentified) clerics, his rebuke is much less barbed than eighteenth-century accusations of deliberate trickery or betrayal. Although Michaud maintains the Enlightenment belief in the clerical initiation of the enthusiasm, he perceptibly softens the harshness of its censure. In fact, it is the tone of Michaud's version of the Children's Crusade which is new; and it is this tone which so well illustrates the romantic historical sensibility. For here the dominant note is one of sympathetic tenderness towards these victims and martyrs, espousing high ideals, who came to grief at such an early age:

> Most of the faithful... thought that Jesus Christ... to confound the pride of the greatest captains and of the... powerful of the earth, had placed his cause in the hands of simple and timid infancy (*enfance*). Many women of bad character and dishonest men insinuated themselves amongst the crowd of these new soldiers of the cross to seduce and plunder them.... Many of these young crusaders lost themselves in forests, then so abundant and large, and wandering about at hazard, perished... Many, say the old chronicles... offered the infidels the edifying spectacle of the firmness and courage the Christian religion is capable of inspiring at the most tender age as well as at the more mature.

Evoking the lamentable fate of "these young crusaders" as they expired against the spectacular backdrop of vast primeval forests, or were slain by infidels, Michaud's sympathy for these child-martyrs quickly yields to "terror" and "astonishment" (reactions which he ascribes to others, but which reflect his own indignation) at the failure of civil or ecclesiastical authority to intervene and "to stop or prevent the madness."[7]

Supplementing Michaud's account of the Children's Crusade is an essay marking the first attempt at a scholarly discussion, as opposed to narrative, of the *pueri*. The essay took the form of a "Lettre à M. Michaud sur la croisade d'enfans de 1212," written by the rising young orientalist Amable Jourdain (1788–1818). Jourdain, as a learned orientalist, might have been expected to qualify the chroniclers' reports of what the *pueri* suffered at the hands of the Saracens and Assassins. Jourdain is aware of such an expectation, but admits that, in the absence of a "more extended examination," the accounts of the thirteenth-century chroniclers cannot be rejected. So this modern orientalist makes no attempt to banish the medieval stereotype of the cruel Muslims.[8]

Yes, there was a Children's Crusade. This is something which Jourdain feels compelled to affirm, despite his initial disbelief. And like the medieval chroniclers, both Michaud and Jourdain also stress just how untypical, indeed unique, this popular crusade was. History's plausibility as a truthful account of real experience must not be jeopardized.

Academic professionalism in nineteenth-century Germany

Michaud was a man of letters who became a historian. In contrast to Michaud, Friedrich Wilken (1777–1840), whose crusade scholarship Michaud knew and admired, was a university-trained academic historian. His professional career was successful—Professor at Heidelberg and Berlin, librarian of the Royal Library of Berlin[9]—at a time when the German ascendancy in European historiography was poised for take-off. With the next generation, dominated by Leopold von Ranke, German historical scholarship would triumph, and with it the seminar, the Ph.D., and the footnote.

Wilken's unfeigned sympathy for the Middle Ages links him firmly to the scholars of the romantic school. Heinrich von Sybel, Ranke's student and the leading crusade historian of his generation, critical as he was of Wilken's inadequate control over his materials and his failure to establish sufficient distance between past and present, nevertheless appreciated his considerable gifts as a crusade historian. "Wilken," said von Sybel, "unquestionably far surpasses all his predecessors."[10]

In Volume 6 of his *Geschichte der Kreuzzüge* (*History of the Crusades*) (seven vols., 1807–32), Wilken devotes about twelve pages to the Children's Crusade, making it the first comprehensive scholarly account of the *pueri*.[11] The result was that for later writers, scholarly as well as popular, Wilken's narrative was the logical starting point. The relevant historical literature was slight, but Wilken, like a good academic historian, went directly to the primary sources, which he plundered in the most inclusive, and also the most indiscriminate fashion. One moment he was closely following a reliable chronicler; then, disconcertingly, the next moment he was paraphrasing an arch-mythistorian. Yet this does not seem to have diminished Wilken's authority. Numerous scholars and popular writers who, intellectually intimidated perhaps, or intellectually lazy, took his account of the Children's Crusade and served it up as their own.

Wilken's fundamental narrative pattern would remain standard until the 1960s. Choosing not to encumber his discourse with excessive rhetoric or affecting set-pieces, Wilken was still sympathetic to the *pueri* and what he perceived to be their aims. The origins of their crusading fervor he situates in the midst of Innocent III's activities to assist the Holy Land. While the great and the powerful absented themselves from the crusades, he argues, many (unspecified) pilgrimages and processions took place to implore divine assistance for the liberation of Jerusalem. All of this agitation, he believes, must have worked into the minds and hearts of the children, so that they believed they would accomplish what kings and princes had failed to do. Freeing the Holy Land was their primary motive. The resulting debacle is recounted according to the mythistorians, save for a few objections or qualifications inserted in the notes.[12] Innocent III summons a great crusade the following year. To Wilken, therefore, the plight of the Holy Land created an intelligible and symmetrical framework for the crusade of the *pueri*.

One or two points from Wilken's classic reconstruction of the Children's Crusade are worth noting. According to him, the enthusiasm arose in France (Stephen) and afterwards spread to Germany (Nicholas), but there is no indication of how the crusading enthusiasm traveled from France to the Rhineland. Nevertheless, the French and the German movements remain distinct. The social dimension of the movement is almost wholly ignored. Yet Wilken does note that the laity and clergy had opposing attitudes towards the *pueri*, and that led to tension between them.[13]

Most remarkable about Wilken's Children's Crusade—and where it differs sharply from previous versions, medieval or modern—is the author's refusal to draw any explicit moral from his story. This was his calling card as a professional historian. In his narrative, the outcome is more than sufficient to convey its meaning.

Justus Friedrich Karl Hecker (1795–1850) was a German physician, and a historian of medicine and pathology.[14] Medieval epidemics like the Black Death interested him, but medieval "epidemics" more so. These were seemingly inexplicable, collective phenomena, such as the late-fourteenth-century dancing mania, as it was known.[15] Hecker's approach combined the developing medical science of his day with a broad interest in the history of behavior. He seems to have been in search of a new discipline. It would be a kind of crowd psychopathology based on historical research. Voltaire's reference to the Children's Crusade as a *maladie épidémique* was metaphorical and ironic. Conversely, for the sober, literal-minded Dr. Hecker, movements of medieval collective enthusiasm were contagious "nervous disorders" attributable to religious emotions.

Hecker believed that such movements had just as much right to be called epidemic diseases as "the English sweat" (sweating sickness). Hecker's "historical-pathological" study of medieval child-pilgrimages first appeared in 1845, supplemented by extracts from selected medieval chroniclers of the *pueri*.[16] It was translated into English in 1859 as a chapter of his *Epidemics of the Middle Ages*.[17] Hecker's work thus belongs to a period of experimentation in historiography, as it does to the age of Louis Pasteur.

Hecker's Children's Crusade was unquestionably one of "those morbid phenomena" which are "often nothing more than the physical consequences of a nervous irritant," namely, "the religious emotions on their pathological side."[18] Hecker names no historical sources, primary or secondary, but his leading authority was presumably Wilken. Says Hecker: "in the year 1212... some outbreak of... overstrained feelings could not be long deferred." This "religious intoxication" was centered on the plight of Jerusalem, which "took hold of men's minds at that time...." And who are known to be among the most susceptible to religious emotionalism? Children, of course:

> Whoever observes children attentively sees readily that they in their own fashion decidedly sympathize with all the excitements of adults and for this reason that the strongest impulse in them is that of imitation.

Because of their tender nervous systems, children are readily overcome by "religious and political passions."[19]

Tracing the *pueri* to Genoa, Hecker accepts a variant of James of Varagine's mythistorical text, so that Hecker's German noblemen kindly provide their crusading young sons not only with guides and nurses, but also with "the usual swarms of sisters-errant." But why? The answer is simple. "In Genoa it was believed that thoughtful parents had... been mindful of the entertainment which companions of this sort could offer them."[20] The founding father of psychohistory was not J.F.K. Hecker.

Nineteenth-century popular history and historical fiction

Johann Sporschil (1800–1863) was an Austrian writer and prolific popular historian of quickly-written and soon-forgotten works.[21] His *Geschichte der Kreuzzüge* (1843), copiously illustrated with engravings by J. Kirchhoff, recounts the history of the crusading movement from Peter the Hermit to the fall of Acre. In his 578 pages, he devotes a little more than two of them, plus an illustration (Figure 12), to the Children's Crusade. Yet into his two and a quarter pages Sporschil crams six primary sources, along with Pietro Bizzarri, although he is chiefly indebted to Wilken. Sporschil ventures a single original observation. Commenting on the Anonymous chronicler of Laon, he remarks that if Stephen of Cloyes had truly received letters for the King of France, then, in an age when the clergy alone were literate, priests were involved in it.[22]

Not Wilken's, but Hecker's psychology of the Children's Crusade must have rubbed off on James M. Ludlow's popular *The Age of the Crusades* of 1897.[23] A Victorian author who specialized in historical romances,

Figure 12 J. Kirchhoff, *Kreuzzug der Kinder*, steel engraving from Joh. Sporschil, *Geschichte der Kreuzzüge* (1843).

Ludlow, as Hecker did, stressed the imitative capacity of children. Crusading, and the Albigensian crusade in particular, was child's play: "Boys practised their sword-thrust at one another's throats, built their pile of faggots about the stake of some imaginary heretic, and charged in mimic brigades upon phantom hosts of Infidels."

Then, after "the impassioned appeals of unwise preachers," the Children's Crusade sallied forth. Did Ludlow come under the spell of Charles Dickens's *Oliver Twist* (1839)? Ludlow's Children's Crusade includes Fagin-esque vultures: "The real leaders... seem to have been men and women of disorderly habits, who... adopted the lives of tramps, and used the pitiable appearance of the children to secure the charities of the towns and cities they passed through."

Earlier in the Victorian era, the Rev. William E. Dutton wrote a popular *History of the Crusades* (1877), sentimentalizing the Children's Crusade according to the prevailing myths of childhood. "Child-preachers" used "language of so much tenderness and force" that "vast numbers" of children enrolled, and "devoted mothers willingly gave up their little ones." Medieval chroniclers would have been astounded.

Stephen of Cloyes' portrait is just as original:

> [The] shepherd-boy... wore a garb of sheepskin, and bore a banner, embroidered with a picture of the Lamb of God.... [H]e was a child of wondrous gifts, possessing a wild, sweet voice, and such a marvellous power of oratory that not only children, but strong men and women were moved....[24]

So far as we know, no "Lamb of God" banner was ever unfurled in the Children's Crusade. It belongs to the Shepherds' Crusade. The beauty of Stephen's voice and his crowd-captivating eloquence belong to the Rev. Dutton.

The poet Alfred des Essarts (1811–1893), "attached by inspiration and style to the romantic school," published his feeble, highly fictionalized *Croisade des enfants (1213)* in 1862; but it failed to secure the Children's Crusade a niche in French literature.[25] That honor belongs to the symbolist writer Marcel Schwob (1867–1905), the translator of Robert Louis Stevenson and co-translator of *Hamlet*. Schwob's "miraculous little book" *La croisade des enfants* appeared in 1896. Later, it was rewritten for Gabriel Pierné's oratorio of the same name (1905).[26]

History was what excited the romantic imagination of this lyrical writer, and from his *Croisade des enfants* it is clear that Schwob read at least some of the Latin chroniclers of 1212. Not unexpectedly, given the way one storyteller instinctively responds to another, he was particularly taken by the mythistorian Alberic of Trois-Fontaines.

There are eight very short chapters, all *récits* or tales told by a single character who encounters the children: the goliard, the leper, Pope Innocent III ("Lord, I am very old, and here before Thee I stand, dressed in white, and my name is Innocent"), three little children ("We have been walking a long time. White voices called us in the night"), François Longuejoue (the clerk of one of Alberic's Marseilles villains), the Calendar's tale—the children as viewed by a Muslim beggar and holy man, little Allys, and Gregory IX, the Pope who, says Alberic, dedicated a church to the New Innocents.

A passage from the *récit* of the goliard illustrates the affecting simplicity and naive lyricism of Schwob's evocative prose poem, which, on the whole, is remarkably free of what Flaubert called *haschich historique*:

> All these children seemed nameless to me. And it is certain that Our Lord Jesus prefers them. They filled the road like a swarm of white bees. I know not whence they came. They were very small pilgrims.... They have faith in Jerusalem.[27]

The theme of whiteness, beloved of symbolists, runs through the book like a refrain. When Schwob sent his friend Paul Claudel a copy of the *Croisade des enfants*, Claudel replied with a Proust-like reflection on the difficulty of seizing the sense of times past, of capturing the "pity of that which no longer is." He thought this "whiteness of the little children" not so much "the ingenuousness of innocence" as "absolution."[28]

The author of a book on biblical doctrine and another on the theory of marriage, George Zabriskie Gray (1838–1889), Professor of Systematic Divinity and Dean of the Episcopal Theological School in Cambridge, Massachusetts, was well-liked by his students and "a broad and liberal-minded churchman."[29] He was not, however, a historian, and certainly no medievalist.

Gray, nevertheless, was correct in thinking that no one before him had set out to produce a single volume of history on the popular crusade of 1212. Furthermore, out of fairness to him, it should be remembered that at the time he was carrying out his research the earliest scholarly article written for the learned journals, Röhricht's (1876), was still to come. Yet, in spite of all his industrious reading of German scholars like Wilken and Hecker, he has rightly been accused of using "good, bad, and indifferent sources with equal confidence."[30] All in all, it has to be said that Gray's *The Children's Crusade: An Episode of the Thirteenth Century* is at best popular history—a simple tale, simply told.[31] The one bee buzzing in Gray's broad church bonnet is anti-Romanism. In *The Children's Crusade* his anti-Roman prejudice was sufficiently undisguised for an anonymous contemporary reviewer of the London *Saturday Review* to decry "Mr. Gray's gratuitous, not to say absurd, suggestion that the movement [of the *pueri*] was deliberately planned by the emissaries of Innocent III"; in fact, Pope Innocent is "Mr. Gray's *bête noire* throughout."[32]

Following Wilken, Gray looks to the beleaguered Holy Land, where Christian prisoners were groaning in captivity, to discover the crusading background of the Children's Crusade. Hence Stephen attends the major litanies on St. Mark's Day (April 25), at which, Gray supposes, the martyrs who died to defend the Holy Land were commemorated with black crosses, and God's mercy was invoked on the suffering eastern Christians.[33] In reality, these black crosses—the *croiz noires* which Joinville refers to in his life of St. Louis—had nothing whatsoever to do with crusading martyrs.[34] Then, when Stephen returns home he encounters a man posing as a pilgrim, who "undoubtedly" was "a disguised priest." Stephen then goes to Saint-Denis, where his preaching and his miracles cause his message to spread quickly eastwards to Cologne, where Nicholas, the emulator of Stephen, also preaches. "All the chroniclers agree," Gray asserts, "Stephen indicated Vendôme as the place of assembling and of united departure for Palestine."[35] None of the chroniclers say anything of the sort. Borrowing the motif from Matthew Paris's mythistorical account, Gray has Stephen travel towards the Holy Land in a splendid, canopy-draped chariot; around it, "to guard him... there rode a band of chosen youths of noble birth" (Figure 13).[36] In presenting the traditional picture of the sad fate of the enthusiasm, Gray remains unswervingly faithful to the tragic tale of Alberic of Trois-Fontaines. He milks the pathos of their situation for all it is worth.

However severely limited it was as history, Gray's *Children's Crusade* did much to familiarize the English-speaking world with the story of the *pueri*, and it was a story which would be remembered. At one time many readers—including historians—drew their knowledge and impressions of the popular crusade of 1212 exclusively from Gray. Since then, things have moved on.

A dreadful warning? The *pueri* in children's literature

There is no room for them here, alas, but the many children's encyclopedias which continued to appear were undoubtedly important in keeping the memory of the *pueri* alive. More important still were the undisguised

STEPHEN ENLISTING BOYS AND GIRLS FOR THE CHILDREN'S CRUSADE.

Figure 13 Stephen enlisting boys and girls for the Children's Crusade from A.J. Church, *The Crusaders: A Story of the War for the Holy Sepulchre* (1905).

fictions of children's books. Perhaps their lasting significance lies in the fact that children occasionally turn into adults. A degree of exposure to the story in childhood—or as parental or grandparental readers to children—familiarized adults with at least its rough outlines.[37] As a result, the mythistory of the *pueri* gradually became part of the baggage of western culture, like traditional fairy stories or the classical myths. So, from the mid-nineteenth to the late twentieth century, the way children's authors re-imagined the *pueri* not only tells us something about these writers, but about their readers as well.

René the Young Crusader was originally published in German by the Rev. Christian G. Barth (1799–1862), an author of church histories and Christian tracts. An English translation appeared in 1844.[38] The hero, René, is a youthful French Waldensian forced to flee to Germany, when Pope Innocent III preached a crusade against heretics in 1209. René hears about Stephen's Children's Crusade which spreads to Germany, and he joins it, despite Waldensian disapproval. Enslaved by an Egyptian emir, René eventually becomes convinced that "God took no pleasure in this enterprise." Joining it had been wrong. Even though the emir treats him like a beloved and trusted servant, René refuses to convert to Islam and remains his captive to the end. The author views René's plight as the consequence of irrational fanaticism which the medieval Waldensians never embraced. They were proto-Protestants. The Rev. Barth thought well of them.

Dedicated to the author's Canadian grandchildren, *The Crusaders: A Story of the War for the Holy Sepulchre* (1905) was written by another minister, the Rev. A.J. Church, formerly professor of Latin in University College, London. Ingeniously, Church makes use of the Wandering Jew—a figure introduced into English mythistoriography by Matthew Paris's visiting Armenian bishop[39]—to relate the story of the crusades. When we reach "the children crusaders," the Wandering Jew is residing in Baghdad with a Christian former slave, a Frenchman, who long ago had been Stephen's friend and companion. He tells him Stephen "thought overmuch of himself, and was too much bent on gaining fame and power for himself." This tale of overweening ambition naturally ends in disaster. After the Wandering Jew leaves Baghdad, he learns that the Christians of the city have been slaughtered.[40]

Evelyn Everett-Green's *The Children's Crusade: A Story of Adventure* (1905) begins when a foreign lad, Angelo, announces: "I come with a message to the boys of England. The Holy Father has called upon the children of Christendom, and by their thousands they are answering the call."[41] Sadly, the boys of England fail to heed the call, save for Eric and Roy, who embark upon a long series of mishaps and escapes in the East. They fight alongside Prince Firuz until the crusader Sir Julian Montjoy rescues them. Eric becomes Sir Eric. This is a book which gives the reader exactly what it promises—the Children's Crusade as a *Boy's Own* adventure.

"The most wonderful crusade of all—that of the children" was preached by "a half-crazy priest named Nicholas." The tale of the *pueri* in Estelle Blyth's *Jerusalem and the Crusades* (1913) starts out as an adventure. Then misery is piled upon misery. It makes quite an edifying bedtime story:[42]

> After these helpless little crusaders there crept a dark stream of thieves, cut-throats, and bad people of all sorts, who robbed and murdered them without mercy. Many of the children died of the hardships of the journey, the long hours of trudging over rough ground, and wading through ice-cold streams... Many of them must have longed for the safe shelter of homes and mothers, as they huddled together, trembling and afraid, through the long dark night.[43]

Still to come were the slave markets of Egypt and a lifetime of servitude.[44] Pleasant dreams, children.

Henry Bordeaux, member of the Académie française, sets his pious *Nouvelle croisade des enfants* (1913) in the Savoyard village of Avrieux, basing it upon an actual Roman pilgrimage of young French Catholics that had taken place the previous year. This child-pilgrimage of 1912 calls to mind the child-crusaders of 1212. Thus Bordeaux cleverly situates the medieval pilgrimage of the *pueri* within the contemporary context of the pilgrimage of modern Catholic youths. The latter culminates in far happier circumstances with a benevolent discourse from the pope at the Sistine Chapel. The imagination of the Savoyard children who come to participate in this "new children's crusade" is kindled at school. It is at school that they discover the story of the enthusiasm of the medieval child-pilgrims from "the learned and picturesque work of M. Luchaire."[45] What is remarkable here is not so much the explicit link between the medieval past and the early-twentieth-century present, but the complete rehabilitation of the *enfants* of 1212, whose idealism is implicitly held up as a model for Christian youth.

In Eileen Heming's *Joan's Crusade* (1947), two village girls, Joan (aged nine) and Wendy (aged eight), after a history lesson at school, start reading a book about the Children's Crusade. In it, a monk preaches to a crowd of youngsters, declaring that "he'd take an army of children, because children hadn't had time to grow wicked." Says Wendy: "he must have been bats! Most of the children I know are wickeder than grownups. The boys are, anyway." When "something, somewhere" goes wrong with the Children's Crusade, the two girls decide to go on a crusade of their own to help people. Things then become Sunday-Schoolish....[46]

After the General Assembly of the United Nations proclaimed 1979 the "International Year of the Child,"[47] UNESCO invited the Scottish Youth Theatre to stage Paul Thompson's *The Children's Crusade*, a play first performed in London six years earlier. So it was during the "Year of the Child" that the Children's Crusade arrived in Edinburgh. Thompson is perceptive ("It is almost impossible to separate the myth [of 1212] from the reality"), but disclaims fidelity to historical facts. His play focuses exclusively on the German enthusiasts, and his premise is that the enthusiasm began out of disillusionment with the Fourth Crusade. He treats his medieval play "as a modern subject—the story of a generation in revolt against the corrupt world of their elders."

This means that the key dramatic encounter of the play occurs between the commercially-minded Genoese (evidently modeled upon the Venetians of the Fourth Crusade) and the idealistic German *pueri*, who in the Edinburgh production were led, not by Nicholas, but—a nice touch this—by Nicola of Cologne. Paul Thompson's *Children's Crusade* is a play imbued with the spirit of the generational conflict and revolutionary fervor of the late Sixties. Or as Ron Daniels, its London director, puts it: "*The Children's Crusade* is a story about growing up—of starting out in life full of ideals... [then] being... destroyed in a society which values only the power of money."[48]

To judge from children's literature over the past 150 years or so, the meaning of the Children's Crusade was constantly open to negotiation. Whether due to authorial intentions or historical circumstances or a combination of both, there were radical changes of perspective. Child readers or hearers of the story learned that it was really religion gone mad, an ego trip, great fun, a sentimental tear-jerker and cautionary tale, an inspiration, a voluntary project, or a protest song. Surviving so many metamorphoses relatively unscathed testifies to a powerful storyline, for somehow the *pueri* retained their identity. And everyone knows that children's literature makes an excellent adhesive—perfect for sticking things in the memory.[49]

Twentieth-century voices: historians, poets, composers

These are solo voices, not a choir. Nor is it an all-inclusive roll call. For the historians alone, a proper historiographical survey would have to stretch from Paul Alphandéry to Jean Richard in France, and from Adolf Waas to Hans Eberhard Mayer in Germany. For other countries, similar lists of respected crusade historians could easily be compiled. Instead, here is an eccentric trio of British historians, one rank amateur sandwiched between two professionals. The reason for their selection is uncomplicated. What they wrote was read far beyond the Groves of Academe.

Sir Ernest Barker (1874–1960), principal of King's College, London (1920–28), and professor of political science at Cambridge (1928–39) was a remarkable English polymath. It was said that his career, as a classical scholar, medievalist, educationalist, and political and social theorist, represented "a protest against excessive departmentalism in learning."[50] Barker's article on the "Crusades" appeared in the classic eleventh edition of the *Encyclopaedia Britannica* (1910). Essentially unchanged, it was reissued as a small book under the title *The Crusades* and reprinted as late as 1939.[51] Historiographically, what sets it apart is its author's aphoristic judgments ("It is simplest, as it is truest, to say that the crusades did not fail—they simply ceased; and they ceased because they were no longer in joint with the times"),[52] together with his efforts to seize the crusading movement as more than a series of events.

In the course of his exposition he includes a short synopsis of the Children's Crusade, which begins with Innocent III (who "could never consent to forget Jerusalem, as long as his right hand retained its cunning") and ends with Innocent as well ("the pathos of the children's crusade of 1212 only nerved him to fresh efforts"). With unusual insight he counts it among those "outbursts of the revivalist element, which always accompanied the crusades" and sees its "after-echo in the legend of the Pied Piper of Hamelin."[53] His concise narrative is shorn of the chroniclers' moralizing over the movement's supposedly miserable outcome. Yet "the pathos of the children's crusade" is neither Innocentian, nor especially medieval. It is Barker's.

H.G. Wells's (1866–1946) unlikely best-seller, *The Outline of History* (1920), was never intended to be more than a work of democratic popularization. Its scholarship was third-hand. Yet it became "immensely popular," selling "over two million copies in England and America alone." Easily surpassing the sales of all of Wells's previous novels and short stories, *The Outline of History* made him a rich man and transformed him into a humanitarian sage with a global vision.[54] Wells acknowledged four consultants as having assisted him in the writing (i.e. the compilation) of *The Outline*. Heading the list is Sir Ernest Barker.[55]

Wells was no Gibbon. Nevertheless, his aims in *The Outline* were humanistic, and his ambition, to show mankind the way forward after the carnage of the Great War, was courageous.[56] Wells curiously resembles the medieval universal chroniclers who began with Creation and slowly proceeded to their own times, borrowing whatever was needed along the way from a succession of writers, biblical or secular, famous or obscure, until first-hand experiences or contemporary anxieties started to bite. So Wells's liberal variant on the Christian providential scheme commences, not with Creation, but with its perfect modern analogue, the post-Darwinian origins of life on earth. His world-historical climax is what amounts to the European Apocalypse ("the catastrophe of 1914"). Concluding *The Outline of History* is a millenarian chapter dedicated to "the possible unification of the world into one community of knowledge and will" which offers a utopian vision of "the leadership of man... unified, disciplined, armed with the secret powers of the atom...."[57] Such was the inter-war optimism of Wells's prophetic vision.

During his trans-Siberian voyage across human history, Wells finds time for a six-sentence précis of Barker's Children's Crusade, calling it "a dreadful thing," a "strange business."[58] What H.G. Wells gave his popular readership was journalism—the digest of a lurid medieval crime—and an image of crusading worthy of Hecker ("an excitement that could no longer affect sane adults"). But the huge sales of Wells's *The Outline of History* guaranteed that this bizarre incident was now securely locked in the public memory of Anglo-American culture.

The internationally celebrated Byzantinist and crusade historian Sir Steven Runciman (1903–2000) was the aristocratic heir to the nineteenth-century English tradition of romantic philhellenism. He was blessed (or cursed) with an enviably readable, fluent narrative style. Unsurprisingly, Runciman's sympathies in his acclaimed *History of the Crusades* (three volumes, 1951–54, reissued several times, and still in print) are rooted in the Byzantine East. A ringing denunciation of the entire crusading tradition concludes his final volume ("the Holy War itself was nothing more than a long act of intolerance in the name of God...").[59] His moral imperative is never in doubt.

Runciman devotes six pages in the final volume of his crusade epic to the Children's Crusade. The only chronicler he names is Albert of Stade; nor are there signs of his having exploited the two twentieth-century studies of the Children's Crusade that he cites.[60] Unfortunately, his "story of the children's crusade" is just that—mythistory, not history. The events are uncontextualized, no historical problems are located, so none can be addressed, and trustworthy information is indiscriminately conflated with the colorful, unverifiable assertions of the classic mythistorians. Runciman's picturesque details cannot be found in the medieval sources.

Two examples: Stephen's *pueri* were to assemble at Vendôme to set off for the East together; and each band of *pueri* had a leader "carrying a copy of the Oriflamme, which Stephen took as the device of the crusade."[61] So where did Runciman unearth these "facts"? Almost certainly they came from a book which is nowhere cited. That is so because by the time Runciman was writing, that book was no longer considered respectable—George Gray's *The Children's Crusade*.[62] Fate has not been kind to Sir Steven's Children's Crusade. "A somewhat fanciful version," says one scholar; "singularly fantastic," says another.[63]

Questions of its historicity—or mythistoricity—aside, Sir Steven's tale is very well-told. Innumerable readers would find it memorable. Following in the footsteps of Matthew Paris and Thomas Fuller, Runciman remained as faithful to the English tradition of mythistoricizing the Children's Crusade as he was to nineteenth-century English romantic philhellenism.[64]

Even more artful than the fictions of historians are those of the poets and composers who have clasped the Children's Crusade to their bosoms. The Italian poet Gabriele D'Annunzio wanted to collaborate with Puccini on an opera based on the *pueri* of 1212, but after reading the rough draft which D'Annunzio sent him in early 1913, the great composer bowed out of the project. D'Annunzio's drama, Puccini felt, lacked one thing. Drama.[65] Set in the days of St. Francis, D'Annunzio's tremulously lyrical, Schwob-like *La crociata degli Innocenti: mistero in quattro atti* (1920) was never completed. Only the first two acts survive.[66]

Without any doubt the most illustrious twentieth-century literary figure to summon up the memory of the *pueri* must be the German Marxist playwright, Bertolt Brecht. Improbable as it may seem, while he was writing about it, he was residing in Los Angeles. Brecht's ballad-like, powerful anti-war poem *Kinderkreuzzug 1939* (1941) was originally conceived as a story for a film, a film which he later deemed suitable for the postwar denazification of his fellow countrymen. The actress Elisabeth Bergner recited *Kinderkreuzzug 1939* in German at two New York anti-fascist cultural gatherings held in 1943. Among those translating it into English were W.H. Auden and the poet Naomi Replansky, whose version Brecht preferred. Replansky challenged Brecht regarding "a stanza in *Children's Crusade 1939* about a rich Jewish child by pointing out that all Jews were not wealthy." Brecht agreed to her emendation.[67]

Brecht's poem of thirty-five quatrains evokes the terrible aftermath of the Nazi invasion of Poland. In Poland troops of hungry, orphaned, refugee children displaced by the war take to the roads to avoid the slaughter, searching for a peaceful land. This bitterly ironic "new crusade of the children" attracts boys and girls, Germans and Poles, Jews, Catholics and Protestants, Nazis and Communists, Spaniards, Frenchmen, and children with "yellow faces." The lost and famished fifty-five children trudge on, sending a dog out for help with a placard round its neck. The dog starves; presumably, so do the children.[68]

Setting Brecht's translated words to music, Benjamin Britten's *Children's Crusade / Kinderkreuzzug Op. 82* ("a ballad for children's voices and orchestra") was written for the Wandsworth School Boys' Choir to perform, fittingly, on the fiftieth anniversary of the Save the Children Fund (1969). Sidney Nolan's striking images in washed-out purple or muddy brown show ghostly, forlorn figures resembling escapees from a death camp.[69] Brecht's evocation of the high-minded, voluntary crusade of the medieval *kinder* provides a mocking contrast to the wretched forced-march of the starving Polish refugee children, even if both crusades could serve as symbols of human futility. It is a fair instance of Brecht's Marxist dialectical view of history and of the scope of his historical memory. Brecht remembers the past for its resonances; but also in order to judge the present.

Gian Carlo Menotti (1911–2007) was an Italian-born, classically-trained musician widely known for writing the first opera for American television—frequently rebroadcast at Christmas time—the child-centered *Amahl and the Night Visitors*. Menotti was commissioned to write a cantata for the Cincinnati May Festival, which became *Death of the Bishop of Brindisi*, first performed in 1963.[70] Taking as his source Adolf Waas's account of the Children's Crusade, Menotti imagines the sleepless, dying Bishop of Brindisi hearing the voices of the drowning *pueri*. The bishop, despite doing all he could do to persuade the children not to sail off to the Holy Land, was put under great pressure to bless them, and he yielded to it. Now he hears their voices. Wracked by guilt, he begs God for an answer, which, when it comes, is as ambiguous as that given to Job. Bleak and self-recriminatory, Menotti's *Bishop of Brindisi* implicitly makes fallible adults, however well-meaning, inadvertent accomplices in their doomed enterprise. These are the death-throes of failed dreams.[71]

Twentieth-century voices: novelists

Twentieth-century novelists writing for adults have by no means ignored the narrative of the medieval *pueri*. Utilizing it in various ways, they have either imaginatively reworked its plot, or, perhaps more fruitfully, employed it as an allusive point of reference to enrich other, far different stories.

Born in Warsaw, Jerzy Andrzejewski's (1909–1983) literary career mirrors the turbulence of Polish history. He was in successive stages a Catholic journalist, an anti-Nazi, a Communist convert, and an ideologically disillusioned post-Stalinist.[72] His experimental Polish novella *The Gates of Paradise*, originally published in 1959, consists of two sentences, the first stretching almost the entire length of the book; the second—five words. Andrzejewski's complex poetic vision is sensitive, lyrical, and lustful. The innocence is childlike; the sexual passions, heterosexual and homo-erotic, not so. Individual human needs and guilty secrets demanding confession co-exist with Catholic-romantic feelings about Christ's tomb far, far away. Crusade ideology and emotional subjectivity intermix. The picture of the long, endless march of the children, thousands of them, their robes, their smocks, their crosses, moving slowly across the horizon, is such a powerful image that it could be cinematic.[73]

The most popular twentieth-century American work of fiction to nourish itself from the Children's Crusade is Kurt Vonnegut's acclaimed anti-war novel *Slaughterhouse-Five or the Children's Crusade: A Duty-Dance with Death* (1969), which was both a best-seller and a critical success. If the horror of the World War II fire-bombing of Dresden overshadows *Slaughterhouse-Five*, the book's alternative title demands to be taken just as seriously.[74]

Kurt Vonnegut's time-traveling hero Billy Pilgrim, a young, naive GI in wartorn Europe is a true American innocent abroad. Given the childlike diminutive of his first name and the medieval *peregrinus* of his last, he makes an excellent symbolic child-crusader. His comrades in arms, and indeed some of the German troops, are likewise represented as youngsters. Their forty-three-year-old U.S. colonel admits he forgot that wars were fought by babies. Looking at their freshly shaved faces, he gets a shock. "My God, my God," he exclaims, "it's the Children's Crusade."[75] As much the innocent victims of war as the German civilians, these young American GIs fighting World War II in Europe are the new child-crusaders.

Slaughterhouse-Five fuses the absurd inhumanity of mass destruction—which the attack on Dresden exemplifies—with the theme of the Slaughter of the Innocents. Calling it "the Children's Crusade" allows Vonnegut to give an anti-heroic twist to the notion that World War II had been a *Crusade in Europe*. That was the title Dwight David Eisenhower chose for his military memoirs (1948),[76] and in retrospect, his choice of title seems inevitable. Four years earlier, on the eve of the Normandy invasion, General Eisenhower delivered a solemn address to the Allied Expeditionary Forces which began: "You are about to embark upon the Great Crusade...."[77] During the war the minumum age of conscription for American servicemen fell from twenty-one to eighteen, as it was for the British.[78] These were boy-soldiers. Boy-crusaders, some might say.

Was it, as one critic suggests, Herman Hesse's *Journey to the East* (1932) which supplied Vonnegut, an admirer of Hesse, with his motif of the Children's Crusade? Hesse called his eastern journey a pilgrimage and a Children's Crusade.[79] But another critic points out that Vonnegut had to look no further for boy soldiers than the great anti-war classic of World War I, Erich Maria Remarque's *All Quiet on the Western Front* (1929). Its German troops were "little more than boys."[80] An example closer to home for Vonnegut would be Stephen Crane's novel of the American Civil War, *The Red Badge of Courage* (1895), with its youthful protagonist and his young friend.[81] These Union soldiers were the "brave boys in blue." There was also the World War II refrain—"Turn the dark clouds inside out, Till the boys come home."[82] Fighting men were now "the boys." Vonnegut's boy-soldiers did not lack military antecedents.

To find out about the actual Children's Crusade, Vonnegut and his friends in *Slaughterhouse-Five*, turn to Charles Mackay's *Extraordinary Popular Delusions and the Madness of Crowds* (1841).[83] Mackay, a Scottish journalist and man of letters (1814–1889), wrote in the spirit of Voltaire that "vile monks" preaching to "deluded children" set it in motion.[84] Vonnegut may have used Mackay to relocate the *pueri* in his World War II American Children's Crusade, but he jettisoned Mackay's cynical perspective. His child-crusaders were naive, not "deluded."[85] Consciously or not, Vonnegut was exploiting the mythic theme of childhood innocence which nineteenth-century America shared with medieval Europe.[86]

Widespread and intense opposition to the war in Vietnam was commonplace across the campuses of America when *Slaughterhouse-Five* appeared in 1969. So Vonnegut's idea of a Children's Crusade spoke to the politicized, activist, anti-war students of America's colleges, who, by then, were already veterans of their own abortive Children's Crusade on behalf of Senator Eugene McCarthy.[87] The climactic moment of the anti-war campus rebellion, the shooting of students at Kent State (1970), came only a year after *Slaughterhouse-Five* was published.

France too, had its student uprising in 1968, but "the events" (*les événements*), as they are called, of May and June of that year were potentially far more radical and destabilizing—culturally, socially, and politically—than the anti-Vietnam student protests in the United

States. There were demonstrations and sit-ins at Nanterre, the Sorbonne, and in many French cities. One banner headline read: "STUDENTS: INSURRECTION."[88] In France, as in America, a mass movement of young people awakened memories of the medieval Children's Crusade, while at the same time reshaping perceptions of it.

Although Bernard Thomas's intelligent, well-researched historical novel *La croisade des enfants* (1973) is plausibly set in medieval peasant society and makes some acute historical deductions, the spirit of "the events" of 1968—disenchantment and an ardent desire to change the system—infuse the text.[89] The very first question which hostile clerics ask the *enfants* is: "why are you rebelling against the order of nature?" The response of the young crusaders is pure Sixties. In the kingdom of adults, disorder reigns, but "our kingdom will be founded on justice, trust, and love."[90]

Other signs of 1968 include a thorough-going animus against the upper strata of the medieval establishment, along with an unconcealed generational antipathy towards most of the parents of the peasant children who follow Stephen of Cloyes. These parents are generally portrayed as poor specimens. They lack courage, are unable to dare, and seem to be defeated by the system. The interrogation scene where Stephen of Cloyes appears before King Philip Augustus and the doctors of the University is a medieval version of a classic confrontation between a starry-eyed 1968 student leader, a disbelieving secular magistrate, and an angry disciplinary board of professors.

In the novel, Stephen of Cloyes returns to France after many painful years of incarceration in the Saracen East. His message to the listening *enfants* is "Rouse yourselves!"[91] Calmly looking towards the future (1968?), Thomas's novel concludes with prophecies of children's crusades to come—indeed, of children's crusades that will occur until the end of time.

In her decidedly unsentimental *The Children's Crusade* (1989), the American novelist and academic Rebecca Brown digs deep into the miseries of parent versus child. Narrated by a shrewd young girl caught up in domestic warfare, the novel has three interlocking parts, the third of which draws explicitly upon the medieval Children's Crusade. The *pueri* are realistically introduced into the narrative when the narrator together with her classmates see a mediocre scholastic film of their crusade as part of a history lesson. At first, the child-actors in their obviously fake costumes and false goody-goody attitudes inspire nothing but cutting reactions from the school children, quite contrary to the moralizing didacticism of the film-makers. To a perceptive minority in the class—

the narrator and her friends—the film's high-flown sentiments are just as absurdly unbelievable as the child-actors' medieval wardrobe. Then the school kids make an amazing discovery. The child-actors in the film (and by extension the medieval *pueri*) are really sending them a hidden message:

> Because we knew, in the secret code of kids adults forget, what the child crusaders were really up to. They secretly told us in code, in the special way they held their wrists, the blue and purple smudges on their hands, that they were a tough, rebellious band of runaways.... The kid crusaders weren't marching to redeem a has-been plot of real estate; they'd simply, suddenly, in the dark when their moms and dads weren't looking, flipped their parents off and hit the road.[92]

The wanderings of the medieval child-crusaders are re-imagined by these disenchanted American school kids as a dream of freedom. Running away speaks to them; the redemption of the Holy Land does not.

The urge to run away and break free of all restrictions is, of course, a recurring theme in classic American tales of childhood like *Huckleberry Finn*.[93] Perhaps, too, there may be an echo of the international youth culture of the late Sixties and early Seventies. Brown's emphasis upon the departure of the medieval children, rather than upon the miseries or failure of their journey, or their supposed ultimate misfortune, extends the story in a provocatively subversive direction, making it something of a modern utopian escapist fantasy for suburban youth. Rebecca Brown's reinterpretation of the mythistory of the Children's Crusade shows what the story is capable of in the hands of a creative artist.

The persistence of social memory

One year after the carnage of World War I, Archibald Jamieson published a pamphlet entitled *The Holy Wars in the Light of Today*. Parallels were drawn: "The Crusade of Children A.D. 1212—Conscription of the Young." Lessons were learned: rightly do we condemn the "hallucination" of 1212; so why do we "recruit the boy-life of our nation, and organise our youth in school and church for military purposes in the sacred name of 'patriotism'?"[94]

The medievalist T.S.R. Boase published his *Kingdoms and Strongholds of the Crusaders* in 1971. Summing up the Children's Crusade, he writes: "It was a protest of youth against the inaction and indifference of their elders, a representation in medieval terms of demonstrations very familiar today."[95] Thus the *pueri* of 1212 prefigured the youthful protesters of the Sixties. Thus they were—the great totemic word of former times—relevant. Just as the past speaks to the present, so, too, the present, if it cannot speak to the past, then at least can be read into it.

The continuing existence of the Children's Crusade in the collective memory of western society is not only a remarkable fact, but one which should be seen as integral to its history. More remarkable still is that the social memory of the *peregrinatio puerorum* is independent of formal public acts of commemoration.[96] Although the French may view it as fundamentally French, the Germans as German—and both may be right—the historical memory of the Children's Crusade lacks a national dimension. National histories largely ignore it, perhaps rightly so, for its scope was European.[97] One key to its memorability is that those who wrote about it, and those who read about it, universalized its meaning. Emancipated from historical particularity, its thematic universality and metaphorical richness were released.

The simple and arresting tale of the *pueri* possessed memory's great fixative—an intelligible narrative structure, culminating in a catastrophic ending, which was pitiable, heroic, or well-deserved, depending on one's point of view. Nor did the Children's Crusade, with its two named protagonists, Stephen of Cloyes, Nicholas of Cologne—and now a third: Otto, the last *puer*—lack individual faces among the vast army of nameless young peasants. Personalist to its core, western culture is driven by a biographical imperative. Mass movements without faces in the crowd are drowned in a sea of anonymity. Peter the Hermit commands far more attention than his horde of peasant, knightly, and clerical adherents. Would that we knew more about the real Stephen, the real Nicholas, the real Otto.

Up to a point this argument for the inherent memorability of the narrative of the Children's Crusade is persuasive. Yet as the product of cultural transmission, the mythistory of the Children's Crusade was a construct, creatively formed and re-formed in successive reincarnations. For memory, while reappropriating the past, simultaneously transforms it. "Memory is the artist that individualizes and remodels its subject."[98] So if the memorability of the *pueri* was to a certain extent independent of its historicity, its perceived historicity was crucial to its survival.

Undoubtedly, the preservation of the social memory of the *pueri* has always been at the mercy of culturally privileged agencies of transmission with historians claiming the lion's share. Yet historians, too, are obliged to include material which their readers have learned to expect or else face the charge of wilful omission. Consequently, historians of the crusades were (and are) forced by historiographical convention to say something about the *pueri*. Social memory has not surrendered its power to compel.

The twentieth century did not forget the Children's Crusade; nor is the twenty-first likely to do so. A dialogue between past and present lasting eight hundred years will not come to a halt when it reaches 2012.

Chronology

1095	November 27: Pope Urban II, Council of Clermont, calls First Crusade
1095–96	Peter the Hermit's Crusade; Jews massacred in Rhineland
1099	Jerusalem conquered by the crusaders
1145	Cathedral building revival at Chartres ("cult of carts")
1145	December 1: Eugenius III issues bull for the Second Crusade
1179–1223	Reign of Philip Augustus, King of France
1181–1226	Life of St. Francis of Assisi
1182–c. 1184	Durand of Le Puy and his peace militia, the "White Hoods"
1183–1217	Reginald of Bar (or Mouçon), Bishop of Chartres
1187	July 4: Saladin's victory at Hattin; loss of the True Cross
	October 2: Fall of Jerusalem
	October 29: Gregory VIII proclaims the Third Crusade
1191	July 12: Crusaders retake Acre
1194	June 10: Fire at Cathedral of Chartres
1198–1216	Pontificate of Innocent III
1199	August 15: Innocent III summons Fourth Crusade
1202	Death of Joachim of Fiore
1204	April 13–15: Constantinople sacked by the Latin crusaders
c. 1206	Death of Amalric of Bène
1208	January 14: The papal legate Peter of Castelnau is assassinated
	March 10: Innocent III initiates the Albigensian Crusade
c. 1209–12	"Pilgrimage of the 300 Rabbis": Jews leave Europe for the Holy Land
1210/11	Autumn–Winter: Bishop Reginald of Chartres in Languedoc
1210	November 20: Burning of the heretical Amalricians at Paris
c. 1211–12	Master Godin, Amalrician intellectual, sent to the stake at Amiens
1211	Early September: Salvatierra falls to the North African Almohads
1211/12	Winter: Preaching of Albigensian Crusade in N. France and Rhineland
	Archbishop Jiménez de Rada's journey beyond the Pyrenees
1212	January 31: Innocent III writes to Archbishop of Sens
	March 18: St. Clare of Assisi runs away from home
	March 25: Easter
	Late March/early April: de Rada returns to Spain
	April c. 15–30: N. French crusade recruits arrive in Languedoc
	May 13: Pentecost (octave ends May 20)
	May 16: Innocent III's Roman processions for the Spanish cause
	May 20: Similar processions in France: Chartres
	After May 20: Post-Chartres revivalist processions in France
	June c. 8–24: Lendit fair. Stephen of Cloyes' *pueri* at Saint-Denis

June c. 30–2 July (?): Saint-Quentin, riot at Rocourt
July c. 8–9: *pueri* in Liège (?)
July c. 10–12: *pueri* in Aachen (?)
July c. 14–18: *pueri* in Cologne
July 16: Battle of Las Navas de Tolosa
July c. 22: *pueri* in Mainz
July c. 22: *pueri* in Trier (?)
July 25: *pueri* in Speyer
August 20: *pueri* in Piacenza
August 25: *pueri* in Genoa
August c. 30: *pueri* in Pisa (?)
September c. 15: *pueri* in Rome (?)
October: Francis of Assisi in Ancona
October (late): Nicholas of Cologne in Brindisi (?)

1213 April 19–29: Innocent III announces the Fifth Crusade
June 18: Royal judgment on Saint-Quentin disturbances
June 23: Death of Mary of Oignies

1215 November 11–30: Fourth Lateran Council

1216 May 1: Innocent III preaches Fifth Crusade at Orvieto
July 16: Death of Innocent III at Perugia

1217 June 1: Fifth Crusaders to gather in Messina and Brindisi
Late summer: Cardinal Pelagius sets sail from Brindisi to Acre

1218 June 25: Simon of Montfort killed at siege of Toulouse
Autumn: Cardinal Pelagius, Nicholas of Cologne, Francis of Assisi at the siege of Damietta

1219 November 5: Capture of Damietta

1220 August 19: Papal register refers to Otto, former *puer*, as a *pauper scolaris*

1221 August 30: Surrender of Damietta ending the Fifth Crusade

1251 The *Pastores* or Shepherds' Crusade

1284 June 26: Legend of Pied Piper at Hameln

1968 U.S. Presidential campaign: American "Children's Crusade"; student-led upheaval in France—*les événements*, "the events"

Europe of the *Pueri*

Abbreviations of Frequently Cited References

Primary sources

Admont: *Continuatio Admuntensis* (to 1250) (ed. W. Wattenbach) *MGH. SS.* 9: 592.
Alberic of Trois-Fontaines: *Chronica Albrici monachi Trium Fontium* (to 1241) (ed. P. Scheffer-Boichorst) in *MGH. SS.* 23: 893–4.
Albert of Stade: *Annales Stadenses* (to 1256) (ed. L.M. Lappenberg) *MGH. SS*, 16: 355.
Andres: *Willelmi chronica Andrensis* (to 1234) (ed. I. Heller) in *MGH. SS.* 24: 754.
Austrian Rhymed Chronicle: *Chronicon rhythmicum Austriacum* (to 1267) (ed. W. Wattenbach) in *MGH. SS.* 25: 356.
Cantimpré: Thomae Cantipratani, *Bonum universale de Apibus* (Baltazaris Belleri: Douai, 1627), pp.140–1.
Cologne Continuator: *Chronicae regiae Coloniensis continuatio prima* (to 1220) (ed. G. Waitz) *MGH. SS.* 24: 17–18.
Ebersheim: *Chronicon Ebersheimense* (to 1235) (ed. L. Weiland) in *MGH. SS.* 23: 450.
Floreffe: *Annales Floreffiensis* (to 1289) (ed. D.L.C. Bethmann) *MGH. SS.* 16: 626.
Hecker: J.F.C. Hecker, *The Epidemics of the Middle Ages* (trans. B.G. Babington) 3rd edn., includes *Treatise on Child-Pilgrimages* (trans. Robert H. Cooke) (Trübner & Co.: London, 1859), "Authorities," pp.354–60.
Henry of Heimburg: *Annales* (to 1300) (ed. W. Wattenbach) in *MGH. SS.* 17: 714.
Herman of Niederaltaich: *Hermanni Altahensis annales* (to 1273) (ed. P. Jaffé) in *MGH. SS.* 17: 386.
Jumièges: *Annales Gemmeticenses* (to 1216) (ed. O. Holder-Egger) in *MGH. SS.* 26: 510.
Laon: *Chronicon universale anonymi Laudunensis 1154–1219* (ed. A. Cartellieri and W. Stechele) (Leipzig, 1909), pp.70–1.
Le Long: Iohannis Longi, *Chronica monasterii sancti Bertini* (to 1294) (ed. O. Holder-Egger) in *MGH. SS.* 25: 828.
Marbach: *Annales Marbacenses* (to 1220) (ed. H. Bloch) in *MGH. SS. Rerum Germ. In usum scholar.* 9: 82–3.
Matthew Paris: *Chronica Majora* (to 1259) (ed. H.R. Luard) 2 (London, 1874), 558.
MGH. SS.: *Monumenta Germaniae historica, Scriptores* (ed. G.H. Pertz) (Hanover, 1826–1913), 1–32.
Migne, *P.L.*: *Patrologiae cursus completus, series Latina* (ed./publ. J.-P. Migne) (Paris, 1844–55), 1–215.
Mortemer: *Auctarium Mortui Maris* (to 1234) (ed. D.L.C. Bethmann), *MGH. SS.* 6: 467
Mousket: Ex Philippi Mousket, *Historia Regum Francorum* (to 1243) (ed. Adolfus Tobler), *MGH. SS.* 26: 806.

Panis: Ogerius Panis, *Annales* (to 1219) in *Annali Genovesi di Caffaro e de' suoi continuatori* (ed. L.T. Belgrano and C. Imperiale) (Ist. Stor. Ital., Fonti, 12) (Rome, 1901) Vol. 2, p.123.

Paris preacher: Nicole Bériou, *L'avènement des maîres de la Parole: la prédication à Paris aux XIIIe siècle* (Collection des Études Augustiniennes, Série Moyen Âge et Temps Modernes, 31), Vol. I (Paris, 1998), p.60, n.188.

Peterborough: *Chronicon Petroburgense* (to 1225) (ed. Thomas Stapleton), Camden Society, ser. 1, Vol. 47 (London, 1849), p.6.

Piacenza: *Annales Placentini guelfi* (to 1235) (ed. G.H. Pertz), *MGH. SS.* 18: 426.

Renier: *Annales Sancti Iacobi Leodiensis* (to 1230) (ed. L.C. Bethmann) (Liège, 1874), pp.95–6.

RHGF: *Recueil des Historiens des Gaules et de la France* (ed. Martin Bouquet-Léopold Delisle) (Paris, 1738–1904), 1–24.

Richer: *Richeri Gesta Senoniensis Ecclesiae* (to 1264) (ed. G. Waitz), *MGH. SS.* 25: 301.

St. Médard: *Annales s. Medardi Suessionensibus* (to 1249) (ed. G. Waitz), *MGH. SS.* 26: 521.

St. Pantaleon's Chronicler: *Chronica regia Coloniensis continuatio IIIa* (to 1219) (ed. G. Waitz), *MGH. SS. rer. Germ. in usum schol.* 18: 234.

Salimbene de Adam: *Cronica* (ed. Giuseppe Scalia) (Corpus Christianorum, Continuatio Mediaevalis series, 125 and 125A), Vol.1 (Turnholt, 1998). Translation: *The Chronicle*, edited by Joseph L. Baird, MRTS, Volume 40 (Binghamton, New York, 1986). Copyright © Arizona Board of Regents for Arizona State.

Salzburg: *Annales sancti Rudberti Salisburgenses* (to 1286) (ed. W. Wattenbach), *MGH. SS.* 9: 780.

Schäftlarn: *Annales Scheftlarienses maiores* (to 1247) (ed. P. Jaffé), *MGH. SS.* 7: 338.

Shinners: John Shinners (ed./trans.), *Medieval Popular Religion, 1000–1500: A Reader* (Broadview Press: Peterborough, Ont., 1997), pp.395–400.

Sicard: *Sicardi Episcopi Cremonensis Cronica* (to 1212) (ed. O. Holder-Egger) in *MGH. SS.* 31: 180–1.

Speyer: *Annales Spirenses* (to 1259) (ed. G.H. Pertz) in *MGH. SS.* 17: 84.

Trier: *Gestorum Treverorum cont. iv.* (to 1242) (ed. G. Waitz), *MGH. SS.* 24: 398–9.

Varagine: *Iacopo da Varagine e la sua chronica di Genova* (to 1297) (ed. G. Monleone) (Ist. Stor. Ital., Fonti, 85), 2 (Rome, 1941), 373–4.

Vincent of Beauvais: *Speculum Historiale* (Graz, reprint 1965), lib. xxx, cap. v: 1238.

Secondary literature

Alphandéry, *d'enfants*: Paul Alphandéry, "Les croisades d'enfants," *Revue de l'Histoire des Religions*, Vol. 73 (1916), pp.259–82.

Alphandéry, *La chrétienté*: Paul Alphandéry and Alphonse Dupront, *La chrétienté et l'idée de croisade*, 2 vols. (Albin Michel: Paris, 1954, 1959) reissued in one vol. (Albin Michel: Paris, 1995), pp.339–72. The one-vol. edition is cited here.

Cardini-Del Nero, *Fanciulli*: Franco Cardini and Domenico Del Nero, *La Crociata dei Fanciulli* (Giunti: Florence, 1999).

De Janssens: Gaston de Janssens, "Étienne de Cloyes et les croisades d'enfants au xiiie siècle," *Bulletin de la société dunoise*, Vol. 90 (1891), pp.109–33.

Dickson, *Amalricians*: Gary Dickson, "The Burning of the Amalricians," *Journal of Ecclesiastical History*, Vol. 40 (1989), pp.347–69; reprinted in *Religious Enthusiasm in the Medieval West: Revivals, Crusades, Saints* (Variorum Collected Studies Series) (Ashgate: Abingdon, October 2000), cap. 3.

Dickson, *Clare*: Gary Dickson, "Clare's Dream," *Mediaevistik, Internationale Zeitschrift für interdisziplinäre Mittelalterforschung*, Vol. 5 (1992), pp.39–55; reprinted in *Religious Enthusiasm in the Medieval West: Revivals, Crusades, Saints* (Variorum Collected Studies Series) (Ashgate: Abingdon, October 2000), cap. 7.

Dickson, *Crowds*: Gary Dickson, "Medieval Christian Crowds and the Origins of Crowd Psychology," *Revue d'Histoire Ecclésiastique*, Vol. 95 (2000), pp.54–75.

Dickson, *Encounters*: Gary Dickson, "Encounters in Medieval Revivalism: Monks, Friars, and Popular Enthusiasts," *Church History*, Vol. 68, no. 2 (1999), pp.265–93.

Dickson, *Genesis*: Gary Dickson, "The Genesis of the Children's Crusade," English version of "La genèse de la croisade des enfants (1212)," *Bibliothèque de l'École des chartes*, Vol. 153 (1995), pp.53–102; reprinted in *Religious Enthusiasm in the Medieval West: Revivals, Crusades, Saints* (Variorum Collected Studies Series) (Ashgate: Abingdon, October 2000), cap. 4.

Dickson, *Genre*: Gary Dickson, "Revivalism as a Medieval Religious Genre," *Journal of Ecclesiastical History*, Vol. 51 (2000), pp.473–96.

Dickson, *Innocent*: Gary Dickson, "Innocent III and the Children's Crusade," *Innocenzo III. Urbs et orbis*, Vol 1, ed. Andrea Sommerlechner (Rome, Istituto storico italiano per il Medio Evo e Società romana di storia patria, 2003), pp.586–97.

Dickson, *Pastores*: Gary Dickson, "The Advent of the *Pastores* (1251)," *Revue Belge de Philologie et d'Histoire*, Vol. 66 (1988), pp.249–67; reprinted in *Religious Enthusiasm in the Medieval West: Revivals, Crusades, Saints* (Variorum Collected Studies Series) (Ashgate: Abingdon, October 2000), cap. 6.

Dickson, *Prophecy*: Gary Dickson, "Prophecy and Revivalism: Joachim of Fiore, Jewish Messianism and the Children's Crusade of 1212," *Florensia*, 13/14 (1999–2000), V Congresso Internazionale di Studi Gioachimiti: Comunicazioni, pp.97–104.

Dickson, *Stephen*: Gary Dickson, "Stephen of Cloyes, Philip Augustus, and the Children's Crusade of 1212," in B.N. Sargent-Baur (ed.), *Journeys Toward God: Pilgrimage and Crusade* (Medieval Institute Publications: Kalamazoo, Mich., 1992), pp.83–105; reprinted in *Religious Enthusiasm in the Medieval West: Revivals, Crusades, Saints* (Variorum Collected Studies Series) (Ashgate: Abingdon, October 2000), cap. 5.

Hansbery, *Children's Crusade*: Joseph E. Hansbery, "The Children's Crusade," *Catholic Historical Review*, Vol. 24 (1938–39), pp.30–8.

Miccoli, *Fanciulli*: Giovanni Miccoli, "La 'crociata dei fanciulli' del 1212," *Studi Medievali*, 3rd series, Vol. 2.2 (1961), pp.407–43.

Raedts, *Children's Crusade*: Peter Raedts, "The Children's Crusade of 1212," *Journal of Medieval History*, Vol. 3 (1977) pp.279–323.

Zacour, *Children's Crusade*: Norman P. Zacour, "The Children's Crusade," in Kenneth M. Setton (ed.), *A History of the Crusades* (University of Pennsylvania Press: Philadelphia, 1962), Vol. 2, pp.325–42.

Notes

Preface

1. Patrick Harpur, *The Philosophers' Secret Fire: A History of the Imagination* (Penguin Books: London, 2002), p.82. Jacques Le Goff's *The Medieval Imagination* (trans. Arthur Goldhammer) (University of Chicago Press: Chicago and London, 1992), pp.1–17, omits the mythistoriographical imagination, whether medieval or modern.

Chapter 1 Introduction

1. Janet Morgan, *Agatha Christie: A Biography* (Collins: London, 1984), pp.362–5. ©HarperCollins Publishers Ltd. Reprinted by permission.
2. *Passenger to Frankfurt* (Collins: London, 1970), pp.216–17. *Passenger to Frankfurt* © 1970 Agatha Christie Limited, a Chorion company, all rights reserved.
3. *Ibid.*, p.88.
4. *Ibid.*, pp.104–5, 121.
5. Varagine, p.374. Hecker, p.358.
6. Renier, p.96. Hecker, p.358.
7. St. Médard, p.521. Hecker, p.359.
8. *Mythistory and Other Essays* (University of Chicago Press: Chicago, 1986), especially, pp.19, 23.
9. University of Chicago Press: Chicago and London, 1963.
10. In *Mythologies* (ed. and trans. A. Lavers) (Jonathan Cape: London, 1972), p.143.
11. See *The Oxford English Dictionary* (2nd edn.), Vol.10 (Oxford University Press: Oxford, 1989), p.178.
12. Cf. Galit Hasan-Rokem and Alan Dundes (eds.), *The Wandering Jew: Essays in the Interpretation of a Christian Legend* (Indiana University Press: Bloomington, 1986).
13. On William of Newburgh and the Green Children, see Nancy Partner, *Serious Entertainments: The Writing of History in Twelfth-Century England* (University of Chicago Press: Chicago, 1977), p.121.
14. Peterborough, p.6.
15. B. Lacroix, *L'historien au Moyen Âge* (Institut D'Études Médiévales: Montréal and Paris, 1971), p.17.
16. Cited from Memo, Helms to the President (November 15 1967) in Rhodri Jeffreys-Jones, *Peace Now! American Society and the Ending of the Vietnam War* (Yale University Press: New Haven and London, 1999), p.78 and n.94, p.251.
17. Arthur Marwick, *The Sixties* (Oxford University Press: Oxford, 1999), p.666.

18. Lewis Chester, *et al.*, *An American Melodrama—the Presidential Campaign of 1968* (Viking Press: New York, 1969), p.325.
19. Todd Gitlin, *The Sixties: Years of Hope, Days of Rage* (Penguin Books: Toronto, 1987; originally published by Bantam Books, a division of Random House), p.205.
20. Reprinted by William Morrow & Co., Inc., New York, 1972. Foreword by Thomas Powers (pp.5–9), here at p.7.
21. *Ibid.*, pp.8–9.
22. From Jefferson's letter to George Wythe in Gordon C. Lee (ed.), *Crusade against Ignorance: Thomas Jefferson on Education* (Teacher's College Press: New York, 1967), p.100.
23. Cited from F.G. de Fontaine, *American Abolitionism from 1787 to 1861* (D. Appleton & Co.: New York, 1861), p.52 in Louis Filler, *The Crusade against Slavery, 1830–1860* (Harper: New York, 1960), p.276.
24. For the historical background, see Carole Hillenbrand, *The Crusades: Islamic Perspectives* (Edinburgh University Press: Edinburgh, 1999).
25. See Gary Dickson, "Crusade as Metaphor" in "Crusades, The," *Encyclopaedia Britannica* (15th edn., 26th printing) (Encyclopaedia Britannica: Chicago, 2003), Vol. 16, pp.822–39, here at p.838.
26. George Lakoff and Mark Johnson, *Metaphors We Live By* (University of Chicago Press: Chicago and London, 1980), p.154.
27. For a brief overview, see, for example, "trope/figuration" in Alun Munslow, *The Routledge Companion to Historical Studies* (Routledge: London and New York, 2000), pp.214–15.
28. Gray, *Children's Crusade*, p.9.
29. Current scholarly opinion holds that Gray's work is "fanciful and unreliable": F.H. Russell, "Crusade, Children's," in *Dictionary of the Middle Ages*, Vol. 4 (Charles Scribner's Sons: New York, 1984), pp.14–15.
30. *The Crusades* (trans. J. Gillingham) (Oxford University Press: Oxford, 1972), p.302, note 77. The original German edition was published in 1965.
31. Witness the Weller Grossman production of *History's Mysteries: The Children's Crusade*, broadcast over the History Channel on July 26, 2000.
32. A semi-popularization is Corrado Pallenberg's *La Crociata dei Bambini* (Mondadori: Milan, 1983). Franco Cardini and Domenico Del Nero, *La crociata dei fanciulli* (Giunti: Florence, 1999) surveys much of the existing scholarly literature, but does not delve deeply into the sources.
33. The thorough bibliography in Raedts, *Children's Crusade* (see pp.320–3) also includes chronicles later than 1301, such as the *Chronica monasterii sancti Bertini* (*ad.* 1294) by Jean le Long (d. 1383) (ed. O. Holder-Egger).
34. Annals, chronicles, histories: for a succinct discussion of the genres of medieval historiography, see Antonia Gransden, "The Chronicles of Medieval England and Scotland," in her *Legends, Traditions and History in Medieval England* (Hambledon Press: London, 1992), pp.199–210, reprinted from *Journal of Medieval History*, Vol. 16 (1990), p.129ff.
35. Herman of Niederaltaich, p.386.
36. Sicard, pp.180–1. For information on Sicard's whereabouts in 1212, I am grateful to Dr. Eddie Coleman of University College Dublin who bases his conclusions, cited above from personal correspondence, on Innocent III's papal letters, in Migne, *P.L.* 216, cols. 650, 657, 667, 723, 726, 730.

37. Salzburg, p.780.
38. Ebersheim, p.450.
39. Examples include the Cologne Continuator, the Marbach Annalist, and the Chronicler of St. Pantaleon.
40. Albert of Stade, p.355. Translation slightly modified from Shinners, p.397. Reproduced by permission.
41. See Thomas of Celano, *First Life of St. Francis*, in Marion A. Habig (ed.) *St. Francis of Assisi: Writings and Early Biographies* (The Society for Promoting Christian Knowledge: London, 1979), pp.237–40; chronology, p.xi.
42. See Dickson, *Clare*, pp.42–4.
43. See Dickson, *Innocent*, pp.594–5.
44. *Austrian Rhymed Chronicle*, p.356.
45. Hayden White, "The Historical Text as Literary Artifact," in Geoffrey Roberts (ed.), *The History and Narrative Reader* (Routledge: New York and London, 2001), pp.221–36, here at p.222. The original source of the essay is not given, cf. pp.xi–xii.
46. Achille Luchaire, *Social France at the Time of Philip Augustus* (trans. E.B. Krehbiel) (John Murray: London, 1912), p.25.
47. Cologne Continuator, pp.17–18. Shinners, p.399.
48. Trier, p.398. Shinners, p.398.
49. Mortemer, p.467. Hecker, p.354.
50. Laon, pp.70–1. Hecker, p.354.
51. Renier, p.95. Hecker, p.358.
52. Piacenza, p.426. Shinners, p.398.

Chapter 2 History: The Pope and the Pueri

1. See Dickson, *Innocent*.
2. Excerpt from Salimbene de Adam, *The Chronicle* (ed. Joseph L. Baird), Medieval and Renaissance Texts and Studies, Vol. 40 (Binghamton, New York, 1986), p.5. © Arizona Board of Regents for Arizona State.
3. Michele Maccarrone, "Innocenzo III prima del pontificato," *Archivio Romano di Storia Patria*, Vol. 66 (1943), pp.59–134, here at p.132, n.2.
4. Letter to Abbot Arnold of Citeaux cited in Helene Tillmann, *Pope Innocent III* (trans. Walter Sax) (North-Holland Publishing Co.: Amsterdam, 1980), p.301.
5. Reinhard Bendix, *Max Weber: An Intellectual Portrait* (Doubleday & Co.: Garden City, New York, 1962), p.310ff.
6. Gerhart B. Ladner, *Die Papstbilnisse des Altertums und des Mittelalters* (Pontifical Institute of Christian Archaeology: Vatican City, 1970), Vol. II, pp.53–79, here at pp.55, 64–5.
7. For the Subiaco fresco, *ibid.*, pp.68–71; Innocent III's vestments, p.69. For all of these vestments, see Giacomo Lecaro, *A Small Liturgical Dictionary* (ed. J.B. O'Connell) (Burns & Oates: London, 1959).
8. On James of Vitry, see Ernest W. McDonnell, *The Beguines and Beghards in Medieval Culture with Special Emphasis on the Belgian Scene* (Octagon Books: New York, 1969). There is a biographical summary by M. Coens, "Jacques

de Vitry," *Biographie Nationale de Belgique*, Vol. 31, Supple. 3 (1962), cols. 465–74.
9. McDonnell, *Beguines and Beghards*, p.37.
10. Thomas Aquinas, *Summa Theologiae*, Vol. 40 (2ae2ae. 92–100) (eds. T.F. O'Meara and M.J. Duffy) (Blackfriars: Eyre & Spottiswoode: London, 1968), pp.80–3 (96.4.3).
11. R.B.C. Huygens (ed.), *Lettres de Jacques de Vitry* (E.J. Brill: Leiden, 1960), pp.73–4. His letter from Genoa dates from early October 1216.
12. Discussing this incident, Agostino Paravicini-Bagliani speculates that the expression *fere nudum*, "almost nude," might mean that Innocent was discovered "dressed only in his white shirt." See his *The Pope's Body*, (trans. D.S. Peterson) (University of Chicago Press: Chicago and London, 2000), p.123.
13. Text of the Perugian chronicler in Massimo Petrocchi, "L'ultimo destino perugino di Innocenzo III," *Bollettino della Deputazione di Storia Patria per l'Umbria*, 64 (1967), pp.201–7, here at pp.206–7.
14. Petrocchi, "L'ultimo destino perugino," pp.206–7.
15. *Ibid.*, p.206.
16. James M. Powell (trans.), *The Deeds of Innocent III, by an Anonymous Author* (Catholic University of America Press: Washington, D.C., 2004), p.3.
17. *De miseria humane conditionis*: Donald R. Howard (ed.), *On the Misery of the Human Condition* (Bobbs-Merrill: Indianapolis, 1969).
18. Geoffrey Barraclough, *The Medieval Papacy* (Thames and Hudson: London, 1968), pp.112–17, here at p.113.
19. Walter Ullmann, *A Short History of the Papacy in the Middle Ages* (Methuen: London and New York, 1982), pp.207–26.
20. See the extract from St. Bernard's apologia, his *De consideratione*, translated in Louise and Jonathan Riley-Smith (eds./trans.), *The Crusades: Idea and Reality, 1095–1274* (Edward Arnold: London, 1981), pp.61–3.
21. *The Chronicle of Henry of Huntingdon*, (trans./ed. Thomas Forester) (H.G. Bohn: London, 1853), p.286.
22. See James A. Brundage, "Prostitution, Miscegenation and Sexual Purity in the First Crusade," in Peter W. Edbury (ed.), *Crusade and Settlement* (University College Cardiff Press: Cardiff, 1985), pp.57–65.
23. Extract from Howden in Thomas A. Archer (ed.) *The Crusade of Richard I* (D. Nutt: London, 1912), p.118.
24. Dickson, *Prophecy*, pp.98–9.
25. Cited from Riley-Smith and Riley-Smith, *The Crusades*, p.120.
26. See Dickson, *Amalricians*.
27. The translated decrees or canons (abbreviated "can.") of the Fourth Lateran Council appear in *English Historical Documents*, Vol. 3, 1189–1327 (ed. H. Rothwell) (Eyre & Spottiswoode: London, 1975), pp.643–76, here at p.645.
28. Powell, *The Deeds of Innocent III*, pp.269–70. Martin of Troppau, however, mistakenly attributes authorship of the *Peri Fiseon* to Amalric.
29. Nicole Lèvis-Godechot, *Chartres* (Zodiac: Paris, 1987), pp.155–7, pl. 61.
30. See Malcolm Lambert, *Medieval Heresy* (3rd edn.) (Blackwell Publishers: Oxford, 2002).

31. See Max Josef Heimbucher, *Die Orden und Kongregationen der katholischen Kirche* (F. Schoningh: Paderborn, 1907–08), 3 Vols.
32. In general, see Dickson, *Clare*. For this citation: *La Leggenda di Santa Chiara d'Assisi* (Angelo Signorelli: Rome, 1953), p.14.
33. *Ibid.*, pp.21–2.
34. For a discussion of Clare and her abstention from food, see Caroline Walker Bynum, *Holy Feast and Holy Fast: The Religious Significance of Food to Medieval Women* (University of California Press: Berkeley and Los Angeles, 1987), pp.99–101, 343 n.173.
35. Maccarrone, "Innocenzo III prima del pontificato," p.83 n.1.
36. See the map folded into Daniel Waley, *The Papal State in the Thirteenth Century* (Macmillan & Co.: London, 1961).
37. *English Historical Documents*, Vol. 3, p.673.
38. See Michele Maccarrone, *Studi su Innocenzo III* (Editrice Antenore: Padua, 1972), pp.129–39.
39. See Denys Hay, *Europe: The Emergence of an Idea* (rev. edn.) (Edinburgh University Press: Edinburgh, 1968).
40. Gabriel LeBras, "Sur l'histoire des croix rurales," in *Miscellanea Historica in honorem Alberti de Meyer* (Bibliothèque de l'Université: Louvain, 1946), Vol. 1, pp.319–36.
41. Piacenza, p.426. Panis, p.123.
42. Mortemer, p.467.
43. See Alphandéry, *La chrétienté*, pp.339–72.
44. Raedts, *Children's Crusade*, p.297.
45. See W.M. Lindsay (ed.), Isidori Hispalensis, *Etymologiarum sive originum*, Vol. 2 (Oxford, 1911), XI. ii. 3–4. For the various medieval schemes, note J. de Ghellinck, "Iuventus, gravitas, senectus," in *Studia Mediaevalia in honorem R.J. Martin* (Bruges, n.d.), pp.39–59 and, more recently, Michael E. Goodich, *From Birth to Old Age: The Human Life Cycle in Medieval Thought, 1250–1350* (University Press of America: Lanham, MD, 1989), p.59ff., 105–43.
46. See Duby's "Les pauvres des campagnes dans l'occident médiéval jusqu'au xiiie siècle," *Revue d'histoire de l'église de France*, Vol. 52 (1966), pp.25–32, here at pp.30–2.
47. Note the remarks of William C. Jordan, *The French Monarchy and the Jews* (University of Pennsylvania Press: Philadelphia, 1989), n.119, pp.310–11, and Raffael Scheck, "Did the Children's Crusade of 1212 Really Consist of Children?" *Journal of Psychohistory*, Vol. 16 (1988), pp.176–82, here at p.178. The present writer arrived at his position before encountering theirs.
48. Robert Fossier, *Peasant Life in the Medieval West* (trans. Juliet Vale) (Blackwell: Oxford, 1988), p.10.
49. J.C. Russell, "Population in Europe, 500–1500," in *Fontana Economic History of Europe* (ed. Carlo M. Cipolla) (London, 1969), Vol. I, cap. 1, pp.31, 49.
50. Antonia Gransden, "Childhood and Youth in Mediaeval England," *Nottingham Mediaeval Studies*, Vol. 16 (1972), pp.3–19, here at pp.11, 17–18.
51. See Goodich, *From Birth to Old Age*, p.197.
52. See Christopher Tyerman, "Who Went on Crusades to the Holy Land?" in B.Z. Kedar (ed.), *The Horns of Hattin* (Israel Exploration Society: Jerusalem, 1992), pp.13–26, here at p.21.

53. "L'Enfant dans la société chrétienne aux xie–xiie siècles" in *La Cristianità dei Secoli XI e XII in Occidente* (Miscellanea del Centro di Studi Medievali, X) (Pubblicazioni dell'Università Cattolica del Sacro Cuore: Milan, 1983), pp.281–302, here at p.282.
54. Personal communication from Professor André Chédeville of the University of Rennes 2, to whom I owe a debt of gratitude.

Chapter 3 History: Birthpangs of the Children's Crusade

1. See J.C. Webster, *The Labors of the Months in Antique and Mediaeval Art* (Northwestern University: Evanston and Chicago, 1938), p.67, *passim*. In general, note Wilhelm Ganzenmüller, *Das Naturgefühl im Mittelalter* (B.G. Teubner: Leipzig and Berlin, 1914).
2. Y. Delaporte (ed.), "L'ordinaire chartrain du xiiie siècle," *Société archéologique d'Eure-et-Loir, Mémoires*, Vol. 19 (1952–53), p.130; William Durand, *Rationale Divinorum Officiorum* (Corpus Christianorum, Continuatio Mediaevalis, 140A) (Brepols S.A.: Turnhout, 1998), pp.526–7.
3. Cologne Continuator, pp.17–18.
4. A. Lecoy de la Marche, *La chaire française au moyen âge* (Paris, 1868), p.249ff., 250 n.1.
5. See André Chédeville (ed.), *Histoire de Chartres et du pays chartrain* (Privat: Toulouse, 1983), pp.63–97. *Idem.*, *Chartres et ses Campagnes* (Editions Klincksieck: Paris, 1973), *passim*.
6. Marc Bloch, *The Ile-de-France, the Country around Paris* (trans. J.E. Anderson) (Routledge and Kegan Paul: London, 1971), pp.19–21.
7. Michel Mollat (ed.), *Histoire de l'Ile-de-France et de Paris* (Privat: Toulouse, 1971), p.117.
8. Henri Bouvier, *Histoire de l'èglise et de l'ancien archidiocèse de Sens*, Vol. 2 (A. Picard et fils: Paris, 1911), p.192.
9. U. Berlière, "Les processions des croix banales," *Bulletins de la classe des lettres et des sciences morales et politiques*, Académie Royale de Belgique (Brussels), 5th series, Vol. 8 (1922), pp.419–46, here at pp.419, 426ff., 430.
10. See Dickson, *Stephen*, pp.90–1 and n.37. Described in a 1389 tractate as the *sancta Camisa in qua Filium peperit* in *Cartulaire de N.-D. de Chartres* (ed. E. de Lépinois and L. Merlet) (Société archéologique d'Eure-et-Loir: Chartres, 1862), Vol. 1, pp.1 n.1, 58.
11. For the phenomenon, see Carl F. Barnes, "Cult of Carts," in *The Dictionary of Art* (ed. Jane Turner), Vol. 8 (Macmillan: London, 1996), pp.257–9. Here note Léopold Delisle, "Lettre de l'abbé Haimon sur la construction de l'église de Saint-Pierre-sur-Dive en 1145" in *Bibliothèque de l'École des Chartes*, Vol. 21, 5th series, (1860), pp.113–39; Benedicta Ward, *Miracles and the Medieval Mind* (Scolar Press: London, 1982), pp.150–3; George Henderson, *Chartres* (Penguin Books: Harmondsworth, 1968), p.34ff.
12. From Delisle, "Lettre de l'abbé Haiman," p.123, translated by George G. Coulton (ed.), *Life in the Middle Ages* (Cambridge University Press: Cambridge, 1967), part ii, p.22.
13. Alphandéry, *La chrétienté*, pp.360–2.

14. W.R. Cross, *The Burned-Over District* (Cornell University Press: Ithaca, 1950), p.3.
15. In general, see C. Métais, "Croisés chartrains et dunois: documents inédits," *Bulletins de la Société Dunoise*, Vol. 8 (1894–96), pp.198–216. Especially see James A. Brundage, "An Errant Crusader: Stephen of Blois," *Traditio*, Vol. 16 (1960), pp.380–95.
16. Jonathan Riley-Smith, *The First Crusaders, 1095–1131* (Cambridge University Press: Cambridge, 1997), pp.88, 100, 155–6. Chédeville, *Histoire de Chartres*, p.327.
17. Fulcher of Chartres, *A History of the Expedition to Jerusalem, 1095–1127* (trans. F.R. Ryan and ed. H.S. Fink) (W.W. Norton: New York, 1969), pp.139, 271.
18. *Ibid.*, p.97.
19. Rosalind Hill (ed.), *The Deeds of the Franks* (Thomas Nelson and Sons: Edinburgh, 1962), p.63.
20. Fulcher of Chartres, *History of the Expedition to Jerusalem*, p.165.
21. *Ibid.*, pp.169, 58.
22. Jonathan Riley-Smith, *The Crusades: A Short History* (Yale University Press: New Haven, 1987), p.90. *Idem.*, *First Crusaders*, p.165.
23. Riley-Smith, *First Crusaders*, p.165.
24. Métais, "Croisés chartrains et dunois," p.209.
25. *Ibid.*, p.199.
26. Chédeville, *Chartres*, p.328. John W. Baldwin, *The Government of Philip Augustus* (University of California Press: Berkeley, 1986), p.67.
27. The first edition of Donald E. Queller's *The Fourth Crusade* (University of Pennsylvania Press: Philadelphia, 1977), is more useful here than the second (Philadelphia, 1997). For the men of the Chartrain: Métais, "Croisés chartrains et dunois," pp.199–206; Jean Longnon, *Les Compagnons de Villehardouin: recherches sur les croisés de la quatrième croisade* (Librarie Droz: Geneva, 1978), pp.79–115.
28. Geoffrey of Villehardouin, *Conquest of Constantinople* (trans. M.R.B. Shaw) (Penguin Books: Harmondsworth, 1963), p.29.
29. I.e., the new Latin emperor of Constantinople. *Ibid.*, p.121.
30. Pierre de Vaux-de-Cernai, *Histoire Albigeoise* (trans. P. Guébin and H. Maisonneuve) (Librairie Philosophique J. Vrin: Paris, 1951), cap. 104, p.48.
31. Villehardouin, *Conquest of Constantinople*, p.54.
32. P.E.D. Comte de Riant, "Les dépouilles religieuses enlevées à Constantinople au xiiie siècle," *Mémoires de la Société Nationale des Antiquaires de France*, 4th series, Vol. 6 (1875), pp.1–214, here at pp.200, 202, 206.
33. For the Albigensian crusade, see text and references in Dickson, *Genesis*, pp.19–25; Malcolm Barber, *The Cathars* (Longman: Harlow, England, 2000), pp.120–40; Malcolm Lambert, *The Cathars* (Blackwell Publishers, Ltd: Oxford, 1998), pp.102–7.
34. De Vaux-de-Cernai, *Histoire Albigeoise*, cap. 142, p.62.
35. Y. Dossat, "Simon de Montfort," in *Paix de Dieu et guerre sainte en Languedoc au xiiie siècle, Cahiers de Fanjeaux*, Vol. 4 (Toulouse, 1969), pp.281–302.
36. Laon, p.85.
37. Note M. Zerner-Charavoine and H. Piéchon-Palloc, "La croisade albigeoise, une revanche: des rapports entre la quatrième croisade et la croisade albigeoise," *Revue Historique*, Vol. 267 (1982), pp.3–18.

38. De Vaux-de-Cernai, *Histoire Albigeoise*, caps. 174, 186; pp.72–8.
39. Pierre Belperron, *La croisade contre les Albigeois et l'union du Languedoc à la France, 1209–49* (Plon: Paris, 1946), p.159.
40. De Vaux-de-Cernai, *Histoire Albigeoise*, cap. 286, p.117.
41. *Ibid.*, caps. 285, 310; pp.115–16, 124. Cf. Michel Roquebert, *L'épopée cathare, 1198–1212: l'invasion* (Toulouse, 1970), p.453.
42. De Vaux-de-Cernai, *Histoire Albigeoise*, cap. 298, p.120.
43. Dickson, *Genesis*, pp.25–31; Joseph F. O'Callaghan, "Innocent III and the Kingdoms of Castile and Leon," in John C. Moore (ed.), *Pope Innocent III and his World* (Ashgate: Aldershot, 1999), here at pp.327–40.
44. See A. Jeanroy (ed.) (re-ed./trans. by J. Boelcke), *Anthologie des troubadours* (Paris, 1974), pp.281–6; S. Stronski, *Le troubadour Folquet de Marseille* (Cracow, 1910), pp.83–6, 134ff.
45. J. Rupp, *L'Idée de Chrétienté dans la pensée pontificale des origines à Innocent III* (Paris, 1939), p.102.
46. A. Huici Miranda (ed.), *Colección de Crónicas Arabes de la Reconquista*, Vol. 2:1. *Los Almohades* (Tetuán, 1953), p.271.
47. E. de Lépinois, *Histoire de Chartres*, Vol. 1 (Chartres, 1854), pp.125, 129, is hesitant; more recent historians accept it as fact.
48. Innocent III, *Opera omnia* in J.-P. Migne, *Patrologiae latina*, Vol. 216 (Paris, 1855), col. 514, no. 155; date corrected by A. Potthast, *Regesta Pontificum Romanorum*, Vol. 1 (Berlin, 1874), p.377, no. 4373.
49. See Michael McCormick, "Liturgie et guerre des Carolingiens à la première croisade," *"Militia Christi" e Crociata nei secoli xi–xiii* (Miscellanea del Centro di Studi Medioevali, 30) (Milan, 1992), pp.209–38.
50. See Christoph T. Maier, "Mass, Eucharist and the Cross: Innocent III and the Relocation of the Crusade," in John C. Moore (ed.), *Pope Innocent III and his World* (Ashgate: Aldershot, 1999), here at pp.352–6.
51. D. Mansilla (ed.), *La Documentacion pontifica hasta Innocencio III* (Monumenta Hispaniae Vaticana, sec.: registros, 1) (Rome, 1955), pp.503–4, no. 473.
52. *Recepimus litteras dolore* in Migne, Vol. 216, col. 514, no. 155; date corrected by Potthast, p.377, no. 4373.
53. Alberic of Trois-Fontaines, p.894.
54. Cf. Baldwin, *Government of Philip Augustus*, pp.359–62.
55. O'Callaghan, "Innocent III and the Kingdoms of Castile and Lyon," p.332.
56. See n.3.
57. "Ritual and crisis" in Edward Shils, *Center and Periphery: Essays in Macrosociology*, Vol. 2 (University of Chicago Press: Chicago, 1975), pp.153–63, here at p.158.
58. Le Long, p.828.
59. The two grounds are: first, two lines of Le Long's seven-line notice on the Children's Crusade are taken from the chronicle of William of Andres; and second, whatever John says "is of little authority" because he was writing so many years after the events in question. The counter-arguments are these. First: out of Le Long's seven-line notice on the Children's Crusade, five of those lines, including those cited on the Spanish stimulus for the Chartres diocesan processions, come from a source which even Le Long's learned *Monumenta* editor has failed to identify. So, which is more likely—that John

took it from a well-informed contemporary source that has not come down to us, or that he personally fabricated the link between the Spanish crisis and the processions at Chartres? A minor point such as this did not appeal to the mythistorical imagination; nor would it have been of special interest to anyone. Second: Léon van der Essen, a fine scholar, has confirmed that in order to compose his chronicle of Saint-Bertin, John Le Long carried out genuine research into the history of the monastery of which he was then the abbot. John consulted "antiquities," older chronicles, archives, and official documents (see his "Jean d'Ypres ou de Saint-Bertin (+1383)," *Revue Belge de Philologie et d'Histoire*, Vol. 2 (1922), pp.475–94). Le Long's account is necessarily derivative, that goes without saying, but from whom did he borrow?

60. Dickson, *Genesis*, p.39ff., with full references.
61. See R. Merlet (ed.), *Collection de cartulaires chartrains, Vol. 1: Cartulaire de Saint-Jean-en-Vallée de Chartres* (Chartres, 1906), p.85, no. 174 (March, 1212), p.86, no. 176 (May, 1212).
62. For discussion, see Dickson, *Genesis*, p.35ff., n.140. Cf. *Annalium Rotomagensium continuationibus* (ed. O. Holder-Egger) in *MGH. SS.* Vol. 26, p.501.
63. Latin text: Mortemer, p.467. English translation adapted from Hecker, p.354.
64. See n.52.
65. Medieval *adolescentia* was usually reckoned to end at twenty-eight: see James A. Schultz, "Medieval Adolescence: The Claims of History and the Silence of German Narrative," *Speculum*, Vol. 66 (1991), pp.519–39, here at p.531.
66. Note "*pueri et puellae* with (*cum*)...."
67. Dickson, *Genesis*, p.46ff, with full references, but note the crusade associations of "exalt Christendom!" for which, see especially the definitive essay by Jean Flori, "'Pur eshalcier sainte crestiënté': Croisade, guerre sainte et guerre juste dans les anciennes chansons de geste françaises," *Le Moyen Age*, Vol. 97 (1991), pp.171–87.

Chapter 4 History: Charisma

1. Max Weber, "The Sociology of Charismatic Authority" in H.H. Gerth and C. Wright Mills (eds.), *From Max Weber: Essays in Sociology* (Routledge & Kegan Paul: London, 1970), pp.245–52, here at p.246.
2. The bibliography on Weberian charisma is very extensive. Here are a few titles: Reinhard Bendix, "Reflections on Charismatic Leadership," in Dennis Wrong (ed.), *Max Weber* (Prentice-Hall: Englewood Cliffs, New Jersey, 1970); S.N. Eisenstadt (ed.), *Max Weber on Charisma & Institution Building* (University of Chicago Press: Chicago, 1968); Edward Shils, "Charisma," in his *Center and Periphery: Essays in Macrosociology*, Vol. 2 (University of Chicago Press: Chicago, 1975), pp.127–34.
3. *The Letters of St. Bernard of Clairvaux* (ed./trans. Bruno Scott James) (Burns Oates: London, 1953), no. 391, p.461.
4. René Crozet, "Le voyage d'Urbain II et ses négociations avec le clergé de France," *Revue Historique*, Vol. 179 (1937), pp.271–310, and "Le voyage

d'Urbain II en France (1095–96) et son importance au point de vue archéologique," *Annales du Midi*, Vol. 49 (1937), pp.42–69.

5. Extract from Guibert's *Dei Gesta per Francos* in August C. Krey (ed./trans.), *The First Crusade* (Peter Smith: Gloucester, Mass., 1958), pp.47–8.
6. Hippolyte Delehaye, "Note sur la légende de la lettre du Christ tombée du Ciel," *Bulletins de l'Académie Royale de Belgique*, Classe des lettres... no. 2 (Brussels, 1899), pp.172–212, here at p.187.
7. See *Gesta Francorum* (ed./trans, Rosalind Hill) (Nelson: Edinburgh, 1962), pp.33, 66, 94. Jean Flori, who makes a good case for "rehabilitating" Peter, nevertheless believes that the claim that Peter later founded the abbey of Neufmoustier at Huy is "a legend without a historical basis." See his *Pierre l'ermite et la première croisade* (Fayard: Paris, 1999), p.494.
8. For bibliography on the *Caputiati*, see Dickson, *Crowds*, pp.62–3.
9. For Stephen's pilgrimage to St. Denis, see especially Dickson, *Stephen*.
10. Mortemer, p.467.
11. Le Long, p.828. Adapted from Hecker, p.356.
12. Guy Fourquin, *Les campagnes de la région parisienne à la fin du Moyen Age* (Presses Universitaires de France: Paris, 1964), p.78.
13. Marie-Thérèse Kaiser-Guyot, *Le berger en France aux xiv*[e] *et xv*[e] *siècles* (Editions Klincksieck: Paris, 1974), pp.116–17.
14. Dr. Michael L. Ryder, author of *Sheep and Man* (Duckworth: London, 1983), kindly supplied this information.
15. Andres, p.754. Le Long's citation from William of Andres begins where William begins; Andres has no idea how or where the Children's Crusade originated. Translation modified from Hecker, p.356 and Shinners, p.397.
16. See Norbert Backmund, *Die mittelalterlichen geschichtsschreiber der Prämonstratenersordens* (Bibliotheca Analectorum Praemonstratensium, 10, Louvain, 1972), pp.267–72.
17. Laon, pp.20–2, 29–30, 37–40, 67, 69–70, 68.
18. *Ibid.*, pp.70–1. Translation revised from Hecker, p.354.
19. Jumièges, p.510. Two later Norman chronicles copy Jumièges.
20. Kaiser-Guyot, *Le berger en France*, pp.23–5.
21. See André Chédeville, *Chartres et ses Campagnes* (Editions Klincksieck: Paris, 1973), pp.60–1; A. Peschot, *Recherches historique sur Cloyes-sur-le-Loir* (reprinted Le Livre d'Histoire: Autremencourt, 1989), *passim*.
22. See Marie-Luce Chéramy, *Notre Dame d'Yron* (Publications de la Société Dunoise, Vol. 19, 1976), p.46.
23. See *Aucassin and Nicolette and other Medieval Tales* (trans. Pauline Matarasso) (Penguin Books: Harmondsworth, 1971), p.40.
24. Chédeville, *Chartres*, p.459; Kaiser-Guyot, *Le berger en France*, p.49; Ryder, *Sheep and Man*, p.412.
25. See Émile Mâle, *Notre-Dame de Chartres* (Flammarion: Paris, 1963), pp.28–9.
26. *Bond Men Made Free—Medieval Peasant Movements and the English Rising of 1381* (Temple Smith: London, 1973), p.101.
27. Paul Alphandéry suspects that the Laon chronicler's account of Stephen was contaminated by hagiographic motifs in the saint's life (*vita*) of the youthful St. Bénézet (d. 1184), the shepherd boy who reputedly built a bridge across the Rhône at Avignon in 1177 after Christ had ordered him to do so,

and an angel had visited him in the guise of a poor pilgrim: Alphandéry, *d'enfants*, p.273; taken up again in Alphandéry, *La chrétienté*, pp.341–2. These suspicions, however, are misconceived. The Laon Anonymous does indeed discuss the career of St. Bénézet (Laon, p.28), but his brief notice is markedly different from Bénézet's *vita* (cf. *Acta Sanctorum*, Victor Palmé: Paris, 1866, *Aprilis*, Vol. 2, pp.254–63). Note especially that in the Laon chronicle: (1) Bénézet is called *juvenis* and not *puer*; (2) there is no mention of sheep or shepherds in connection with Bénézet; (3) there is no vision or voice of Christ; (4) there is no angel; (5) and no pilgrim dress. Compared to the *vita*, the Laon chronicler's report is more sober in tone, and more plausible in many other respects. Finally, there is a strong presumption that the legend of St. Bénézet was composed c. 1270–80, long after the death of the Laon Anonymous (cf. F. Lefort, "La légende de saint Bénézet," *Revue des questions historiques*, Vol. 23 (1878), pp.555–70, here at pp.556–7).

28. *The Children's Crusade: An Episode of the Thirteenth Century* (Hurd and Houghton: New York, 1870), p.30.
29. *La Crociata dei Bambini* (Mondadori: Milan, 1983), p.97. Cloyes was on the Santiago pilgrimage route from Chartres to Tours, according to Kenneth J. Conant, *Carolingian and Romanesque Architecture, 800 to 1200* (Penguin: Harmondsworth, 1959), p.xxxiii.
30. A motif not unknown to *exempla* literature: see Frederic C. Tubach, *Index Exemplorum: A Handbook of Medieval Religious Tales* (Suomalainen Tiedeakatemia: Helsinki, 1969), p.80, no. 987.
31. Sometimes known as the *Memoriale* of Walter of Coventry or the "Barnwell" chronicle, it derives from the Crowland annals (to 1224–25) from which it was copied into the Peterborough chronicle. See Richard Kay, "Walter of Coventry and the Barnwell Chronicle," *Traditio*, Vol. 54 (1999), pp.141–67, here at p.156. Peterborough, p.6.
32. See James Lea Cate, "The English Mission of Eustace of Flay (1200–1201)," in *Études d'Histoire dédiées à la mémoire de Henri Pirenne* (ed. François Louis Ganshof, *et al.*) (Nouvelle Société d'Éditions: Brussels, 1937), pp.67–89.
33. Michel Mollat (ed.), *Histoire de l'Ile-de-France et de Paris* (Privat: Toulouse, 1971), p.117.
34. See Anne Lombard-Jourdan, "Les foires de l'abbaye de Saint-Denis," *Bibliothèque de l'École des chartes*, Vol. 145 (1987), pp.273–338. Professor Elizabeth A.R. Brown kindly directed me to this essay; Mme. Lombard-Jourdan graciously commented on an earlier version of my ideas, although I alone am responsible for errors and misinterpretations.
35. "Center, Kings, and Charisma: Reflections on the Symbolics of Power" in Joseph Ben-David, *et al.* (eds.), *Culture and its Creators: Essay in honor of Edward Shils* (University of Chicago Press: Chicago, 1977), pp.150–71, here at p.151.
36. See Gabrielle M. Spiegel, "The Cult of Saint Denis and the Capetian Kings," *Journal of Medieval History*, Vol. 1 (1975), pp.43–70; *idem.*, *The Chronicle Tradition of Saint-Denis: A Survey* (Classical Folia Editions: Brookline, Mass., 1978).
37. Elizabeth A.R. Brown and M.W. Cothren, "The Twelfth-Century Crusading Window of the Abbey of Saint-Denis," *Journal of the Warburg and Courtauld Institutes*, Vol. 49 (1986), pp.1–40 and pls 1–12.

38. Dickson, *Genre*, pp.482–5.
39. *Ex chronico Lyrensis coenobii* (to 1249) (ed. M.J.J. Brial), *RHGF*, Vol. 18, p.352.
40. Professor John W. Baldwin most kindly provided me with information concerning Philip Augustus's itinerary during June, 1212. Any inferences I have drawn from this are my own.
41. On Innocent III and Paris, note Gordon Leff, *Paris and Oxford Universities in the Thirteenth and Fourteenth Centuries* (Wiley: New York, 1968), pp.21–7.
42. Lombard-Jourdan, "Les foires de l'abbaye de Saint-Denis," p.238.
43. Most notably, Zacour, *Children's Crusade*, pp.330–1.
44. See n.30.
45. Lombard-Jourdan, "Les foires de l'abbaye de Saint-Denis," p.327.
46. Jumièges, p.510.
47. See n.15.
48. Heinrich Gross, *Gallia Judaica: dictionnaire géographique de la France d'après les sources rabbiniques* (reprinted with a supplement by Simon Schwarzfuchs), (Philo Press: Amsterdam 1969), pp.151, 454, 602–4.
49. Alexandre Teulet, Henri-François Delaborde, and Elie Berger (eds.), *Layettes du Trésor des Chartes*, I (Paris, 1863), item no. 1049, pp.392–3. The document is headed: "Paris. 1213. 18 juin. *Sententia lata adversus majorem et cives S. Quintini de querelis in dicta urbe contra capitulum S. Quintini motis occasione puerorum.* (J.232-Saint-Quentin, n.1-Original scellé)." The key portion of the text reads: "…*ad querelas, que orte fuerant occasione puerorum inter D. decanum et capitulum, et R. de Sunville et O. de Sancto-Symone, canonicos Sancti Quintini, ex una parte, et burgenses Sancti Quintini, ex altera*…." Note also L.-P. Colliette, *Mémoires pour servir à l'histoire ecclésiastique, civile, et militaire de la province de Vermandois* (Cambrai, 1772), 2, pp.548–49. Colliette does not understand the meaning of *occasione puerorum*: "pour les causes que nous ignorons," p.481.
50. Also Raucourt, Rocour, and presently Rocourt, nowadays a suburb of Saint-Quentin.
51. De Janssens, "Étienne de Cloyes," pp.117–19. Cf. Zacour, *Children's Crusade*, p.325.
52. De Janssens, "Étienne de Cloyes," p.117.
53. Teulet, no.967, pp.366–7. Colliette, Vol. 2, pp.479–80.
54. Alphandéry, *d'enfants*, pp.261–2; Alphandéry, *La chrétienté*, p.345. Pallenberg, *La Crociata dei Bambini*, pp.20–3, situates Rocourt near Liège!
55. Marbach, p.82. Hecker, p.357.
56. See n.44.
57. Marbach, p.82. Shinners, pp.399–400.
58. Mousket, p.806.

Chapter 5 History: On the Road

1. See the entry on D.C. Munro by E.P. Cheyney in the *Dictionary of American Biography* (ed. Dumas Malone), Vol. 13 (Oxford University Press: London, 1934), pp.330–1. An edited version of Munro's unfinished work was published as *The Kingdom of the Crusaders* (ed. A.C. Krey) (D. Appleton-Century: New York, 1935).

2. "The Children's Crusade," *American Historical Review*, Vol. 19 (1913–14) pp.516–24, here at p.518. Krey praises this essay as perhaps "the best example of [Munro's] rigorous critical scholarship," *The Kingdom*, p.208.
3. The formula "all of Germany and France" (Cologne Continuator, p.17) is reversed as "all of France and Germany" (St. Pantaleon's Chronicler, p.234), but this has nothing to do with precedence. The chroniclers were ignorant about where it began, and eventually the spread of the revival made it appear to be everywhere at once.
4. Renier, p.95; *Ibid.*; Ebersheim, p.450; Marbach, p.82–3, adds Burgundy.
5. Jumièges, p.510; Andres, p.754; Albert of Stade, p.355; Marbach, p.82–3.
6. Mortemer, p.467; Marbach, p.82–3.
7. Mortemer, p.467; Cologne Continuator, p.17.
8. Andres, p.754; Cologne Continuator, p.18.
9. See Jonathan Riley-Smith, "The First Crusade and the Persecution of the Jews," in W.J. Sheils (ed.), *Persecution and Toleration* (Studies in Church History, 21) (Basil Blackwell: Oxford, 1984), pp.51–72.
10. See Jonathan Riley-Smith (ed.), *The Atlas of the Crusades* (Times Books: London, 1991), pp.30–1.
11. On Renier, see Nicolaus Dupuis, "Les 'Annales de Renier de Saint-Jacques,' (1194–1230). Une oeuvre et son auteur," in *Annuaire d'Histoire Liègeoise*, Vol. 29 (1998), pp.1–219, which supersedes Joseph Demarteau, *Le chroniqueur Renier* (Liège, 1874) and Sylvain Balau, *Les sources de l'histoire du Pays de Liège* (Brussels, 1903), pp.426–28.
12. Jacques Stiennon (ed.), *Histoire de Liège* (Privat: Toulouse, 1991), cap. 4 (by Jean-Louis Kupper), here at pp.76–87.
13. *Actes des Princes-Évèques de Liège* (ed. Édouard Poncelet) (Brussels, 1946), p.xvi; note also p.L.
14. Renier, pp.95–6.
15. There are some variations. Parental opposition: the Cologne Continuator says that their parents "tried to hold them back," not that some managed to do so. Intent: with Renier it is the Holy Sepulchre that the *pueri* desire to recover; with Cologne it is Jerusalem itself. Those who previously tried and failed: with Renier it is "the powerful and kings," while with the Cologne Continuator, it is "kings, dukes, and countless people."
16. Cologne Continuator, p.17. Shinners, p.399.
17. Miccoli, *Fanciulli*, p.415, n.32: around 25km. per day: 16 miles; John W. Nesbitt, "The Rate of March of Crusading Armies in Europe," *Traditio*, Vol. 19 (1963), pp.167–81, here at p.173: 28.5km. for Peter's *pauperes* (average daily marching rate): 18 miles; Raedts, *Children's Crusade*, pp.291, 319, n.21, 35km. per day: 22 miles; Dickson, *Pastores*, p.254, n.24: 20–25 miles per day.
18. Figures of mileage are approximate; and miles as well as miles per diem have been rounded off.
19. Erich Meuthen, "Aachen in der Geschictsschreibung," in *Speculum Historiale* (ed. C. Bauer, *et al.*) (Freiburg and Munich, 1966), p.378ff.
20. Ernst Kantorowicz, *Frederick II, 1194–1250* (trans. E.O. Lorimer) (Constable & Co.: London, 1957), pp.72–3.
21. Ernst G. Grimme, *Der Karlsschrein und der Marienschrein im Aachener Dom* (Einhard: Aachen, 2002), p.20.

22. Clark Maines, "The Charlemagne Window at Chartres Cathedral: New Considerations on Text and Image," *Speculum*, Vol. 52 (1977), pp.801–23; but cf. Colette Manhes-Deremble, *Les vitraux narratifs de la cathédrale de Chartres* (Corpus Vitrearum, France, 2) (Léopard d'or: Paris, 1993), p.10.
23. Of these, only the designs of two scenes survive: Louis Grodecki, *Les Vitraux de Saint-Denis: étude sur le vitrail au XIIe siècle* (C.N.R.S.: Paris, 1976), pp.115–21.
24. Glyn S. Burgess and Anne E. Cobby, *The Pilgrimage of Charlemagne* (Garland: New York and London, 1988), pp.1–3.
25. *Ibid.*, p.13; Carl Erdmann, *The Origin of the Idea of Crusade* (trans. M.W. Baldwin and W. Goffart) (Princeton University Press: Princeton, 1977), p.298.
26. Jonathan Riley-Smith, *The First Crusade and the Idea of Crusading* (The Athlone Press: London, 1986), pp.25, 111–12; *Gesta Francorum* (ed./ trans., Rosalind Hill) (Nelson: Edinburgh, 1962), p.2.
27. Robert Folz, *Le souvenir et la légénde de Charlemagne dans l'Empire germanique médiéval* (Les Belles Lettres: Paris, 1950), pp.180–1.
28. Erich Meuthen (ed.), *Aachener Urkunden, 1101–1250* (Bonn, 1972), pp.247–8. Also note Heinrich Schiffers, *Karls des Grossen Reliquienschatz und die Anfänge der Aachenfahrt* (Verlag J. Volk: Aachen, 1951), pp.60–1, n.194.
29. Her prized relic, the *sainte chemise*, some authors suggest, is the garment she wore while breastfeeding the baby Jesus.
30. A.W. Wybrands (ed.), *Gesta abbatum Orti Sancte Marie* (Leeuwarden, 1879), pp.3–4.
31. See Georges Duby, "Les pauvres des campagnes dans l'occident médiéval jusqu'au xiiie siècle," *Revue d'histoire de l'église de France*, Vol. 52 (1966), pp.25–32.
32. Rodney Hilton, *Bond Men Made Free—Medieval Peasant Movements and the English Rising of 1381* (Temple Smith: London, 1973), pp.37–8; Guy Fourquin, *Le Paysan d'Occident au Moyen Âge* (F. Nathan: Paris, 1972), pp.88–101; Günther Franz, *Geschichte des deutschen Bauernstandes vom frühen Mittelalter bis zum 19. Jahrhundert* (Deutsche Agrargeschichte, 4) (Ulmer: Stuttgart, 1970), pp.46, 49.
33. Paul Freedman, *Images of the Medieval Peasant* (Stanford University Press: Stanford, California, 1999) provides an up to date, balanced analysis.
34. Panis, Vol. 2, p.123. Hecker, pp.357–8 (based on Varagine).
35. Paris preacher, Vol. 1, p.60, n.188.
36. Mousket, p.806: *Que croisiet furent li enfant* (l.29207); "firmly fixed" (ll.29214–15).
37. Marbach, p.82; St. Pantaleon's Chronicler, p.234.
38. Raedts, *Children's Crusade*, p.283.
39. Piacenza, p.426.
40. *Ibid.*
41. Schäftlarn, p.338.
42. Cologne Continuator, pp.17–18.
43. A conflation of the texts of three chroniclers: Ebersheim, p.450; Schäftlarn, p.338; Richer, p.301.
44. On medieval French Jewish communities, see H. Gross, *Gallia Judaica* (reprinted Amsterdam 1969), pp.151, 454, 602–4.

45. On the "pilgrimage of the 300 rabbis," see Dickson, *Prophecy*, pp.99–102.
46. Cited in Joshua Prawer, *History of the Jews in the Latin Kingdom of Jerusalem* (Clarendon Press: Oxford 1988), pp.75–6.
47. *Ibid.*, pp.77–8.
48. Piacenza, p.426.
49. Trier, pp.398–9; Shinners, p.398.
50. Albert of Stade, p.355; Shinners, p.397.
51. Mortemer, p.467. Cf. Peterborough, p.6; St. Médard, p.521.
52. Schäftlarn, p.338: *crucem dominicam liberaturus....*
53. See, for example, Penny J. Cole, "Christian Perceptions of the Battle of Hattin (583/1187)", *Al-Masaq*, Vol. 7 (1993), pp.9–39.
54. Note the discussion in A. Frolow, *La Relique de la vraie croix* (Archives de l'Orient Chrétien, 7) (Paris, 1961), pp.97, 383, 494–5.
55. *Ibid.*, p.287.
56. For this paragraph, see Alan V. Murray, "'Mighty against the Enemies of Christ': the Relic of the True Cross in the Armies of the Kingdom of Jerusalem," in *The Crusades and their Sources* (ed. John France and William G. Zajac) (Ashgate: Aldershot, 1998), pp.217–38.
57. On the anonymous chronicle of the *Libellus de Expugnatione Terrae Sanctae per Saladinum*, see Helen J. Nicholson (trans.), *The Chronicle of the Third Crusade, the Itinerarium Peregrinorum et Gesta Regis Riccardi* (Ashgate: Aldershot, 1997), p.4. Translated text: James A. Brundage (ed. and trans.), *The Crusades: A Documentary Survey* (The Marquette University Press: Milwaukee, 1962), pp.158–9.
58. Cited from Ibn al-Athīr (d. 1233) in Francesco Gabrieli (ed./trans.) *Arab Historians of the Crusades* (trans. from the Italian by E.J. Costello) (Routledge & Kegan Paul: London, 1969), p.122.
59. Cole, "Christian Perceptions of the Battle of Hattin," pp.10–11.
60. H.-F. Delaborde (ed.), *Oeuvres de Rigord et de Guillaume le Breton*, Vol. 1 (Société de l'Histoire de France: Paris, 1882), pp.82–3, item no. 55.
61. See Peter W. Edbury (ed./trans.), *The Conquest of Jerusalem and the Third Crusade: Sources in Translation* (Scolar Press: Aldershot, 1996), pp.162–3.
62. October–November, 1187; cited from Louise and Jonathan Riley-Smith (eds./trans.), *The Crusades: Idea and Reality, 1095–1274* (Edward Arnold: London, 1981), pp.64–7.
63. Kate Norgate, *Richard the Lion Heart* (Macmillan: London, 1924), p.71. Cf. Nicholson, *Chronicle of the Third Crusade*, p.47: "Richard... was the first to receive the sign of the cross to avenge the Cross's injury."
64. Edbury, *Conquest of Jerusalem*, pp.179–80.
65. Yves M.-J. Congar, "Henri de Marcy," *Studia Anselmiana*, Fasc. 43, 5th series, pp.1–90, here at pp.53–7.
66. J.-P. Migne, *Patrologiae Latina*, Vol. 204 (Paris, 1855), col. 353.
67. *Sigeberti Gemblacensis continuatio Aquicinctina* (to 1237) (ed. D.L.C. Bethmann) in *MGH.SS.* 6: 424.
68. There is a considerable bibliography; two useful titles are: Richard Barber, *The Holy Grail: Imagination and Belief* (Allen Lane: London, 2004); Roger S. Loomis, *The Grail: From Celtic Myth to Christian Symbol* (Princeton University Press: Princeton, 1991).

69. Henri Pirenne, "Philippe d'Alsace," in *Biographie Nationale de Belgique*, Vol. 17 (Brussels, 1903), cols. 163–76.
70. Cf. Frederick W. Locke, *The Quest for the Holy Grail* (Stanford University Press: Stanford, 1960), pp.3–5.
71. Ebersheim, p.450.
72. See Michael E. Goodich, *From Birth to Old Age: The Human Life Cycle in Medieval Thought, 1250–1350* (University Press of America: Lanham, MD., 1989), p.60, referring to Isidore of Seville's *Etymologiae*: "*Pueritia* comes from pure (*purus*), the period just before puberty, which ends at fourteen." Cf. Shulamith Shahar, *Childhood in the Middle Ages* (Routledge: London and New York, 1992), p.22.
73. Cologne Continuator, p.17. Shinners, p.399.
74. See Kenneth M. Setton (ed.), *A History of the Crusades*, Vol. 1 (University of Pennsylvania Press: Philadelphia, 1958), pp.260–4, 472–7; Vol. 2 (1962), pp.89–90, 119–20, 164.
75. Full documentation in Dickson, *Genesis*, pp.20, 22–3; 25.
76. *Ibid.*, pp.27–31.
77. Raedts, *Children's Crusade*, p.290. As Raedts has astutely pointed out, Nicholas was not mentioned by any of Cologne's chroniclers: "This discrepancy can be explained if we assume that the movement originated near Cologne, and that Nicholas was... accepted [only] later as leader."
78. St. Pantaleon's Chronicler, p.234. By following his account of the *pueri* with an event known to have happened in July (*Circa idem tempus*), he effectively places the movement of the *pueri* within the month of July.
79. See Manfred Groten, *Köln im 13. Jahrhundert* (Böhlau: Köln, 1998); Jonathan W. Zophy (ed.), *The Holy Roman Empire* (Greenwood Press: Westport, Conn., 1980), pp.84–7.
80. See Richard C. Trexler, *The Journey of the Magi: Meanings in the History of a Christian Story* (Princeton University Press: Princeton, 1997), pp.74–9; Bernard Hamilton, "Prester John and the Three Kings of Cologne," reprinted in *Prester John, the Mongols, and the Ten Lost Tribes* (ed. C.F. Beckingham and B. Hamilton) (Ashgate: Aldershot, 1996), pp.171–85; Hans Hofmann, *Die heiligen drei Könige* (Ludwig Röhrscheid Verlag: Bonn, 1975), pp.130–4; and for the Latin prayer, Karl Meisen, *Die heiligen drei Könige* (Cologne, 1949), p.17.
81. St. Pantaleon's Chronicler, p.234. Revised from Hecker, p.358.
82. Cologne Continuator, p.17. Adapted from Shinners, p.399. This very slightly modifies the estimated date of their departure from Cologne in Dickson, *Genesis*, pp.16–18.
83. Cologne Continuator, p.18. The scholarly dispute over the place-name *Maguntie* (Mainz? Metz? Monza?) is best resolved in favor of Mainz. See Johann Graesse, *Orbis Latinus* (rev. H. Plechl), Vol. 2 (Braunschweig: Klinkhardt and Biermann, 1972), p.574.
84. Here the scholarly disagreement between "turned back" and "were turned back" is complicated by the list of three cities, Mainz, Piacenza, and Rome, all linked to a single verb, *revertebantur* "were turned back" which, if accurate, probably pertains only to Rome. Cf. the sensible remarks of Raedts, *Children's Crusade*, p.291: "The trip was obviously too hard for some, and they turned around at Mainz and went home."

85. Otto of Freising, *The Deeds of Frederick Barbarossa* (trans. Charles C. Mierow) (W.W. Norton: New York, 1966), pp.45–6.
86. Ludwig Falck, *Mainz in Frühen u. Hohen Mittelater* (Walter Rau Verlag: Düsseldorf, 1972), pp.161–2; *Idem.*, "Die erzbishchöfliches Metropole, 1011–1244," in Franz Dumont, *et al.*, *Mainz: Die Geschicte der Stadt* (Verlag P. von Zabern: Mainz, 1998), pp.130–2, 138.
87. On the Trier chronicler, see Petrus Becker, *Die Benediktinerabtei St. Eucharius-St. Matthias von Trier* (Germania Sacra, n.f., 34, Erzbistum Trier, 8) (Berlin, 1996), p.467; Fr. Bertheau, *Die Gesta Treverorum, 1152–1259* (R. Peppmüller: Göttingen, 1874), pp.40–1; W. Wattenbach and Franz-Josef Schmale, *Deutschlands Geschictsquellen im Mittelalter*, Vol. 1 (Darmstadt, 1976), pp.350–1.
88. P.B. Gams, *Series Episcoporum Ecclesiae Catholicae* (reprinted Graz, 1957), p.318; *Handbuch des Bistums Trier* (Paulinus: Trier, 1952), p.37.
89. Piacenza, p.426.
90. See Dickson, *Crowds.*
91. See Miccoli, *Fanciulli*, p.416.
92. Trier, pp.398–9. Translation adapted from Shinners, p.398.
93. Augustus Potthast (ed.), *Regesta Pontificum Romanorum*, Vol. 1 (reprinted Graz, 1957), p.146; Latin text in J.-P. Migne (ed.), *Patrologiae Latina*, Vol. 214 (Paris, 1855), col. 1012; English translation in James M. Powell (trans.), *The Deeds of Innocent III, by an Anonymous Author* (Catholic University of America Press: Washington, D.C., 2004), cap. 115, pp.214–15.
94. See n.42.
95. On the Exodus theme and the *tau*, see Miccoli, *Fanciulli*, p.420ff.; Damien Vorreux, *Un symbole franciscain: le Tau* (Paris 1977), p.18.
96. Speyer, p.84. On this chronicler, see Miccoli, *Fanciulli*, p.415, n.32, Raedts, *Children's Crusade*, p.286, and Wattenbach and Schmale, *Deutschlands Geschictsquellen im Mittelalter*, p.128.
97. *Ellenhardi annales* (to 1297) (ed. P. Jaffé) in *MGH.SS.* 17: 101. Cf. Raedts, *Children's Crusade*, p.290.
98. Ebersheim, p.450. Adapted from Shinners, p.398.
99. Zacour, *Children's Crusade*, p.335.

Chapter 6 History: The Great Migration

1. Marbach, p.82. Revised from Hecker, p.357 and Shinners, pp.399–400.
2. The calculation of Raedts, *Children's Crusade*, pp.290–1, seems generally the most reasonable. Also see Zacour, *Children's Crusade*, pp.333–4, and Cardini-Del Nero, *Fanciulli*, pp.25, 42–3.
3. Sicard, pp.180–1; and note cap. 1, *Introduction*. Cf. Zacour, *Children's Crusade*, p.334 and Jonathan Riley-Smith (ed.), *The Atlas of the Crusades* (Times Books: London, 1991), pp.82–3.
4. Piacenza, p.426.
5. Giacomo C. Bascapé, "Le vie pellegrinaggi medioevali attraverso le Alpi Centrali e la pianura lombarda," *Archivio Storico della Svizzera Italiana*, 11 (July–December 1936), pp.129–69, here at pp.160–1.

6. See David Abulafia (ed.), *Italy in the Central Middle Ages* (Short Oxford History of Italy) (Oxford University Press: Oxford, 2004).
7. Panis, Vol. 2, p.123. Hecker, p.357.
8. The late French verse chronicler, Philippe Mousket (d. early 1240s), initially says that no one knew how many ran off on crusade; then he relents—there were 10,000 of them. Mousket, ll.29210, 29224. Mousket does not appear in Raedts's bibliography.
9. James of Varagine's Genoese chronicle (to 1297) misdates the coming of the *pueri* to 1222 and derives partially from Pane. It includes interesting mythistorical elements.
10. Michel Balard, "Le film des navigations orientales de Gêne du xiiie siècle" in *Horizons Marins, Itinéraires Spirituels* (ed. H. Dubois, *et al.*) (Publications de la Sorbonne: Nancy, 1987), pp.99–122, here at pp.100, 104. Records for 1212 are incomplete, but in 1213 a sailing for *outre-mer* is recorded for September 30.
11. Richer, p.301.
12. Cf. Steven A. Epstein, "Urban Society," in *The New Cambridge Medieval History*, Vol. V (ed. David Abulafia) (Cambridge University Press, 1999), pp.26–37.
13. Cologne Continuator, p.18. Shinners, p.399.
14. A. Montreuil, "Moeurs et institutions marseillaises au Moyen-Age. L'Esclavage," *Revue de Marseille*, Vol. IV (1858), pp.153–74, and more generally, Jacques Heers, *Esclaves et domestiques au Moyen-Age* (Fayard: Paris, 1981).
15. For example, see John W. Baldwin, *Masters, Princes, and Merchants: The Social Views of Peter the Chanter and his Circle* (Princeton University Press: Princeton, 1970), Vol. I, p.267.
16. See Leon Festinger, *When Prophecy Fails: A Social and Psychological Study of a Modern Group that Predicted the Destruction of the World* (Harper & Row: New York, 1964).
17. See David Herlihy, *Pisa in the Early Renaissance: A Study in Urban Growth* (Yale University Press: New Haven, 1958), *passim*.
18. Richer, p.301. Translated by A.B.E. Hood.
19. Whereas Hansbery, *Children's Crusade*, p.36, n.40, correctly, I think, is hesitant about them sailing from Pisa, Zacour, *Children's Crusade*, p.334, has no such reservations. Hansbery, however, makes an egregious toponymic blunder with Richer, mistaking his monastery of Sénones in the Vosges, for Sens, southeast of Paris. Hence he argues that Sens was "one of the points of origin of the real children's crusade" (p.32)!
20. Bascapé, "Le vie pellegrinaggi," p.135.
21. Robert Brentano, *Rome before Avignon* (Longman: London, 1974), p.13.
22. For the Jubilee of 1300, see Gary Dickson, "The Crowd at the Feet of Pope Boniface VIII: Pilgrimage, Crusade and the First Roman Jubilee (1300)," *Journal of Medieval History*, Vol. 25, no. 4 (1999), pp.279–307.
23. Marbach, p.82; cf. Alberic of Trois-Fontaines, p.893.
24. Léopold Delisle, "Itinéraire de Innocent III d'après les actes de ce pontife" in *Bibliothèque de l'École des chartes*, Vol. 18 (1857), pp.500–34, here at p.529. See Dickson, *Innocent*, p.590ff. On Segni, note John C. Moore, *Pope Innocent III (1160/61–1216): To Root Up and to Plant* (Brill: Leiden and Boston, 2003), pp.2, 200ff. Moore says "we do not know" if "any of these 'crusaders' [i.e.

the *pueri* of 1212] saw Innocent in Segni" (p.201), but Segni is less plausible than Rome as a possible meeting place.

25. Salzburg, p.780.
26. See n.23 and Albert of Stade, p.355. A leading Innocentian scholar takes it for granted that Innocent III knew about it, see Michele Maccarrone, *Studi su Innocenzo III* (Editrice Antenore: Padua, 1972), pp.97–9.
27. Latin text of Innocent's sermon *Desiderio desideravi* in Migne, *P.L.*, Vol. 217, cols. 673–80. English translation in Marshall W. Baldwin (ed.), *Christianity through the Thirteenth Century* (Harper & Row: New York, 1970), p.298.
28. Damien Vorreux, *Un symbole franciscain: le Tau* (Paris, 1977), pp.5–6. For a good illustration, see John V. Fleming, *From Bonaventure to Bellini: An Essay in Franciscan Exegesis* (Princeton University Press: Princeton, 1982), fig. 25.
29. This is the interpretation of Vorreux, *Uni symbole franciscain*, p.15.
30. See the *Second Life of St. Francis* by Thomas of Celano (trans. Placid Hermann) in Marion A. Habig (ed.), *St. Francis of Assisi: Writings and Early Biographies* (The Society for Promoting Christian Knowledge: London, 1979), cap. 72 (106), p.450.
31. Luke Wadding (ed.), *Annales Minorum*, Vol. 1 (Quaracchi, 1931), p.149. Cf. Vorreux, *Uni symbole franciscain*, p.9: pre-1217.
32. See John Moorman, *A History of the Franciscan Order* (Franciscan Herald Press: Chicago, 1988), pp.24–5, 25 n.3.
33. Note E. Randolph Daniel, *The Franciscan Concept of Mission in the High Middle Ages* (University of Kentucky Press: Lexington, 1975), pp.37–54. A classic example, pertaining directly to Francis's spiritual motives at Ancona, comes from the *First Life of St. Francis* by Thomas of Celano (trans. Placid Hermann) in Habig *St. Francis of Assisi*, cap. 20 (55), p.274.
34. *Life of St. Francis of Assisi* (Longmans, Green & Co.: London, 1927), p.184.
35. *Ibid.*, p.185.
36. L. Di Fonzo, "Per la cronologia di S. Francesco gli anni 1182–1212," *Miscellanea Francescana*, Vol. 82 (1982), pp.1–115, here at pp.106–7. Roberto Rusconi entertains the same possibility in his excellent "Francesco d'Assisi," *Dizionario Biografico degli Italiani*, Vol. 49 (1997), pp.664–78, here at p.666.
37. Wadding, *Annales Minorum*, Vol. 1, pp.146–7, based on a late chronicler.
38. Thomas of Celano, *First Life of St. Francis*, cap. 20 (55), pp.274–5.
39. Daniel Waley, *The Papal State in the Thirteenth Century* (Macmillan & Co.: London, 1961), pp.87–8.
40. It was at the start of Francis's second journey from Ancona that Bartholomew of Pisa's *De conformitate vitae b. Francisci ad vitam domini Iesu* (composed 1385–99) places the saint's encounter with a "little boy" (*parvum puerum*), whom he asks to decide which of his friars should go with him. The boy does so, declaring it was "God's will." This is the *topos* of childhood innocence and purity—a "little boy" voicing the voice of God. See *Analecta Franciscana*, Vol. 4 (1906), p.481. Translation in Habig, *St. Francis of Assisi*, pp.1841–2.
41. Kenneth M. Setton (ed.), *A History of the Crusades*, Vol. 1 (University of Pennsylvania Press: Philadelphia, 1958), pp.278, 358, 491.
42. Translation of *Ad liberandam* from Louise and Jonathan Riley-Smith (eds./trans.), *The Crusades: Idea and Reality, 1095–1274* (Edward Arnold: London, 1981), pp.124–9.

43. Kenneth M. Setton (ed.), *A History of the Crusades*, Vol. 2 (University of Pennsylvania Press: Philadelphia, 1962), p.382.
44. Trier, p.399. Translation modified from Shinners, p.398.
45. His name is uncertain. See C. Eubel (ed.), *Hierarchia Catholica Medii Aevi*, Vol. 1 (rev. edn.) (Librariae Regensbergianae: Monasterii, 1913), p.149. Vincent of Beauvais (d. 1264) also places the *pueri* at Brindisi: see cap. 7.
46. St. Pantaleon's Chronicler, p.234.
47. Admont, p.592.
48. Eubel, *Hierarchia Catholica Medii Aevi*, p.149.
49. Joseph P. Donovan, *Pelagius and the Fifth Crusade* (University of Pennsylvania Press: Philadelphia, 1950), pp.44–6.
50. See James M. Powell, *Anatomy of a Crusade, 1213–21* (University of Pennsylvania Press: Philadelphia, 1986), p.144.
51. Setton, *History of the Crusades*, Vol. 2, p.428.
52. *The "Historia Occidentalis" of Jacques de Vitry: A Critical Edition* (John F. Hinnebusch, ed.) (University Press: Fribourg, Switzerland, 1972), p.161ff. Passage translated in John R.H. Moorman, *Sources for the Life of St. Francis of Assisi* (Manchester University Press: Manchester, 1940), p.56.
53. Martiniano Roncaglia, "San Francesco d'Assisi in Oriente," *Studi Francescani* Vol. 50 (1953), pp.97–106, here at pp.98–9.
54. Cf. James Powell, "Francesco d'Assisi e la Quinta Crociata: una Missione di Pace," *Schede Medievali*, Vol. 4 (1983), pp.68–77, well-argued, although the link with Joachist teaching is untenable, but also note Benjamin Z. Kedar, *Crusade and Mission: European Approaches toward the Muslims* (Princeton University Press: Princeton, 1984), pp.119–26, and especially the contrary opinions, pp.129–31.
55. Thomas of Celano, *Second Life of St. Francis*, cap. 4 (30), pp.388–9.
56. Hinnebusch, *"Historia Occidentalis" of Jacques de Vitry*, p.162. Moorman, *Sources for the Life of St. Francis*, p.56.
57. James of Vitry substantially confirms Illuminato's account; for Ernoul, note Kedar, *Crusade and Mission*, pp.122–3.
58. Bonaventure, *Major Life of St. Francis*, in Habig, *St. Francis of Assisi*, cap. 9 (8), pp.703–5.
59. *Verba S. Francisci*, cap. 5, in *Documenta Antiqua Franciscana* (ed. Lemmens), Vol. I, p.104, cited in John Moorman, *Church Life in England in the Thirteenth Century* (Cambridge University Press: Cambridge, 1945), p.366.
60. For Nicholas, see Admont, p.592. Francis may have contracted trachoma while in the East: see Rusconi, "Francesco d'Assisi," p.668.
61. Archivio Segreto, Reg. Vat. 11, epist. 52, fol. 13r; cf. *Regesta Honorii Papae III*, ed. P. Pressuti, no. 2627. Dr. Jessalynn Bird alerted me to this document and kindly transcribed the passage from the Ms.
62. Professor Brundage informs me that "the *locus classicus* is in Gratian's *Decretum* at C.20 q.1 c.1 *Firma autem* and C.20 q.1 d. a. c.9" and Gratian's basic teachings concerning vows were elaborated by the early decretists to include the ratification of vows made by minors below the age of fourteen.
63. James A. Brundage, *Medieval Canon Law and the Crusader* (University of Wisconsin Press: Madison, 1969), pp.75, 81, 105, 133.

64. A preliminary investigation of what it meant to be a *scolaris pauper* in medieval universities is Jacques Paquet, "L'Universitaire 'pauvre' au Moyen Age: problèmes, documentations, questions de méthode," in Jozef Ijsewijn and Jacques Paquet (eds.), *The Universities in the Late Middle Ages* (Leuven, 1978), pp.399–425. I owe this reference to Professor James Brundage.
65. Laon, pp.70–1.
66. Points raised by Professor James Brundage.
67. See "Aquilée: liste des Patriarches," *Dictionnaire d'histoire et de géographie ecclésiastiques*, Vol. 3 (Paris, 1924), p.141.
68. C. Cecchelli, "Aquileia," *Enciclopedia Cattolica*, Vol. 1, col. 1725 (Florence, 1948).
69. The informed judgment of Professor Andrea Tilatti, whose erudite assistance in tracking down documents in Friuli has been invaluable. I alone, however, am responsible for interpreting them.
70. See J.E. Tyler, *The Alpine Passes* (Blackwell: Oxford, 1930), pp.127, 135ff.
71. See C. Scalon (ed.), "Introduzione," *Necrologium Aquileiense* (Udine, 1982), p.44. I was directed to this text by Andrea Tilatti.
72. Zacour, *Children's Crusade*, p.339.
73. The mythistoricizing Alberic of Trois-Fontaines speaks of "four hundred [enslaved *pueri*], eighty of them priests and all of them clerics" purchased by the caliph; see Alberic of Trois-Fontaines, pp.893–4.
74. Scalon, *Necrologium Aquileinse*, p.44, n.24 *bis*.
75. C. Scalon (ed.), *Libri, Scuole, e Cultura nel Friuli* (Antenore: Padua, 1987), pp.23–4, n.56. Andrea Tilatti alerted me to this text also.
76. Scalon, *Necrologium Aquileiense*, p.44, n.24 *bis.*, pp.99–100.
77. St. Pantaleon's Chronicler, p.234. Revised from Hecker, p.359. Also note Schäftlarn, p.338.
78. Richer, p.301; Ebersheim, p.450.
79. Marbach, p.82. Translation revised from Hecker, p.357, and Shinners, pp.399–400. A later chronicler pretty much echoes these remarks: Richer of Sénones, p.301, notes that such a dispersal took place in Italy, with the new migrants becoming servants and laborers: *per regiones Ytalie et Tuscie dispersi, ad serviendum gentibus illius terre vel ad laborandum....*
80. Marbach, p.83, Shinners, p.400; Ebersheim, p.450.
81. Floreffe, p.626; Marbach, p.82; Trier, p.399; Ebersheim, p.450; Mousket, p.806, ll.29220–4.
82. Albert of Stade, p.355.
83. Cologne Continuator, p.18. Shinners, p.399.
84. Albert of Stade, p.355. Shinners, p.397.
85. Schäftlarn, p.338.
86. Cologne Continuator, p.18. Shinners, p.399.
87. Under certain circumstances, Christians could still enslave Christians, especially for debt: see Heers, *Esclaves et domestiques*, pp.17–20ff.
88. Marbach, p.82. Translation revised from Hecker, p.357, and Shinners, p.400.
89. As recently as 1950, a reputable Catholic historian (*nihil obstat*), dismissed the Children's Crusade as "that mass movement of child delinquency in 1212." Donovan, *Pelagius and the Fifth Crusade*, p.26.

90. Latin text: Mortemer, p.467. English translation revised from Hecker, p.354.
91. M. and C. Dickson, "Le cardinal Robert de Courson," *Archives d'Histoire Doctrinale et Littéraire du Moyen Age*, Vol. 9 (1934), pp.53–142, here at pp.64, 85–7, 90–1.
92. Note Powell, *Anatomy of a Crusade*, pp.20–2.
93. *Ibid.*, p.35. Guilelmus Brito, *Historia Philippi Augusti, RHGF*, Vol. 17, p.108, *s.a.* 1214, cited in R. Röhricht (ed.), *Testimonia minora ed quinto bello sacrpo e chronicis occidentalibus* (Publications de la société de l'orient latin, série historique), 3 (Geneva, 1882), pp.78–9.
94. *Item ad crucesignatos*: ff.233ra–234rb in Ms. Paris BNF n.a.l. 999. See Nicole Bériou, *L'avènement des maîtres de la Parole: la prédication à Paris aux XIIIe siècle* (Collection des Études Augustiniennes, Série Moyen Âge et Temps Modernes, 31), Vol. I (Paris, 1998), pp.58–62; Vol. II (Paris, 1998), pp.681–2. Professor Bériou kindly transcribed this Ms. passage for me before her book appeared.
95. *Ibid.*, Vol. I, p.60, n.188 for the extract quoted. "In another /the other year" (*alio anno*), meaning last year, or shortly thereafter, Nicole Bériou dates precisely to 1213.
96. Contrary to Zacour, *Children's Crusade*, pp.330–2, and Raedts, *Children's Crusade*, pp.292–3.
97. Unless we think of it in Aristotelian terms as a material cause.
98. There is no evidence that the *pueri* imagined themselves as part of a spiritual elite called "the poor." Nor did representative churchmen at the time confuse the socio-economic poor with Christ's poor. Preaching the Third Crusade in 1189, Alan of Lille denounced sinful prelates, knights, burgesses, merchants—along with the plebs, the common people (amongst whom were the poor). Only Christ's poor would be the Lord's crusaders, and they were *the poor in spirit*. Here he cites Matthew 5:3: *Beati pauperes spiritu....* See Marie-Thérèse d'Alverny (ed.), *Alain de Lille: textes inédits* (J. Vrin: Paris, 1965), pp.142–3, 279–83.
99. On medieval revivalism, see Dickson, *Genre*; and Gary Dickson, "Medieval Revivalism," in Daniel Bornstein (ed.), *Medieval Christianity* (Vol. 4 of *The People's History of Christianity*) (Augsburg Fortress Publishers, forthcoming).
100. See Jonathan Riley-Smith, "The First Crusade and the Persecution of the Jews," in W.J. Sheils (ed.), *Persecution and Toleration* (*Studies in Church History*, Vol. 21) (Oxford, 1984), pp.51–72, and *idem.*, *The Crusades: A Short History* (Yale University Press: New Haven and London, 1987), pp.18–20.
101. For bibliography, see Gary Dickson, "Shepherds' Crusade, First (1251)" and "Shepherds' Crusade, Second (1320)," in Alan Murray (ed.) *The Crusades: An Encyclopedia* (ABC-CLIO, 2006), Vol. 4, pp.1093–4, 1094–5.
102. For bibliography, see Gary Dickson, "Popular Crusades," in Murray, *The Crusades: An Encyclopedia* (ABC-CLIO, 2006), Vol. 3, pp.975–9.
103. On medieval youth movements after 1212, see Dickson, *Genre*, pp.487–90. For 1333, see *Chronicon Abrincense* (to 1359) excerpted in *RHGF*, Vol. 23, De Wailly, *et al.* (eds.) (Paris, 1894), pp.569–70, at p.569. *Quartum Chronicorum Librum... vulgo Anonymus Cadomensis* (to 1343) in E. Chantel (ed.), *Mémoires de la Société des Antiquaires de Normandie*, Vol. 33 (1892), p.170.

104. Note Vidal Chomel, "Pèlerins languedociens au Mont Saint-Michel à la fin du moyen âge," *Annales du Midi*, Vol. 70 (1958), pp.230–9, here at p.234.
105. *Ibid.*, pp.232, 234–7 (Latin text of Soybert's letter at pp.237–9).
106. The fullest account is found in Ulrich Gäbler, "Die Kinderwallfahrten aus Deutschland und der Schweiz zum Mont-Saint-Michel, 1456–59," *Zeitschrift für schweizerische Kirchengeschichte*, Vol. 63 (1969) pp.221–331.
107. The most recent discussion is that of Dominique Julia, "Le pèlerinage au Mont-Saint-Michel du XVe au XVIIIe siècle," in Pierre Bouet, *et al.* (eds.), *Culte et Pèlerinages à Saint Michel en Occident* (École Française de Rome: Rome, 2003), pp.271–320; for contemporary interpretations, see pp.282–7; allusion to the Children's Crusade, p.285, n.40.

Chapter 7 Mythistory: The Shape of a Story

1. See Nancy F. Partner, "Historicity in an Age of Reality-Fictions," in Frank Ankersmit and Hans Kellner (eds.), *A New Philosophy of History* (Reaktion Books: London, 1995), pp.21–39, here at pp.23–5.
2. The classic text is Hayden White, *Tropics of Discourse: Essays in Cultural Criticism* (Johns Hopkins University Press: Baltimore, 1978), but also note Frank Kermode, *The Sense of an Ending* (Oxford University Press: New York, 1967), p.36, who writes, "historiography has become a discipline more devious and dubious because of our recognition that its methods depend to an unsuspected degree on myths and fictions."
3. Evelyn B. Vitz, *Medieval Narrative and Modern Narratology* (New York University Press: New York, 1989), p.111.
4. For the text, see G.G. Coulton (ed.), *Social Life in Britain from the Conquest to the Reformation* (Kegan Paul: London, 2004), pp.537–8. For commentary, see Nancy Partner, *Serious Entertainments: The Writing of History in Twelfth-Century England* (University of Chicago Press: Chicago, 1977), p.121.
5. St. Médard, p.521; translation modified from Hecker, p.359. Literary mockery of the count of Champagne's military defeat in 1230 at his castle of Mont-Aimé is supposedly the source of the battle of the dogs; see Jacques Berlioz, "Il Rogo del Mont-Aimé," *Storia*, Vol. 3, no. 22 (October 1988), pp.30–3, here at p.33. The author kindly supplied me with his article. A later chronicler adds that a great assembly of birds also slaughtered one another: Geoffrey de Courlon, *Chronique de l'abbaye de Saint-Pierre-le-vif de Sens* (to 1294) (M.G. Julliot, ed./trans.) (Sens, 1876), pp.518–19.
6. See Migne, *P.L.*, Vol. 213, col. 539.
7. O. Holder-Egger, "Ueber die verlorene grössere Chronik Sicards von Cremona I," *Neues Archiv*, Vol. 29 (1903–04), pp.177–245, here at p.241, nn. 3–4.
8. Salimbene de Adam, Vol. 1, p.44. Translation excerpted from Salimbene de Adam, *The Chronicle* (ed. Joseph L. Baird), Medieval and Renaissance Texts and Studies, Vol. 40 (Binghamton, New York, 1986), p.4. © Arizona Board of Regents for Arizona State.
9. Peterborough, p.6.
10. See Dickson, *Prophecy*, pp.98–9. Traditional scriptural commentary: Raymond E. Brown, *The Birth of the Messiah* (new edn.) (Geoffrey Chapman: London, 1993), pp.473–91.

11. Ernest R. Curtius, *European Literature and the Latin Middle Ages* (trans. W.R. Trask) (Bollingen Series, 36) (Pantheon Books: New York, 1953), pp.98–100. Cf. Brown, *Birth of the Messiah*, pp.488–9.
12. Aelred of Rievaulx, *De Jesu puero duodenni/"Quand Jésus eut Douze Ans"* (ed./ trans. A. Hoste and J. Dubois) (Sources Chrétiennes, 60) (Cerf: Paris, 1958). Brown recognizes that there is a problem here, but fails to resolve it satisfactorily, *Birth of the Messiah*, pp.489–90.
13. Attribution of authorship to the Franciscan friar (who was not St. Bonaventure) and the newly edited Latin text: Johannes de Caulibus, *Meditaciones vite Christi* (ed. M. Stallings-Taney) (Corpus Christianorum, 153) (Brepols: Turnhout, 1997). English translation: *Meditations on the Life of Christ* (trans. Isa Ragusa) (Princeton University Press: Princeton, 1961), pp.75–94, here at p.89 and pp.92–3.
14. See Josephus, *The Jewish War* (trans. G.A. Williamson) (Penguin: Harmondsworth, 1959), pp.319–20. Cf. Lamentations, 2:20 and 4:10. For a medieval version (1003), see Rodulfus Glaber, *Opera* (ed./trans. John France) (Clarendon Press: Oxford, 1989), pp.81–3.
15. Varagine, Vol. 2, pp.373–4. But Varagine is mistaken about their departure and Genoa's attitude towards Frederick II in 1212: see Teofilo Ossian De Negri, *Storia di Genova* (Giunti: Florence, 2003), p.333.
16. Henry of Heimburg, p.714; Richer, p.301; Andres, p.754.
17. See W.M. Lindsay (ed.), Isidori Hispalensis, *Etymologiarum sive originum*, Vol. 2 (Oxford, 1911), XI. ii. 10.
18. Trevisa's translation of the thirteenth-century encyclopedia of Bartholomaeus Anglicus, *De proprietatibus rerum*, Book VI, cap. vi, p.lxxii verso (T. Berthelet: London (?), 1535).
19. See Gregory IX, *Decretales, De delicitis puerorum*, lib. V, tit. xxiii, cap. I.
20. Anselm of Laon, *Enarrationes in Matthaeum*, Migne, *P.L.*, Vol. 162, col. 1413.
21. See J.B. Pitra (ed.), *Analecta Novissima Spicilegii Solesmensis. Altera Continuatio*, 2 (Paris, 1888; reprinted Farnborough, 1967), sermo 73, *ad pueros et adolescentes*, pp.439–42, here at p.440. See also T.F. Crane (ed./trans.), *The Exempla of Jacques de Vitry* (Publications of the Folk-Lore Society, 26) (London, 1890), pp.120–1 (Crane's translation is faulty).
22. Laon, p.71. Nicole Bériou, *L'avènement des maîtres de la Parole: la prédication à Paris aux XIII*[e] *siècle* (Collection des Études Augustiniennes, Série Moyen Âge et Temps Modernes, 31), Vol. I (Paris, 1998), p.60, n.188.
23. Vincent of Beauvais, citing Peter Comestor, in his *Speculum Historiale* (Bibliotheca Mundi, IV) (Douai, 1624; reprinted Graz, 1965), Book VI, cap. xi, p.205.
24. Matthew 2:16–18. R.M. Woolley (ed.), *The Canterbury Benedictional* [c. 1025–50] (London, 1917), p.78: ...*primitias martyrum ab innocentia paruulorum*. See also Martin R. Dudley, "*Natalis Innocentum*: The Holy Innocents in Liturgy and Drama," in Diana Wood (ed.), *The Church and Childhood*, Studies in Church History, 31 (Oxford, 1994), pp.233–42, here at p.237.
25. Further on, Alberic describes the eighteen enslaved Christian *infantes* who were executed at Baghdad for failing to convert to Islam as *martirii*. Alberic of Trois-Fontaines, *Chronicon*, n.31 above, 893.

26. *Richeri Gesta Senoniensis Ecclesiae* (*ad* 1264) (ed. G. Waitz), *MGH. SS.* 25, 301.
27. See Gavin I. Langmuir, *Towards a Definition of Antisemitism* (University of California Press: Berkeley, 1990), pp.282–4.
28. Renier, pp.95–6.
29. Richer, p.311.
30. See Richard Kieckhefer, *Magic in the Middle Ages* (Cambridge University Press: Cambridge, 1990), pp.181–7.
31. Trier, p.399.
32. Cited in Jeffrey B. Russell, *Witchcraft in the Middle Ages* (Cornell University Press: Ithaca and London, 1972), p.146.
33. Admont, p.592.
34. Cantimpré, pp.139–41.
35. Ebersheim, p.450. Translation adapted from Shinners, p.398.
36. Henry of Heimburg, p.714.
37. St. Pantaleon's Chronicler, p.234.
38. *The "Opus Majus" of Roger Bacon* (ed. J.H. Bridges), Vol. 1 (Clarendon Press: Oxford, 1897), p.401; translated in *Roger Bacon, Opus Majus* (trans. R.B. Burke), Vol. 1 (University of Pennsylvania Press: Philadelphia: 1928), p.417.
39. See Dickson, *Crowds*, pp.70–4.
40. Latin text and German translation in Hans Dobbertin, *Quellensammlung zur Hamelner Rattenfängersage* (Schriften zur Niederdeutschen Volkskundee, 3) (Göttingen, 1970), pp.15–16; earlier texts, pp.11–15. Note Zacour, *Children's Crusade*, pp.340–1.
41. Useful as well, especially for diverse interpretations, is Heinrich Spanuth, *Der Rattenfänger von Hameln* (C.W. Niemayer: Hameln, 1951; reprinted 1981), pp.108–28; for Leibniz, pp.111–12.
42. E. Louis Backman, *Religious Dances in the Christian Church and in Popular Medicine (*trans. E. Classen) (London, 1952), pp.181–90, here at p.186.
43. See Gérard Sivéry, "Rural Society," cap. 1c of *The New Cambridge Medieval History*, Vol. 5 (ed. David Abulafia) (Cambridge University Press: Cambridge, 1999), pp.38–49, here at p.39.
44. On Alberic of Trois-Fontaines, see Dr. Wilmans, "Über die Chronik Alberich's", *Archiv für Altere Deutsche Geschichtskunde*, Vol. 10 (1849), pp.174–246; U. Berlière, "Albéric de Trois-Fontaines," in *Dictionnaire d'Histoire et de Géographie Écclesiastique*, Vol. 1 (Paris, 1912), col. 1413; M. Prevost, "Aubry de Trois-Fontaines," in *Dictionnaire de Biographie Française*, Vol. 4 (Paris, 1948). Note especially Mireille Schmidt-Chazan, "Aubry de Trois-Fontaines, un historien entre la France et l'Empire," *Annales de l'Est*, 5th series, Vol. 36 (1984), pp.163–92, and André Moisan, "Aubry de Trois-Fontaines à l'écoute des chanteurs de geste," in *Actes du IX*[e] *Congrès International de la Société Rencesvals*, Vol. 2 (Mucchi: Modena, 1984), pp.949–76.
45. Jumièges, p.510.
46. Peterborough, p.6.
47. Laon, pp.70–1.
48. Raedts, *Children's Crusade*, p.297. He argues that a known interpolator supplied the additional material. That may be so, although the "interpolator of Huy" or Maurice of Neufmoustier seems to have been mainly preoccupied

by local matters. Cf. Sylvain Balau, *Les sources de l'histoire du Pays de Liège* (Brussels, 1903), pp.467–75.

49. Zacour, *Children's Crusade*, pp.338–9. Yet it could be that Alberic "or, after so many years, his informant" (postulates Zacour) confused William Porcus with William of Posquères, who was at the siege of Acre with Hugo in 1190. Zacour is here reiterating a hypothesis of Röhricht's.
50. Edouard Baratier (ed.), *Histoire de Marseille* (Privat: Toulouse, 1973), p.69.
51. The most recent and most dubious claim dates from 1867 and was reaffirmed in 1938–39: see the disparaging remarks of Zacour, *Children's Crusade*, pp.337–8. The earliest such claim was made in 1737 and needs to be verified: see the comments in Cardini-Del Nero, *Fanciulli*, p.32, n.7.
52. Note A. Mortreuil, "Moeurs et Institutions Marseillaises au Moyen-Age. L'Esclavage," *Revue de Marseille*, Vol. 4 (1858), pp.155–6.
53. Cologne Continuator, p.18. Shinners, p.399.
54. Ebersheim, p.450.
55. It is at this point in the text that the mythistorical hanging of Hugo and William appears.
56. Alberic of Trois-Fontaines, pp.893–4. Translation revised from Hecker, pp.355–6, and Shinners, p.296.
57. Admittedly, it is bad form to quote oneself: Dickson, *Innocent*, p.592. Cf. Zacour, *Children's Crusade*, pp.339–40.
58. For a general overview, see Simon Lloyd and Rebecca Reader, "Matthew Paris," in *The Oxford Dictionary of National Biography*, Vol. 42 (Oxford University Press: Oxford, 2004), pp.620–8; Antonia Gransden, *Historical Writing in England, c.550 to c.1307* (Routledge & Kegan Paul: London, 1974), pp.356–72.
59. Richard Vaughan, *Matthew Paris* (Cambridge University Press: Cambridge, 1958), p.134.
60. Vivian Hunter Galbraith, *Roger Wendover and Matthew Paris* (Glasgow University Publications, no. 61) (Glasgow, 1944), p.24.
61. *Ibid.*, p.37.
62. Suzanne Lewis, *The Art of Matthew Paris in the "Chronica Majora"* (Scolar Press: Aldershot, 1987), p.2.
63. *Chronica Majora* (Rolls Series) (ed. H. R. Luard), Vol. 5 (1857), pp.246–53. Translation revised (defective, especially on the crucial identification of the youthful leader of 1212 as the future Master of Hungary): *Matthew Paris's English History* (trans. J.A. Giles) (H.G. Bohn: London, 1852–54), pp.451–7. For bibliography, see Gary Dickson, "Shepherds' Crusade, First (1251)," in Alan Murray (ed.) *The Crusades: An Encyclopedia* (ABC-CLIO, 2006), Vol. 4, pp.1093–4.
64. See Evelyn B. Vitz, "The Apocryphal and the Biblical, the Oral and the Written in Medieval Legends of Christ's Childhood: The Old French *Evangile de l'Enfance*," in *Satura* (ed. Nancy M. Reale and Ruth E. Sternglantz) (Shaun Tyas: Donington, 2001), pp.124–49.
65. There it appears as an addendum at the bottom of the page, in a later hand—clearly the same hand in both the British Library Cotton MS Nero D V and the Parker Library, MS 16 Corpus Christi, Cambridge. Note the comments of Luard, *Chronica Majora*, "Preface," Vol. 1 (1872), p.xi; Vol. 5, p.558, n.1.

66. Laon, pp.70–1.
67. See Shulamith Shahar, *Childhood in the Middle Ages* (Routledge: London and New York, 1992), p.187.
68. Mortemer, p.467; *Ex annalium Rotomagensium continuationibus* (to 1280) (ed. O. Holder-Egger) in *MGH. SS.*, Vol. 26, p.501. As a source for Matthew Paris, it could be that Rouen is the better bet.
69. Dickson, *Crowds*, pp.66–70.
70. Matthew Paris, p.558. Translation revised from Hecker, pp.354–5, and *Roger of Wendover's Flowers of History* (trans. J.A. Giles), Vol. 2 (H.G. Bohn: London, 1849), p.28.
71. Matthew Paris, p.246.
72. Jeffrey B. Russell, *Lucifer: The Devil in the Middle Ages* (Cornell University Press: Ithaca and London, 1984), p.207.
73. On Vincent of Beauvais, see B.L. Ullman, "A Project for a New Edition of Vincent of Beauvais," *Speculum*, Vol. 8 (1933), pp.312–26; Beryl Smalley, *Historian of the Middle Ages* (Thames and Hudson: London, 1974), pp.175–9; Monique Paulmier-Foucard, "Ecrire l'histoire au xiiie siècle: Vincent de Beauvais et Helinand de Froidmont," *Annales de l'Est*, Vol. 33, 5th series, pp.49–70; English summary of J.B. Voorbij's Groningen Ph.D. thesis on Vincent of Beauvais—*Het "Speculum Historiale van Vincent van Beauvais* (1991)—in the *Vincent of Beauvais Newsletter*, Vol. 16 (1991) (unpaginated).
74. Ullman, "Project for a New Edition," p.323; Gregory G. Guzman, "A Growing Tabulation of Vincent of Beauvais' *Speculum Historiale* Manuscripts," *Scriptorium*, Vol. 29 (1975), pp.122–5. Personal communication from Dr. J.B. Voorbij of the University of Utrecht (August 12, 1996). I am also grateful to him for extensive material on Vincent.
75. The printed text reads "*Arsacidae*" but a shoulder note indicates "*Assassini*" is what is meant. Cf. the Lanercost chronicle which copies Vincent on the *pueri*: *Chronicon de Lanercost* (to 1346) (ed. J. Stevenson) (Maitland Club: Edinburgh, 1838), p.14: *Assisinos*.
76. Vincent of Beauvais, *Speculum Historiale* (Douai, 1624; reprinted Graz, 1965), cap. 5, p.1238. Translation revised from Hecker, p.356.
77. Quotation cited from F.M. Chambers, "The Troubadours and the Assassins," *Modern Language Notes*, Vol. 64 (1949), pp.245–7 in Dorothee Metlitzki, *The Matter of Araby in Medieval England* (Yale University Press: New Haven and London, 1977), p.223. On the Assassins, see Robert Irwin, "Assassins," in Murray, *The Crusades: An Encyclopedia* (ABC-CLIO, 2006), Vol. 1, pp.113–15; M.S.S. Hodgson, *The Order of Assassins* (Mouton: The Hague, 1955); Bernard Lewis, *The Assassins* (Weidenfeld and Nicolson: London, 1967).
78. Arnoldi Abbatis Lubeccensis, *Chronica Slavorum* (ed. L.M. Lappenberg), *MGH.SS.* Vol. 21, p.240. Text in English: Lewis, *The Assassins*, pp.2–3 (close paraphrase); Metlitzki, *The Matter of Araby*, pp.223–4 (translation).
79. Charles E. Nowell, "The Old Man of the Mountain," *Speculum*, Vol. 222 (1947), pp.497–519, here at pp.516–17. Cf. Hodgson, *The Order of Assassins*, pp.133–9.
80. Nowell, "Old Man of the Mountain," p.519.
81. Alphons Lhotsky, *Quellenkunde zur Mittelalterlichen Geschichte Oesterreichs* (Mitteilungen des Instituts für Oesterreichische Geschichtsforshung, ergb., 19) (Hermann Böhlaus: Graz-Cologne, 1963), pp.190–1; Gerlinde Möser-

Mersky, "Das österreichische 'Chronicon rhythmicum'," *Mitteilungen des Instituts für Oesterreichische Geschichtsforshung*, Vol. 73 (1965), pp.17–38. Also note *Repertorium Fontium Historiae Medii Aevi* (Rome, 1970), p.277.

82. But see Möser-Mersky, "Das österreichische 'Chronicon rhythmicum'," pp.19; 27, n.32. It is possible that the *ARC* chronicler learned Nicholas's name from Admont, p.592.
83. Alphandéry, *La chrétienté*, p.349.
84. See Karl Young, *Ordo Rachelis*, University of Wisconsin Studies in Language and Literature, 4 (Madison, 1919), 18: I. *Processio Puerorum*; II. *Interfectio Puerorum*; III. *Lamentatio Rachelis*.
85. *Austrian Rhymed Chronicle*, p.356. Revised from the French translation of Alphandéry, *La chrétienté*, p.349; Latin: assisted once again by Mr. Alan Hood. Passage discussed in Miccoli, *Fanciulli*, p.419.
86. Möser-Mersky, "Das österreichische 'Chronicon rhythmicum'," p.38.
87. On the supposed pilgrimage songs of the German *pueri*, see Reinhold Röhricht, *Beiträge zur Geschichte der Kreuzzüge*, Vol. 2 (Weidmann: Berlin, 1878), p.257, n.14.
88. *Austrian Rhymed Chronicle*, p.356.

Chapter 8 Memory: the echo of the centuries—fourteenth to eighteenth

1. Varagine, p.374. Hecker, p.358.
2. See Hans Eberhard Mayer's classic bibliography of crusade historiography, *Bibliographie zur Geschichte der Kreuzzüge* (Hahnsche Buchhandlung: Hanover, 1960).
3. See his *The Uses of Enchantment: The Meaning and Importance of Fairy Tales* (Penguin: London, 1991).
4. To take one example of mistaken chronology (1208), see *Annales SS. Udalrici et Afrae Augustenses* (to 1334) (ed. P. Jaffé), *MGH. SS.*, Vol. 17, p.431, a notice based on Herman of Niederaltaich (to 1273), p.386, where the movement of the *pueri* is correctly dated.
5. See Christine Knowles, "Jean de Vignay," in *Dictionnaire des Lettres Françaises: le Moyen Age* (Fayard: Paris, 1964), pp.431–3. Note B.L. Ullman, "A Project for a New Edition of Vincent of Beauvais," *Speculum*, Vol. 8 (1933), pp.312–26, here at p.323.
6. C. Hegel (ed.), *Die Chroniken der oberrheinishcen Städte: Strassburg* (*Die Chroniken der deutschen Städte*, 8), Vol. 1 (Leipzig, 1875), p.101. I owe the translation to Malcolm Burnett. Closener refers to the enthusiasm of 1212 at a point in his Strasbourg chronicle where he was drawing from the Ellenhard annals, which had also been compiled in Strasbourg. In Latin, under the year 1211, the Ellenhard annals record the "journey (or crusade) of the foolish *pueri*": *Annales Ellenhardi* (to 1297) (ed. P. Jaffé), *MGH. SS.* Vol. 17, pp.101–4.
7. *Practica Inquisitionis Heretice Pravitatis*, for which, see G. Mollat (ed.), *Bernard Gui, Manuel de l'Inquisiteur*, 2 Vols. (Champion: Paris, 1926).

8. See Bernard Guenée, *Between Church and State: The Lives of Four French Prelates in the Late Middle Ages* (trans. Arthur Goldhammer) (University of Chicago Press: Chicago, 1991), cap. 1, pp.37–70. Note also Antoine Thomas, "Bernard Gui, frère prècheur," *Histoire littéraire de la France*, Vol. 35 (Paris, 1921), pp.139–232.
9. *Vita Innocentii Papae III* in L.A. Muratori (ed.), *Rerum Italicarum Scriptores*, Vol. III (Milan, 1723), p.482.
10. Cf. n.7. Since neither Gui's text nor Vincent's is found in a properly critical edition, one or both may be inaccurate as we have them.
11. For Gui as a historian of the *pueri* (1212), *pastores* (1251), and *pastoureaux* (1320), see Dickson, *Encounters,* pp.270–4.
12. *Anonymi Leobiensis Chronicon* (to 1343) (ed. H. Pez), *Scriptores Rerum Austriacarum*, Vol. 1 (J.P. Krauss: Vienna, 1743), col. 802. See Augustus Potthast, *Repertorium Fontium Historiae Medii Aevii, Fontes*, Vol. 2 (Rome, 1967), pp.360–1. Note Alphons Lhotsky, *Quellenkunde zu Mittelalterlichen Geschichte Oesterreichs* (Mitteilungen des Instituts für Oesterreichische Geschichtsforshung, ergb., 19) (Hermann Böhlaus, Graz-Cologne, 1963), p.301ff.; *Idem.*, *Oesterreichische Historiographie* (Verlag R. Oldenbourg: Munich, 1962), p.32. Cf. *Anonymi Chronicon Austriacum* (to 1327) (ed. Adrianus Rauch), *Rerum Austriacarum Scriptores*, Vol. 2 (Vienna, 1793), p.231.
13. Revelations 1:9.
14. See Donald E.R. Watt, "Abbot Walter Bower of Inchcolm and his *Scotichronicon,*" *Records of the Scottish Church History Society*, Vol. 24, part 3 (1992), pp.286–304. I owe this reference to Professor Geoffrey Barrow. The complete publication of the *Scotichronicon* must count amongst Scottish historiography's "great historical enterprises."
15. John of Fordun's *Chronica Gentis Scotorum* (ed. W.F. Skene) 2 vols. (Edinburgh, 1871–72); supplementary notes on Scottish history bring it up to Fordun's own day (c. 1380s).
16. This is my own translation of *Non Scotus est, Christe, cui liber non placet iste.*
17. Watt, "Abbott Walter Bower," pp.293–5, comments that Bower, as a preacher, liked *exempla*, taking some from Vincent of Beauvais and some from Thomas of Cantimpré.
18. Cf. Alan MacQuarrie, *Scotland and the Crusades, 1095–1560* (John Donald Publishers Ltd.: Edinburgh, 1985), pp.100–1, 132–3.
19. Walter Bower, *Scotichronicon* (D.E.R. Watt, gen. ed.), Vol. 5 (Simon Taylor, D.E.R. Watt, with Brian Scott, eds.) (Aberdeen University Press: Glasgow/Aberdeen, 1990), pp.38–9. As Bower used an Ms. of Vincent, this discussion, along with the comments on his interpolations, depends upon his having utilized, at libraries in Edinburgh or St. Andrews (cf. Watt, p.290), a Ms. which corresponds to the early printed editions. There is always the possibility that Bower, like Gui, used a Ms. of Vincent which contained no reference to the Old Man of the Mountain.
20. Scriptural citations have been modified to conform to the King James version (©University of St. Andrews: reproduced by permission).
21. Watt, "Abbott Walter Bower," p.288
22. See Paul Rousset, *Histoire d'une idéologie: la croisade* (L'Age d'Homme: Lausanne, 1983), pp.120–4.

23. Other fifteenth-century chroniclers reiterated opinions which had long been conventional. For example, the Dominican archbishop of Florence, St. Antoninus (d. 1459), except for adding Brindisi and Genoa to the list of reported destinations of the *pueri*, virtually reproduces the text of Vincent of Beauvais: *Chronica Antonini* (Lyons, 1543), tit. xix, cap. 2, sec. iv.
24. On Rolewinck, see *Allgemeine Deutsche Biographie*, Vol. 29 (Leipzig, 1899), pp.72–3, and Hugo Wolffgram, "Neue Forshungen zu Werner Rolevincks Leben und Werken I," *Zeitschrift für vaterländische Geschichte und Altertumskunde*, Vol. 48 (1890), pp.85–136; on the *Fasciculus Temporum*, pp.114–36. I am grateful to Dr. Gadi Algazi for bibliography and essays on Rolewinck.
25. Werner Rolewink [*sic*], *Fasciculus Temporum* (to 1484) in *Germanicorum Scriptorum* (J. Pistorius, ed.), Vol. 2 (Hanover, 1613), p.80.
26. A. Petrucci, "Accolti, Benedetto" in *Dizionario Biografico degli Italiani*, Vol.1 (Rome, 1960), pp.99–101. See Robert Black, *Benedetto Accolti and the Florentine Renaissance* (Cambridge University Press, Cambridge, 1985), especially pp.224–6, 298ff. Cf. Norman Housley, *The Later Crusades* (Oxford University Press: Oxford, 1992), pp.106–9, 388–9.
27. Andreas Burckhardt, "Herold(t), Johannes," in *Neue Deutsche Biographie*, Vol. 8 (Berlin, 1968), p.678.
28. William of Tyre, *Belli sacri historia…* [and] Johannes Herold, *De bello sacro continuate* (both edited by P. Poyssenoti) (N. Brylingerum and I. Oporinum: Basle, 1549?). 1549 is the date of Herold's preface. It is not known whether both books were published at the same time, or later bound together to form a single volume, as they are in the copy held by Edinburgh University Library's Special Collections.
29. Herold, *De bello sacro continuate*, book three, cap. 1, pp.88–9.
30. *Ibid.*, p.ii.
31. Varagine, pp.373–4.
32. S. Menchi, "Bizzarri, Pietro," in *Dizionario Biografico degli Italiani*, Vol.10 (Rome, 1968), pp.738–41. Note also Eric Cochrane, *Historians and Historiography in the Italian Renaissance* (University of Chicago Press: Chicago, 1981), pp.244–5, 549. The full title of Bizzarri's work is *Senatus Populique Genuensis Rerum Domi Forisque Gestarum Historiae atque Annales* (Antwerp, 1579).
33. *Ibid.*, p.30.
34. S.C. Roberts, *Thomas Fuller: A Seventeenth Century Worthy* (University of Manchester Press: Manchester, 1953), pp.3–6. James W. Thompson, *A History of Historical Writing*, Vol. 1 (Macmillan: New York, 1942), p.634.
35. E.K. Broadus (ed.), *Thomas Fuller, Selections with Essays by Charles Lamb, Leslie Stephen, etc.* (Clarendon Press: Oxford, 1928), pp.ix–xi, 10–12, 13ff. Cf. Walter E. Houghton, Jr., *The Formation of Thomas Fuller's "Holy and Profane States"* (Harvard University Press: Cambridge, Mass., 1938), pp.3–9.
36. See Aziz S. Atiya, *The Crusade: Historiography and Bibliography* (Indiana University Press: Bloomington, 1962), p.31.
37. See James A. Brundage (ed.), *The Crusades: Motives and Achievements* (D.C. Heath & Co.: Boston, 1964), pp.1–3.
38. Thomas Fuller, *The Historie of the Holy Warre*, 3rd edn. (R. Daniel: Cambridge, 1647), pp.151–2. Cf. *Table*, book iii, cap. 24.
39. Towards the beginning of that century Bongar's important collection of crusading texts appeared, patriotically bearing the same title which Guibert

of Nogent gave to his twelfth-century chronicle of the crusade, *Gesta Dei per Francos* (1611). Also adding lustre to the seventeenth century was the outstanding philological scholarship of Du Cange (d. 1688), which he displayed in his editions of the crusade historians Villehardouin and Joinville, and in his indispensable dictionary of medieval Latin. Seventeenth-century French medievalism had strong literary as well as scholarly aspects to it. See Nathan Edelman, *Seventeenth-Century Attitudes of France towards the Middle Ages* (King's Crown Press: New York, 1946).

40. *Ibid.*, pp.64, 86. J.-E. Fidao-Justiniani, *Qu'est-ce qu'un classique?* (Firmin-Didot: Paris, 1930), pp.11–13. On the young Leibniz and the papacy, see *History of the Church* (Hubert Jedin and John Dolan, eds.), *the Church in the Age of Absolutism and Enlightenment*, Vol. 6 (W. Müller) (trans. G.J. Holst) (Burns & Oates: London, 1981), pp.122–3.
41. On Gallicanism and Maimbourg, Jedin and Dolan, *History of the Church*, p.119. See also N.A. Weber, "Maimbourg, Louis," in the *Catholic Encyclopedia*, Vol. 9 (London, 1910), p.540.
42. Eduard Fueter, *Histoire de l'historiographie moderne* (trans. E. Jeanmaire) (Paris, 1914), p.332.
43. Jefferson owned the four-volume edition of 1682: Hans Eberhard Mayer, "America and the Crusades," *Proceedings of the American Philosophical Society*, Vol. 125 (February 1981), p.38. Seven years earlier, in 1675, the two-volume edition had been published. Further editions and translations into Dutch, Italian, and English (1685) followed.
44. Louis Maimbourg, *Histoire des croisades pour la delivrance de la Terre Sainte*, 3rd edn., Vol. 3 (Paris, 1680), pp.288–91.
45. *Ibid.*, pp.293–4.
46. In general, see Lionel Gossman, *Medievalism and the Ideologies of the Enlightenment: The World and Work of La Curne de Sainte-Palaye* (Johns Hopkins University Press: Baltimore, 1968). The great Italian scholar Ludovico Antonio Muratori (1672–1750) referred to the Children's Crusade in his *Annali d'Italia* (Milan, 1744–49). He did so because the enthusiasm came to Genoa, whose chronicle he used. "Pious enthusiasm" prompted this "novelty" to leave Germany: Vol. 10, 2nd edn. (Milan, 1753), p.252.
47. On Voltaire as a historian and medievalist, see J.H. Brumfitt, *Voltaire Historian* (Oxford University Press: Oxford, 1958); Furio Diaz, *Voltaire Storico* (Einaudi: n.p., 1958); Ludovico Gatto, *Medioevo Voltairiano* (Bulzoni editore: Rome, 1972).
48. The Abbé Claude Fleury (1640–1723) wrote an influential twenty-volume *Histoire ecclésiastique*, published between 1691 and 1737. In it he summarizes the Children's Crusade, based on two German chronicles: Vol. 16 (Paris, 1728), p.323. On Voltaire and Fleury, see Larissa Albina, "Voltaire et ses sources historiques", *Dix-Huitième Siècle*, Vol. 13 (1981), pp.349–59, here at pp.350–1.
49. On this I disagree with Albina, p.351 and Brumfitt, p.45, n.3 (but not on Voltaire's positive economic-historical approach to the crusades, pp.68–9); Diaz, *Voltaire Storico*, emphasizes Fleury's Gallicanism and gives the best discussion of Voltaire and the crusades, pp.191–9.
50. In the *Mercure de France*, Vol. 1 (1750), September, pp.9–31; October, pp.30–50, December, pp.91–110, and Vol. 2 (1752), February, pp.47–59. I owe this reference to Professor John Renwick.

51. Voltaire, *Le Micromégas avec une histoire des croisades* (London, 1752), p.103.
52. Cf. Susie I. Tucker, *Enthusiasm. A Study in Semantic Change* (Cambridge University Press: Cambridge, 1972), cap. 11, pp.144–61 on metaphors of enthusiasm, including heat, disease, madness, etc. What is strange—and amusing—is that, when, in a later publication, Voltaire uses the word "crusade" figuratively, he uses it to combat a disease—"a crusade against the pox!" See *L'Homme aux quarante écus* (c. 1767–68) in his *Oeuvres Complètes/ Complete Works*, Vol. 66 (The Voltaire Foundation: Oxford, 1999), p.385. (Again, I am indebted to Professor Renwick.) Voltaire's positive metaphorical usage of "crusade" may lie behind Thomas Jefferson's "crusade against ignorance," for a complete set of Voltaire's works was lodged in Jefferson's library (Mayer, "America and the Crusades," p.38). But the claim to the earliest metaphorical use of "crusade" may belong to J.G. Hamann's *Die Kreuzzüge des Philologen* (1762): Rousset, *Histoire d'une idéologie*, p.208.
53. D. Diderot and D'Alembert, *Encyclopèdie ou Dictionnaire raisonné des sciences des arts et des mètiers*, Vol. 4 (Paris, 1754), "Croisades" pp.502–5, here at p.504.
54. See Richard N. Schwab, "Inventory of Diderot's *Encyclopèdie*, II", *Studies on Voltaire and the Eighteenth Century*, Vol. 83 (1971), "Croisades," p.302. Once more, my gratitude to John Renwick.
55. Claude F.X. Millot, *Élémens de l'historie de France*, Vol. 1, 10th edn. (Paris, 1817), p.300.

Chapter 9 Memory: the echo of the centuries—nineteenth to twentieth

1. Note Edward W. Said, *Orientalism: Western Conceptions of the Orient* (Penguin: London, 1995) pp.42–3, 76, 84ff., *passim*.
2. See Heinrich von Sybel, *The History and Literature of the Crusades* (Lady Duff Gordon, trans. and ed.) (Chapman and Hall: London, 1861), p.341, n.55, p.344, n.57. Cf. A.C.E. Franquet de Franqueville, *Le premier siècle de l'Institut de France*, Vol. 2 (J. Rothschild: Paris, 1895–96), p.402.
3. George Peabody Gooch, *History and Historians in the Nineteenth Century* (Beacon Press: Boston, 1959), p.157.
4. *Génie du Christianisme* (new edn.), Vol. 1, part 2, cap. 2 (Garnier Frères: Paris, 1871), pp.173–4. In his history-saturated book of travel meditations, the *Itinéraire de Paris à Jerusalem* (1811), the negative views of the *philosophes* on the crusades are thrust aside.
5. On the publishing history and reception of Michaud's *Histoire des Croisades*, see Jean Richard, "De Jean-Baptiste Mailly à Joseph-François Michaud: un moment de l'historiographie des croisades (1774–1841)," *Crusades*, Vol. 1 (2002), pp.1–12. On Chateaubriand and Pope Gregory, see "Michaud, Joseph," in *Nouvelle biographie générale*, Vol. 35 (1861), cols. 329–33 by J.J. Poujoulat, his secretary and travel companion to the East.
6. My discussion of Michaud owes much to David Denby, "Les croisades aux xviiie et xixe siècles: une historiographie engagée," in *Les champenois et la*

croisade (eds. Yvonne Bellenger and Danielle Quéruel) (Aux amateurs de livres: Paris, 1989), pp.163–70, here at pp.168–9.

7. Joseph-François Michaud, *Histoire des Croisades*, 4th edn. Vol. 3 (Paris, 1826), pp.380–3. *Michaud's History of the Crusades* (trans. W. Robson), Vol. 2 (G. Routledge: London, 1852), pp.202–3.
8. Sédillot, "Jourdain, Amable-L.-M.-M.-B.," in *Biographie Universelle (Michaud) Ancienne et Moderne* (new edn.) Vol. 21 (Paris, n.d.), p.241. "Lettre à M. Michaud sur la croisade d'enfans de 1212," in J.F. Michaud, *Histoire des Croisades*, Vol. 3, 5th edn. (Paris, 1838), pp.605–13 and *Michaud's History* (trans. Robson), Vol. 3, pp.441–6.
9. See A. Stoll, "Wilken, Friedrich," in *Allgemeine Deutsche Biographie*, Vol. 43 (Leipzig, 1898), pp.236–41.
10. On von Sybel, see Eduard Fueter, *Histoire de l'historiographie moderne* (trans. E. Jeanmaire) (Paris, 1914), pp.668–9; Gooch, *History and Historians*, pp.120–1. For von Sybel's critique of Wilken, see his *History and Literature of the Crusades*, pp.339–44. Note Gooch, *History and Historians*, p.67.
11. Vol. 6, pp.71–83.
12. For example, he cites Alberic's disclaimer (*ut dicitur*), Vol. 6, p.81, n.53, and calls two of Alberic's assertions "false" and "very doubtful," p.82, n.55.
13. Vol. 6, pp.74–5, n.26.
14. A. Hirsh, "Hecker, Justus Frederick Karl," in *Allgemeine Deutsche Biographie*, Vol. 11 (Leipzig, 1880), pp.211–13.
15. Now see Madeleine Braekman, "La dansomanie de 1374: hérésie ou maladie?, *Revue du Nord*, Vol. 63 (1981), pp.339–55. For a hitherto unpublished text on the dancers of 1374, see Markus Müller, "Eine Trierer Bistumschronik aus der Zeit des Grossen Schismas," *Archiv für Mittelrheinische Kirchengeschichte*, Vol. 49 (1997), pp.335–77.
16. *Die Kinderfahrten* (Berlin, 1845). It was later included in his posthumous German collection *Die Grossen Volkskrankheiten des Mittelalters* (ed. August Hirsh) (Berlin, 1865; reprinted Hildesheim, 1964) pp.124–34; Latin extracts from the sources, pp.135–42.
17. J.F.C. Hecker, *The Epidemics of the Middle Ages* (trans. B.G. Babington) 3rd edn., includes *Treatise on Child-Pilgrimages* (trans. Robert H. Cooke) (Trübner & Co.: London, 1859). The translator of Hecker's treatise on medieval child-pilgrimages was a suitable choice: R.H. Cooke was the author of *Epidemic Mental Diseases of Children*.
18. Hecker, pp.346–8.
19. *Ibid.*, p.349.
20. *Ibid.*, pp.351–2. Hecker and his translator must have been drawing on a faulty version of James of Varagine containing the word *meretricibus* rather than *nutricibus*.
21. Wegele, "Sporschil, Johann," in *Allgemeine Deutsche Biographie*, Vol. 35 (Leipzig, 1893), pp.277–8.
22. *Geschichte der Kreuzzüge* (Leipzig, 1843), pp.445–7.
23. J.M. Ludlow, *The Age of the Crusades* [Eras of the Christian Church] (T. & T. Clark: Edinburgh, 1897), pp.298–300.
24. Rev. W.E. Dutton, *History of the Crusades* (John Hodges: London, 1877), pp.218–20.

25. L. Martal, "Essarts, Alfred des" in *Dictionnaire de biographie française*, Vol. 10 (Paris, 1965), cols. 1324–5. Des Essarts, *Croisade des enfants* [*Bibliothèque de la famille*] (Paris, 1862). Inexplicably, Röhricht cites him in his learned article (the Paris, 1875 edn.).
26. See Iain White's introduction to his translation and edition of *The King in the Golden Mask and Other Writings by Marcel Schwob* (Carcanet: Manchester, 1982), p.12. White also includes a chronology of Schwob's life, pp.2–5, and a new English translation of Schwob's *The Children's Crusade*, pp.168–86. An earlier English translation is that by H.C. Greene (Portland, Maine, 1907). For the French text, see *Les oeuvres complètes de Marcel Schwob, La Lampe de Psyché* (ed. Pierre Champion) (François Bernouard: Paris, 1928), pp.131–54. Note also Janine R. Dakyns, *The Middle Ages in French Literature, 1851–1900* (Oxford University Press: London, 1973), pp.231, 277–8.
27. Schwob, *The Children's Crusade*, H.C. Greene (trans.), p.33.
28. Cited in Pierre Champion, *Marcel Schwob et son temps* (Bernard Grasset: Paris, 1927), p.270, and the short discussion of the *Croisade des enfants*, on which I have drawn, pp.118–19.
29. See the encyclopedia entries in the *American Biographical Archive* (Microfiche, 644, 78–83).
30. Dana C. Munro, "The Children's Crusade," *American Historical Review*, Vol. 19 (1913–14), pp.516–24, here at p.517, n.17. Munro further comments: "In his bibliography... he cites as a contemporary a man who died before the movement began; he quotes the same account under two different names in three instances; and he has many other errors."
31. London, 1871; Hurd & Houghton: New York, 1872.
32. *Saturday Review*, Vol. 31 (1871) (February 11), pp.187–8.
33. Gray, *The Children's Crusade*, p.27.
34. See C. du Fresne, Ducange (ed.), *Mémoires du sire de Joinville*, Vol. 1 (London, 1785), "Observations," n.2. pp.193–4. Medieval liturgists like Durandus traced their origins to the plague victims of late-sixth-century Rome.
35. Gray, *The Children's Crusade*, p.129. Other assertions include Nicholas as a shepherd (p.60). The best of them is that the Old Man of the Mountain "was the famous Aladdin, the story of whose wonderful lamp is told in the *Arabian Nights*" (p.54).
36. *Ibid.*, p.137.
37. For a brief overview, see Elizabeth Siberry, *The New Crusaders: Images of the Crusades in the 19th and early 20th centuries* (Ashgate: Aldershot, 2000), here at p.157.
38. Rev. C.G. Barth, *René the Young Crusader* (trans. S. Jackson) (S. Lingham: London, c. 1844).
39. See George K. Anderson, *The Legend of the Wandering Jew* (Brown University Press: Providence, 1965), p.18ff.
40. Rev. A.J. Church, *The Crusaders: A Story of the War for the Holy Sepulchre* (Seeley & Co., Ltd.: London, 1905), cap. 25, pp.234–47.
41. E. Everett-Green, *The Children's Crusade: A Story of Adventure* (Thomas Nelson & Sons: London, 1905), pp.26–7.
42. E. Blyth, *Jerusalem and the Crusades* (T.C. & E.C. Jack: London, 1913), pp.198–205.
43. *Ibid.*, p.202.

44. *Ibid.*, p.205.
45. H. Bordeaux, *Annette et Philibert ou la nouvelle croisade des enfants* (Ernest Flammarion: Paris, 1913). See cap. 4, "La croisade des enfants", pp.65–81. The reference would either be to Ernest Lavisse's *Histoire de France*, Vol. 3.1 by Achille Luchaire (Hachette: Paris, 1901), pp.311–13, or to Luchaire's *Social France at the Time of Philip Augustus* (translated from the 2nd French edn. by B. Krehbiel) (John Murray: London, 1912), p.25ff.
46. E. Heming, *Joan's Crusade* (Lutterworth Press: London, 1947), pp.5–7. See the comments of Elizabeth Siberry, "Children and the Crusades," in *Church and Childhood* (Studies in Church History, 31) (Blackwell: Oxford, 1994), pp.417–26, here at p.425 (with references to further titles).
47. *Keesing's Contemporary Archives*, 1977, Vol. 23, p.28251: Resolution 31/169.
48. Program of the 1979 Edinburgh production: Paul Thompson, *The Children's Crusade: A Play*; music by Robert Campbell (Samuel French: London, 1975); Thompson: pp.ix–x; Daniels: p.xii.
49. Comprehensiveness in such a survey is a vain hope; additional titles include: Eileen and Rhoda Power, *Boys and Girls of History* (Cambridge University Press: Cambridge, 1926), cap. 5, pp.53–63; Daphne Muir, *The Lost Crusade* (Chatto and Windus: London, 1930) (also published as *Pied Piper* (?) (Henry Holt: New York, 1930)); Henry Treece, *The Children's Crusade* (Bodley Head: London, 1958) (frequently reprinted); Evan H. Rhodes, *An Army of Children* (Dial Press: New York, 1978).
50. G.E.G. Catlin in *The Dictionary of National Biography, 1951–60* (ed. E.T. Williams and H.M. Palmer) (Oxford University Press: Oxford, 1971), pp.62–4.
51. *The Crusades* (Oxford University Press: London, 1923; reprinted 1925, 1936, 1939). The 1939 reprint is the last listed in the *National Union Catalog (pre-1956 imprints)*, Vol. 35, p.464.
52. E. Barker, *The Crusades*, p.92.
53. *Ibid.*, pp.74–5.
54. "Immensely popular": *The Columbia Encyclopedia*, 3rd edn. (Columbia University Press: New York, 1963), p.2305. See John Batchelor, *H.G. Wells* (Cambridge University Press: Cambridge, 1985), pp.125, 168; Michael Draper, *H.G. Wells* (Macmillan: Basingstoke, 1987), p.7. Note also Anthony West, *H.G. Wells: Aspects of a Life* (Penguin: Harmondsworth, 1985), pp.67–8.
55. H.G. Wells, *The Outline of History, being a Plain History of Life and Mankind*, 2 Vols. (revised edn.) (George Newnes Ltd.: London, 1920).
56. Cf. J.H. Huizinga's penetrating comments on Wells and Spengler, "Two Wrestlers with the Angel," in his *Dutch Civilisation in the 17th Century and Other Essays* (ed. Pieter Geyl, *et al.*) (Collins: London, 1968), pp.158–218.
57. Wells, *Outline of History*, Vol. 2, pp.758–9.
58. *Ibid.*, Vol. 2, pp.459–60.
59. S. Runciman, *History of the Crusades*, Vol. 3 (Cambridge University Press: Cambridge, 1955), p.480.
60. These four studies are by Röhricht (1876); Winkelmann on Frederick II (1889–97) in which there is nothing on the *pueri*; Munro (1913–14) (Raedts wonders if he read it, p.282); and Alphandéry (1916): Runciman, *History of the Crusades*, Vol. 3, p.144, n.1.

61. *Ibid.*, Vol. 3, p.140.
62. Cf. Gray, *The Children's Crusade*, pp.129–30.
63. Zacour, *Children's Crusade*, p.325; Raedts, *Children's Crusade*, p.282.
64. Gile Constable's biographical memoir is a fine, balanced appreciation of Runciman: see *Proceedings of the American Philosophical Society*, Vol. 147, no. 1 (2003), pp.96–101.
65. See Cardini-Del Nero, *Fanciulli*, pp.160–2.
66. See *Tutti le opere di Gabriele d'Annunzio*, Vol. 2 (Verona, 1950), pp.1143–69.
67. For all these details, see James K. Lyon, *Bertolt Brecht in America* (Princeton University Press: Princeton, 1980), pp.74 (and nn.9–10, p.361), 74, 77, 108, 238, 243, 244, 274.
68. See *Bertolt Brecht: Plays, Poetry & Prose; Poems: part three, 1938–56* (John Willett and Ralph Manheim, eds.) (Eyre Methuen: London, 1976), pp.368–73.
69. Faber Music Ltd. in association with Faber & Faber: London, 1973. Brecht translated by Hans Keller.
70. See Bruce Archibald and Jennifer Barnes, "Menotti, Gian Carlo," in *The New Grove Dictionary of Music and Musicians* (ed. Stanley Sadie), 2nd edn., Vol. 16 (Macmillan: London, 2001), pp.432–4, and the obituary by Peter Dickinson in *The Independent*, February 3, 2007, p.44.
71. G.C. Menotti, *Death of the Bishop of Brindisi* (G. Schirmer: New York, 1963). I wish to thank Paul Freedman of Yale for alerting me to Menotti's work.
72. E.J. Czerwinski (ed.), *Dictionary of Polish Literature* (Greenwood Press: London, 1994), p.2ff; Czeslaw Milosz, *History of Polish Literature*, 2nd edn. (University of California Press: Berkeley, 1983), pp.490–3.
73. J. Andrzejewski, *The Gates of Paradise* (trans. James Kirkup) (Weidenfeld & Nicolson: London, 1962).
74. K. Vonnegut, *Slaughterhouse-Five or the Children's Crusade: A Duty-Dance with Death* (Triad Panther: London, 1979; frequently reprinted). Among the many critical studies, see Jerome Klinkowitz, *Kurt Vonnegut* (Methuen: London, 1982), p.63ff.; Richard Giannone, *Vonnegut: A Preface to his Novels* (Kennikat Press: Port Washington, New York, 1977), pp.82–97.
75. Vonnegut, *Slaughterhouse-Five*, pp.73–4.
76. D.D. Eisenhower, *Crusade in Europe* (Wm. Heinemann: London 1948). Cf. p.3: "by V-J Day in the Pacific, 322,188 of [America's] *youth* [my italics] had been lost in battle... and approximately 700,000 more had been wounded."
77. A.D. Chandler, Jr. (ed.), *The Papers of Dwight David Eisenhower: The War Years*, Vol. 3 (Johns Hopkins Press: Baltimore, 1970), no.1735, p.1913.
78. See Paul Fussell, *Wartime: Understanding and Behaviour in the Second World War* (Oxford University Press: New York, 1989), p.53.
79. See Tony Tanner in Robert Merrill (ed.), *Critical Essays on Kurt Vonnegut* (G.K. Hall: Boston, 1990), pp.126–30. Hesse alludes to the *Kinderkreuzzug* in *Die Morgenland-fahrt* (S. Fischer Verlag: Berlin, 1932), p.54.
80. E.M. Remarque, *All Quiet on the Western Front* (trans. A.W. Wheen) (Putnam: London, 1929), p.31, and cf. 22. See Clark Mayo, *Kurt Vonnegut: The Gospel from Outer Space* (Borgo Press: San Bernardino, 1977), p.46.
81. S. Crane, *The Red Badge of Courage* (ed. F. Bowers) (University of Virginia edition of the Works of Stephen Crane, 2) (University Press of Virginia: Charlottesville, 1975). Note pp.4–5, 125.

82. "Boys: men of the armed forces," *Oxford English Dictionary*, Vol. 2, 2nd edn. (Clarendon Press: Oxford, 1989), p.467, def. 6c.
83. Vonnegut, *Slaughterhouse-Five*, pp.17–18.
84. See *The Dictionary of National Biography* (ed. Leslie Stephen and Sidney Lee), Vol. 12 (Oxford University Press: London, 1959–60), pp.564–5. C. Mackay, *Extraordinary Popular Delusions and the Madness of Crowds* (1841; Farrar, Straus and Giroux: New York, 1972), pp.438–40.
85. Cf. Robert A. Hipkiss, *The American Absurd* (Faculty Press: Port Washington, New York, 1984), p.52
86. Note, especially, Albert E. Stone, Jr., *The Innocent Eye: Childhood in Mark Twain's Imagination* (Yale University Press: New Haven, 1961), p.154 (Huck Finn as a runaway), p.202ff. (the Middle Ages in America; Joan of Arc and youth and purity); Leslie A. Fiedler, *No! In Thunder. Essays on Myth and Literature* (Stein and Day: New York, 1972), see his "The Eye of Innocence," pp.253–93.
87. See Klaus Mehnert, *The Twilight of the Young: The Radical Movements of the 1960s and their Legacy* (Secker and Warburg: London, 1978), pp.35–6, 365.
88. For general background, see Arthur Marwick, *The Sixties* (Oxford University Press: Oxford, 1999), pp.602–18, here at p.607.
89. B. Thomas, *La croisade des enfants* (Fayard: Paris). In 1988, the novel was screened as a television film. During his career, as well as writing historical novels, Bernard Thomas was for many years a journalist for *Canard Enchaîné*. The author's historical annotations and references are commendable, if at times difficult to trace.
90. *Ibid.*, p.124.
91. *Ibid.*, p.253.
92. Rebecca Brown, *The Children's Crusade* (Pan Books: London, pb, 1990), p.110. See p.108ff.
93. Cf. Stone, Jr., *The Innocent Eye*, p.154.
94. A. Jamieson, *The Holy Wars in the Light of Today* (Headley Bros.: London, 1919), pp.17–18.
95. T.S.R. Boase, *Kingdoms and Strongholds of the Crusaders* (Thames and Hudson: London, 1971), p.172.
96. Paul Connerton, *How Societies Remember* (Cambridge University Press: Cambridge, 1989), cap. 2, p.41ff.
97. Cf. James Fenton and Chris Wickham, *Social Memory* (Blackwell: Oxford, 1992), p.ix, citing Maurice Halbachs on the importance of group identity to social memory. Note also memory of events as a set of images, p.58.
98. Karl Lamprecht, *What is History?* (trans. E.A. Andrews) (Macmillan: New York, 1905), p.9.

Bibliography: Specialist Scholarship

Alphandéry, Paul, and Alphonse Dupront, *La chrétienté et l'idée de croisade*, 2 vols. (Albin Michel: Paris, 1954, 1959); reissued in one vol. (Albin Michel: Paris, 1995), pp.339–72.

Alphandéry, Paul, "Les croisades d'enfants," *Revue de l'Histoire des Religions*, Vol. 73 (1916), pp.259–82.

Cardini, Franco, and Domenico Del Nero, *La Crociata dei Fanciulli* (Giunti: Florence, 1999).

De Janssens, Gaston, "Étienne de Cloyes et les croisades d'enfants au xiiie siècle," *Bulletin de la société dunoise*, Vol. 90 (1891), pp.109–33.

Dickson, Gary, "La genèse de la croisade des enfants (1212)," *Bibliothèque de l'École des chartes*, Vol. 153 (1995), pp.53–102; reprinted in English in *idem.*, *Religious Enthusiasm in the Medieval West: Revivals, Crusades, Saints* (Variorum Collected Studies Series) (Ashgate: Abingdon, 2000), cap. 4.

—— "Innocent III and the Children's Crusade," *Innocenzo III. Urbs et orbis*, ed. Andrea Sommerlechner (Rome, Istituto storico italiano per il Medio Evo e Società romana di storia patria, 2003), Vol. 1, pp.586–97.

—— "Prophecy and Revivalism: Joachim of Fiore, Jewish Messianism and the Children's Crusade of 1212," *Florensia*, 13/14 (1999–2000), V Congresso Internazionale di Studi Gioachimiti: Comunicazioni, pp.97–104.

—— "Stephen of Cloyes, Philip Augustus, and the Children's Crusade of 1212," in B.N. Sargent-Baur (ed.), *Journeys Toward God: Pilgrimage and Crusade* (Medieval Institute Publications: Kalamazoo, Mich., 1992), pp.83–105; reprinted in *idem.*, *Religious Enthusiasm in the Medieval West: Revivals, Crusades, Saints* (Variorum Collected Studies Series) (Ashgate: Abingdon, 2000), cap. 5.

Gäbler, Ulrich, "Der 'Kinderkreuzzug' vom Jahre 1212," *Schweizerische Zeitschrift für Geschichte*, Vol. 28 (1978), pp.1–14.

Hansbery, Joseph E., "The Children's Crusade," *Catholic Historical Review*, Vol. 24 (1938–39), pp.30–8.

Menzel, Michael, "Die Kinderkreuzzüge in geistes- und sozial-geschichtlicher Sicht," *Deutsches Archiv für Erforschung des Mittelalters*, Vol. 55 (1999), pp.117–56.

Miccoli, Giovanni, "La 'crociata dei fanciulli' del 1212," *Studi Medievali*, 3rd series, Vol. 2.2 (1961), pp.407–43.

Munro, Dana Carleton, "The Children's Crusade," *American Historical Review*, Vol. 19 (1913–14), pp.516–24.

Raedts, Peter, "The Children's Crusade of 1212," *Journal of Medieval History*, Vol. 3 (1977) pp.279–323.

Röhricht, Reinhold, "Der Kinderkreuzzug 1212," *Historische Zeitschrift*, Vol. 36 (1876), pp.1–8.

Zacour, Norman P., "The Children's Crusade", in Kenneth M. Setton (ed.), *A History of the Crusades*, Vol. 2 (Philadelphia, 1962), pp.325–42.

Index

Aachen, 87, 89
Abel and Cain, 90
Admont abbey, monastic chronicler of, 117–18
Accolti, Benedict (Renaissance historian), 164
Aelred of Rievaulx (Cistercian writer), 135
Agnes of Assisi (Franciscan nun), 12, 28
Albert of Stade (abbot, chronicler), 11–13, 188
Alberic of Trois-Fontaines (chronicler and mythistorian), 13, 52, 111, 143–7, 168, 181, 182
Al-Kāmil (Egyptian sultan), 119–20
Alpais of Cudot (ascetic), 65
Alphandéry, Paul (historian of religion and the crusades), 40–1, 80, 155, 187
Amalric of Bène (theologian, heretic, d. c.1206), 25–6, 65
Amalricians, 25–6, 65
Ancona, 115
Andrzejewski, Jerzy (Polish writer), 191
Anselm of Laon (exegete), 137
Aquileia,
  Berthold de Méran patriarch of, 121–2
  schools of, 123
Arnulf of Chocques (Latin Patriarch of Jerusalem), 96
Assassins, *see* Old Man of the Mountain
Austrian rhymed chronicle (*Chronicon rhythmicum Austriacum*), 14, 24, 155–7

Backman, Louis (historical writer), 142
Bacon, Roger (Franciscan philosopher), 141, 142, 150
Barker, Sir Ernest (1874–1960, English polymath), 187
Barth, Rev. Christian G. (German author of religious books), 184
Bernard of Clairvaux (saint, Cistercian abbot, crusade preacher), 23–4, 43–4, 60, 99, 137
Bettelheim, Bruno (psychologist), 159
Bizzarri, Pietro (early modern historian), 166, 178
Blyth, Estelle (children's author), 185
Boase, T.S.R. (medieval historian), 194–5
Bonaparte, Napoleon (1769–1821, French general and emperor), 173
Bonaventure (Franciscan saint, hagiographer of St. Francis), 119
Bordeaux, Henry (French writer), 185
Bower, Walter (late medieval Scottish abbot and historian), 162–3
Brecht, Bertolt (German dramatist), 189–90
Brenner pass, 108
Brindisi, 116–17, 152
Britten, Benjamin (English composer), 190
Brown, Rebecca (American novelist and academic), 193–4
"burned-over district", 42

Cathars, 19, 27, 32, 47
Catherine of Siena (saint), 161
charisma, Weberian, 59
  of office, 18
  personal, 18
Charlemagne (emperor, saint, d. 814), 87–9
Chartrain, 35, 52, 63
  and the crusades, 41ff., 45–6
  Dunois, 48–9, 72
  Louis (count of Blois and Chartres), 44–5
  Stephen (count of Chartres and Blois), 42–3
  Theobald V (count of Chartres and Blois), 44
Chartres, 37–41, 52, 53
  cathedral of, 37–8, **38 (fig. 4)**, 41
  "cult of carts" (*croisade monumentale*), 40–1
  place of pilgrimage, 39

Chartres *continued*
processions (1212), 52–4, 66, 67
representation of shepherds, cathedral, 67, **69–70 (fig. 6)**
Chateaubriand, François René de (1768–1848; French writer), 173
Chédeville, André (French historian), 35
childhood,
myths of 4, 132
puer senex, 4, 135
Children's Crusade,
Children's Crusade, The (1870) *see* Gray, George Zabriskie
aftermath, 123–7
and the Albigensian Crusade, 49, 52–3
and the Fourth Crusade, 46
and the Fifth Crusade, 22–3, 120, 126–7
and Francis of Assisi, 116
and the Spanish Crusade, 52–3
as mythistory, 6, 13
continuities, French and German phases, 83–4
evidence of, varieties, 9–14
"innocence" of the *pueri*, 24, 40, 137–8
also see pueri as new Innocents
later medieval children's crusades, 128–30
name of the, xiii
processional enthusiasm, 52–8, 156–7
rhetoric of revivalism, 16
verdict of the chroniclers, 2
Chrétien of Troyes (Grail poet), 98
Christie, Agatha (crime novelist), 1–2
Church, Rev. A. J. (Latinist, children's author), 184
Cividale del Friuli,
cathedral school, 122–3
Henry, canon of 121–2
Clare of Assisi (saint, founder of the Poor Sisters), 12, 28–9
Claudel, Paul (d.1955, French poet and dramatist), 181
Closener, Fritsche (or Friedrich) (vernacular chronicler), 160
Cloyes, 66–7
Codagnello, John (chronicler), 92, 108
Cologne, 92–3, 100–2
Cologne Continuator (monastic chronicler), 86–7, 98–9, 100, 102, 111, 113, 146
Constantinople,
Ottoman conquest of (1453), 130
sack of (1204), 44, 96
Crane, Stephen (American novelist), 192
crowd, mixed religious, 39
crusades, 41
American metaphorical, 7–8
Albigensian Crusade, 46–9
and the idea of Christendom, 32–3, 49, 57
First Crusade, 42–3
Fifth Crusade and *Ad liberandam*, 22–3, 114, 118–20
Fourth Crusade, 44–7, 186
Rhineland and, 99–100
Second Crusade, 23–4, 43
Spanish Crusade, 49–53, 99
Third Crusade, 30, 44
also see popular crusades, Shepherds' and Children's Crusades
Cuthbert, Father (Franciscan historian), 115

Damietta, 118, 119, 120
Daniels, Ron (English theatrical director), 186
D'Annunzio, Gabriele (Italian poet), 189
De Janssens, Gaston (French historian of the Dunois), 79–80
Devil, *see* Satan
Diderot, Denis (Enlightenment *philosophe* and encyclopedist), 151, 171, 172
Dominicus (bishop of Brindisi, 1203–16), 116–17
Doré, Gustave (artist), xi–xii, **xii (fig.1)**
Du Cange, Charles du Fresne (seventeenth-century French Latinist and medievalist), 168, 169
Durand of Le Puy (leader of the "White Hoods"), 61–2, 65, 103
Dutton, Rev. William E. (Victorian writer of popular histories), 180

Ebersheim chronicler (monk), 106, 146
Eco, Umberto (writer, scholar), 160

Eisenhower, Dwight David (WWII general; U.S. President), 191–2
Essarts, Alfred des (French nineteenth-century romantic poet), 180
Everett-Green, Evelyn (early-twentieth-century children's author), 184–5

Ferreus, Hugo (villain of Alberic), 144–5, 147
Fleury, Claude (1640–1723, ecclesiastical historian), 170, 171
Fourth Lateran Council (1215), 22, 25, 114–15
Francis of Assisi (saint, founder of the Order of Friars Minor), 12, 28, 29, 115–16, 119–20, 189
  also see Tau cross, emblem of
Frederick I Barbarossa (Holy Roman Emperor), 87, 97, 99, 101
Fulcher of Chartres (chronicler), 42–3
Fuller, Thomas (seventeenth-century English writer), 166–8, 189

Galbraith, V. H. (historian), 148
Geertz, Clifford (anthropologist), 73
Genoa, 108–11, 112, 113, 166, 178, 186
Giotto (artist), 120
Godin, Master (Amalrician), 25, 65
Gooch, G.P. (historian), 173–4
Gray, George Zabriskie (churchman and writer of *The Children's Crusade*), 7–9, 71, 181–3, 189
Green children, 4, 132–3
Gregory VIII (pope, 1187), 97
Gregory IX (pope, 1227–1241), 138, 145, 181
Gui, Bernard (Dominican inquisitor, bishop of Lodève, chronicler), 160
Guibert of Nogent (chronicler), 60
Guy of Vaux de Cernay (abbot), 45

Haimo (abbot, chronicler), *see* Chartres, "cult of carts"
Hattin, battle of, 30, 44, 49, 57, 94–7
Hecker, Justus Friedrich Karl (1795–1850, German historian of epidemics), 177–8, 180, 181
Heming, Eileen (children's author), 185–6
Herold, Johannes Basilius (historical writer), 164–5
Henry of Marcy (cardinal-legate), 97–8
Herman of Niederaltaich (chronicler), 10
Hesse, Herman (German writer), 192
Hilton, Rodney (historian), 70
historiography, 4–6
Holy Grail, *see* Chrétien of Troyes
Holy Innocents, 138
  image of, **139 (fig. 10)**
  also see Children's Crusade, "innocence" of the *pueri*
Honorius III (pope, 1216–1027), 14, 121
Humiliati, 65

Île-de-France, 37, 39, 47–8, 50, 52, 56, 57
Illuminato (Franciscan friar), 119–20
imagination, xiii
impossibilism, religious, 23, 26–9, 65, 127
Innocent III (pope, 1198–1216), 12, 13, 17ff., 44, 46, 113, 120, 169, 182, 184, 187
  as a papal crusader, 31ff.
  career and pontificate, 21–2
  crusade preaching at Orvieto, 30–1
  death, grave-robbing, and funeral of, in Perugia, 19–20
  eulogized, 20–1
  image of, 17–19, **18 (fig.3)**
  personal name and papal name, 18
  prophecy, 25
  Roman processions, 50–2
  Segni, Rome, and the *pueri,* 114
  also see Fourth Lateran Council
"International Year of the Child" (1979), 186

James of Varagine (archbishop of Genoa, author, chronicler), 137, 165, 166, 178
James of Vitry (writer of sermons, bishop of Acre), 19–20, 28, 37, 48, 99, 119
Jamieson, Archibald (post-WWI pamphleteer), 194
Jefferson, Thomas (1743–1826) (ambassador to France, U.S. President), 8, 168, 234 n.52
Jerusalem, 44, 88, 94, 156, 157
Jesus, twelve-year-old, 4, **5 (fig.2)**, 75–6, 134–5, **136 (fig. 9)**

Jews
  conversion of the, 156
  Jewish communities and the *pueri*, 78–9, 93
  massacres of the, xiii, 78
  "Pilgrimage of the 300 Rabbis", 93
  ritual murder allegation, 140
Jiménez de Rada, Rodrigo (archbishop of Toledo), 50
Joachim of Fiore (biblical exegete, prophet, d.1202), 24, 134
John de Caulibus (Franciscan writer), 135
John Le Long or John of Ypres (chronicler), 14, 53, 63–4, 210–11 n.59
Joinville, *see* Louis IX
Jourdain, Amable (1788–1818, orientalist), 175

Kent State University, shooting of students at (1970), 7, 192

Laon, Anonymous (chronicler), 64–5, 75–7, 212–13 n.27, 149, 178
Las Navas de Tolosa, battle of, 77, 99, 115
Lewis, Suzanne (art historian), 148
Leibniz (German philosopher), 142
Lendit fair, 72–3, 76
Leobiensis Chronicon (fourteenth-century Dominican chronicle), 161
"*les événements*" ("the events": student demonstrations in France, 1968), 192–3
Liège, 85–7
Louis IX (king of France, 1226–1270, saint), 152, 168, 173
  Joinville, hagiographer of St. Louis, 182
Louis XIV (king of France, 1661–1715), 168
Luchaire, Achille (medieval historian), 15, 185
Ludlow, James M. (Victorian author of historical romances, 178, 180

McCarthy, Eugene (senator), 6–7, 192
Mackay, Charles (nineteenth-century Scottish journalist), 192
McNeill, William H. (historian), 3
Magi *see* Three Kings
magicians, 140
Maimbourg, Louis (seventeenth-century French historian), 168–9
Mainz, 102
Marbach annalist (monastic chronicler), 107, 113
Marseilles, 106, 110, 111, 124, 143, 145, 146, 152
Mary of Oignies (Beguine), 19–20
Matilda (holy woman), 65
Mayer, Hans Eberhard (German crusade historian), 9, 187
memory, social, 16, 158–9, 194–6
Menotti, Gian Carlo (Italian/ American composer), 190
metaphor, 8
Michaud, Joseph-François (French journalist, crusade historian), 174–6
Millot, Claude (eighteeenth-century French historian), 172
Mont Saint-Michel, 129
Mortemer chronicler, 55–7, 126, 150
Munro, Dana Carleton (American crusade historian), 83
mythistory, viii–xiii
  definition and history, 3–56, 131–2
  mythistorians, 13
  prophecy, relation to, 155

Nicholas of Cologne, 14, 182, 185, 186, 195
  at Damietta, 118–20
  his father, 117
  leader of the Rhenish *pueri*, 98, 102–3, 105–11, 116–17
  also see Tau cross, emblem of
Nolan, Sidney (artist), 190

Old Man of the Mountain, 2, 153–5, 160, 165
Orvieto *see* Innocent III
Ordo Rachelis, 156
Otto (*pauper scolaris*), 14, 121–3, 195
  Otto Rufus, 123

Pacifico of the March of Ancona (Franciscan friar), 115
Pallenberg, Corrado, 71
Pane, Ogerio (chronicler), 108–9, 112
Paris, 37, 72, 126
  Paris Masters, 75–6, 193
  sermon of anonymous Paris preacher, 126–7

Paris, Matthew (chronicler and mythistorian), 13, 147–51, 167, 171, 182, 184, 189
for a drawing by Matthew Paris *see* **fig. 7**
for illustration of a motif from Matthew Paris *see* Stephen of Cloyes
Passenger to Frankfurt see Christie, Agatha
Patmos *see Leobiensis Chronicon*
peasants
demography, 90–1
negative image, 91
Pelagius (cardinal and papal legate), 118–19
Pentecost, 36–7, 49–50
octave of, 50, 51, 52
Perugia *see* Innocent III
Peter of Amiens, known as Peter the Hermit, 60–1, 62, 85, 195
Peter of Corbeil (archbishop of Sens), 37, 46, 52
Peterborough chronicler, 134, 152
Philip Augustus (king of France, 1179–1223), 44, 46, 50, 73, 193
Philip of Alsace (count of Flanders), 98
Piacenza, 108, 109, 111
Pied Piper (or Ratcatcher) of Hameln, 4, 141–3, 187
Pierné, Gabriel (French composer), 180
Pisa, 112, 113
Pontebba pass, 122
popular crusades, 40, 56, 84, 128
Porcus, William (villain of Alberic), 144–5, 147
Puccini, Giacomo (Italian opera composer), 189
pueri and *puellae*, 33–5, 54, 56, 57, 73–4
as neo-Israelities, 92–4
as new Innocents, 145, 146, 156
as pilgrims and crusaders, 91–2, 113
Jerusalemites, 94
self-imaginings, 89–94
Prester John, 155

Raedts, Peter (historian), 33–5
Ranke, Leopold von (1795–1886; German historian), 176
Reginald of Bar (or Mouçon) (bishop of Chartres, 1183–1217), 37, 44, 46, 48, 52, 54
Remarque, Erich Maria (German novelist), 192
Renier of Liège (prior, chronicler), 84, 85–7
Richard, Jean (French crusade historian), 187
Riché, Pierre (historian), 35
Richer of Sénones (chronicler), 111–12, 138
Richard Lionheart (king of England, 1189–99, and crusader), 24, 97
Rigord (chronicler), 97
Robert of Courçon (cardinal, papal legate, crusade preacher), 126
Rocourt *see* Saint-Quentin
Roger of Wendover (chronicler), 148–9
Röhricht, Reinhold (late-nineteenth-century German crusade historian), 181
Rolewinck, Werner (Carthusian writer of histories), 163–4
Rome, 51, 111, 112–13
Runciman, Sir Steven (Byzantinist and crusade historian), 188–9

Saint-Denis, 37, 71–2
royal abbey, 72–3, 88
St. Médard's monastic chronicler (France), 133–4
St. Pantaleon's monastic chronicler (Cologne), 101
San Pietro, island SW of Sardinia, 145
Saint-Quentin
social disorder at 79–81
Salimbene (Franciscan chronicler), 17, 24, 134–5
Saladin (Sala-al-Din, general and ruler, 1138–93) *see* Hattin, battle of, and True Cross
Satan, 140–1, 151, 164
Schwob, Marcel (1867–1905, French translator and writer), 180–1, 189
shepherds
Christian narrative and, 67, **69–70 (fig. 6)**, 90
Shepherds' crusades, 70, 128, 148, 150, 160–1, 164
Jacob, Master of Hungary (1251), 141, 148–9
Sicard of Cremona (bishop, papal legate, chronicler), 10–11, 108
Simon of Montfort (crusader), 45–6
Sixties, 1–2, 6–7, 186, 194

Speyer, 105
Sporschil, Johann (1800–63, Austrian writer of popular histories), 178, **179 (fig. 12)**
Stephen of Cloyes, 14, 62, 65–6, 180, 182, 193, 195
  illustration of motif from Matthew Paris, 182, **183 (fig.13)**
  leader of the French *pueri*, 70–6
  reputed portrait of, **68 (fig. 5)**
  shepherd-boy, 63, 64, 67–70, 90
Sybel, Heinrich von (nineteenth-century German historian), 176

Tau cross
  and Innocent III, 114–15
  as a Christian symbol, 105
  emblem of Nicholas of Cologne, 103–4, 110–11, 157
  emblem of Francis of Assisi, 115–16
  St. Antony Abbot holding the Tau Cross, **104 (fig. 8)**
Thompson, Paul (dramatist), 186
Thomas, Bernard (French journalist and novelist), 193
Thomas of Cantimpré (medieval writer), 3
Thomas of Celano (Franciscan hagiographer), 116
Three Kings (Magi), 100–1
Treviso, 114, 122
Trier, 102–3
  anonymous chronicler of, 102–4, 116–17
True Cross, 30, 44, 51, 57
  capture of the True Cross by Saladin, drawing **95 (fig. 7)**
  quest for, 94–8
  unrecovered, 119

UNESCO, 186
Urban II (pope, 1088–99), 60, 88

Vaughan, Richard (historian), 147–8
Vendôme, 65, 66, 143, 182, 189
Venice, 114, 122
Vienne, 106
Villehardouin, Geoffroy de (chronicler), 44, 45, 109
Vincent of Beauvais (encyclopedist), 13, 151–5, 159–60, 161, 162–3, 165
Voltaire (Enlightenment *philosophe*), 169, **170 (fig. 11)**, 171–2, 177, 192
Vonnegut, Kurt (American novelist), 191–2

Waldensians, 27, 65, 184
Wandering Jew, 4, 184
Waas, Adolf (German crusade historian), 187, 190
Weber, Max (sociologist), 18, 59, 62
Wells, H.G. (English novelist and popular historian), 187–8
White, Hayden (theorist of history), 15
Wilken, Friedrich (1777–1840, German crusade historian), 176–7, 178, 181, 182
William of Andres (chronicler), 64
William the Breton (chronicler), 126
William of Newburgh (chronicler), 132–3
William of Tyre (archbishop, historian), 164, 165

Zacour, Norman (crusade historian), 145, 147